Jacques Tagher

Christians in Muslim Egypt

An Historical Study of the Relations
between Copts and Muslims
from 640 to 1922

Arbeiten zum spätantiken und koptischen Ägypten

Herausgegeben von
Prof. Dr. Martin Krause

10

Jacques Tagher, **Christians in Muslim Egypt. An Historical Study of the Relations between Copts and Muslims from 640 to 1922.** Oros Verlag, Altenberge 1998, XX+294 S., DM 80,-.

ISBN 3-89375-157-2

Jacques Tagher

Christians in Muslim Egypt

An Historical Study of the Relations
between Copts and Muslims
from 640 to 1922

A Translation from the Arabic of Jacques Tagher's

Copts and Muslims from the Arab Conquest to 1922
(Aqbāṭ wa Muslimūn mundhu al-fatḥ al-'arabī ḥattā 'ām 1922)
Translated and Annotated by
Ragai N. Makar
Edited and Introduced by
S. Kent Brown
Foreword by
Lee L. Bean

Umschlag: D. Rayen, Altenberge

Oros Verlag
Postfach 11 45
D 48337 Altenberge
Tel./Fax (02505) 3534

ISBN 3-89375-157-2

CONTENTS

V

PREFACE

I am neither a Muslim nor a Copt. I have discussed the relations between the Copts and the Muslims with the viewpoint of the historian who records the events as they happened, not with the viewpoint of the judge who issues a verdict between two litigants. It is obvious that this research will raise some comments and I welcome the views and comments of everyone.

The Author

FOREWORD

Jacques Tagher concluded his historical analysis of Copts and Muslims by recognizing two opposing views of the future.

> "In fact we are now going through a transitional period that will come to an end. During this period we have discovered two currents that oppose one another: some thinkers—looking to the past—do not acknowledge the progress that has taken place in Egyptian society, others believe that modernism will eventually prevail over conservatism."

Tagher, himself, appears to be optimistic, suggesting that Egypt in the early 1920s had embarked on a path which would lead to the reduction or elimination of the patterns of conflict and repression that had marked centuries of Copt-Muslim relations. He wrote, "Modern Egypt chose the right path when she adopted the 1922 constitution." Half a decade later we have enough data to understand not simply that the "right path" has been marked by detours, political and religious empediments, but also the reason why this volume is important enough to be translated into languages that will reach audiences far beyond the Middle East.

Many political and social theories developed during the second half of the nineteenth century and the first half of the twentieth century predicted the declining importance of ethnic differences within all nations. Events of the third quarter of this century initiated questions about the validity of these arguments, and events of the last quarter of this century have required a complete reassessment.

Marxist-Leninist ideology predicted the submersion of ethnicity, religion, and nationalism to an international political ideology.[1] By the end of the 1930s,

---

1. M.I. Kulichenko, for example, writes: "The unification, more than half a century ago, of big and small peoples in a single Soviet multinational state on the basis of a socialist type of national relations ensured a qualitatively new character of universal internationalization of their economic, political, and cultural life. The common territory of each nation or nationality, in conjunction with the common territory of the entire Soviet people as a new internationalist community, has become an important factor in their coming closer together for the purpose of helping each people to solve common problems.

the bastian of Marxist-Leninist theory, the Soviet Union, had defeated and integrated a wide range of nationistic and ethnically dominated states into a single, great nation state committed to ever expanding its ideological base. As late as the beginning of this last decade of the twentieth century, no one would have predicted that it would be the re-emergence of nationalist demands in the Baltic States, ethnic conflicts in the Caucus, and ethnic—and in some cases religious—demands for independence in the central Asian republics which would serve as the foundation for the ongoing restructuring of the Soviet Union. Clearly Marxism was wrong: ethnicity—broadly defined to include religious groups as well as tribal or cultural communities—could not be overridden by a particular form of universalistic political ideology.[2]

At the other end of the political spectrum, capitalist theories reached the same conclusion as Marxist-Leninism with respect to ethnic communities—but through a different path. Industrialization and modernization were assumed to provide a new, general, universalistic basis for social organization. In the views of sociologists espousing structural-functional theory, achievement would replace ascription, obviating religious, racial, and national identities. The United States was held up as a model, and the concept of the "melting-pot" structured the work of social scientists seeking evidence for integration and assimilation—or the barriers which once identified should be removed through legal action.

For many social scientists, assimilation, integration, and eventual amalgamation were seen as simply the end result of a natural pattern of linear,

---

"The social role of such an important ethnic feature of nations and nationalities as national culture has become a qualitatively new factor in the conditions prevailing in the Soviet Union. Based on Marxist-Leninist ideology and incorporating mankind's achievements of the past, national culture has become a major factor in the progress of nations and nationalities and their contribution to the treasure house of world culture." ("Socialism and Ethnic Features of Nations: The Example of the Peoples of the Union of Soviet Socialist Republics," in Regina E. Holloman and Serghei A. Arutiunov [eds.], *Perspectives on Ethnicity,* The Hague: Mouton Publishers, 1978, pp. 421–428, especially pp. 421–22.)

2. A reasonable definition of ethnic groups is provided by Horowitz (1985: 17–18): "The groups are defined by ascriptive differences, whether the indicium of group identity is color, appearance, language, religion, some other indicator of common origin, or some combination thereof. This is an inclusive conception of ethnicity." Religious groups such as the Copts may be also treated as an ethnic group, for as Guidieri and Pellizzi note, "A critical assessment of the revival of nationalist and ethnic movements in our time must include their religious component, both as an expression of 'spontaneous,' fundamentalist *faiths* and as a remarkably vigorous, often controversial, commitment by venerable religious institutions." (Remo Guidieri and Francesco Pellizzi, "Introduction: Smoking Mirrors—Modern Polity and Ethnicity" in Remo Guidieri, Francesco Pellizzi, and Stanley J. Tambiah [eds], *Ethnicities and Nations: Processes of Interethnic Relations in Latin America, Southeast Asia, and the Pacific.* Austin: University of Texas Press, 1988, pp. 7–38.

evolutionary change. Ethnic, racial, or religious conflicts were identified as archaic impediments to progress.[3]

Questions regarding the validity of assimilationist models of American society emerged in the 1950s. One of the earliest studies to question the disappearance of religious differences in the United States was Herberg's *Protestant, Catholic and Jew* (1955). In the early 1960s, Glazer and Moynihan detailed the persistence of racial and ethnic differences in *Beyond the Melting Pot* (1963). However, it was another decade, or longer, before American scholars began to address systematically the reality of continuing and increasing inequality and competition, evidenced by the race riots of Watts and other focal points of conflagration. The reality of ethnic differences and their historical importance became codified in the 1980s with the emergence of multi-culturalism as a theory and as a policy for social action.

Elsewhere in the world the real-politik of plural societies[4] was mirrored in ethnic conflicts which became open wars regardless of levels of development and modernization: Burundi, Nigeria, Sri Lanka, Lebanon, Armenia, Azerbaijan, Yugoslavia, and others. The conclusion of the Gulf war and the revolts by the Shi`a population in southern Iraq and the Kurdish population in northeastern Iraq are but two other illustrations of essentially the same process.

These underlying cleavages and conflicts, which now appear to be ubiquitous, have stimulated an expansion of studies by political scientists and others to assess the role of ethnicity in political and economic change.[5] Examples include a volume by Donald L. Horowitz, one by Dennis L. Thompson and Dov Ronen, and Milton J. Esman and Itamar Rabinovich's edited volume focusing on the Middle East.[6] Published in the 1980s, these volumes represent a growing set

---

3. The arbitrary division of regions by European colonial powers is clearly reflective of the ideology which denigrated the reality of ethnic territories in Africa as well as in the Middle East.

4. For perhaps the earliest analysis of pluralism, see M.G. Smith, "Pluralism in Precolonial African Societies," in Leo Kuper and M.G. Smith (eds), *Pluralism in Africa*, Berkeley: University of California Press, 1969.

5. For a summary of the development of scholarship dealing with ethnicity in the Middle East, beginning with Albert Hourani's *Minorities in the Arab World* (London: Oxford University Press), see Milton J. Esman and Itamar Rabinovich, "Ethnic Politics in the Middle East," in Milton J. Esman and Itamar Rabinovich (eds), *Ethnicity, Pluralism, and the State in the Middle East*, Ithaca: Cornell University Press, 1988, pp. 3–24.

6. Donald L. Horowitz, *Ethnic Groups in Conflict*; Dennis L. Thompson and Dov Ronen (eds.), *Ethnicity, Politics, and Development*; Milton J. Esman and Itamar Rabinovich (eds.), *Ethnicity, Pluralism, and the State in the Middle East*.

of books and articles which focus on ethnic groups in conflict. Such theoretical reconfigurations, however, following by some years the concept of plural societies, applied explicitly to ex-colonial states.[7]

The issue of ethnic conflict or simply the struggle to accommodate different racial, ethnic, and religious groups is not new, nor is it simply a product of arbitrary national boundaries created by Western colonial powers, as some writers have suggested with respect to a number of countries in which conflict has been particularly intense at various times: Nigeria and its Biafran civil war of the 1960s, the most recent Lebanese civil war which extended from 1975 to 1990, and the continuing Tamil revolution in Sri Lanka. Clearly ethnic differences and ethnic conflicts are ones which will continue to demand evaluation, understanding, and experimentation in order not to attempt to eliminate the reality of such differences but rather to accommodate such differences with a minimum of conflict.

A basis for understanding ethnic and religious differences requires a historical perspective. Such a focus has been missing from much of the literature on ethnic and religious minorities. Amnon Cohen, for example, is particularly critical of H.A.R. Gibb and Harold Brown's monumental 1962-63 study, *Islamic Society and the West*. He writes:

> "The topic which, unlike many others, did not have to wait for any reaction from the outside was the *millet* system: here criticism stated at home. Not only was it consciously left for the last chapter in the second volume but the authors also deemed it necessary to start this chapter—"The Dhimmis"—with an apologetic remark: "We could not exclude from our survey a chapter devoted to these communities, even if it had to be based on secondary sources to a much greater extent than the other chapters." (1982, p.7)[8]

Nevertheless, it is important to note that the literature on various religious groups and ethnic groups in the Middle East is rather large. The number of

---

7. See the studies by Sammy Smooha for an application of the concept of pluralism to Israel.

8. A necessary corrective to the ignoring of "ethnic groups" in the Middle East is represented by a number of important new publications on religious communities in the Middle East: Braude and Lewis' edited two-volume work is simply representative: Benjamin Braude and Bernard Lewis (eds.), *Christians and Jews in the Ottoman Empire*, 2 Vols., New York: Holmes & Meier Publishers, Inc., 1982.

studies on the Kurds, Druze, Maronites, Baha'i, Shi`a, Alawites, Armenians, Copts, and others is, indeed, extensive. This body of literature, however, tends to focus on more contemporary issues with an often brief and incomplete introduction to the history of these groups and their interactions with subordinate or dominate groups over centuries. Much of the literature, for example, on the Kurds and Armenians focuses on the period beginning in the late nineteenth-century when these groups sought independence within the frenzy of emergent nationalism dominating political ideology in western Europe—tempered, of course, by the need to protect colonial empires.

-        Among the few classical studies of intergroup relationships in the Middle East is Jacob Mann's *The Jews in Egypt and in Palestine under the Fatimid Caliphs,* published originally in 1920. Tagher's study of Copts and Muslims, published approximately thirty years later, might be seen as a parallel to Mann's study. Both face the problem of detailing a history based upon incomplete information. As Mann acknowledges,

> "They (the reference materials) are of course incomplete, and do not yet render possible a connected and detailed account of the vicissitudes of these Jewries. But where till now there was almost a blank page of Jewish History, every additional line, every new word, as it were, that help to cover up this blank are of importance."

One is constantly reminded in Tagher's volume of the limited, fragmentary, and often incomplete body of information from which a fascinating history is woven, more chronologically ordered than Mann's study in some respects, but more cursory in part because of the longer time frame and the absence of a corpus of written materials of the form utilized by Mann. Yet given these limitations, one must argue in Tagher's case, as Mann did for himself, "every additional line, every new word . . . that help to cover up this blank are of importance."

Tagher's book should not be viewed as a theoretical contribution nor as a test of a particular hypothesis dealing with ethnic group relations over time. Rather it provides the detail necessary to understand patterns of conflict and accommodation in one particular case. Added to other documents, the studies of Jews in Palestine, Istanbul, or Baghdad, one finds increasing documentation from which one might anticipate developing more theoretically satisfying explanations of accommodation in the face of continuing subordination, extending over centuries, under a variety of political regimes. There is evidence from Mann's study of the Jews and Tagher's study of the Copts, that minorities frequently occupied a critical occupation niche from which minority members were able to provide support for or protection of their co-religionists.

Tagher and Mann, for example, reference the same individuals performing such roles, although their interpretations differ when speaking of a Copt or a Jew. In chapter 6, "The Rise and Fall of the Copts During the Reign of the Fatimids," Tagher describes the role of Isa ibn Nastoros (a Melchite) who became a vizier under al-Aziz. A mention of Menasha is made by Tagher, but Mann devotes more attention to Isa ibn Nastoros's chief deputy, "the Jew Menasse." A comparison of these two independent references to the same two individuals reveals the emphasis and selectivity which emerges from specialized studies of Copts and Jews, and the differences—perhaps biases—which intrude. While Tagher emphasizes the protective intermediary role of Nastoros, Mann sees him in a different light: "Isa was hard-hearted and an usurer who grasped for himself every lucrative business, and augmented very much the taxes" (p. 16). The interpretive views of Tagher and Mann may be different, but the individuals, the events, and the roles remain constant in each case, with Tagher expanding our knowledge of the Copts and Mann performing a similar service for the Jews during the same periods, in the same region.

In the view of this writer the translation of Tagher's volume is important for historians and social scientists. It moves the history of the Copts of Egypt back beyond the period of the Ottoman empire and its unique political, theological approach to structuring a plural society.[9] The issues have been well documented in a number of significant volumes and enter, even if peripherally, in many histories of the Middle East. While the history of the Jews as a subordinate group in the Middle East is increasingly well documented[10], the Copts, a population much larger in size than the Jews of Israel, and their survival as a subordinate group has been less well documented. Incomplete though the picture may be, Tagher begins to fill some blanks.

Finally, in a broader context, the growing publication of volumes which deal with the history of ethnic persistence in the Middle East must be seen as a simple parallel to modifications in Western social science, history, and literary analyses. The realities of ethnic persistence and conflict in Eastern Europe, the

---

9. The recent publication of *The Coptic Encyclopedia* under the editorship of the late Prof. Aziz S. Atiya provides a considerable body of information on the Copts—their theology, architecture, saints, history, scholars and scholarship. But the interweaving of Coptic and Muslim history in Egypt is less complete than one will find through a careful reading of Tagher's study.

10. See Bernard Lewis's *Jews of Islam* (Princeton University Press, 1984) as a recent addition to the literature.

Soviet Union, South Africa, Canada, and the United States demands it. In addition, while multi-culturalism is leading to a rewriting and reinterpretation of American history, Mann, Tagher, and others initiated this task for the Middle East half a century ago.

Lee L. Bean, Ph.D.
Department of Sociology
and the Middle East Center,
University of Utah

EDITOR'S INTRODUCTION

Only occasionally does a work of broad historical sweep succeed in capturing both large issues and small nuances that have affected people for generations, even centuries. In the case of medieval and modern Egypt, only the history written by Jacques Tagher has come close to this aim. Except for the last decades of the thirteen-century period that Tagher examines (640–1922), Egypt was ruled by leaders from outside whose chief aim was to extract as much wealth as possible from the country. Tagher has succeeded in tracing a rather consistent pattern of repression and financial tyranny by foreign rulers, continuing a system incidentally that goes back to Roman and Byzantine times (30 B.C.–640 A.D.).

The principal focus of Tagher's work rests on those Copts who sat closest to the seats of Muslim power. For the most part it is difficult if not impossible to measure accurately the impact of Muslim policies on those who lived at substantial distances from the capital city. One must simply assume that the lot of these Copts was largely as good or as bad as that of their Muslim neighbors. On the one hand, they simply were not as deeply subject to the occasionally whimsical winds of fortune that blew over those who were in one way or another associated with government services in Cairo. On the other, official policies enforced at the center were not always carried out fully, or even at all, in Egypt's hinterland.

In the first three chapters of his book, Mr. Tagher surveys the general situation of Coptic Christians before and just after the Arab invasion of Byzantine Egypt. In those initial pages, he has probed important issues such as (1) the reasons behind the Islamic invasion of Egypt, (2) the question whether the Copts really welcomed the Arab invaders, and (3) how the Ahl al-Dhimma (Christians and Jews) were treated under *shari`a* (Islamic law).

In the next chapter, the author has scrutinized the conditions of the Copts under the *wulat*, the Muslim representatives of the Umayyad and Abbasid caliphs (640–868 A.D.). Here he has examined the character of the Arab occupation of Egypt, the policy of `Amr ibn al-`As who was the first Muslim *wali*, the fiscal policy of the *wulat*, the first Coptic revolution in 725, and the colonial policy during the time of the *wulat*.

The fifth chapter, though brief, deals with the independent *walis*, the Tūlūnids and the Ikhshīdīds, who generally ruled more responsibly and even-handedly (868–969 A.D.). In chapter six, "The Rise and Fall of the Copts during the Reign of the Fatimids," Tagher has examined the undulation in relationships between Copts and the successive Fatimid caliphs, all Shi`ites, who are to be distinguished from the Sunnite Muslim majority in Egypt. Significantly, he is the

XV

first Arab historian to analyze the nature of the connection between a religious majority led by foreign rulers—who in this case belonged to a different Islamic sect—and the native religious minority in a clearly documented, analytical manner.

In the seventh chapter, he has studied not only the policies of Salāh al-Dīn and the Ayyubids towards Christians but also the disservice rendered by the crusaders towards Christians of the region. The Copts had learned through centuries of experience how to get along with their overlords, and the coming of the crusaders was an unwelcome intrusion. Further, because the Copts sensed rightly that the crusader presence was temporary, they consequently refused to be led into accepting favors from their European co-religionists.

In chapter eight, he has penetrated "the catastrophic condition of Christianity under the Mamlūk sultans" (1250–1517 A.D.). In his judgment, Christianity in the Middle East, both in general and particularly in Egypt, suffered most under the rule of the Mamlūks (the "slave sultans"). Like their predecessors, all these rulers were foreigners who humiliated Christians to legitimize their authority within a population whose native majority was now Muslim. All of them confiscated money and property of Christians and Jews, particularly to meet the financial needs of their mercenary armies who were in a continual state of war.

In chapter nine, Tagher discusses briefly the conditions of the Coptic Christians between the Ottoman conquest in 1517 and the French invasion in 1798. It is his view that "justice in Egypt did not change its course under Ottoman rule."

In the tenth chapter, he has probed the impact of the French presence in Egypt (1798-1801) on relations between Muslims and Christians. The author concludes that Napoleon "sacrificed the Copts to prove his support of Islam."

In chapter eleven, Tagher explores first the reasons for the improved conditions of the Copts during the reign of Muhammad `Ali. While "in spite of the many aspects of tolerance during Muhammad `Ali's reign, the Christians could not claim equality with the Muslims," the new spirit of tolerance breathed new life into relationships between Muslims and Copts. To be sure, Christians held the government responsible for not recognizing "publicly the equality between Christianity and Islam." But progress had nonetheless been achieved.

In a second stage, between 1882 and 1922, the British occupation strained ties between Muslims and Christians. As a result, the first Coptic prime minister, Boutros Ghali, was assassinated by a Muslim in 1911. Although Coptic Christians were responsible for certain sectarian incidents during that period, their situation improved tremendously at the urging of Saad Zaghlul, leader of the 1919 revolution against the British; he achieved a national unity of Muslims and Christians, a circumstance never seen before.

The next-to-last chapter is devoted to an examination of topics closely related to the main thrust of the study, including the spiritual condition of Coptic Christians under Islamic rule, the effects of Islam on the religion and customs of Copts, the character of the competition between the two oldest Christian groups in Egypt, Melchites and Copts, and the attitudes of Copts towards Europeans. The final chapter is devoted to Tagher's conclusions.

At this point, it is important to make three observations. First, Tagher's work is the best study to appear on Egypt's Christian minority for the period covered, 642 to 1922 A.D. Its scope alone underscores the importance of its contribution. Next, his documentation rests entirely on primary sources in Arabic, French, English and German—which he could read—as well as others translated from Coptic, Latin, Syriac and Greek. Last, as a result of his painstaking documentation, Tagher's study still possesses validity today. While the volume exhibits weaknesses typical of early scholarly work that focuses on impoverished regions, the author's serious effort at objectivity and the character of his supporting data go a long way in limiting such shortcomings. Our task has been to turn frailties into strengths by carefully focusing and buttressing his observations with additional explanatory notes.

There is the further issue of what this annotated translation of Tagher's volume will do for a reading audience. First and foremost it will respond to a fundamental need to understand more fully the complexities of the forces and interests that shape developments in Egypt, America's principal Arab ally, located in the strategic Middle East. Second, concern for minorities and their place in various societies has become a serious issue in our time. And Tagher's work documents best and most objectively the long, complicated story of the heights and depths experienced by Egypt's Christian minority, which was frequently an accurate barometer of the situation faced by the Muslim majority ruled by foreigners. Third, the intriguing story of the Coptic Christians of Egypt, the oldest and largest Christian minority in the Middle East, remains basically untold to English readers. Of course, there are many reasons for this. After the Council of Chalcedon in A.D. 451, at which one of the major disagreements in the Christian church took place, the Coptic community in Egypt—which represented almost the whole population of the country at the time—became virtually isolated from the western world. This isolation was then made more complete by the Islamic conquest of Egypt in 642 A.D. Moreover, Copts soon applied themselves to learn to read and write in Arabic, a language unknown in the West. In addition, over the centuries the Copts feared to reach out and associate with representatives of the

West lest their Muslim rulers accuse them of effectively "cooperating with the enemy."

In the broad sense, my associates and I believe that this one book will constitute a valuable addition to public libraries and the libraries of schools, colleges, and universities in the English speaking world, as well as to the private libraries of all who share an interest in the Middle East. But perhaps more significantly, it will do more by dispelling views that have gained a certain amount of respect in recent decades concerning the relation between religious communities in Egypt. For instance, in an essay in *The Atlantic Monthly*, James Pittaway, an American author, described the "domestication" and maturation of the Muslim Brotherhood ("Egypt: A Benign Brotherhood?" [Jan. 1989], pp. 25-33). While he may have been correct in his assessment of the current relationship of the Brotherhood to the Egyptian government and to the wider movement of Islamic fundamentalism, he and his sources–all reflecting positive biases toward the Brotherhood–were absolutely wrong in their view of how the Christian minority of the country would respond to the imposition of Islamic law, a goal of the Brotherhood. For the essay pointed out that all dimensions of Egyptians' lives had been and continued to be congruent with Islamic law, including and especially religious aspects, even for orthodox Coptic Christians. Such an observation exhibits a fundamental naiveté on this issue which undermines the otherwise well researched conclusions of a person who interacts regularly with the Western diplomatic community in Egypt and, by his own admission, also influences their views on Egypt and the Middle East. This type of misunderstanding, with potentially weighty consequences among those who formulate and carry out policies for western governments in Egypt, underscores the difficulties facing outsiders of coming to a reasonable, informed, even empathetic view of actions and reactions in a region of global importance.

While studies and students have sought to answer questions regarding turns of events that have led to the current state of affairs in Egypt, by and large none have possessed sufficient scope to serve as a reliable guide, particularly for the earlier religious backdrop which continues to inform the modern Egyptian situation–and the relevance of the religious element cannot be deemphasized. Except one book. That book was published just once, in Arabic. It is this volume.

The author, who was neither a Coptic Christian nor an adherent of Islam, was the librarian who had charge of the royal library of King Farouk of Egypt (1936–1952). Mr. Tagher was a Lebanese historian who had earned a degree in Middle Eastern history in France. While he wrote other books, this was his best and most thorough.

As a historian, the author quickly determined that many of the extant works about Christians of Egypt covered aspects of their religious history and development but avoided related political and social dimensions. Prior serious investigation of the fluctuations in relationships between the majority (Muslims) and the minority (Christians) was almost non-existent. He also noted that previous publications had not included citations and analyses of the sources on which their authors depended. Hence, Tagher focused his research on political and social aspects of the history of the Christians in Egypt, employing an extensive array of primary resources. Discounting the polemical bent of many modern Coptic writers, he sought to uncover the historical veracity of majority-minority relations in Egypt's past, "however bitter this truth might be." In his brief introduction, he observed that "this study does not aim, as some people might think, at reviving the old hatreds because of what it reveals of conflicts and painful events. The fact is that volatile religious attitudes in the Middle East have not diminished among Muslims and Christians in the middle and lower classes, although they seem quiet on the surface. . (Even) if I fail to suggest solutions for that problem, I shall be satisfied with studying some of its aspects."

One must assess, of course, how successful Tagher's study really was. If one compares its scope to the fifty pages devoted to the same period in Sohirin Mohammed Solihin's *Copts and Muslims in Egypt, A Study in Harmony and Hostility* (Leicester, England: The Islamic Foundation, 1991), one will quickly conclude that this more recent work suffers both from brevity and from overgeneralization. It is worthwhile noting that, among Westerners who study Arab society, the award-winning French author, Jean-Pierre Péroncel-Hugoz, has observed that "the only serious historical study of the Copts, based principally on Muslim sources, was written by Jacques Tagher" (*The Raft of Mohammed: Social and Human Consequences of the Return to Traditional Religion in the Arab World* [New York, 1988], p. 88).

S. Kent Brown, Ph.D.
Department of Ancient Scripture
and the David M. Kennedy Center
for International Relations,
Brigham Young University

TRANSLATOR'S NOTE

Because the work of Tagher is more than forty five years old and because further research and publication has enriched the detail and broadened the sources that are available for students of the medieval and modern Middle East in general and Egypt in particular, I have sought to provide further helpful documentation where the author's work seemed to be lacking. In addition, at times the author has assumed that his Middle Eastern readership possesses a certain level of acquaintance with dates and events, features with which most westerners are not familiar. I have tried to fill in these gaps with dates and relevant notes as aids to the reader. All such additions to the author's own work appear in brackets, [ ], thus indicating what is not original in his book.

It has to be stated that as I am not a historian, I am not in a position to condone or refute the author's views and/or conclusions.

Ragai N. Makar, M.A., M.L.S.

Marriott Library,

University of Utah

Chapter 1

CHRISTIANITY IN EGYPT BEFORE
THE ARAB CONQUEST

Christianity appeared in Egypt six hundred years before the Islamic conquest. We will not attempt here a detailed review of its appearance because such a study is beyond the scope of this book. Nor will we try to discuss the conclusions reached by some orientalists such as Lefebvre, Schmidt and Schultze,[1] who have stated that Christianity was alien to native Egyptians and that the success of the Arab conquest of Egypt was generally due to the fact that Islam attracted the Copts of Egypt who were tired of the rigidity and oppression of their church.[2] It is sufficient to observe that Egyptian Christianity before the Islamic conquest was, for the Egyptian people, a vehicle for political liberation and a way to shed the yoke of the Byzantine rule.

After the spread of Christianity under the Romans and Byzantines, the Copts continued enthusiastically to worship their pharaonic gods and to revere their glorious past. They refused to make any offerings to the Roman and Greek gods. They accepted Christianity with reserve because it came to them from outside their borders. In this way they attempted to convince themselves that they had not been subjugated by a foreign invader as long as they resisted its beliefs and religious practices.

Egyptian Christians abandoned the religion of their forebears reluctantly because the religion, temples and gods of the pharaohs continually reminded them of the eras of the glorious past of Egypt. It is no wonder that ancient beliefs remained strong in their minds and hearts even after their conversion to Christianity. An example of this persistence can be found by reading the *Synaxarion* (*History of the Saints*) which reports, "In the temple of Caesar which was built by Cleopatra, wherein stood a large copper idol called Mercury, an annual festival was celebrated and sacrifices were offered to Mercury. These customs were practiced until the days of Father Alexander, i.e., for over three hundred years [after the arrival of Christianity]. When Alexander became the Coptic patriarch he decided to destroy that idol, but the people of Alexandria revolted against his decision saying, `We have been accustomed to celebrating this

1. Gustave Lefebvre, *Recueil des inscriptions grecques-chrétiennes d'Égypte*, Cairo, 1907, p. xxiv; Carl Schmidt, *Zeitschrift für die Kunde des Morgenlandes* 32 (1919):52; Viktor Schultze, *Geschichte des Untergangs des griechisch-römischen Heidentums*, Jena, 1887–92, p. 234.

2. See Muhammad Abduh, *Risalat al-Tawhid (Theology of Unity)*, Cairo, 1897 (in Arabic).

idol's festival. Twelve patriarchs have sat on that throne and not one of them dared to make us abandon that custom."[3]

When idolatry ceased to exist and the ruling authority gave up protecting it, the Egyptians could not avoid adopting Christianity and they tried, as Jean Maspero has correctly observed, "to confiscate it for their own interest" by claiming that everything beautiful and great in Christianity was Egyptian. From that time onward the clergy and the people tended to take over the government and to secede from Byzantium. This tendency became clear after the first Council of Nicea[4] where the star of the Alexandrian Coptic church emerged and glittered.

After the Nicene council, the patriarchs of Alexandria felt that the Christian world sympathized with them and valued their knowledge and genius. The pope of Rome began to show them respect and consideration, and the emperor of the eastern empire showered them with gifts and donations. The reason for this change in attitude was that the Copts had refuted the claims of the Arian secessionists[5] and preserved both the unity of Christianity and good relations between the two halves of the Roman Empire. Sensing the mood, the Egyptian patriarchs seized the opportunity to get rid of the emperor's religious guardianship; and they cooperated in clarifying their views concerning their religious affairs, even if these views were sometimes contrary to the views of the patriarch in Constantinople [whose authority was derived from that of the emperor].

The Coptic people, who were disquieted about the passing greatness of the pharaohs, suffered under Roman and Byzantine occupation. Burdensome taxes, which were imposed on them by the ruling authority, increased their despair. The Coptic people tried to express their desire for political freedom by revolting against oppressive and tyrannical rulers. However, more paths were available to them than that of religious schism. They resorted to it only after the patriarch of Alexandria became prominent in the religious and political arenas. The patriarch was the one person of authority who had not been imposed on the

---

3. Émile C. Amélineau, *La Géographie de l'Égypt à l'epoque copte*, Paris, 1893, pp. 43–44.

4. [The first Council of Nicea was held in 325 A.D. in opposition to Arianism and was reaffirmed by the Council of Constantinople in 381 A.D. (Tr.)]

5. [In Egypt, two major heresies appeared successively and gained considerable ground throughout the country. One was gnosticism, which arose in the second century, and the other was Arianism which unsettled both Egypt and the empire in the fourth. Arius himself was a presbyter of the church of Alexandria (d. 336 A.D.). Arianism was a theological movement initiated by Arius which won strong support during the fourth century, chiefly in the eastern churches, but was condemned in the general councils of Nicea (325 A.D.) and Constantinople (381 A.D.). In the view of Arianism, Jesus Christ is not truly God. See further Aziz S. Atiya, *History of Eastern Christianity*, Millwood, N.Y.: Kraus Reprint, 1980, pp. 40, 42–44, 55, 60, 174. (Tr.)]

Egyptian people by civil authorities: he had been elected by Egyptians. As a result, the patriarch was a true representative of the Egyptian people. He was able to express publicly their ambitions and hopes, and became the only person who could stand against the authority of the emperor and his representatives.

We would like to remind the reader that religious affairs were at that time the sole topic of public discussion, hence the only topic on which disagreement would become severe. Consequently, under the leadership of their religious leaders, the Coptic people declared their departure from the principle of the united [Byzantine] church. The Coptic schism was religious in appearance only. Although religious factors have largely lost their influence today, it would be useful to refer to past religious schisms which will help us to understand the reasons for the tragedy that took place in Chalcedon in 451 A.D.

Patriarch Dioscorus, whose name is always mentioned along with the Council of Chalcedon, used to say "This country `Egypt' belongs to me more than the emperors and I request sovereignty over it." He never faltered and waited patiently for the opening to put his words into action. The opportunity came when the patriarch of Constantinople made an unintentional mistake.

When Eutyches the monk announced his doctrine [which is followed by the orthodox Copts at present] concerning the dual nature of Christ, the divine and the human,[6] the Egyptian clergy rushed to refute that doctrine. There was nothing in the air that warned of serious trouble. But fate intervened when Flavian, the patriarch of Constantinople, officially announced the excommunication of the advocate of the new doctrine [Eutyches the Monk] which in turn made Dioscorus[7] [the Patriarch of Alexandria] disapprove publicly of his colleague's condemnation of one of the members of the church because Flavian's behavior gave more prestige to the patriarch of Constantinople than to the patriarch of Alexandria. Because Flavian condemned Eutyches the monk publicly, Dioscorus officially adopted the view of the monk.

The patriarch of Alexandria put the Egyptian clergy in an awkward position by his sudden and late pronouncement, because the Egyptian bishops had disapproved of Eutyches without any serious opposition on the part of the patriarch, who had the last word. How could they contradict their decision without exposing themselves to ridicule? While the bishops stood puzzled in the face of this odd situation, Dioscorus ordered them to join him and support his

---

6. [Eutyches held that there were two natures before, but only one after, the union of Christ incarnate. The issue whether Christ possessed two natures became controversial and precipitated numerous discussions and arguments in the Christian world. (Tr.)]

7. [The twenty-fifth Patriarch, 444–454 A.D. (Tr.)]

position, which they did because they had no choice but to submit to the patriarch's orders. When the matter was discussed at the council of Chalcedon with other bishops, they said, "Has not the council of Nicaea decided that all Egypt would fall under the jurisdiction of the patriarch of Alexandria and that the bishops could not dispose of any matter without consulting with him?" When the council ordered them to submit to the will of the Byzantine patriarch, they grudgingly answered, "If we did that we would not be able to stay in our country because the people would kill us. If you want to dismiss us from our dioceses you can do that; we are reluctant to stay, and all that we want is not to die."

The Egyptian people did not hesitate for a moment to support their patriarch because they believed that the courage of their religious leader had helped them to realize their most cherished hopes. When the council of Chalcedon condemned Dioscorus and ordered him into exile, the Egyptian people, along with the monks, refused to recognize the authority of the new patriarch [of Alexandria] whom the emperor of Constantinople had appointed. Thus the schism in the Church opened, and later it widened after the doctrine of monophysitism, i.e., the monk Eutyches' doctrine, gained prominence. The dissidents in Egypt in 600 A.D. numbered six million and only 200,000 remained loyal to the Catholic patriarch, whose authority derived from the emperor in Constantinople. Naturally, the dissidents were natives of Egypt while the supporters were either Byzantines living in Alexandria, who were influenced by Greek culture, or their Coptic employees whose interests mandated that "they receive communion from the hands of their 'atheist' ruler."

We should not try to explain the doctrine of monophysitism because the Egyptians did not care for the advocate of the doctrine nor for his teachings. Their main goal was to secede from Byzantium. They considered religious dissent the first stage towards liberation.

Byzantium was well aware of the aims of Dioscorus and the reasons behind the people's enthusiastic support of him. Therefore, the emperor tried to convince the patriarch to change his extremist position and seek reconciliation. The emperor was embittered to see the unity of the empire collapse because of a conflict unsupported by strong reasons.

The emperor resorted to force to keep the secessionists under the authority of the Catholic pope. But he first did his best to settle the dispute in a way satisfactory to the two conflicting parties. The Emperor Zeno[8] suggested a

---

8. [Zeno (426–491 A.D.), from Isauria, was emperor of the eastern Roman Empire (474–491 A.D.). (Tr.)]

solution known as *henoticon*.[9] Later, Emperor Heraclius[10] suggested another solution known as *ecthesis*.[11] But the Egyptian people rejected both solutions because they were not ready to resume their relationship with the emperor after they had made great efforts to terminate it. The Egyptian clergy were not the only supporters of Patriarch Dioscorus. The whole Egyptian nation followed him. Internal peace in Egypt was disturbed after the council of Chalcedon and a new era of persecution was started which the Copts called "catholic terror." The Egyptian people and the Egyptian monks considered that Cyrus the patriarch, whom Heraclius had appointed in Egypt before the Arab conquest, was the enemy of Christ because he tried to force them to accept the doctrine of *ecthesis*, which the emperor had mandated in Constantinople.

However, after the council of Chalcedon the Copts made no effort to push on towards their goal of independence, nor did they continue their struggle to achieve that goal. While religion occupied a very high position in their national consciousness, they strongly believed that if they won their religious independence they would achieve the most important part of their political freedom. Hence, they did not try to deepen the schism which they had created. Moreover, they were not qualified to take over the government because they had no experience in governing. If the Copts had tired of the oppressive Byzantine rule, their long years in serfdom had made them doubt their ability to free themselves from foreign guardianship. Deep in their hearts they merely wanted a change in government that might consolidate religious peace and ensure the reduction of the heavy taxes that they had to pay. They always expressed their readiness to support the enemies of the government in power if those enemies appeared ready to carry out their wishes.

In 609 A.D. when Nicetas, a deputy of Heraclius,[12] invaded Egypt, many Egyptians volunteered to help him without knowing exactly what benefits they would reap from the new ruler. They had no other incentive to support him than their hatred for the government in power. Nicetas wanted to follow a wise policy

---

9. [Henoticon was a theological formula that sought union of monophysites and other Christians by omitting reference to the number of natures in Christ. (Tr.)]

10. [Heraclius (575–641 A.D.) was emperor of the eastern Roman Empire (610–641 A.D.). (Tr.)]

11. Ecthesis was a formula written by Sergius, patriarch of Constantinople, and published by the emperor Heraclius in 638 A.D. both forbidding further debate about the existence of one or two energies in Christ and asserting the doctrine of the two natures of Christ united in a single will. (Tr.)]

12. [Phocas was then emperor of the eastern Roman Empire (602–610 A.D.). After being defeated and murdered by Heraclius in 610, the latter became emperor. (Tr.)]

towards the Egyptians after his victory. Therefore, he refused to interfere in the religious dispute and postponed collecting taxes for three years. As a result the Egyptians remained content and historians agree that peace prevailed throughout the country.

In 619 A.D. the Persians, under the Sassanid king Khosrow or Chasroes, invaded Egypt and committed terrifying atrocities. However, they did not involve themselves in religious matters. Consequently, the Copts did not feel uncomfortable with their presence nor did they protest against their authority. In fact, they were unhappy that the Persians left after ruling the country for nine years (619–627 A.D.). It is worth mentioning that the people did not help the Persians against the Byzantines. Moreover, they did not show any resistance when the latter came back to rule Egypt.

In summary, the Egyptian people had not hoped for more than national independence based on religious freedom and low taxes, a policy followed by `Amr ibn al-`Āṣ[13] when he invaded Egypt. Surely, `Amr was assisted by Heraclius' behavior. A few years before the Islamic conquest Heraclius had tried to bring the Copts back to the domain of the Byzantine Catholic church. This attempt angered the people and made them cooperate with the Arab invaders, while they continued to be loyal to Christianity to the extent that the defeat of the Byzantines appeared to be a punishment against deviant Christians and an assertion of the doctrine of monophysitism "which enjoyed God's blessings." The Jacobite Bishop Hanna al-Naqyusi [John of Nikiou] wrote, "Let us praise our master Jesus Christ and praise his holy name all the time, because he has protected us, we Christians, until this moment, from the evil of the pagans and the apostates and he has defeated the atheists, the traitors."[14] The same historian was more explicit when he added that the deviant Christians, the followers of the doctrine of the council of Chalcedon,[15] were the ones who hurried to adopt Islam, not the followers of monophysitism.[16] I do not go too far if I say that consolidating Arab sovereignty in lieu of the Byzantine sovereignty in Egypt brought a glimpse of hope to the Christians of the east. Michael the Syrian, patriarch of the Jacobites of Antioch, wrote, "The God of revenge brought from the southern regions the sons of Ishmael to save us from the hands of the Greeks. Although we have suffered some losses, because the

---

13. [`Amr ibn al-`Āṣ: 575–663 A.D. (Tr.)]

14. Hermann Zotenberg, ed. and trans., *Chronique de Jean, Évêque de Nikiou*, Paris, 1883, p. 586.

15. [i.e., Duophysites. (Tr.)]

16. Zotenberg, *op. cit.*, p. 585.

churches taken from us and given to the followers of the council of Chalcedon remained in their hands after the Arab invasion, yet we still gained a little by being liberated from the cruelty of the Romans and their evils and anger, and from their rancor against us; moreover, peace has prevailed among us."[17] What actually happened was that the Jacobite [and Coptic] church was revived and strengthened under `Amr ibn al-`Āṣ. For some time, the native population believed that the victory of the Muslims would help Christianity. More explicitly, if we want to be precise, the doctrine of monophysitism regained its influence.

---

17. J. B. Chabot, ed. and trans., *Chronique de Michel le Syrien Patriarch Jacobite d'Antioche, 1166–1199 A.D.*, 4 vols., Paris, 1899–1924, 3:417.

Chapter 2

THE ARAB CONQUEST

The Attitude of the Arabs toward the Copts, the Nature of Their Invasion and the Copts' Attitude toward Them.

Muslim legislators issued a number of laws for the Ahl al-dhimmah,[1] i.e., "Copts," inspired by the Qurān and Hadith.[2] But the Fuqahā'[3] [scholars of jurisprudence] were not always able to impose their views on the rulers who avoided adopting such views whenever circumstances or interests forced them to do so.

The differences between principle and reality, and the hesitation of the Muslim administration vis-à-vis the Ahl al-dhimmah during the conquest, had their effects on the relations between the defeated people and their new masters, that is between Copts and Muslims.

In order for us to explain the relationship between these two elements of one and the same people, it is not enough for us to go back to the roots of the Islamic invasion. We should put ourselves in the atmosphere of the events of that time. We cannot understand the position of the Arabs nor the reaction of the Copts unless we know the hidden and declared intentions of both parties. We also cannot distinguish between the measures taken by the Arabs relating specifically to the Copts and measures of a general character.

The first period of the Islamic conquest is full of vagueness and ambiguity. Therefore, we should try to throw some light on it to elucidate the

---

1. [Ahl al-dhimmah refers to the dhimmis, people of the covenant or obligation. According to Muslim common law, at the conquest of a non-Muslim country by Muslims, the population that does not embrace Islam and that is not enslaved is guaranteed life, liberty, and in a modified sense property. The dhimmis' status involves temporal rights apart from Muslims and duties towards Muslims. But such a dhimmah is strictly open only to the people of scripture (Ahl al-Kitab), thus to Jews, Christians, and Sabeans, which has been interpreted to cover Zoroastrians. Each adult dhimmi—male, free, sane—must pay a poll-tax (jizyah). See "Zimmah" in *Hughes' Dictionary of Islam* (London, 1885) and "Dhimma" in *First Encyclopedia of Islam 1913-1936* (Leiden, 1987). (Tr.)]

2. [Hadith are the sayings of Prophet Muhammad which are often referred to as the Traditions. (Tr.)]

3. [*Fuqahā'*, plural of *faqih* (sing.), denotes scholars of *fiqh* (jurisprudence). Different schools of *fiqh* were founded during the first centuries of Islam, most prominently the Shafi'ī, Hanafi, Hanbalī, and Malikī (Sunnite schools). (Tr.)]

points which might seem at first glance far from the main topic, but in fact had a clear influence on the development of relations between Muslims and Copts.

A. The Attitude of the Arabs towards the Copts.

The Prophet Muhammad had compassion for the Copts.

It seems that the invasion of Egypt was decided before the death of the Prophet. However, Egypt had an important position in the plans of Islam's military expansion. Had not al-Muqauqus[4] [Cyrus] the ruler of Egypt shared—along with the king of the Persians and al-Najachi [the King of Ethiopia] and the Byzantine emperor—the honor of receiving the messenger sent by the Prophet Muhammad, calling them to convert to Islam?[5] Although the Prophet never visited Egypt he had apparent compassion for the Copts. The Hadith says, "I urge you to take good care of the Copts; you will find them the best helpers when fighting your enemies."[6] All the Muslim historians and writers compete in citing the Ahādith[7] that express strong compassion for the Copts. Included in these Ahādith is what he said just before his death: "O God, O God, how good are the Copts! You will prevail upon them and they will be your supporters and followers in the cause of God." In another Hadith he says, "The Copts of Egypt are uncles and in-laws and they are your supporters against your enemies and supporters of your religion." When he was asked, "How could they be supporters of our religion, O Messenger of God?" he said, "They will save you the trouble of

---

4. [This was the name that the Arabs gave to Cyrus the bishop of Phasis and later the governor and patriarch of Alexandria appointed by the Byzantines. The Arabs mistook him for a Copt. He was the one who chose to negotiate the surrender of the fortress of Babylon on April 6, 641 A.D. (Tr.)]

5. [Before the surrender of the fortress of Babylon in Egypt (641 A.D.), the Prophet Muhammad sent letters to the Byzantine emperor, the Persian king, and to Cyrus asking them to convert to Islam. Specifically, he sent Hatib ibn Balt'ah to Cyrus with a letter which said: "In the name of Allah the Merciful, the Compassionate. From Muhammad the messenger of Allah to al-Muqauqus the chief of the Copts. Peace be upon those who follow the right path. I invite you to Islam. If you convert to Islam, you will become safe. If you convert to Islam, God will reward you twice. Say to the People of the Book: Let us agree upon one matter which is the same for you and us, namely, that we worship none but Allah, that we associate no partner with Him, and that some of us accept no others as lords beside Allah. If they turn away, say to them: Bear ye witness that we have submitted to Allah." See Ibn 'Abd al-Hakam, Futūh Misr, Leiden, 1920, p. 46. (Tr.)]

6. Ibn 'Abd al-Hakam, ibid., p. 3.

7. [Ahadith is the plural of hadith, a saying of the Prophet Muhammad. (Tr.)]

doing the work of this world, and you devote yourselves to worship." The Prophet also said, "If Ibrahim lived, I would not have made a Copt pay the *jizyah*."[8]

It is clear that what the prophet says specifically about a people whom he did not know, and was thinking of conquering, may cause surprise and astonishment. However, we are confident that the founder of Islam had every good intention toward the native inhabitants of Egypt. We may ask: Did Maria [Muhammad's Egyptian Christian wife] have a positive influence on the feelings of the Prophet? Was the prophet made aware of the enmity of Copts toward their Byzantine rulers? Did he deduce, based on this enmity, the tendency of the Copts towards cooperating with the Muslim invaders? If we were to believe this interpretation we could explain the meaning of the letter that the Prophet sent to Cyrus, although Cyrus was a subordinate to the Byzantine emperor.

Nevertheless, Egypt was geographically far from the Arabian Peninsula, and the Arabs had crossed the lands of Syria and Lebanon on foot because they had no fleet to cross the Red Sea. On the other hand, when the Prophet defeated Quraysh and entered Mecca victorious, he gave priority to the unification and administration of the Arabian Peninsula. He did not seriously think of spreading his authority over new lands. His successor, Caliph Abu-Bakr (11–13 A.H./632–34 A.D.), spent most of his governing years in consolidating the unity of the Arab tribes and clearing out pockets of resistance from among revolting tribes. The Arabs did not feel confident in pursuing military activities outside the Arabian Peninsula until the Caliphate of `Umar ibn al-Khattab (13–23 A.H./634–44 A.D.).

The Arabs found no political reason to conquer Egypt.

Many writers have tried to determine the reasons that led the Arabs to invade Egypt. It is difficult to find political justification for the invasion, and Muslim historians in particular have not troubled themselves over the matter.

In fact, the Persians and the Romans sought rest from the wars which had exhausted them. They were certainly not afraid of the tribes that inhabited the vast Arab deserts. If we look into the works of the Arab historians who have shown interest in the two letters that the Prophet Muhammad sent to the emperors of Persia and Byzantium, we come to agree with them that the Byzantine emperor did not want to respond to the invitation sent to him, while the Persian king tore the message to pieces in public, declaring his spite for the Arab race. We say this to illustrate that the Arab conquests were not for defensive purposes. Is it not a

---

8. Ibrahim was the Prophet Muhammad's son from Maria the Copt. He died at the age of nine. [*Jizyah* was the poll tax paid by the dhimmis in an Islamic state. (Tr.)]

simple matter to learn the reasons for these conquests? Islam unified the Arab tribes that used to wage war against each other. They also used to plunder and loot because of bad economic conditions. When the spirit of reconciliation, which Islam spread among them, replaced the common state of enmity, it was natural for the people of Arabia to look for a less arid land from which to make a living. The Muslims readily left their country and took by force the rich lands of the "pagans" and "polytheists," pushed by their strong religious belief and their conviction that the people who did not adopt Islam concealed enmity for them.

It has been said that need justifies every aggressive deed. History tells us that long before the advent of Islam the Arabs were very aggressive in looking for food. [They had invaded Egypt during the pharaonic period, had resided for some time in Assyria, and were also successful in invading Ethiopia]. These [early] conquests were not accompanied by the appearance of a new religion or mission. Dr. Sulayman Huzayyin, the Egyptian geographer, once said that there is a connection between these successive invasions and climatic conditions. Supporting his theory of climatic changes and their effects, he held that there was proof that the climate of northern and southern Arabia, in the period between the twelfth century B.C. and the third century A.D., was more humid than it is now and that rainfall diminished, starting in the third century A.D. It gradually decreased until the sixth century when the drought reached its apex. But he later added that it would be an exaggeration to hold that the Arab expansion was due to the climate of the Peninsula. Nevertheless, the drought must have had its influence on the expansion.[9]

The reasons for the Islamic invasion were not religious only.

Some scholars have tended to portray the early Arab invaders as if they were missionaries driven by their hope of conquering the whole world. There is no doubt that religious enthusiasm was a strong factor in the activities of the newly converted to the new religion. But we cannot say for sure that the desire to preach was the main reason behind the conquests. Ibn Khaldūn[10] tells us that when

9. Huzayyin, Sulayman, *Bilad al-'Arab wa al-Sharq al-Adna*, Cairo, 1924, pp. 11–12 (in Arabic). [See also his "Spread of the Arabs and of Islam: Its Relations to Climatic Changes and other factors." *Bulletin of the Geographical Society of Egypt*. Vols. LI and LII, 1978-79, p.p. 5-22. (Tr.)]

10. [Ibn Khaldūn, 'Abd al-Rahman (1332–1406 A.D.), was an Arab historian, philosopher and sociologist from North Africa. (Tr.)]

`Umar ibn al-Khattab[11] was selected as the caliph of the Muslims, he stood to talk to the audience and urged the truly faithful to invade Iraq, saying, "The Hijaz [Arabian Peninsula] is not a suitable home for you except for grazing your sheep. Its people cannot stay in it except by grazing their animals. Where are the immigrants who were given a promise? Rove the earth which God promised in the Book[12] to give you as an inheritance."[13]

The policy of the Arab leaders changed completely after contacting the outside world. We know that, when the Christian emperor Heraclius conquered the pagan Persians, the Prophet Muhammad congratulated him publicly, disregarding the negative results that that victory might have on the Islamic religion. In the second year of the *Hejira*,[14] we also see him at the battle of Badr[15] fighting one thousand of the Quraysh tribe with only three hundred fighters. But the responsibility of governing made his successors look carefully before taking any steps. Political considerations replaced sentimental ones.

The expansion of the Arab empire east and west lessened the influence of the religious factor. The Caliph `Umar ibn al-Khattab was forced to follow a wise policy that contradicted the enthusiasm and courage characterizing the early converts to Islam. At least this is what we understand from Muslim historians. They have described the conquest of Egypt as a military action decided on by Arab leaders after long hesitation. They have also assured us that the approval of `Umar was not obtained easily, but in fact he was forced to give that approval. One contemporary writer has objected to this assessment by saying that it was against the nature of the famous caliph. He said, "It is unbelievable that `Umar—who subjugated the Persians and the Romans and caused the greatest kings on the earth to flee before his [invading] armies—permitted the army to march to conquest and

---

11. [`Umar ibn al-Khattab was the second of the four Guided Caliphs (13–23 A.H./634–644 A.D.). (Tr.)]

12. [The Qurān. 14:14 (Tr.)]

13. Ibn Khaldūn, *al-Muqqadimah (Prolegomenon)*, Cairo, 1284, 1:122 (in Arabic).

14. [*Hejira* or *hijra* refers to the migration of the Prophet Muhammad from Mecca to Medina in 622 A.D. The term "Anno Hejira" (abbreviated A.H.) is now applied to the Muslim calendar that began in 622 A.D. (Tr.)]

15. [The Battle of Badr was the first major encounter between the Muslims and the Meccans, taking place on the 19th of Ramadan 2 A.H. (March 17, 623 A.D.). (Tr.)]

Jihad,[16] then reneged and ordered the fighting to be stopped, while knowing that his orders might result in weakening the will of the fighting men and encouraging the enemy."[17]

But `Umar, who was known for his wisdom and farsightedness, could not voluntarily jump into a raging war. Did the Arabs know anything about Egypt? They were mostly ignorant of everything related to that country. Because they did not have geographical maps, they took the route followed by other invaders which `Amr ibn al-`Aṣ[18] had come to know during his travels to Egypt. Do not the historians tell us that the Arab forces were totally ignorant of the Fayyum region and that a guide showed them the way indirectly? Did not Hanna al-Naqyusi [John of Nikiou] prove that the Muslims did not know Medinat Misr [the capital of Egypt]?[19] We believe that, except for `Amr's persistence, the conquest of Egypt would have been delayed for a long time. In fact, `Amr was the first to induce the Arabs to invade Egypt, and he entered it as a victorious conqueror.

In the Jahiliya,[20] `Amr ibn al-`Aṣ used to trade with Egypt.[21] Legend has beautified the reality when it refers to one of `Amr's meetings that took place coincidentally in Palestine, and made him continue his travel to Alexandria where he attended a festival at which participants played a game wherein a ball was thrown among them. The one on whom the ball fell was believed to be the future

---

16. [*Jihād* literally means "an effort" or "a striving," and comes to mean a religious war against those who do not believe in the mission of Muhammad. To pursue *jihād* is an incumbent religious duty, established in the Qurān and in the Traditions as a divine institution, and is enjoined especially for the purposes of advancing Islam and repelling evil from Muslims. Muslim fundamentalists consider *jihād* one of the major duties of a Muslim. See *Hughes' Dictionary of Islam* under "Jihad" and *Encyclopedia of Islam* under "Jihād;" see also A. J. Abraham and George Haddad, *The Warriors of God, Jihad (Holy War) and the Fundamentalists of Islam*, Bristol, Indiana, 1989. (Tr.)]

17. Akush, Mahmud, *Misr fī `Ahd al-Islam, Fath Misr wa al-Iskandariyah (Egypt in the reign of Islam, the conquest of Cairo and Alexandria)*, Cairo: National Library, 1941, pp. 26–27 (in Arabic).

18. [`Amr died in 42 A.H./663 A.D. "He passed for one of the most wily politicians of his time." See *First Encyclopedia of Islam*, vol. 1, pp. 334–335. (Tr.)]

19. John of Nikiou, *op. cit.*, p. 557.

20. [Originally, *jahiliya* meant "days of ignorance," which refer to the period of Arab history before Islam. But some contemporary writers believe in Sayyid Qutb's definition of *jahiliya*. He says, "The Jahili society is that which does not follow Islam." See *Milestones* by Sayyid Qutb (Rev. ed., Cedar Rapids, Iowa, 1980), p. 93. (Tr.)]

21. al-Kindī, Abi `Umar Muhammad ibn Yusuf, *Kitab al-Wulah wa al-Qudah (The Governors and Judges of Egypt)*, edited by Rhuvon Guest, Leiden, 1912, p. 7.

13

ruler of Egypt. The ball fell on `Amr who was just a spectator. This incident stirred the curiosity of the players, who were the elite of Alexandria.

`Amr doubtless studied the conditions of the country during his repeated travels to Egypt. He probably noticed the hatred that the people harbored for their Byzantine rulers and observed both the chaos that had spread in the administration and the weakness of the forces responsible for defending the country. The fertility of the earth and the attendant affluence fascinated him. He described that country for `Umar ibn al-Khattab at the right time, saying, "Conquering Egypt is a source of power and support for the Muslims. It is the most affluent land, and the least competent, when it comes to fighting and war."[22]

When Palestine fell under Arab control, `Amr asked `Umar privately for permission to march to Egypt, saying, "I know it and its roads. It is the least resisting, but it is the richest." However, "The Emīr al-Mu'minīn [the Prince of the Faithful] hated to attack the Romans who were in Egypt, and `Amr tried to make the invasion of Egypt look easy to `Umar."[23] This is exactly what al-Kindī said, from which we understand that in the beginning `Umar refused `Amr's request. But, "'Amr continued to attach great importance to Egypt for `Umar ibn al-Khattab, and to tell him about its conditions, and to make invading Egypt look easy, until `Umar became convinced and authorized him to lead four thousand men who were all from Ak. It was said they were three thousand five hundred."[24] Ibn `Abd al-Hakam repeats the words of `Umar: "March and I will seek God's protection for your march."[25] Ibn `Abd al-Hakam added that `Amr did not hesitate a moment in carrying out the order of `Umar, marching with his army at night without anyone being aware of his movement. Ibn `Abd al-Hakam also tells us[26] that when `Uthmān ibn `Affan[27] went to see `Umar, the latter informed him of `Amr's march to Egypt. It was said that `Uthmān commented on that news by saying, "O Emīr al-Mu'minīn, 'Amr is daring and venturesome and has a love for

---

22. Ibn `Abd al-Hakam, *op. cit.*, p. 56.

23. al-Kindī, *op. cit.*, p. 7.

24. Ibn `Abd al-Hakam, op. cit. p. 56. Ak was a town in Yemen.

25. Ibn `Abd al-Hakam, *op. cit.*, p. 56.

26. *Ibid.*, pp. 56–57.

27. [`Uthman ibn `Affan was the third of the four Guided Caliphs (23–35

A.H./644–45 A.D.). (Tr.)]

authority. I am afraid he goes without a reliable group to support him, thus exposing Muslims to death, hoping for an opportunity which may or may not come."[28] 'Umar redrafted his letter to 'Amr for fear of what 'Uthmān said, writing the following: "If you receive my letter before you enter Egypt, return to where you were, and if you have entered it, go ahead."[29]

Most Arab historians mention that 'Amr received the message of 'Umar, and they claim that 'Amr did not open the message until he entered the land of Egypt for fear that the message might contain an order canceling the march.

If these events are true, they indicate that the Arabs tried to achieve a compromise between their religious beliefs and their military and economic goals when they started their contacts with the outside world. Jihad wars [holy wars] were not the incentives behind the conquests, but were the results of these conquests. We shall see, when we talk about the Arab administration, that Arab rulers were seeking material gain besides urging the conquered peoples to convert to Islam.

There is a third point that needs to be clarified in order for us to understand the meaning of events that followed the Arab conquest of Egypt, that is, the Arab sense of superiority toward conquered peoples. The Arabs of the Arabian Peninsula were a racially conscious people, and they prevented foreigners from relating to their tribes. The orientalist Poliak[30] has said in one of his studies, supported by solid evidence and by the observations of Abu Yusuf al-Faqih,[31] that "residence in the Arabian Peninsula, and speaking the Arabic language were not sufficient to consider the residents of Arabia Arabs, if they were immigrants, even if they had immigrated centuries previously.[32] Further, the native Arab did not lose his nationality after his stay in a foreign country, even if his stay lasted several centuries."[33] Poliak adds, "The word Arab did not have the same nationalistic

---

28. Ibn 'Abd al-Hakam, op. cit., pp. 57–58.

29. We can consider 'Uthmān's statements, as retold by Ibn 'Abd al-Hakam, valid. The proof is that 'Uthmān forced the resignation of 'Amr, after he became a caliph under 'Umar ibn al-Khattab, and appointed Abdallah ibn S'ad in his stead.

30. [Poliak, Abraham N., "L'arabisation de l'Orient semitique," La Terre d'Islam, 1938, Cahiers 1. (Tr.)]

31. [Yaqub ibn Ibrahim ibn Habib al-Ansari (Abu Yusuf al-Faqih), 113–82 A.H./731–98 A.D. He was one of the disciples of Abu Hanifah the Muslim jurist. (Tr.)]

32. [This is true to the present time. (Tr.)]

33. Poliak, op. cit.

meaning which it has today because the Arabs did not know what citizenship and lack of citizenship meant. The Muslim who lived before the Abbasid revolution[34] considered the Arabs a hereditary social tribe which ensured its members of some privileges as well as duties.[35] Racial origin was not the reason for its unity, but the same habitat [i.e., the Arabian Peninsula], which was [also] the reason for this revolution."

The Arabs of the Peninsula continued to adopt this principle until the Abbasids came to power. Father Janot noted that the converts to Islam from the Mawali—Christians, Jews, and Samaritans who were not of Arab origin—were not fully integrated into the Arab Muslim society when they converted to Islam, but had to seek a relationship to an Arab tribe, and paid dearly for that relationship. Even so, they were considered second class Muslims.[36]

We deduce that the conquered peoples who converted to Islam during the early years of the Islamic call were not cordially received by the Arabs or in a brotherly manner. Arabs put them in a lower social position compared to their own. We are also surprised when we compare the inferiority of the position of Muslims who were not of Arab origin with the excellent treatment allotted to Arab tribes that remained Christian after the advent of Islam. This treatment was a logical extension of a real condition which goes back to the time of Jahiliya [the "days of ignorance"]. With regard to this matter, we know that Syrian merchants in Medina were working publicly to propagate their beliefs. Muhammad the Prophet was seen frequenting the Christian communities. It was never reported that the syndicate of the Qurashite merchants expressed fear at the presence of [Christian] monks among them nor of them propagating their religion in the markets close to their city. A small number of the Christian Qurashites continued

---

34. [The Abbasid revolution against the Umayyads was begun in June 747 A.D. by Abu Muslim near Merv. In September 749 A.D., Abbasid troops took Kufa and in November 749 A.D. Abu al-Abbas (al-Saffah) was proclaimed caliph. In June 750 A.D., the massacre of most Umayyad family members by the Abbasids took place. The Abbasid dynasty ruled from 750 to 1258 A.D. in Baghdad. (Tr.)]

35. The Abbasid caliphs tried hard to facilitate the integration of the Mawali [supporters or clients], who had converted to Islam, into the genuine Arab tribes. In this light, the books of *Fiqh* which were written during the Abbasid period did not differentiate between the status of the Mawali [who knew the Arabic language and culture well] and the native Arabs.

36. Father Janot, "Les chrétiens devant l'Islam," in *La Terre d'Islam*, 1945, Cahier 3. With respect to this matter we mention an incident which irritated some Copts in Egypt who claimed kinship to one of the big Arab families in the Arabian Peninsula. They surely had bought that relationship. Their claim stirred public opinion and they took their case to the judge al-Imari who approved their kinship relation. But some people took their case to the Baghdad judge, al-Bakri, who disappointed them by not granting their request. See al-Kindī, *op. cit.*, pp. 399, 413, 415.

to enjoy a privileged status for which they were qualified by their birth and skills. The proof is that the tribe of Bani Asad, which particularly sympathized with Christianity, continued to have their homes near the Ka`ba, while the foreigners [i.e., non-original Arabs] moved to distant sections of the city or to the suburbs.[37]

When the Prophet Muhammad dominated the Arabian Peninsula, he wanted to include the Christian tribes. He [thereby] unintentionally raised the problem of Christian Arabs. No one could discredit their Arab nationality, and they were determined to maintain their prestige and dignity. Further, they refused to allow the Muslims to treat them as second class Arabs.

The Prophet was the first to write to the Christians of Najran, inviting them to sign a pact with him in the tenth year of the Hejira. The tribe of Najran sent a delegation to negotiate with the Prophet to get the best terms and to bring him to understand that the tribe would never abandon its creed, whatever the price might be.

No one dared to impose *jizyah* [poll tax] on those Arabs. However, the tribe of Najran agreed to some of the conditions later imposed on conquered peoples[38]. Nevertheless, the Muslims were very careful, when they wrote the pact, not to hurt the feelings of the Christian citizens by not putting the pact into effect. The following are examples which support this observation:

1. The Prophet was entitled to have control of the property and slaves of the tribe, but he actually left the investing of these resources to the tribe in return for an annual levy of one thousand she-camels.

2. The Christian people of Najran had to host the Prophet's emissaries (without special reference to soldiers) for twenty days or less, and not exceeding thirty days.

3. If war broke out in Yemen, they had to lend thirty horses and thirty camels.

4. They had to give up lending money at interest.

5. No one was entitled to force the members of the tribe to abandon their religion under any circumstance.[39]

---

37. Father La Mens, "Les chrétiens à la Mecque à la veille de l'Hegire," in *Études orientales de l'Academie francaise*, vol. 16.

38. [The texts of the agreements between the Prophet and the tribe of Najran can be found in Muhammad Hamid Allah's "Majmu'at al-Watha'iq al-Siyasiyah lil-'Ahd al-Nabawi wal-Khilafah al-Rashidah." Beirut: Dar al-Irshad, 1969. Document numbers 93-96, 99-104 and 106. (Tr.)]

39. Abu Yusuf (113–82 A.H./731–98 A.D.), *Kitab al-Kharaj*, Cairo: Bulāq Press, 1302 A.H./1884 A.D., p. 40 (in Arabic). See appendix one for the complete text of this covenant.

Moreover, no one thought of imposing *jizyah* on the Christians of the tribe of Bani Taghlib. They were only requested to pay double what Muslims pay of *zakat*[40] on condition that women should pay this tax. From this we deduce that what the Muslims imposed upon the Arabs in the form of *zakat* was imposed on the Christians of conquered countries in the form of *jizyah*.[41]

Aside from these conditions, we can say that for a long time the Arab Christians enjoyed certain privileges which the Arab [Muslims] denied some other peoples who adopted Islam. For example, the Christians of Arabia joined the army and fought with the brigades which invaded Persia and marched to Egypt, while the Copts who adopted Islam were not immediately accepted into the Arab army. When they were later accepted, they were enrolled in the foot soldier brigades which meant that, in case of the army's victory, they were entitled to only half the horsemen's share of the war spoils.[42] Finally, we note that the conversion of Arab pagans was by force. Those who did not respond to this obligation were punished by death, if they were men, or by slavery, if they were women or children. But the Christians of Arabia were able to remain Christians while the Muslim leadership was doing its best to convert them to Islam.

We cannot deny that the presence of the Christian elements among the Muslim population of the Arabian Peninsula was unwanted. It is said that before his death the Prophet expressed his desire that Arabia should not have two religions. The Christians of Najran became worried when they heard this news. They immediately sent a delegation to Abu Bakr who assured them that the pact that they had concluded with the Prophet was still in effect.

`Umar ibn al-Khattab followed another policy towards the Christians of Arabia, and he started to antagonize them, claiming that they practiced usury.[43] He later attacked the Bani Taghlib and tried to impose the *jizyah* on them. They had no alternative but to leave Arabia for Iraq. During that time, a man called al-Nu`aman ibn Zur`ah ibn al-Nu`aman went to see the caliph to criticize his policy towards the Christians, saying, "By God, Bani Taghlib are Arab people who are above the *jizyah*, and their vindictiveness is great. Do not let your enemy push you

---

40. [*Zakāt* is the obligatory alms tax on all Muslims. See *Hughes' Dictionary of Islam* and *First Encyclopedia of Islam* under "zakāt." (Tr.)]

41. Abu Yusuf, *op. cit.*, p. 68.

42. Leone Caentani, *Annali dell' Islam*, vol. 2, no. 1, "Events of 10 A.H.," pp. 311ff.

43. Abu Yusuf, *op. cit.*, p. 41.

against them."[44] When 'Umar heard this, he sent for them and offered them the following conditions: "not to mark a child,[45] not to force their religion on a child, and to pay double the alms."

We do not know whether the members of the tribe accepted these conditions. In fact, they paid no attention to them, which made 'Ali ibn Abu Talib announce, "If I had had time for the Bani Taghlib, I would have killed their fighters and taken their children as prisoners of war. They have breached the covenant and, since they have baptized their children, I have no obligation toward them."[46]

Although the Muslims of Arabia were sorry that some of their compatriots were still Christians, they never tried to hurt them. But that contradictory position gradually disappeared. When the Muslim victories [abroad] came one after the other and grew in importance, the Arab conquerors considered the loyalty to Christianity of some of their compatriots as a challenge to them. 'Ali ibn Abu Talib threatened them several times, but he could not put his threats into effect. The Umayyads succeeded in achieving what he could not do. Surprisingly, Mu'awiya thought seriously of preventing the Copts of Egypt from converting to Islam, claiming that if they all converted to the true religion [Islam] they would cause the treasury a great loss in income from the *jizyah*. But during the later reign of the Caliph al-Walid ibn 'Abd al-Malik,[47] "the Ta'is' leader,[48] called Muhammad, wanted the Christian Arabs to convert to Islam after he had acted evilly in Iraq and killed many of its people. He ordered the leader of the Taghlibis, named Ma'az, to be brought to him. He requested that he abandon his religion, but Ma'az refused, in spite of every inducement. As a result, he ordered him to be thrown into a ditch full of mud and killed. He did not allow his body to be buried."[49]

---

44. al-Baladhūrī, Ahmad Ibn Yahya (d. 892 A.D.), *Kitab Futūḥ al-Buldan*, edited by M. J. De Goeje, Leiden, 1865, p. 181.

45. [By tattooing the sign of the cross on the wrist or arm, and baptizing the child. (Tr.)]

46. al-Baladhūrī, *op. cit.*, p. 183. It seems that the religious aspect was just a pretext because the Bani Taghlib were friends of Caliph 'Ali and later supporters of the Umayyads.

47. [al-Walid ibn 'Abd al-Malik was an Umayyad caliph (86–96 A.H./705–15 A.D.). (Tr.)]

48. The Arab Syrians are known by the name Ta'is who were related to a tribe called Tay'i.

49. Michael I, Jacobite Patriarch of Antioch (1125–99 A.D.). See J. B. Chabot, ed. and trans., *Chronique de Michel le Syrien Patriarche Jacobite d'Antioche*, 3 vols., Paris, 1899–1924

(continued...)

We have never found violent religious incidents like this among the Arabs of that time. The Arab Muslims' anomalous position with regard to the Christians of the Arabian Peninsula was due to the sense of racial superiority among Arabs. The following sentence from Michael the Syrian supports that statement: "al-Walid, the Caliph, told the monk Sam'a Allah al-Taghlibi, `Your worship of the cross, although you are the head of an Arab tribe, makes your people ashamed of you.'"[50]

B. Was the Arab Victory Great?

Before we study the position of the Copts after the Islamic invasion, we should like to strip the military actions of `Amr ibn al-`Āṣ of their exaggerations. Historians and orientalists alike have portrayed the Arab conquest of Egypt as an easy military operation against a well-fortified country that was defended by several well-trained army divisions. Is it not an exaggeration to say that conquest was achieved "with lightning speed" or that it was "one of the miracles?"[51] We look in vain for effusive enthusiasm in the writings of the Arab historians when they describe the Islamic victories in Egypt. When recording the events of the invasion, they did not try to belittle the difficulties that the Arabs faced nor their heavy losses.[52] They never claimed that the resistance of the enemy was insignificant, nor that their own army was like lightning, nor that the population hurried to sign a treaty with the invader. It is true that they tended to exaggerate when they mention the numbers of the enemy, but they did so with good intentions because they were ignorant of the real conditions of the Byzantine empire. It was the Byzantine historians who continued to hide the catastrophe that had befallen their armies. Now we can clarify the approximate condition of both parties.

49(...continued)
(reprinted by Culture et Amblisation, Brussels, 1963), 2:480–81.

50. *Michel le Syrien*, 2:480–81.

51. Wiet, Gaston. *L'Égypte musulmane de la conquête arabe à la conquête ottomane.* Cairo: L'Institute français d'archéologie orientale du Caire, 1932, vol. 2, p. 113.

52. The Muslims who attacked the Babylon fortress consisted of twelve thousand three hundred soldiers, not including those who died or were killed during the siege. See al-Kindī, *op. cit.*, p. 9.

A comparison between Alexander the Great and 'Amr ibn al-'Āṣ.

The Nile Valley has been an easy and attractive prey for anyone who has wanted to invade it. Many a time neighboring countries took the opportunity, during the weakness of the controlling authority, to invade the valley. The Hyksos, Libyans, Ethiopians, Assyrians, and Persians invaded it in different periods.[53]

Led by Alexander the Great, the Greek invasion was doubtless the most successful. Briefly speaking, Alexander arrived at al-Farama[54] after taking over Tyre and Gaza; he then proceeded to Memphis, the capital, without shooting one arrow, and evicted the Persians. The people were happy because they had suffered under the yoke of the [Persian] tyrants, and they showed enthusiasm for the new invader. Afterwards, Alexander went north and laid out the city of Alexandria. He marched westward along the Mediterranean Sea coast until he arrived at Mersa Matrouh, then southward to the Siwa Oasis before he returned to Memphis. Alexander was able, in less than a year, to conquer Egypt and control it. To a great extent, the Arab conquest of Egypt resembled the Greek one.

'Amr ibn al-'Āṣ, like Alexander, knew that the people wanted new rulers. He also knew that the country was not well-fortified and that he could easily invade it. In this light, he invaded with the 3500–4000 soldiers put at his disposal by the Caliph 'Umar. However, it seemed that 'Amr was not ready to go to war against fortifications because, in spite of the two reinforcements sent to him by the caliph from Arabia, he was able to overcome the resistance only after three years of fighting. Moreover, it seems that the Arab invasion was not a military picnic, as some have imagined, nor was the morale of the fighters high. Ibn Kathīr said, "When 'Amr ibn al-'Āṣ met Cyrus, many Muslims withdrew from the march and 'Amr called them back by blowing a horn and urged them to remain steadfast. One of the Yemeni soldiers told him that they were not made of stone or iron. 'Amr retorted, 'Shut up, you are a dog.' The man said, 'Then you are prince of the dogs.'"[55]

---

53. The Hyksos ruled Egypt about 1660–1555 B.C. (15th–16th Dynasties). The Libyans ruled Egypt about 945–715 B.C. (22nd Dynasty). Persian domination included a first period, about 525–404 B.C. (27th Dynasty); second period, about 343–332 B.C. (31st Dynasty); and a third period, about 628–39 A.D. The Ethiopian and Nubian Dynasty ruled about 747–656 B.C. The Assyrians invaded Egypt in 671 B.C. and again in 677 B.C. Their rule of Egypt ended in 656 B.C.

54. [Pelusium or al-Farama lies to the south-east of the lake Manzala. (Tr.)]

55. Ibn Kathir, Ismail ibn 'Umar (1301-1373 A.D.), *al-Bidayah wa al-Nihayah*, Cairo: Matb'at al-S'ādah, 1932, vol. 7, p. 99 (in Arabic).

If we were to study the strength of the forces sent to Egypt, we would learn that 'Umar was correct to complain of the slowness of the military operations on the Egyptian front.[56]

The Arab army.

The data that has reached us concerning the number of Arab army divisions that invaded Egypt is not accurate; but no historian has previously objected to it.

The Arab divisions included at first four thousand soldiers whom the Caliph 'Umar put under the leadership of 'Amr ibn al-'Āṣ. Those divisions proved to be unqualified to carry out the operation that they were charged with. During the siege of the fortress of Babylon, 'Amr ibn al-'Āṣ twice requested reinforcements from the caliph. 'Umar sent him eight thousand fighters in two installments under the leadership of al-Zubayer ibn al-'Awām. Thus the number of the fighters under 'Amr's leadership grew to twelve thousand. Some sources on which al-Kindī has depended say that the fighters totaled 15,500 soldiers.[57]

No one doubts the value of those fighters and their courage, because their good qualities were the major reason for the lowering of morale among the Byzantine forces. They were daring horsemen who knew well how to use arms. Nevertheless, they did not perform well except on flat battlefields. If they were obstructed by fortified walls, they camped in front of them for longer or shorter periods, according to the circumstances. For example, they were forced to fight in front of the city of al-Farama [Pelusium] for about a month; the fortress of Babylon resisted them for seven months; and Alexandria resisted them for fourteen months.

The leaders of the campaign, especially 'Amr and al-Zubayer, did not have war as their profession. But they were trained in Syria in the arts of war and they did not lack ability to maneuver.

---

56. 'Umar the caliph wrote to 'Amr ibn al-'Āṣ during his siege of Alexandria saying, "I have been surprised because of your slowness in conquering Egypt. You have been fighting them for two years." (Ibn 'Abd al-Hakam, *op.cit.*, p. 79).

57. al-Kindī, *op. cit.*, p. 9.

The Byzantine army.

We knew little about the organization of the Byzantine army until Jean Maspero published his book, *The Military Organization in Byzantine Egypt*.[58] Ten years before Maspero published his work, Alfred Butler stated in his book, which included much information about that army, "The Copts were wholly out of action—crushed by Cyrus; and it is untrue to represent them as capable of combining among themselves or of fighting or dealing with the Arabs."[59]

Jean Maspero has been able to give us an authoritatively accurate and important picture of the organization of the Byzantine army in Egypt. The emperor Justinian[60] reorganized the Byzantine army in Egypt by abolishing the unified leadership of the army for fear of a revolt against the central government by the chief of the colonial army. He also destroyed the administrative unity of the country maintained by the Romans during their rule. Instead of the diocese of Egypt, he established five duchies governed by five governors or dukes appointed by the emperor and directly responsible to him. These governors were at first foreigners; later they were selected from natives. They held both civil and military authority.

Headed by civilians, the army's responsibility was clear. Surely it was entrusted with defending the land of Egypt. But it proved incapable of doing so when the Persians invaded Egypt in 619 A.D., a short time before the Islamic invasion. This was due to the fact that the army was overburdened by policing functions, such as chasing thieves, maintaining internal peace, helping tax collectors, and supporting the position of the empire in a doctrinal schism. There was no army that could devote all its time for defense. What was mistakenly called an army was nothing but a police force which had no unified leadership, nor a military leader. The leadership was divided among five civil chiefs who enjoyed equal authority.

Maspero states that the army consisted of 23,000 men who were enough, or more than enough, to repulse the twelve or fifteen thousand fighters put under `Amr's leadership, especially because the [Byzantine] army was protected behind fortifications. However, while the Arabs were under a unified leadership and attacked their enemy in large numbers, the Byzantines never thought of effecting

---

58. Maspero, Jean, *L'Organization militaire de l'Egypte byzantine*, Publications de la Bibliothèque des Hautes-Études, no. 201, Paris, 1912 (reprinted by G. Olms, New York, 1974).

59. Butler, Alfred J., *The Arab conquest of Egypt and the last thirty years of the Roman Dominion*, Oxford, 1902, p. 252.

60. [Justinian I was the east Roman emperor (483–565 A.D.). (Tr.)]

a plan for defense based on cooperation [between the different governors]. Thus, while the Arabs were increasing their pressure on the fortress of Babylon, not one single governor came to the rescue of the besieged units. Each of them was awaiting his turn to repulse the enemy's attacks, effectively making the Arabs outnumber the Byzantines.

Maspero summarized the reasons for the victory of the Arabs—and the Persians before them—stating, "The collapse of Egypt, in the face of the invasions in the seventh century, was not due to the lack of men. Moreover, the fortifications set up at the points exposed to invasion were in a condition that would support their holding out.

"The army of Egypt was divided and the leadership responsibilities were distributed among several leaders, each one of them fighting for his own interest. It is certain that the governor of Libya did not participate in the fighting until the Arabs attacked him directly after occupying the Nile Valley.

"The Byzantines were known for their indifference to the public interest, their schisms, and their uncooperativeness. They did not have officers whose job was to fight.

"The Egyptian army had only a small number of foreign mercenaries. It consisted of—in its major part—Egyptians (Copts) who had lost their military skills centuries ago.

"We conclude from what the historian John of Nikiou reported that the Byzantine army included leaders who lacked both knowledge of military science and fighting experience. Most of them panicked in the face of the danger and were unable to follow a well-coordinated plan. Each one of them fought for his personal interests without any discipline. The soldiers also were not trained nor were they loyal to their leaders.

"The main reason for the defeat of the Byzantines in the Nile Valley was the low level of [coordination in] the army that was charged with the responsibility of defending Egypt under the pressure of circumstances."[61]

The low morale of the Byzantines.

There was another factor that Maspero does not mention. He left it for us to understand it from the context, that is, the low morale of the Byzantines after the Arab victory over the Persians. If we accept what Michael the Syrian reported in his history, we notice that, instead of setting up his camp in the areas exposed to danger and organizing its defense and raising the morale of the people, Heraclius lost hope in victory before he met the enemy in the battlefield. When

---

61. Maspero, *op. cit.*, pp. 116–32.

he witnessed the extent of the destruction and ruin, he sadly left Antioch for Constantinople. It is said that, before he left, his farewell words were, "Stay safe Syria." He later wrote to all the Romans in Iraq, Egypt, and Armenia, warning them against engaging in battles with the Arabs and urging that anyone who was able to keep his job should stay where he was.[62]

Did Cyrus, the governor [and Byzantine patriarch] of Alexandria, understand from this message that the situation was left to his own discretion, and he [therefore] took the opportunity to negotiate with 'Amr? On his part, did the Arab leader think at one time to change his mind about invading Egypt in return for 200,000 dinars to be paid annually by the Egyptians? We should not leave out this assumption. Many details about this matter were reported in the history of Mahbūb.[63] The author reports something that we could not verify, saying, "After signing the treaty, Cyrus ruled the country resolutely for three years during which [time] no Arab came to Egypt. Nevertheless a number of Egyptians went to Heraclius complaining that Cyrus took money from Egyptians and gave it to the Arabs. As a result of their complaint Heraclius fired Cyrus as patriarch and appointed Admiral Manuel instead. When the Arabs claimed the *jizyah* from Manuel he told them, 'I am not Patriarch Cyrus who gave you gold to be safe from your evil. He is a monk who devoted his life to the service of God; but I am a man of fighting, war and courage.'" We can explain the firing of Cyrus by the emperor's temporary regaining his determination and renewed desire to resume fighting.

Actually, the morale of the Persians and the Byzantines dropped when they heard of the early Arab victories. Michael the Syrian reported a story that explains the conditions of those people when they went to war, which says, "Once there was a Persian hero wearing his suit of armor, carrying many arms, and running in front of an Arab who was pursuing him. This Arab did not carry any arms but his spear, holding it in his hand, and wore light clothes. On arriving at a village, the Persian found a man working in a field. He asked him to show him a hiding place for fear of his pursuer. The man hid him believing that there were many pursuing him. After some time a man, who did not seem to be a soldier, arrived riding a horse in a way that showed he was not trained to ride a horse.[64] The farmer was surprised, and his surprise increased when he saw how simple the

---

62. *Michel le Syrien*, 2:424–25.

63. *Kitab al-'Awān* by Mahbūb, translated by A. A. Vasiliev, in *Patrologie Orientale*, vol. 8, Paris, p. 474.

64. He means the bedouin way.

appearance of the man was, and he said to himself, `How did such a big man with his fearful appearance, wearing his suit of armor and carrying different arms, run away from such a thin man?' The farmer was infuriated by the scene, and [yet] he laughed at the Persian and ridiculed him because of fleeing and hiding from the Arab. The Persian responded, `Do not blame me for my behavior, but wait and see in order for you to believe me.' Then he took an arrow and shot it at an iron shovel, which it penetrated. Then he said, `I shot at that Arab with several shots like this one, but he was pushing the arrows away from him as if he were pushing away flies. From this I became sure that God gave them victory, and all I did was turn my back and run away.'"[65]

C. The Position of the Copts.

The Jewish escorts of the Arabs.

When his luck started to decline, Emperor Heraclius dreamed that a people who followed the custom of circumcision would revolt against him, conquer him, and rule the whole world. Heraclius believed that this people would be the Jews. He immediately ordered all Jews and Samaritans residing in every province of the empire to be baptized.[66]

At that time the Jews were not thinking of revolting, nor did they have the means which would allow them to rise against the Byzantine Empire. But when the Arabs marched through the land of their enemies, the Jews remembered the acts of violence and persecution that they had suffered under the Byzantines. They offered their services to the Arabs and gave them useful information, helping them in Syria and Egypt.

In light of these events, can we say that the Copts, like the Jews, wanted to take revenge on their persecutors in those difficult circumstances? Because the Copts were surprised by the unexpected Arab invasion and remained disoriented for a long time, we cannot say that they allowed events to decide their destiny. [But] when they wanted to take a positive stand, they realized that it was too late to make a decision.

Had the Arabs connived with the Copts to participate in the battle, they undoubtedly would have been able to depend on the general cooperation of the Egyptian people. But the people were ignorant of the Arab intentions and were

---

65. *Michel le Syrien*, 2:422.

66. Severus Ben El-Moqaffa', *Historia Patriarchorum Alexandrinorum* I.1, edited by C. F. Seybold, in *Corpus Scriptorum Christianorum Orientalium*, Louvain, 1954, vol. 52, tome 8, p. 107.

afraid of showing their enmity to the Byzantines during the battle, especially before Byzantium was on the verge of collapse.

The Copts wanted to change their rulers.

Heraclius persecuted the Copts by imposing on them the solution that he proposed under the name of "Ecthesis," which aimed at reclaiming them to the Byzantine church. The persecution was increased because of the Copts' hatred for Byzantium. However, persecution was not the only reason that made the people seek change in their government. By decreasing taxes, Heraclius was able to limit the negative effects of his religious policy on the psychology of the people. Nicetas[67] tried this approach after his victory over Phocas[68] by postponing the collection of taxes for three years. John of Nikiou acknowledged the fact that "the Egyptians showed great loyalty to him."[69]

It is known that since ancient times the Egyptians have hated paying taxes. They have shown enmity toward any authority that has imposed taxes on them. Ammianus Marcellinus,[70] the Roman historian of the fourth century, reported that "Egyptians in ancient times considered themselves naive if they paid what they owed the government without being forced, or at least threatened."[71] Gaston Wiet added, "As regards this simple financial matter, the writers limited themselves to that mentioned in Ammianus Marcellinus, or the message from Hadrian.[72] No one ever tried to attract attention to the laws of Patriarch Peter the Martyr [Botras al-Shahid] which imposed some [financial] duties on apostates who wanted to return, a punishment of Christians who willingly paid taxes in an effort to show themselves unblemished because thereby they showed a spite of money."[73]

---

67. [Nicetas was the Byzantine prefect of Egypt, 610 A.D. (Tr.)]

68. [Phocas was the emperor of the eastern empire (602–10 A.D.). (Tr.)]

69. John of Nikiou, *op. cit.*, p. 550.

70. [Ammianus Marcellinus was a Roman soldier and historian (320–91 A.D.). (Tr.)]

71. Gaston Wiet quoted this in his article entitled "Kibt," *First Encyclopedia of Islam*, vol. 4, pp. 994–1003.

72. [Hadrian was a Roman emperor (117–38 A.D.). (Tr.)]

73. Wiet, *op. cit.*

Germaine Rouillard mentions that in the fourth century people boasted about the beatings that they received from the tax collectors[74] and that the emperor's will was broken in the face of the resistance of the Egyptian taxpayers. That resistance increased vis-a-vis any increase in the taxes imposed under Byzantine rule.

Naturally the people listened willingly to the victor's promises of decreasing the taxes or eliminating them completely. But those who were exposed to death and torture for holding fast to their belief in monophysitism denied their belief in Christianity when they were requested to pay taxes to the Muslim invaders."[75]

Did the Copts receive the Muslims as liberators?

When the Arabs penetrated deeply into the Egyptian land, the Copts knew nothing about their intentions. They did not know whether the Arabs would force them to convert to Islam, confiscate their possessions, or maintain the Byzantine tax system. These matters continued to occupy the minds of the Copts. They did not come to realize the intentions of the Arabs until the Arab siege of the fortress of Babylon when the question of a truce was raised among the fighting parties. At that point the Copts felt that the Arab ruler was more tolerant than the Persians or Byzantines because he offered them three choices: (1) converting to Islam and stop paying *jizyah*; (2) accepting the Islamic protection and paying two dinars for every man capable of fighting; or (3) resuming the fight and accepting the results.

Moreover, the Arabs never tried to reassure the Egyptian people concerning their intentions because they did not know the Greek or the Coptic languages. They also abstained from publicizing their military actions. Although they fought with less fury and did not commit actions of destruction, or shed the blood of the people, yet they were sometimes forced to be excessive in committing both disgraceful acts and actions of severe repression, which did not help them to gain the confidence and support of the people.

Bishop John of Nikiou, who is the only contemporary source for the campaign, was more interested in reporting these excesses than in reporting positive things about the invasion. Unfortunately, he reported [only] the bad things in his *Chronicles*. Sadly, we are not able to verify the validity of his

---

74. Rouillard, Germaine. *L'administration civile de l'Égypte byzantine.* 2nd ed. Paris: Geuthner, 1928, p. 184.

75. Duchesne, Louis, *Histoire de l'Église au VIe siecle,* Paris: De Boccard, 1925, p. 425.

statements because the Arab historians did not incorporate all the details of the battles when they wrote their works. John of Nikiou, for example, reports, "`Amr ordered that the Roman judges be arrested and bound hand and foot in chains tied to wooded stakes; and he usurped the properties and doubled the taxes imposed upon the peasants whom he forced to supply fodder for the horses. He also committed many acts of violence."[76]

Religious zeal might be a reason for committing some acts of violence. John of Nikiou says, "When the Muslims entered a city accompanied by Christian apostates they took over the property of the Christians who ran away, and they called the servants of Christ the enemies of God."[77]

By and large, the Copts were unable to receive the Arabs as liberators because the invaders belonged to a different religion. It is true that the Arabs liberated them from the Byzantine yoke. But they were never comfortable with rulers who adopted a religion other than Christianity.

If we study the behavior of the Copts during all the stages of the battle, we shall be able to throw some light on their position. But before we do that we should mention something about the ambiguous identity of Cyrus.

The difficulty of verifying the identity of Cyrus.

The person whom the Arabs call al-Muqauqus (Cyrus) is still ambiguous. Was he Copt? Was he of Greek origin? Was the Cyrus who surrendered Cairo to the Arabs the same person who signed the treaty of Alexandria? Orientalists have not yet reached satisfactory answers to these questions after more than a century of research and investigation. Surely, we are closer to reality than people such as Champollion-Figeac[78] who portrayed Cyrus as a restless corrupt priest who succeeded Patriarch George in 630 A.D., while Egypt was ruled by a Copt. He was of noble origin and one of the richest in the country of those named al-Muqauqus. But the documents that we have been able to procure do not help us to solve decisively this historical mystery.

Historians have used the word Muqauqus as if it were a proper name. But we are sure of the origin of this word: Patriarch Cyrus, who was appointed by Emperor Heraclius as governor of the duchy of Alexandria, was before that the

---

76. John of Nikiou, *op. cit.*, p. 560. We shall refer later to the papyri related to the invasion.

77. John of Nikiou, *ibid.*

78. "L'Égypte ancienne," in *Collection L'Universe Pittoresque*, p. 480a. The author was the brother of F. Champollion who deciphered the Rosetta stone.

bishop of Faz, a city in Caucasia. In Egypt he was given the title al-Quqius (the Caucasian). A rare Coptic document, which was discovered and brought to our attention by Amélineau, testifies that "al-Quqius, that so-called bishop, allowed spite to grow in his heart until he arrived at al-Fayyūm,[79] . . . and when Father Samuel felt he was near death he told al-Quqius, `You [are] the deceptive Chalcedonian.'"[80]

It is likely that the Arabs corrupted the name, which is not a serious matter. What is serious is the confusion they fell into when they spoke of the different governors of Egypt. It seems that they neglected the fact that each governor was directly responsible to Byzantium and he had to submit his reports to the eastern administration only. It is true that Cyrus, the patriarch and duke of Alexandria, enjoyed a privileged status among all the other dukes because he was charged with collecting the taxes in addition to his other responsibilities. But he was unable to function outside the system, nor was he able to impose his own policies upon his colleagues, nor sign agreements with the conquerors on their behalf. We tend to believe—without being absolutely sure—that al-Muqauqus who negotiated the surrender of Babylon was a person other than the patriarch Cyrus who signed the Alexandria treaty, and that he was a Coptic governor. The Arab historians have abstained from verifying the identity of that governor. The Catholic historian Ibn al-Bitriq refers to al-Muqauqus as "a Jacobite who hated the Romans, but he was afraid to show his Jacobite belief lest they should kill him." Moreover Ibn al-Bitriq accused him of "cutting off the income from Egypt after the siege of Constantinople by Kisra.[81] He was fearful of falling into the hands of Heraclius lest he should kill him."[82]

What did the historians mean by the name "Misr?" Did they mean all of Egypt? I do not think so. Those who wrote the history in Arabic used the word "Misr" in the beginning to mean the "City of Cairo." Later al-Maqrizi,[83] who tried

79. al-Fayyūm was at that time an administrative district of the Alexandria duchy.

80. "Fragments coptes pour servir à l'histoire de la conquête de l'Égypte par les Arabs," *Journal Asiatique*, Nov.-Dec. 1888, pp. 361–410.

81. Kisra is the designation for the Persian kings in general. [This siege took place in 619 A.D. (Tr.)]

82. Ibn al-Bitrīq, Sa`id, *Tarikh Sa`id ibn Bitrīq*, edited by Louis Cheikho, Beirut, 1909, p. 22.

83. [Ahmad ibn `Ali al-Maqrizi, the medieval Arab historian (1364–442 A.D.). (Tr.)]

to be more accurate, distinguished between the land of Misr [i.e., the whole country of Egypt] and Fustāt[84] Misr [i.e., the city of Cairo].

What makes us believe that during the campaign the governor of Babylon was a Copt is the conspicuous difference between the Cairo and Alexandria treaties. While the Alexandria treaty concerned itself with the destiny of the Greeks, the Babylon one concerned itself only with the destiny of the natives [Copts]. Ibn ʿAbd al-Hakam[85] left no doubt about this matter. After mentioning the Babylon agreement, he added, "All this is about the Copts in particular." On the other hand, Cyrus wanted to talk to ʿAmr before the treaty came into effect. He told him, "My authority is on behalf of myself and on behalf of those who obey me. The peace with the Copts was reached between you and them, and this [Alexandria agreement] shows no sign of abrogating it. Concerning the Romans, I have nothing to do with them."[86] Ibn al-Bitriq tells us that al-Muqauqus "deceived the Romans" and told ʿAmr secretly, "As for the Romans, I have nothing to do with them; my religion is not theirs and my belief is not theirs either. But I was fearful that they might kill me; therefore, I hid my religion and belief from them."[87]

The suspicion and uncertainty of the Copts.

Because we have failed to learn the true identity of the governor who negotiated with the Arabs during the siege of Babylon, and therefore it is impossible for us to find a relationship between his position and the feelings of his compatriots towards the Arab invaders, we can be sure that the attitude of the Copts during the invasion was passive. Father Janot summarized their position as follows: "They made no effort to stop the catastrophe, and they hid behind the

---

84. [al-Fustāt was a city built by ʿAmr ibn al-ʿĀṣ in 640—41 A.D. with the permission of Caliph ʿUmar ibn al-Khattab. It was built in the area between the Nile and the Mokattam hills near the Babylon fortress. It flourished during the Umayyad period and beyond until Ibn Tulūn built the city of Qatāʾi. When the Fatimids built Cairo in 969 A.D., al-Fustāt deteriorated and was burned down in 1169 A.D. (Tr.)]

85. [Ibn ʿAbd al-Hakam, ʿAbd al-Rahman ibn ʿAbdallah (d. 870 A.D.), is the Arab historian whose book *Futūh Misr* is the earliest surviving account, from Arab sources, about the Arab conquest of Egypt and North Africa, the first Arab settlements in and about al-Fustāt and Alexandria, and allied topics concerning the occupation and early history of Egypt under Arab rule. (Tr.)]

86. Ibn ʿAbd al-Hakam, *op. cit.*, p. 72.

87. Saʿid ibn al-Bitriq, *op. cit.*, p. 24.

walls of the cities which the Arabs did not dare to invade, and waited for their attack."[88]

After an extended study of the period of the Guided Caliphs, based on original Arabic sources, one modern Egyptian writer states, "Doubtless the Copts did not help the Romans in fighting the Arabs, except to the extent they were forced, due to their reluctant submission to the hated authority of Caesar and his representatives. Doubtless they also did not help the Arabs, except in individual cases. Beyond that the people of Egypt took a position between the two fighting parties of a very inquisitive spectator."[89] Because the Egyptian people were spoiled by enslavement, they bore indifferently with the changing of their rulers, in spite of their nationalistic feelings.

Let us go back to the main topic. While 'Amr's armies were making their way to al-Farama, on the eastern border of Egypt, after making efforts that resulted in very high casualties, the Egyptian people remained quiet. As for the [Coptic] patriarch Benjamin, he was living in hiding. Some historians claim that, when that patriarch learned of the Arab invasion, he sent a message to all the bishops asking them to support the invaders.[90] But the events that followed belie that claim, a circumstance overlooked by subsequent historians.

The Arabs besieged the fortress of Babylon for a long time, forcing the Byzantines to be on the defensive rather than the offensive because of their small numbers and the weakness of their military planning. Reinforcements did not reach the besieging army. However, we do not find even one text that indicates that the Copts offered any assistance to 'Amr's army during the prolonged siege.

al-Muqauqus came out to address the garrison, saying, "The Arabs have received a reinforcement which is difficult to resist. We are afraid that they will overcome the fortress [Babylon] and kill us. But we can lock the doors of the fortress and station some fighters at them. Then we can depart to the island and stay there protected by the water." The Romans left with Cyrus, followed by a group of notables of the Copts, through the southern door of the palace, leaving behind them a group to fight the Arabs. They took the boats to the island and destroyed the bridge. This happened during the Nile flood.[91] This might have been a ploy by al-Muqauqus to get the Romans out of the fortress. Nevertheless,

---

88. Janot, *op. cit.* "Les Chretienes devant l'Islam."

89. Muhammad Husayn Haykal, *al-Farouk 'Umar*, Cairo, 1944, 2:94–95.

90. Ibn 'Abd al-Hakam related this statement to one of the prominent Egyptians; *op. cit.*, p. 58.

91. Ibn al-Bitriq, *op. cit.*, p. 22.

Ibn 'Abd al-Hakam does not accuse al-Muqauqus of treason, and he reports that al-Zubayer arrived with his men at the door of the fortress and broke into it. "When al-Muqauqus feared for himself and those with him, he asked 'Amr for peace and invited him to [accept] it in return for two dinars to be paid by every Coptic man."[92] Thus, at that critical moment al-Muqauqus thought of securing the future of his Coptic compatriots at the expense of the Byzantines.

Whatever the case may be, negotiations took a long time. Concerning this matter, Ibn 'Abd al-Hakam and Ibn al-Ditiq state that the leader of the fortress tried to negotiate a peace with the best possible conditions. He addressed the Arabs by saying, "You are the people who have invaded our country and have persisted in fighting us, and your stay has been prolonged. You are a small group and the Romans who are greater in number are ready to meet you with arms and armor. The Nile surrounds you and you are prisoners in our hands. Send us a man to tell us your opinion, hoping that matters will be settled as you and we would like. Thus fighting will stop on both sides before the Roman troops descend upon you."[93] But the Arabs were not deceived by these words and 'Amr sent someone to tell them, "Either you convert to Islam and become our brothers, who will have the same rights, or you refuse that and pay the *jizyah* submissively, or we get into fighting with you—while we are supported by patience and our fighting skills—until God, who is the best Judge, judges between us."

Then 'Ubada, one of the negotiators, added to the second offer the following: "If you refuse to convert to Islam you have to pay the *jizyah* to us submissively. We will agree to a certain amount which may satisfy you and us to be paid every year for life. We will also fight your enemies who transgress against your land or yourselves or possessions. We will do this on your behalf when you come under our protection, and if there is an agreement between us about it."[94]

Muslim historians have informed us that the Copts were unenthusiastic—if not resentful—about this offer, although they felt that they had lost the battle. Ibn 'Abd al-Hakam added that some members of Cyrus' entourage responded, "Does anyone accept this humiliation? That they want us to convert to their religion will never happen. We will never abandon the religion of Christ and adopt another one which we do not know. That they want to take us as prisoners of war and enslave us, death is easier than that. If they are satisfied with doubling what we have given them repeatedly, it would be easier for us to do

---

92. Ibn 'Abd al-Hakam, *op. cit.*, p. 63.

93. *Ibid.*, p. 65.

94. *Ibid.*, p. 68.

that."[95] Cyrus tried to help them think rationally by telling them, "`Let me tell you that I do not order you to convert to another religion; but I know that you would not be able to conquer them, nor do you have their endurance, and the third option is a must.' They said, `Shall we become their slaves forever?' He said, `Yes, you become slaves to a [foreign] power in your own country, safeguarding yourselves, possessions and children. This is better than dying to the last person or becoming slaves sold and dispersed in the world, forever slaves, you, your relatives and your descendants.' But they responded, `Death is easier for us.'"[96]

The situation ended with the Copts accepting the protection of the Arabs and `Amr promptly signing the peace treaty. But al-Zubayer ibn al-`Awwām[97] faulted him because he wanted to invade the fortress and enslave the population, distributing their properties among the Mujahedeen [religious fighters].

After the Copts accepted Arab protection, some offered services to the Arabs. History books clearly refer to this. Ibn `Abd al-Hakam states, "`Amr went out with some Muslims, when they were able to do so, accompanied by a group of Coptic notables. They had cleared the roads, built some bridges and opened markets for them. The Copts became their assistants in what remained of the fighting against the Romans."[98] John of Nikiou supports this statement. After he describes the occupation of Babylon and al-Fayyūm, and the attack of Alexandria, he writes, "At this point the Copts started to offer assistance to the Muslims."[99]

The Copts who offered assistance were those who were subdued by the Muslims, that is, those who acknowledged the tolerance of their new rulers. The rest of the Copts continued to be hostile. John of Nikiou noted that during the Arab march to the northern part of the Delta, "Panic spread in all parts of Egypt. The people fled to Alexandria leaving behind them their possessions and cattle."[100]

---

95. *Ibid.*

96. *Ibid.*, p. 69.

97. [al-Zubayer ibn al-`Awwām (593–656 A.D.) was an Arab commander and a companion of the Prophet Muhammad. When `Amr ibn al-`Ās asked `Umar ibn al-Khattab for additional troops to conquer the fortress of Babylon, he was sent several thousand soldiers under the command of Ibn al-`Awwām who succeeded in taking over the fortress. He also participated in the invasion of Alexandria. (Tr.)]

98. Ibn `Abd al-Hakam, *op. cit.*, p. 73.

99. John of Nikiou, *op. cit.*, p. 559.

100. *Ibid.*, p. 560.

Alexandria resisted for fourteen months. It could have resisted the Arabs longer than that, and even have defeated them, if it had received full reinforcements and if its people were not tired of fighting. "Cyrus, the Chalcedonian patriarch, was not the only one who wanted peace. Indeed, the inhabitants, the rulers, and Domentianus, the favorite of Empress Martina, met for consultation with Cyrus the patriarch to sign the peace treaty with the Arabs."[101]

When `Amr entered the city the people received him respectfully, in spite of what had happened to them. Naturally, the Arabs also grew tired of the war. The proof is that `Amr ordered the fighting stopped for eleven months in order to give the garrison of the city enough time to move out of the city with its arms and equipment.[102]

If we were to summarize most concisely our view concerning this matter, we should refer to the passage in which the orientalist De Goeje[103] described the position taken by Syrian citizens toward the Arab invaders. He said, "They were as spectators looking at the Arab forces subduing their country and they followed with curiosity the development of events that imposed upon them one of the two combatants. However, they showed some sympathy towards the Arabs, especially when they became sure that they did not have looting and plundering as their goals and that they dealt leniently and kindly with those who willingly submitted to them."[104]

101. *Ibid.*, p. 573.

102. *Ibid.*, p. 583.

103. [Michael Jan De Goeje (1836–1909) was a Dutch orientalist. (Tr.)]

104. De Goeje, Michael Jan, *Memoire sur la conquête de la Syrie*, 2nd edition, Leiden: E. J. Brill, 1900, p. 30.

Chapter 3

ISLAMIC LAW AND THE AHL AL-DHIMMAH

The Arabs knew little of the art of governing. As a result, the management of occupied territories kept them very busy. Moreover, the Qurān's precise instructions concerning the dhimmis did not make it easy for rulers to shoulder their responsibilities. In fact, they were compelled either to ignore some instructions of the Qurān and the Hadīth or to interpret them according to their own liking.[1] Thus, from the beginning of the invasion these Quranic principles were subject to menacing commentaries that increased the distance between the principles, which were sometimes harsh and humiliating to the dhimmis, and their implementation. It is worthwhile reviewing briefly the position of the Islamic *shari`ā* [or, law] both on employing dhimmis in the Islamic administration and on their style of dress, in order that we understand clearly what happened in Islamic Egypt.

The dhimmis in the Qurān.

The Qurān mentions the dhimmis at times in precise terms and at other times in ways that need explanation. The following are sample verses from the Qurān:

> "Let not believers take disbelievers for intimate friends in preference to believers." (*Sura Āl-Imran*, verse 28.) "O ye who believe, take not Jews and Christians as your helpers, for they are helpers of one another. Whoso from among you takes them as helpers will indeed be one of them. Verily, Allah guides not the unjust people." (*Sura al-Mā`idah*, verse 51.) "How can there be a guarantee for the others, who, if they were to prevail against you, would have no regard for any tie of kinship

---

1. [There has been a wide difference of opinion among the Muslim `Ulamā' about Muslims hiring Christians and Jews throughout Islamic history, including today. Some have interpreted the Quranic texts concerning the dhimmis in a way that forbids hiring them. Others have interpreted the same texts in a way that allows hiring them, with restrictions. Two important works on this subject are the following:

a. Ibn al-Naqqash, Muhammad (723 or 725–63 A.H./1320–61 or 1362 A.D.), *al-Madhammah fi Istimal Ahl al-Dhimmah (Reprehensibility of Hiring Ahl al-Dhimmah)*, Egyptian National Library, manuscript no. 1693, Fiqh Shaf'i, date of copying 858 A.H., p. 44.

b. Ibn al-Durayhim, `Ali (712–762 A.H./1312–1361 A.D.), *Minhāj al-Sāwab fi Qubh Istiktāb Ahl al-Kitah (The Right Way "to Explain" the Ugliness of Hiring the People of the Book "Christians and Jews")*, Egyptian National Library, manuscript no. 1404, Ahmad al-Thalith collection, date of copying 921 A.H., p. 80. (Tr.)]

or pact with respect to you. They seek to please you with words, which their hearts repudiate; most of them are perfidious." (*Sura al-Tauba,* verse 8.)

The conditions of `Umar.

The dhimmis were also subjected to "the conditions laid down by `Umar." We do not know how exactly this legislation was decreed. Historians such as Ibn `Abd al-Hakam, al-Kindī and al-Baladhūrī[2] were unaware of the legislation. No doubt some part of it was included in the history and law books, especially the texts related to one's dress. Al-Qalqashandi was the one who illustrated the official aspects [of `Umar's legislation] when he mentioned it in his book *Subh al-`Asha*.[3] However, we cannot disregard its importance because some of the walis in Egypt and in the Muslim world referred to it in a variety of [legal and social] contexts.

Its conditions did not take the shape of administrative orders. Rather they came out in the form of a letter written to Caliph `Umar by the Christians of a Syrian city seeking his approval of the letter's contents. The following is the text of the letter as it was included in *Subh al-`Asha*:

> "When you came to us we requested of you safety for ourselves, our offspring, our wealth, and our co-religionists. We have pledged that no new house of worship or a monk's cell will be built in our city or its environs; and that none of the collapsing churches or monasteries will be renovated; and that we will not hide any of these buildings located in the Muslim districts; and that we will not prevent any Muslims from residing in our churches for three nights full-board; and not to allow into our homes and churches a spy; and not to teach our children the Qurān; and not to display polytheism nor invite anyone to it, and not to prevent our relatives from converting to Islam if they want to; and to respect Muslims and to leave our seats for them if they want to sit down; and not to emulate them in their dress, in their caps and turbans and in their parting of their hair; and not to talk like them, nor use the same surnames they use; nor to ride on saddles or carry swords or any other arms; and not to engrave Arabic on our stamps; and not to sell alcohol; and to shave the

---

2. [See the bibliography at the end of the book for the full names and works of these three historians. These three sources will be quoted often in the work. (Tr.)]

3. [al-Qalqashandi, Ahmad ibn `Ali (1355 or 56–1418 A.D.), *Subh al-`Asha fi Sin`āt al-Insha*, 14 vols, Cairo: al-Matba`ah al-Amiriyah, 1913-1918, 13:357–60. (Tr.)]

front parts of our heads; and to abide with our religion wherever we go; and to wear girdles around our waists and not to have crosses on our churches; nor should we pursue the ways of Muslims nor emulate their behavior; nor should we ring our bells in our churches except lightly;[4] and not to raise our voices when reading in our churches nor in the presence of Muslims; nor should we celebrate Palm Sunday in the streets nor raise our voices nor light fires at funerals—especially in the streets and markets of the Muslims—nor should we bury our dead close to Muslims; nor should we take slaves selected by the Muslims; nor should we meet them at their homes."

`Abdel Rahman ibn Ghanim said, "When I delivered the letter to `Umar, he added to the previous statement: `We [Christians] will not beat anyone Muslim. This will be our obligation and our co-religionists'; and in return you will ensure our safety. If we did otherwise we will have no dhimmah, and you might do to us what you do to the people of obstinacy and dissension.'"[5]

Al-Qalqashandi added the conditions imposed upon the dhimmis thereafter: [to pay] a special tax (called *jizyah*), to host [Muslims], to submit to the Muslim administration of justice, to ride donkeys by putting both legs on one side of the donkey, to allow Muslims to head meetings and lead the way, to wear different dress from that of Muslims, not to allow their buildings to be higher than those of the Muslims, and not to build a new church in countries newly invaded by Muslims.

Preventing Muslims from employing dhimmis.

The conditions set out by `Umar overlooked a very important issue: Could Muslims employ Christians? There can be no doubt that the caliph missed mentioning this matter and that during his caliphate he consequently adhered to

---

4. The Jesuit Father Sicard wrote about using bells in the monasteries in the seventeenth century in his *Lettres Edifiantes* (p. 225): "There was a two-foot-high bell, two-feet in diameter, hanging in the monastery tower which was used to call us to all group prayers. The rings of these bells sounded a strong music in that desert, especially among the Turks." When were bells used in Egypt? We cannot answer this question. Mr. Habib Zayyat asked the same question in his paper published in *Majallat al-Mashriq* (1938), but he was unable to answer it. The Dominican Father Vansleb mentioned in his book *Nouvelle Relation* (pp. 293–313) that he saw in the church of Saint Paul and Saint Peter in the desert a small bell which was used to call the monks to prayer and to other functions. Because using bells in Lebanon was rare until the beginning of the nineteenth century, al-Zayyat deduced that the use of church bells entered Egypt in the late period.

5. al-Qalqashandi, *op. cit.*, p. 359.

the directions of the Qurān when he realized that the Quranic answer to that question was in the negative. One of the experts in *shari`a*, Muhammad ibn `Ali ibn `Abdel Wahid ibn Yahya, known by the name Ibn al-Naqqash,[6] has offered us several examples:

> "Abu Musa al-Ash`ari told the caliph [`Umar], `I have hired a Christian.' The caliph answered, `What have you done, man? God will punish you. Have you not understood God's saying, "O ye who believe, take not Jews and Christians as your helpers, for they are helpers of one another. Whoso from among you takes them as helpers will indeed be one of them. Verily, Allah guides not the unjust people." [*Sura al-Mā'ida*, verse 51.] I said, `O Prince of the Faithful, I hired him for secretarial work only, and I put aside his religion.' `Umar the Caliph said, `This is not an excuse. I will never honor those who are despised by God, and I will never elevate those who are put by God in a contemptible position, and I will not draw close to those whom God has put at a distance from himself."

One of the generals of the caliph wrote to him inquiring about the policy relating to appointing *infidels* in public positions, saying, "Money is pouring into the treasury in plenty and no one but them can do the accounting. Please let me know what should be done." `Umar responded, "Do not allow the infidels to have a share in your business; do not give them what God has denied them; do not put your money in their hands; and do not forget these principles which should be followed by every man." The caliph also wrote to one of his generals, "He who hires a Christian secretary [or, accountant] should not share his life with him, nor should he sympathize with him, or allow him to sit beside him, or take his advice, because the Prophet and his caliph ordered the dhimmis not to be hired."

The caliph received a letter from Mu'āwiya ibn Abī Sufyān saying, "O Prince of the Faithful, I have employed a Christian without whose help I cannot collect the *kharaj* [land tax]. But I am looking forward to receiving your orders before I let him start the job." The caliph responded, "I beg God to protect me from this evil. I have read your letter concerning that Christian. Please be informed that he has died."

---

6. Ibn al-Naqqash was a noted faqīh [Islamic jurist] and preacher at the Ibn Tulūn mosque in Cairo. He also lectured in that mosque and in other Cairo mosques. He was envied by many for his influence. He died in Syria in 763 A.H. (1362 A.D.). We have quoted him for two reasons. First, he resided in Egypt and spoke about Copts in his works; second, he lived in Egypt when the country was independent and when the Muslims were in complete control of it.

The opinion of the faqih [Islamic jurist] Ibn al-Naqqash is no less candid than that of `Umar himself, although it was expressed several centuries after `Umar's. The faqih was asked,

"What is the opinion of the Muslim ulamā', who are the leaders of the people, concerning hiring dhimmis and seeking their help as secretaries on the staff of the emirs for administering the country and collecting the *kharaj* [land tax]? Is it legal according to Islamic law, or forbidden?" Ibn al-Naqqash answered, "I would like you to know that the *shari`ā* does not allow hiring dhimmis, and this is the opinion of all Muslims. The ulamā' issued a *fatwa* [religious opinion] which forbids hiring dhimmis, absolutely forbidding it, or at least expressing their dissatisfaction with it. God has taught us that the Ahl al-Kitab [Christians and Jews] believe that they do no wrong if they fail Muslims or take over their possessions. In effect God the Sublime has said, `You may find one among the Ahl al-Kitab, with whom you may deposit a qintar [one thousand dinars],[7] and they will return it to you; and you may find among them someone who does not return to you one single dinar unless they are compelled to do so because, they say, `there is no obligation on our part towards Muhammad's followers.'"[8]

We can apply this view to the Copts of Egypt who believed that they were not tied to the Muslims by pledges. They thought that, if they were deprived of their possessions and men, they might even recover a small part of what they had lost in the past of both possessions and men. Ibn Naqqash also said,

"If it is said that the verses I have mentioned relate only to friendship with the Christians, while the real issue relates to their being hired for public positions, I say that one does not hire another except one whom he trusts, because he may find in him the qualities that make him honest. If you hire an honest man and become his friend, this would be an indicator of trust between you, and thus you appoint him. However, God the Sublime has solved the problem of the dhimmis decisively when he

---

7. [A dinar is a Muslim gold coin of varying weight, fineness and value. (Tr.)]

8. Ibn al-Naqqash did not quote the exact words of the Qurān, but he offered his own interpretation of verse 75 of *Sura al-Imran*.

said, 'Whoso among you takes them as helpers will indeed be one of them.'" [*Sura al-Mā'idah*, verse 51.]

Ibn al-Naqqash tried to console those who—in compliance with the Qurān and the orders of the sultan—might be forced to do without their Christian employees by telling them, "Christians are ignorant of the elements of arithmetic. They are even ignorant of its basic elements because they put three units into one and one unit into three."[9]

Interpretating the Qurān is a delicate and difficult task. Some fuqahā' [Islamic jurists] have commented on the Quranic verses that dictate the exclusion of dhimmis from official positions, although the Qurān does not mention it openly. But were not the fuqahā' the advisers to Islamic governments?

External restrictions imposed upon the dhimmis.

Some famous fuqahā' offered extended commentaries on some of the conditions of 'Umar. The judge of Baghdad, Abu Yūssuf Yaqūb ibn Ibrahīm, who was a contemporary of the Caliph Harūn al-Rushīd,[10] spoke of the restrictions imposed upon the dress style of the dhimmis in his book *Kitab al-Kharaj*.[11] We shall discus these restrictions later. Abu Yūssuf told the caliph,

> "To facilitate the collection of the *jizyah*, it is advisable to afix sealable rings on the necks of those liable to pay it as 'Uthmān ibn Hanif did. After the completion of the collection, the rings may be removed upon request. They should not be permitted to emulate Muslims in clothes, in riding horses and donkeys, or in their general appearance. They should wear girdles that resemble thick drapes tied around their waists. They should fix a wooden ball in the shape of a pomegranate [on their saddles] instead of the saddle bow, and double-lace their sandals, and should not

---

9. We could not locate the Arabic manuscript of Ibn al-Naqqash and were forced to depend on its French translation by Belin from which we took these quotations and translated them back into Arabic. [M. Belin's translation of Ibn al Naqqash is found in *Journal Asiatique*, November–December 1851, pp. 417–92, under the title "Fetoua relatif à la condition des Zimmis." The translator has the complete text of Ibn al-Naqqash's manuscript and attests that these quotations made by the author match the original text. Incidentally, Ibn al-Naqqash alludes here to the Christian religious belief in a divine trinity. (Tr.)]

10. Abbasid caliph from 170 to 193 A.H./786 to 809 A.D. (Tr.)

11. Cairo: Bulāq Press, 1302 A.H./1884 A.D., pp. 72–73. There are several editions of this important book.

emulate Muslims. Their women should not be permitted to ride on saddles. They should also be prevented from building new churches in any town except those wherein they had [church buildings] when peace was made with them and they were made dhimmis. Whatever belonged to them at that time, of synagogues and churches, should be left with them and should not be demolished. It is likewise in the case of their fireplaces. They should be permitted to live in the towns of Muslims and in their streets, to buy and sell anything except wine and pigs, and not to make a display of their crosses in the towns. They should wear long roundish caps.[12] Order your governors to require the dhimmis to adopt this dress."

`Umar ibn al-Khattab had also ordered his governors to ask the dhimmis to adopt this dress so that their clothing would be distinct from that of Muslims. Abu Yūssuf also said,

"`Abd al-Rahman ibn Thabit ibn Thawbān related to me on the authority of his father that `Umar ibn `Abd al-`Aziz wrote to his governor, `Do not permit the cross to be displayed in public, but it should be broken. Jews and Christians should not ride on saddles. Nor should any of their women ride on a riding animal, but should ride on pack-saddles. Regarding these matters, you should issue an effective and severe warning. Issue orders that no Christian in your domain should wear a cloak, or silk-clothes, or embroidered Yemeni clothes. It has been mentioned to me that many Christians in your domain have reverted to wearing turbans and have given up the girdles on their waists, and are showing their heads and are becoming accustomed to lengthening their hair. If all this is done before your eyes, then it is because of your weakness and leniency with them. If they are reverting to these practices, they intend to test your attitude towards them. So you should pay

---

12. It seems that clothes played an important role in the culture of the Arabs. al-Kindī relates a story about capes that was about to end in tragedy. The chief judge, Ibn Abi al-Layth, noticed that the judges in his jurisdiction had capes longer than usual. He ordered them shortened and swore that he would cut off the head of anyone who did not comply with his order (al-Kindī, *Kitab al-Wulah wa al-Qudah*, p. 460).

attention to everything that I have forbidden, and prevent people from indulging therein."[13]

---

13. This quotation clearly indicates that these restrictions were violated after their imposition. These violations were due to different reasons. We will return to this subject when we talk about the era of the *wulat*.

Chapter 4

THE REAL CONDITIONS OF THE COPTS
UNDER THE RULE OF THE WALIS

A. The Character of the Arab Occupation.

Good treatment by the invaders.

How did the Arabs treat the Egyptians when they occupied their country? The Arab historians were uninformed about this issue. But John of Nikiou portrayed a gloomy picture of the occupation, incorporating into it incidents of killing, looting, plundering, and destruction. Violence accompanies military campaigns, especially if their leaders are motivated by the enthusiasm of faith. Although John of Nikiou assures us of the Arabs' mismanagement of their victories, newly discovered papyri which go back to the time of the Islamic invasion prove that the Arabs' treatment of the dhimmis was not horrible. We have two documents, discovered by Professor Grohmann, that attest to this state of affairs.[1]

These documents go back to 22 A.H. [642 A.D.]. The first says, "In the name of Allah, I am Emir `Abd-Allah. I am writing to both of you, Christophorus and Theodorakios, of the province Heracleopolis. I have taken from you sixty-five sheep—not more—to feed my soldiers. I repeat, sixty-five sheep—no more—and all are expected to be informed about what I have done. I have dictated this acknowledgement, written by Yuhanna the deacon, the registrar of contracts, on the 30th of Bermuda of the first term."[2] This document was written in Greek. An Arabic text was attached which said, "In the name of Allah, most Gracious, ever Merciful, this is what `Abd-Allah ibn Jabir and his fellow fighters have taken of sheep for slaughtering in Heracleopolis. We took from the agent of Theodorakios, second son of Apa Kyras, fifty sheep for slaughtering and fifteen others. `Abd-Allah took them to feed his boatmen and horsemen and his infantry. Dated Jumada 1, 22 A.H. and written by Ibn Hadid." On the back of the document appeared the following statement: "An acknowledgement of giving the sheep to

---

1. Grohmann, Adolf, "Aperçu de Papyrologie arabe," in *Études de papyrologie*, Cairo: Imprimerie de l'Institute français d'Archéologie orientale, 1932, 1:23–95.

2. [Probably he meant the term of the tax year. Bermuda is the 4th month of the Coptic calendar (April). (Tr.)]

the fighters and others who came to this country; the price of these sheep will be deducted from the *jizyah* due in the first term."[3]

While nowadays wars occur in which combatants compete in committing savage acts,[4] we should mention that during war, at a time when the nations of the world were known for violence and cruelty, the Arab tribes respected personal ownership.

The following is the text of the other document. "In the name of Allah I, Emir `Abd-Allah, am writing to you, the chief merchants of Psaphthis city. Please sell fodder to `Umar ibn al-`Asl`a for the Quta division in the amount of three gold dirhams,[5] each of the [measures of fodder] for two aroures.[6] Each soldier should receive three kinds of food."[7] Grohmann concluded by observing, "This [positive] treatment of a conquered people is rarely shown by a victorious people."

The Arabs lacked a consistent policy.

It was really unfortunate that the greed created by both Egypt's wealth and the caliphs' suspicion of their viceregents had sinister consequences. Statistics indicate that the Guided Caliphs, along with the Umayyad and the Abbasid Caliphs—from 20 to 252 A.H. [641 to 866 A.D.], that is, from the waliship of `Amr ibn al-Ās to the waliship of Ibn Tulūn—appointed one hundred and eleven walis in a period of two hundred twenty-five years. Although some walis were appointed two or three times, yet the short periods that they were allowed to rule did not permit them to follow a constructive policy or, at least, to think of specific [constructive] plans.

Gaston Wiet[8] offers an interesting statistic that starts with the death of `Amr ibn al-Ās [43 A.H./644 A.D.] as follows:

"During the Umayyad Caliphate twenty-one walis ruled Egypt. Two of them ruled twice and one ruled three times. One of them ruled the country by the name Ibn al-Zubayer; but the caliph removed him after a

---

3. Grohmann, *op. cit.*; Papyrus Rénier, pp. 41-42.

4. [The author wrote this book towards the end of World War II. (Tr.)]

5. [A dirham was a Muslim silver coin of varying weight and value. (Tr.)]

6. [An aroure was a Muslim copper coin. (Tr.)]

7. Grohmann, *op. cit.*, pp. 44–46.

8. Wiet, Gaston (1887–1971), *Les Mosques du Caire*, Paris: E. Leroux, 1932, p. 19.

short period. Five of the walis were relatives of the caliphs. Six of these walis died during their tenure. The caliphs transferred or removed eleven walis. One of them resigned, another was forced out by his soldiers because he reduced their salaries. The last wali was probably killed by the Abbasids. One of them stayed on the job for a mere sixteen days[9] while another ruled for twenty years, which is the longest period that any wali ruled Egypt.[10] The Abbasid caliphate appointed sixty-four walis for Egypt. Nine of them ruled twice and one three times. During al-Ma'mūn's reign, the army units which remained loyal to the memory of Caliph al-Amin appointed five of them. Twelve of the walis were from the caliph's family. Ten of them died during their tenure and fifty of them were transferred or removed. Two of them were assassinated. Rebellious soldiers dismissed one wali and another resigned to join these soldiers. It is worth noting that the number of the walis transferred from their positions increased under the Abbasids compared to the Umayyads. This was due to the fact that the central authority, under the Abbasids, was far away in Baghdad. The caliphs did not want to give the walis enough time to be able to win the people to their side. Fear of the power of the walis caused the caliphs to suffer perpetual anxiety. It is most probable that fear led to the killing of the Baramakids,[11] a tragedy which tainted the memory of Caliph Harūn al-Rashīd."

We may add to this that twenty-four walis ruled Egypt during Harūn al-Rashīd's Caliphate alone, a period of twenty-three years. Wiet also indicates that the "instability which accompanied the appointment of the walis was not at all in the interest of the country. How could an employee, who was a foreigner and certain not to stay in his position, be expected to care for the country or manage its resources or worry about its administration?"

There is another characteristic of Arab rule in Egypt, and all countries occupied by Arabs during the period of the Arab invasions: the lack of a plan to

---

9. His name was Hassan ibn 'Atahiya.

10. He was 'Abdel 'Aziz ibn Marwān, son of the caliph Marwān I (64–65 A.H./684–85 A.D.) and brother of the Caliph 'Abd al-Malik ibn Marwān (65–86 A.H./685–705 A.D.). But for his death he would have ruled for a longer period. His brother had appointed him as his successor.

11. [A famous Persian family which played an important role in the affairs of the Abbasid dynasty during the rule of the first four Abbasid caliphs (132–93 A.H./750–809 A.D.). Caliph Harūn al-Rashīd (170–93 A.H./786–809 A.D.) destroyed this family, confiscated its property and killed its head J'afar al-Barmaki. (Tr.)]

be followed. Political, economic and social decisions were haphazard. This was because the Arabs did not, in the beginning, intend to reside in these countries nor to administer their affairs. Their sole goal was to secure the rear of their army in order to pursue new conquests and to obtain enough money to continue their military activities.

As a result, the Arab soldiers did not try to mix with the defeated people, because their leaders kept them from doing so. Ibn `Abd al-Hakam reported Caliph `Umar's words about the occupation army in Egypt: "I do not like Muslims to settle where water separates me from them in winter or summer."[12] This meant that Arab soldiers had to maintain their military character and not think of settling in the country.

If we exclude the orders related to tax collection and sending the money and wheat to the Arabian Peninsula, we in fact can find no plan to bolster the economic growth of the country. "Trajan's Canal was dug again, not to promote trade but to facilitate sending the wheat of Egypt to arid Arabia easily and in a short period of time. It did not take long for the sands to refill the canal—at the beginning of the eighth century A.D. The rulers of Egypt blocked it in 144–45 A.H. [761–62 A.D.] to prevent sending provisions to the city [Cairo] when it became a source of revolution."[13]

Public works were [almost] completely neglected. However, it was necessary to utilize the water of the Nile, which was rich with silt, especially during the flood season. The rulers used forced labor to clear canals, and to build roads and bridges. In return the laborers were exempted from a part of the taxes proportionate to their accomplishments.[14] We can find no evidence of any effort to spread education, even long after establishing Arab colonies in the Nile Delta. On the other hand, the Arabs established a tax system, but they did not think of establishing an accounting office in Medina.

Although building churches was not allowed in cities founded by the Arabs, `Abd al-`Aziz ibn Marwān permitted building one in Helwan [to the south of Cairo]. This tolerance can be explained by the existence of some Melchite

---

12. Ibn `Abd al-Hakam, op. cit., p. 91. Quoted in al-Maqrizi, al-Khitat, vol. 1, p. 296. `Umar was referring to the location of the new capital of Egypt [al-Fustāt].

13. Heyd, W., L'histoire du commerce du levant au moyen-âge, Amsterdam: Adolf M. Hakkert, 1959, 1:40–41 (reprint of Harrassowitz edition, 1885–86).

14. al-Maqrizi, al-Khitat. 1:74.

Christians in the service of the wali.[15] The Caliph al-Ma'mūn's policy was no different when he resided in Egypt and employed Christians who solicited from him the right to build a church near Qubat al-Hawā' [in the Shubra district of Cairo].[16]

Bishop Sawirus ibn al-Muqaff a[17] reported that, when the water level in the Nile went down in 136 A.H. [752 A.D.], the Muslims prostrated themselves in front of God begging him to increase the water level to allow it to overflow the banks of the Nile; then the Jews did the same, in vain. The miracle did not take place until the Christians began praying. The vice-wali, Ba'ūn, decided to reward them by reducing the *jizyah* and giving them assurances of security for their lives and property in all of Egypt.[18]

It seems fitting to give another example to prove our statement about the haphazard policy of the Arab rulers and their contradictory decisions. In 169 A.H. [785 A.D.], the wali 'Ali ibn Sulayman ordered all newly built churches in Egypt to be destroyed. He was offered fifty thousand dinars to abandon the project, but he refused.[19] His successor, Musa ibn Issa, in 171 A.H. [787 A.D.] permitted the reconstruction of these churches for purely financial reasons. He did not make that decision until he sought the opinion of the fuqahā' on the issue. Their *fatwa* [formal legal opinion][20] was that churches were "part of the building trade 'construction' of the country."[21] They added that the wali should not be more excessive than his predecessors because, "most churches in Egypt were built under Islam during the time of the Sahaba [companions] and the followers of the Prophet."[22] We should note that some years before, in 117 A.H. [735 A.D.], a mob

---

15. Ibn al-Bitriq, *op. cit.*, p. 41.

16. *Ibid.*, p. 58.

17. [Sawirus ibn al-Muqaff a was bishop of al-Ashmunīn (fl. 955–87 A.D.). (Tr.)]

18. Ibn al-Muqqaf a, *History of the Patriarchs*, pp. 207–08.

19. al-Kindī, *op. cit.*, p. 131.

20. [A *fatwa* is a published opinion or decision regarding religious doctrine or law made by a recognized authority who is often called a *muftī*. (Tr.)]

21. *Ibid.*, p. 132.

22. *Ibid.*, p. 132. [The number of persons entitled to this distinction at the time of the Prophet's death is said to have been 144,000. The number includes all persons who had ever served as followers of the Prophet and who had actually seen him. Anyone who embraced Islam, saw the Prophet and accompanied him, even briefly, was a Sahabi. (Tr.)]

killed al-Walid ibn Rifā`ah because he permitted the Christians to build Mar Mina church.[23] Probably the Arabs' need for money at that time was not great.[24]

It is clear that the high turnover among authorities, the lack of concern on the part of the Arabs for the people whom they subjugated, and the confused and contradictory policies of the walis created an atmosphere devoid of mutual understanding.

B. The Ambitions of `Amr ibn al-Āṣ and its Results.

Mrs. Devonshire has said, "There is not a single wali of the ninety-eight who were appointed in Egypt[25] who deserves to have his name immortalized."[26] This harsh judgement against the walis of Egypt sets off the strong personality of `Amr ibn al-Āṣ. Because `Amr was the conqueror of Egypt and the first to rule her, he established a special system that we can readily understand, based on his various actions and deeds. `Amr knew how to solve serious problems without depending on clear-cut precedents that did not exist at the time. Because his policy aimed at gaining the support of Christians, he gave the institutions of the country the air of tolerance, which allowed Copts to enjoy some essential privileges.

`Amr sought to rule Egypt in an absolute manner.
Naturally a conquered people received the commander of a victorious army with awe and respect. John of Nikiou acknowledged that, "`Amr's position

---

23. *Ibid.*, pp. 77–78. [Mar Mina church was located in Old Cairo. (Tr.)]

24. Gaston Wiet reports in the *Encyclopedia of Islam* under "Kibt" that the legal theory concerning building new churches goes back to the second century A.H. (eighth century A.D.).
[Two important works exist on the Islamic rules related to the construction and renovation of churches and synagogues in Muslim states. All the rules related to this matter are restrictive and sometimes prohibitive:
a. Ward, Seth, *Construction and Repair of Churches and Synagogues in Islamic Law*, A treatise by Taqī al-Dīn `Ali ibn `Abd al-Kafi al-Subki, 1284–1355 A.D. Yale University, Ph.D. Dissertation, 1984.
b. Pearlman, Moshe, ed. and trans., *Shaykh Damanhūrī on the Churches of Cairo (1739)*, Berkeley: University of California Press, 1975. In English translation, the original title of this work is *Presentation of the Clear Proof for the Obligatory Destruction of the Churches of Old and New Cairo*. (Tr.)]

25. After `Amr ibn al-`Aṣ.

26. Devonshire, H., *L'Egypte musulmane et les fondateurs des ses monuments*, p. 22.

grew stronger day by day."[27] Actually `Amr's reputation became such that Caliph `Uthmān sought his help when the Byzantine armies repeated the attack on Alexandria, despite his hatred for him and his accusations that `Amr was greedy and venturesome. `Amr responded to the caliph's request without hesitation. Did he not consider Egypt to be his own property which the caliph had taken away from him when he relieved him of the viceregency? His return to his former position might enable him to rule the country for his own interests and to disregard the authority of the caliph.

`Amr's ambition was not new. It was first expressed the day that the Babylon fortress surrendered to him. His sympathy for the conquered armies cannot be explained without acknowledging his ambition. Nor can we explain his contracting an honorable peace with his enemies, despite the opposition of al-Zubayer[28] and a good number of his army, and despite the ability of the Arab army to invade the fortress and exploit its victory to the end. We cannot explain his actions without acknowledging his ambitious nature. When we come to Alexandria, we find the same readiness for tolerance, even though the city resisted the invaders for fourteen months, forcing al-Zubayer and his companions to protest once more [to `Amr] because they wanted to apply the *shari`a* principles related to a conquered people.

al-Zubayer was right,[29] especially as the issue related to countries which had forcibly resisted the Muslim invasions. He could have recalled a serious incident, the resistance of the Jews at Khayber.[30] When the Prophet defeated them, he distributed their lands among the members of his victorious army and excluded the members of the tribe. But `Amr, with his shrewdness, wanted to maintain Egypt's unity. He knew that the country had rich resources and he understood that the public interest forbade distributing these resources among the warriors as spoils of war. The public interest also required treating the population and the religious leaders well, respecting the religious feelings of the people, preserving the resources of the country, and not collecting much in taxes in order to prevent a deterioration in the economic condition of the country. Briefly speaking, he

---

27. John of Nikiou, *op. cit.*, p. 584.

28. [al-Zubayer ibn al-`Awwām (593–656 A.D.) was the Arab commander who—at the head of an additional Arab army—was sent to help `Amr ibn al-`Āṣ conquer Egypt. (Tr.)]

29. al-Balladhūrī, *Futūḥ al-Buldān*, p. 214.

30. [Khayber is an oasis in Hijaz, Saudi Arabia, and lies 90 kilometers to the north of Medina. It has several villages, the most important of which is Khayber village where Jews were residing when the Prophet Muhammad invaded it. (Tr.)]

wanted to gain the friendship and love of the people, and not to humiliate and degrade them. In this light, `Amr had two policies. The first was public, inspired by the caliph [`Umar], the second was personal, which deserves our special interest because it saved the Copts many an obligation.

`Amr requests the mediation of `Umar to prevent distribution of the land.

`Amr unhesitatingly requested the mediation of `Umar to prevent the redistribution of the land, because a [serious] problem had erupted after the conquest of Syria and Iraq. "Bilal and his companions asked `Umar ibn al-Khattab about the distribution of what God gave them as booty from Iraq and Syria. They said, `Distribute the land among those who have conquered it, just as booty of the armies is distributed.' But `Umar refused to accept this and recited to them the verses [of the Qurān] alluded to above. He said, `God has made those who would come after you as partners in this booty. If I distribute it [to you], nothing would be left for those who would come after you. If anything remains undistributed, then even a shepherd at Sanā' would get his share of this booty."[31]

> `Umar (may Allah be pleased with him) wrote to Sa'd when he conquered Iraq: "Your letter has arrived. You mentioned in it that people had asked you to distribute amongst them their booty and whatever Allah had given them. As my letter reaches you, see what people have brought to you and to the army of horses, cattle and property. Distribute these amongst those Muslims who are present, and keep all the lands and canals for the governors so that they may be a gift for [all] the Muslims. Because, if you distribute everything among those who are present, there will not be anything left for those who come after them."[32]

> `Umar said on another occasion,

> "`How would it be for those Muslims who come afterwards and find the land already distributed and inherited—by sons from their fathers—and reserved for others, as their own property? How is it in your view?' `Abd al-Rahman ibn `Awf (may Allah be pleased with him) said to him, `What then is your view? The land and the peasants are only what Allah has

---

31. Abu Yūssuf, *op. cit.*, pp. 36–37.

32. *Ibid.*, p. 43.

given to them.' 'Umar said, 'This is what you say, but I do not share this view with you. By God, after me no land would be conquered; and there would not be much benefit in this; but it is likely that [this situation] would all be a burden for the Muslims. Thus, if the land of Iraq and Syria is distributed, by what would the defense of frontiers be managed, and what would there be for their descendants and the widows of this land, and for others of the people of Syria and Iraq?' They debated for a long time with 'Umar (may Allah be pleased with him). And they said, 'Will you hold back what Allah has given for our lot in battle, [holding it] for people who were not present and did not fight, and for the sons of the people and the sons of their sons who were not present?'"[33]

But 'Umar was not convinced, so he sent for ten persons from amongst al-Ansār,[34] five from al-Awas and five from al-Khazraj,[35] who were their elders and notables. He asked them to mediate according to the Arab custom. Those mediators said unanimously, "If these frontiers and towns are not attended by troops, and if they are not given salaries for their sustenance, the unbelievers will recapture their towns."[36]

When 'Amr ibn al-Ās listened to the complaints of al-Zubayer and his men, he relied on the decisions of Caliph 'Umar who wrote to him supporting his decision not to divide the land as al-Zubayer had requested. al-Zubayer was finally calmed by being given some land which satisfied him and he [thereupon] carried out the caliph's orders.

Certainly the problem was of great importance because that which 'Amr gave to al-Zubayer clearly indicates that 'Amr felt it necessary to get rid of al-Zubayer's opposition in order to avoid raising once again the problem of [ownership in] cities occupied by the power of arms.

---

33. *Ibid.*, pp. 44-45.

34. [al-Ansār (Arabic for "supporters") was the name given by the Prophet to the believers among the people of Medina to distinguish them from the Muhajirūn, the immigrants from Mecca. (Tr.)]

35. [al-Khazraj is the name of the tribe who, with their brother-tribe al-Awas, occupyied the region of Medina and farther north to Khaybar and Taima' at the time of the beginning of Islam. Both tribes are identified by the name of "al-Ansār." (Tr.)]

36. Abu Yūssuf, *op. cit.*, p. 46.

Was Egypt conquered by force (`unwah) or by a peace agreement (sulh)?

This matter caused heated discussions after the Arab conquest of Egypt. Some fuqahā' have said that the country was conquered by a peace agreement (sulh), others said by force (`unwah), while a third group supported the opinion of the first, but with reservations.

We should first mention some facts before we present these three views. Nowadays writers call the Arab conquest of Egypt and neighboring countries al-Jihad, that is, a war waged by Muslims against non-Muslims[37] who reject the call to convert to Islam. Moreover, most Muslim historians have accepted the authenticity of the message sent by the Prophet Muhammad to [Cyrus] the ruler of Egypt. If we agree that the Egyptians did not accept [the Prophet's] invitation—nor did they openly reject it, as some writers claim—the slowness of military operations and the presence of Copts in the Byzantine army indicate that the natives resisted the Arab invasion.

Some writers have wanted to explain `Amr's tolerance by referring to the fact that the defending forces at the Babylon fortress [in Old Cairo] and at Alexandria had requested the cessation of fighting. But in both cases they did not proceed until they felt that they had lost control of the situation. In addition, the text of the Qurān is clear concerning such a case. "Then sue not for peace because of your slackness, for you will certainly have the upper hand. Allah is with you, and he will not diminish aught from your works." (*Sura Muhammad*, verse 35.)

In spite of this, some fuqahā' have tried to justify the position of the Arab commanders, which was not in harmony with the Quranic texts. For instance, Hussein ibn Ahmad ibn Muhammad al-Qaddūri, who can be considered one of the ulamā' of Abu Hanifa's school of fiqh, wrote of this matter:

> "If the Imam [the Muslim religious leader] found it suitable to have peace with his antagonists, or some of them, and he saw that it was in the interest of Muslims to do so, there is no objection to it. If he had peace with them for some time and saw that breaking the peace was most

---

37. [For the different meanings of *jihad* in Islam, see the following works:

a. Jansen, Johannes J. G., *The Neglected Duty: The Creed of Sadat's Assassins and Islamic Resurgence in the Middle East*, New York: Macmillan, 1986. It includes an English translation of "al-Faridah al-Gha`ibah" (Literary, *The Absent Duty*).

b. `Abd al-`Ati, Hammudah, *Al-Jihad (Holy War) in Islam*, Cairo: al-Azhar Press, 1963.

c. Peters, Rudolph, ed. and trans., *Jihad in Medieval and Modern Islam: the Chapter on Jihad from Averroes' Legal Handbook "Bidayat al-Mudjtahid" and the Treatise "Koran and fighting" by the Late Shaykh-al-Azhar, Mahmud Shaltut*, Leiden: E. J. Brill, 1977. (Tr.)]

beneficial, he should inform them of breaking the peace and fight them. If they have betrayed him, he should fight them without a prior announcement of breaking the peace. If the imam has conquered a country by force (`unwah), he is free to divide it among the Muslims or to leave its people in peace and impose the *jizyah* on them. He is also free to take them as prisoners of war. He may kill them or enslave them or, if he wishes, he may let them free as dhimmis for the Muslims."[38]

Those who confirm that Egypt was conquered by force (`unwah) depend on the accuracy of statements of events. Ibn `Abd al-Hakam reports statements of some witnesses who said, "`Umar ibn al-Khattab had a cabinet in which he kept every covenant between himself and any other person. No covenant for the people of Egypt was found."[39] Ibn `Abd al-Hakam relates two other events. When Abu Salamah ibn `Abd al-Rahman wanted to go to Alexandria in a boat, he needed someone to steer it. He forced a Copt into doing that. He then said, "They [the Copts] are in the position of slaves when we need them." The other event involved a man who converted to Islam and asked `Umar ibn al-Khattab to exempt his land from the *jizyah*. `Umar told him, "No, your land was conquered by force (`unwah)." Even `Amr himself went to the mosque and said publicly, "I have taken my present position with no covenant or contract between me and any Copt, except the people of Antopolis who have a covenant to be observed. If I wish, I may kill or take a fifth of their property or sell it."[40]

Some fuqahā' reached a final opinion that it would be more appropriate to admit that Egypt was conquered according to a peace treaty [sulhan], with the exception of the towns of "Celtis," "Mazil," "Belheet," and the city of Alexandria, all of which resisted the invasion.[41]

It is clear that this issue has not yet been solved. Those who claim that Egypt was conquered according to a peace treaty [sulhan] have shaped their opinion for military, political and economic reasons; and they have sought the support of the fuqahā' to prove the validity of their views.

---

38. Quoted in Sylvestre de Sacy's *Trois memoires sur la nature et les revolutions du droit de proprieté territoriale en Égypte* (Bibliothèque des Arabisants. Cairo: L'Institute français d'Archéologie orientale, p. 149.).

39. Ibn `Abd al-Hakam, *op. cit.*, p. 89.

40. al-Balladhūrī, *op. cit.*, p. 217.

41. Ibn `Abd al-Hakam, *op. cit.*, p. 83.

`Amr's tolerant administration.

We need no longer affirm that the Arabs' policy was dictated by circumstances. We have an additional example [of their policy]: when the Arabs wanted to secure the southern borders of Egypt during their campaign against Libya, they signed a treaty with the Christian people of Nubia. Arab historians have called this treaty "al-Baqat."[42] However, the Arab commanders found no reason not to abrogate this treaty, saying, "There is no covenant between Egypt and the blacks [Nubians]. It was nothing but a truce between us and them, during which we gave them wheat and lentils and they gave us slaves in return."[43] When Oqba ibn Nafi' invaded Tripoli and conquered it, its people asked him to make peace with them and give them a covenant. But he refused, saying, "We have no covenant for polytheists."[44] Concerning the case of Egypt, `Amr ibn al-Āṣ carried out the orders of Caliph `Umar because they fit his personal ambitions. His tolerance during his tenure as wali over Egypt was a source of amazement and admiration to the Egyptians. He was, in the first place, religiously tolerant. John of Nikiou says, "`Amr did not confiscate church property, nor did he steal or loot [such property], but he made it safe under his administration."[45]

`Amr understood the status of the Coptic patriarch Benjamin among his people, and he sought information about him from them to learn of his hiding place because he had had to escape the persecution of Cyrus. `Amr stated concerning him, "He has a covenant of safety and security from God. Let him return safe and secure to manage the affairs of his church and the politics of his people."[46] Saint Benjamin returned to Alexandria with great joy after fourteen years of absence, ten years under Heraclius the Roman emperor and four years after the Muslims entered Egypt. He had on his head the crown of patience and struggle which characterized the Christian orthodox people when persecuted by opponents. When the people throughout the city expressed joy after his arrival was announced, `Amr ordered that he be brought to meet with him. When he saw him, he honored him and told his companions and confidants, "All the provinces we have taken over before this moment have not seen a man of God like this

---

42. [al-Baqat is an agreement according to which someone grows crops on land owned by someone else in return for a third or a fourth or a fifth of the harvest. (See al-Bustan, *Arabic Dictionary*, under "Baqat.") (Tr.)]

43. Ibn `Abd al-Hakam, *op. cit.*, pp. 188–89.

44. al-Kindī, *op. cit.*, p. 32.

45. John of Nikiou, *op. cit.*, p. 584.

46. Sawirus, *op. cit.*, p. 109 (Seybold edition).

man."[47] Benjamin was handsome; he spoke well and calmly. `Amr turned to him and said, "Take control over the affairs of your church and men. If you invoke God's blessing on me to go to the Maghreb [Morocco] and the five cities [of Libya], and successfully take them over like Egypt, and return safely and quickly to you, I will give you whatever you may request from me." Saint Benjamin invoked God's blessings on him, using words which impressed `Amr and those who were present. There was a moral lesson and much benefit in what he said to those who listened to him. He also suggested a few ideas to him, and he departed in esteem and great respect.

Naturally `Amr was concerned about the great festivity with which the people received their religious leader. He hastened to consult the patriarch about the best way to manage the affairs of the country and to ask him about the most suitable time to collect taxes. He also requested from him a blessing on his campaign against Tripoli. `Amr's aim was to make the patriarch responsible for both the country's security and the loyalty of the people to the Arabs during his absence by giving the patriarch the opportunity to participate in the success of the campaign. He actually rewarded him for his services by letting the Copts take over most of the churches and monasteries of the Melchites [many of which had been given to the Melchites a few years earlier by Cyrus].

`Amr's interest in the Copts made them attach great hopes to their future, causing Bishop Sawirus ibn al-Muqqaf`a to describe their feelings by saying, "The people were as happy as calves when they are released from their ties and rush to suck their mothers' udders."[48]

Sawirus was correct in his characterization of their behavior because the Copts had not been treated with such leniency for a long time. Moreover, the Arabs during `Amr's tenure did not try to pressure the Copts to convert to Islam, nor did he persecute them.

When `Amr studied the conditions of the country he realized that it was impossible to collect taxes without the help of the Copts. He wrote to the caliph saying that, because the Muslims did not know the country very well, they could not calculate the sums of money collected from the taxes. Consequently, he had

---

47. [The hero in this story is the thirty-eighth Coptic patriarch, Benjamin I (623-662 A.D.), who abdicated his position when the Roman emperor Heraclius (575–642 A.D.) appointed Cyrus as patriarch and ruler of Egypt. Benjamin went underground for fourteen years until `Amr ibn al-`Āṣ encouraged him to return and be reinstated as patriarch. A complete biography of this militant patriarch can be found in Sawirus ibn al-Muqaff`a, *History of the Patriarchs of the Coptic Church of Alexandria*, Arabic text edited, translated and annotated by B. Evetts (Paris: P. Fages 1904, vol. 1, pt. 2, pp. 223–54); see also C. Detlef G. Müller, "Benjamin I," *The Coptic Encyclopedia*, 2:375–77. (Tr.)]

48. Sawirus, *op. cit.*, p. 236.

hired a capable Christian of integrity on condition that he be replaced by someone else when he ['Amr] knew the country's conditions well.

'Amr also thought of establishing an apparatus to ensure justice, and he approved Christians having a role in it. He divided the country into a number of provinces and for each province he appointed a Coptic judge responsible for handling religious and civic disputes among non-Muslims. If the dispute was between a Copt and a Muslim, it was referred to a council formed by the judges of the two parties. Criminal cases fell within the jurisdiction of Muslim judges only.

Differences between 'Umar and 'Amr concerning the collection of taxes.

When 'Amr consulted the Copts concerning taxes, they advised him not to collect taxes according to the lunar calendar but according to the Egyptian calendar established long before by the pharaohs according to the seasons. 'Amr agreed, but 'Umar criticized his agent for proceeding thus because he badly needed money. He forcefully ordered him to expedite tax collection and send the money to Medina.

No one ever thought that 'Amr would disobey the orders of the caliph, but this was exactly what happened. The leader and his subordinate exchanged several strongly worded letters concerning the matter. 'Umar did not understand why the taxes imposed on Egypt declined year after year, a result of the decline of the number of people paying *jizyah* owing to the increasing number of Christians converting to Islam. As for the Ahl al-dhimmah, they did not consider it inappropriate to escape the tax collectors whenever they had the chance. We shall talk again about this situation when we discuss finances.

When 'Umar ibn al-Khattab felt that 'Amr ibn al-Āṣ was slow in sending him the *kharaj* [land tax], he wrote to him saying,

> "In the name of God, Most Gracious, Ever Merciful, may the peace of God be with you. I thank God, there is no God but Allah. I have thought of your affairs and the condition you are in. Your land [Egypt] is vast and wide and rich. God has given it a large population with perseverance and power in land and sea. The pharaohs worked hard and did well in it, despite their excessive polytheism and despotism. I have wondered about that. But what has caused me to wonder more is that its *kharaj* has gone down to half of what it was—without drought or lack of fertility. I have written to you several times about the *kharaj*. I thought that we would not receive it in such small amounts. And I had hoped that you would wake up and send the *kharaj*. Instead, you have sent me excuses which do not suit my purpose. I will not accept from you a

kharaj of less than what it was. I do not know why you have not liked my letter to you. If you are really experienced and efficient, you should understand that honesty is the best policy. But you are careless and like to talk too much. The matter is different from what you think. I have forgiven what I suffered from you last year, hoping that you would wake up [and send the *kharaj*]. I know that nothing has prevented you from doing that but your agents, the agents of evil. Because of your fraud and duplicity, they have hidden behind you. But I have a cure for this situation. Do not panic, Aba 'Abdallah, when rights [of others] are taken from you, and your rights are given to them. By shaking we get out the milk [from the cow's udder], and truth is light and I never hesitate to follow it. And what was hidden has come out in the open. Peace be upon you.

'Amr ibn al-Ās replied to him saying,
"In the name of God, Most Gracious, Ever Merciful. To 'Abdullah 'Umar, the Prince of the Faithful, from 'Amr ibn al-Ās. I thank God, there is no God but Allah. I have received the letter of the Prince of the Faithful in which he mentioned that I was slow in sending him the *kharaj*. And he referred to the work of the pharaohs before me, expressing his admiration for the *kharaj* that they collected and the decline of the *kharaj* since the advent of Islam. Upon my life, the *kharaj* at that time was more abundant and the land was better utilized because they were, in spite of their polytheism and despotism, more willing to utilize their land than we have been since the advent of Islam. And you mentioned that by shaking we extract the milk [from the cow's udder], and thus you milked [Egypt] in such a bad manner that you have cut its udder. You were excessive in your letter, and you reprimanded and intimidated me, making a big fuss about something that you hide from me. Upon my life, you have come up with abominable and slanderous remarks. You could have used more calm, decisive, eloquent and truthful words. I have worked for the Messenger of God (may the peace of Allah be upon him) and for those who came after him. We thank God that we have carried out our responsibility honestly, and have preserved the godly rights of our imams. We have considered anything other than this as ugly, and doing such as shameful. We were known for that [attitude] and we have kept our hearts pure. May God protect us from this graft—and from the evil characters and their audacity of committing every sin—to carry out your work. God has kept me unblemished from this lowly graft, and even from desiring it, after receiving your letter in which you did not spare from slander, nor did you honor a brother. By God, Ibn al-Khattab,

58

when I am asked to do something wrong I feel angry out of purity and dignity. I have done nothing blameworthy. But I have learned what you have not. And if I were one of the Jews of Yathrib,[49] I would not have said more than what I have said. May God forgive you and us. I have kept silent about things that I know well; but I have kept silent."

When ʿAmr responded for the second time to ʿUmar, the caliph could not check his anger, and he accused him of stealing a large sum of money.[50] It did not take him long to send Muhammad ibn Maslama al-Ansari to him to receive half of what was due to him from ʿAmr.

It is not surprising that ʿAmr scooped money [from the *kharaj*] for himself because he was an Arab bedouin who found himself suddenly in possession of great wealth. The Arab historians have not discussed this accusation levelled against him. Some of them recount that the caliph questioned an Egyptian Copt about Egypt's *kharaj* before the coming of Islam. The Copt said, "O Prince of the Faithful, nothing was taken out before development work took place. But your agent does not care for development, and he takes what he finds available to him, as if he needs it for just one year."[51]

If we put aside this accusation, we find that ʿAmr wanted to preserve the country's wealth and prevent the caliphs from exploiting the people. It is appropriate to mention ʿAmr's very convincing response to the Caliph ʿUthmān. ʿAmr had estimated the taxes to be twelve million dinars while ʿAbdallah ibn Saʿad raised the estimate to fourteen million. ʿUthmān told ʿAmr, "Aba ʿAbdallah, the she-camel, has given more milk than before." ʿAmr responded, "You have hurt its youngster."[52]

Over and above neglecting the *jizyah*, ʿAmr paid no attention to ʿUmar's instructions concerning the appearance of the dhimmis, in spite of the insistence of some individuals that these instructions be followed. It is true that ʿAmr ordered that crosses not be shown in public, "but these orders were not observed

---

49. [Yathrib is the old name of Medina where the Jews opposed the Prophet Muhammad at an early stage of his mission. (Tr.)]

50. Ibn ʿAbd al-Hakam mentions these correspondences in pp. 158–69 of his book. op. cit.

51. *Ibid.*, p. 146. The English historian Stanley Lane-Poole says, without indicating his source, that after his death ʿAmr left seventy keeses of dinars [equal to ten tons of gold]. His children refused to inherit this sum of money because of their chastity (*The story of Cairo*, London: Dent, 1902, pp. 56–60). al-Yʿaqūbi mentions only that ʿAmr left a great wealth after his death (edition of 1358 A.H., vol. 2, p. 198).

52. Ibn ʿAbd al-Hakam, *op. cit.*, p. 161.

later on and Christians resumed showing their crosses at their weddings and funerals. But in Homs and Damascus such was never permitted, because the conditions of 'Umar spelled that out."[53] Finally, 'Amr allowed the Copts to live in the city of al-Fustāt.

This tolerance formed a serious precedent for the Arabs, from which the Copts benefited a great deal. This was undoubtedly due to the position taken by 'Amr whose aim was to become the absolute ruler of Egypt. Finally, he wanted to make Alexandria his capital city on the pretext of the suitability of the houses left by the Greeks for lodging the occupation army. When 'Umar refused to allow him to reside where he wanted, 'Amr accepted the orders and returned to al-Fustāt.

When Caliph 'Ali ibn Abi Talib [35–40 A.H./656–61 A.D.] took over and the Muslim world was divided into two antagonistic camps, 'Amr ruled Egypt [for the second time] in the name of Mu'āwiya I [41–60 A.H./661–80 A.D.]. He stipulated that the caliph should appoint him the wali of Egypt for life, in return for his important service. It was clear that 'Amr was trying to seize an opportunity to announce his independence and proclaim himself the first caliph of Egypt, after separating it completely from the Arab empire.

C. The Walis Follow a Utilitarian Policy.

The successors of 'Amr did not try to develop the country. Their activities were limited to maintaining security and sending the *jizyah* to the Umayyad and Abbasid caliphs. Since their tenure was generally short, they followed their personal interests. How could these walis follow any other policy since the caliphs did not give them enough time to plan in a positive manner? Whenever they did something useful for the country, they caused suspicion and anxiety within the central authority. The repeated transfers of the walis is clear proof that the caliphs did not care about their agents' efforts to promote the interests of their administrative areas.

Money is the basis of relationships between victor and vanquished.

'Abd Allah ibn Salih described Egypt in a beautiful statement: "He who wants to remember how the heavens look, or to see something like it on this earth, he should look at the land of Egypt when its plants become green and their fruits start to appear."[54] We do not exaggerate if we say that this expression of

---

53. *Michel le Syrien*, 2:432.

54. Ibn 'Abd al-Hakam, *op. cit.*, p. 5.

admiration has been repeated by every Arab who has come to the Nile Valley. It was natural for the desert man, who was victorious in a war that he waged against two empires, to benefit from his victories. The strong proof was the insistence that the victorious armies distribute among themselves the vast areas of land that they conquered in Iraq, Syria and Egypt.

When famine took place in al-Medina al-Munawarrah, `Umar [the caliph] sent word to Egypt to rush the wheat needed to feed the population, saying, "God will ruin Egypt for the sake of the good and the prosperity of Medina."[55] When he was talking about conquered peoples, the same caliph also said, "The Muslims will devour them as long as they are alive. But when we and they perish, then our sons will devour their sons as long as they are alive."[56] These statements betray the intentions of the conquerors.

First taxes imposed upon the Copts.

When representatives of the two parties met near the fortress of Babylon to discuss the conditions for surrender, the greater interest of the Arabs was in the amount of *jizyah* to be imposed upon the conquered. Because the Arabs were not qualified to establish a new tax system, they copied the tax systems of the Byzantines. Even so, the people benefited from a tangible decrease in taxes. The tax system was back to its simplest forms, as in the beginning. The orientalist Van Berchem stated that "taxpayers paid two basic taxes: the *jizyah*, which is a high tax paid in cash, and the *dariba* [levy] which was an in-kind tax collected in the form of wheat. Parallel to the two taxes were two distinct items of expenses in the state budget, i.e., military salaries were paid from the *jizyah*, and what was collected of wheat was distributed among the soldiers and their families." We offer an example that illustrates the relationship between these two kinds of taxes.

"An order for payment [of taxes] by the people of Psyrou. Inv. no. 335. Safar, 91 A.H.; Thot of the eighth indiction (9 December 709, to 7 January 710 A.D.; 29th August to 30th September, 709 A.D.). ([The] homestead of Psyrou [is to pay of] solidi [coins] 104 2/3, [of] artabas of wheat 11 1/3). In the name of God, the Compassionate, the Merciful. This is a letter from Qurra ibn Sharîk to the people of Shubra Psîrû of the

---

55. *al-Tabari*, Leiden edition, 1:257. al-Balladhûrî referred to this statement on p. 216 of his history without comment.

56. Abu Yûssuf, *op. cit.*, p. 141 (chapter on churches, synagogues, and crosses). The rest of this statement reads as follows: "They would thus be reduced to be slaves of the people of Islam as long as the religion of Islam prevails."

district of Isqauh. Verily, it hath fallen upon you (as your part) of the gold-tax of the year eighty-eight, a hundred and four counted dinars and a third of a dinar, and of the corn-tax, eleven artabas and a third artaba of wheat."[57]

Naturally the in-kind *dariba* [levy] was not limited to wheat and flour, but it included vegetables, shirts and other things.[58]

This principle of collecting and disbursing taxes continued only for a short period of time. This explains differences in opinion among Arab historians. These differences are partially due to the contradictory instructions issued by the administration. The Arab historical texts differentiate between *jizyah* and *kharaj*, although the two words refer to the same kind of taxes. Fortunately, the unclear accounts of Arab historians have been complemented by the discovery of papyri which go back to the early centuries of the Hejira. On the other hand, while these historians claim that a tax of two dinars was levied on the Ahl al-dhimmah—except the elderly, women, children, beggars, and handicapped—we later learn that this amount was only the average paid by every taxpayer.

The *jizyah* [in cash] and the *dariba* [in kind] were imposed collectively on the group and were levied by the central authority for each village. Then they were distributed among the taxpayers and collected from the individuals according to the wealth of each. The tax lists written in Greek, which go back to the first century of the Hejira, indicate that sums of less than two dinars were collected. "The sum of one dinar, the minimum referred to in the fiqh for each individual, went down to less than that most of the time during the following centuries, which can be seen in the receipts issued at the time."[59] Generally speaking, at the time these taxes were levied, the tax rates were twelve dirhams for individuals of the middle class, twenty-four dirhams or two dinars for individuals of the upper class, and four dinars for wealthy individuals.

The land tax, called *kharaj*, was not referred to in any agreement between the two parties. What concerned the Arabs was collecting a tax of two dinars from each dhimmi, paid in cash or in kind. With the exception of Alexandria and Babylon and some other cities, "the *jizyah* had to be converted into a land tax; and the amount of tax levied after conducting a population census was supposed to be

---

57. Grohmann, Alolf, *Arabic Papyri in the Egyptian Library*, 3:47–49, document no. 160. The translation of this Arabic document is Grohmann's.

58. *Ibid.*, 1:61.

59. Heyd, *op. cit.*, 1:26.

distributed according to the land overflowed by the [flooding] Nile water, not according to the number of people who pay taxes."[60]

Deterioration of economic conditions and the resulting taxes.

After some years of the spreading of Islam, the Arabs realized that the amount of taxes prescribed by the Qurān would not meet the needs of their great empire. The economic conditions in Egypt deteriorated for several reasons, some of which have been mentioned by the historian W. Heyd: "No one can deny that commercial activities at the beginning of Islam faced many unexpected difficulties because the Jihad had exhausted all the energy of the Muslims and, as a result, the trade movement as well as foreign trade stopped."[61] This dangerous condition brought about serious results in the port of Alexandria where the import and export movement was paralyzed. The people of Alexandria fell into despair because they depended on foreign trade for their living. Added to this was the fact that authorities did not care for the well-being and the affluence of Egypt. The authorities held the people responsible for maintaining the dams and water canals without any effort on their part to support the people's efforts. As a result, dams and canals were seriously neglected and the people benefited little from the Nile flood. al-Maqrizi commented on this situation by indicating that the decrease in the *kharaj* was due to the increase in destruction and ruination year after year.

When agricultural crops declined, taxpayers refused to pay the taxes due. Naturally, they tried to outwit the treasury. The Egyptians enjoyed an unexpected respite. While the Byzantine rulers used to beat people to force them to pay taxes, Islam declared that, if the person could not afford to pay taxes, the ruler should not force him to do so by corporal punishment, either by beating him, or by exposing him to the burning rays of the sun, or by spraying boiling oil on his skin. The only permitted method for punishment was imprisonment [for not paying taxes].

Concerning this issue, Abu Yūssuf stated candidly, "No dhimmi should be beaten or forced to stay in the burning sun, nor be physically hurt because of not paying taxes. They should be dealt with gently and be imprisoned until they pay the taxes due."[62]

---

60. *Encyclopedia of Islam*, see "jizyah."

61. Silvestre de Sacy, *op. cit.*, p. 172.

62. Abu Yūssuf, *op. cit.*, p. 70. But these punishments were later reinstated. One of the papyri, which goes back to third century of the Hejira, contains a candid statement giving taxpayers a three-day grace period to pay taxes or "undergo ten lashes daily by a stick until they pay" (Grohmann, *op. cit.*, 3:104).

Copts preferred imprisonment to paying taxes. Some of them entered the monasteries because monasticism exempted them from *jizyah* for life. The historian Renaudot stated that "the number of monks increased to the extent that they had to build new cells everyday."[63] Some people avoided taxes by changing their place of residence after the authorities completed the census, residing in other regions where their names were not included in tax lists. These were in addition to Copts who converted to Islam to escape paying the *jizyah*. The numbers of these Copts increased over the years.

The Arab historians have stated that the total taxes, which were about twenty million dinars in the past, declined during the tenure of `Umar ibn al-Khattab to twelve million, then rose to fourteen million during the tenure of `Abd Allah ibn Sa`ad.[64] But later it declined rapidly. During the Umayyad and the Abbasid caliphates, the amount of collected taxes did not exceed three million [dinars].[65]

While income was decreasing, expenses were on the increase. The desire for carrying out new conquests and the importance of ensuring the security of the empire necessitated maintaining large, well-equipped armies. Similarly, internal security necessitated the establishment of a police force from the first.

Financial affairs were the foremost concern of the caliphs. They tried initially to reduce the budget. But since the army exhausted the major part of the budget, they tried reducing the pay of the soldiers. But four successive times in the first century of the Hejira they failed drastically. They had to look for other solutions which would not expose them to danger. They resorted to increasing taxes for civilians.

Measures to increase the income.

The Copts had good memories of the rule of `Amr ibn al-Ās, even though he did not hesitate to take illegal measures in order to double the income. Ibn `Abd al-Hakam tells us, "When `Amr ibn al-Ās conquered Egypt, he said to the Copts, `I will kill, if I can, him who hides his treasure from me.'"[66] It was betrayed to `Amr that a Nabatean called Peter from Upper Egypt had a treasure. `Amr summoned the man and asked him about it. But he denied having it, and `Amr

---

63. Renaudot, *op. cit.*, p. 182.

64. Historians agree, in general, to the validity of these figures.

65. al-Maqrizi, *al-Khitat*, 1:98–99.

66. Ibn `Abd al-Hakam, *op. cit.*, p. 87.

imprisoned him. `Amr then asked whether the man was trying to contact anyone, and he was told that he was asking about a monk in al-Tur [the mountain].[67] `Amr summoned Peter and took his name stamp from him. Then he wrote to the monk asking him to send what he had and stamped the letter with Peter's stamp. The messenger returned with a small ceramic water jar sealed with lead. `Amr opened it and found a statement written on a piece of vellum: "Your money is under the big fountain." `Amr sent someone to the fountain who stopped the water from running to it and removed its floor tiles. Under it he found buried fifty-two artabas of minted gold. `Amr executed the man at the door of the mosque. Ibn Ruqayah[68] mentions that the Copts brought out their treasures for fear of being killed like Peter.[69]

We also know that some Copts living in Alexandria, or in lands surrounding it, helped the Byzantines who landed on the north shore of Egypt in the year 23 or 25 of the Hejira. The Arab historians were not surprised at this help, and they explained it by the following incident. The reason for the violation of the Alexandria agreement [between the Arabs and the Alexandrians] was that the representative of Ikhna [near Alexandria] went to `Amr ibn al-Ās and asked him to spell out the *jizyah* requested from each one in his district in order to have it ready. `Amr said, pointing to the support of the church wall, "If you gave me [money] enough to fill the distance between this support and the ceiling I would not tell you, because you are a money-safe for us. If our expenses increase, we will press for more taxes from you. And if our expenses decrease, we will decrease the taxes on you." The representative became angry and left to join the Byzantines.[70]

The caliphs made no statements as candid as those made by `Amr. But they were careful to give elastic interpretations to the law, suitable for their financial needs. It is true that they did not want to infringe upon the laws, but they were surprised at the rapid decline in their income. Since they were reluctant at any time to stop the progress of their conquests or to put limits on the luxury of their lives, they were forced to establish financial measures which resulted in creating a wave of embitterment and discontent among both Muslims and Christians.

For example, during the Byzantine period, before Muslims imposed *jizyah* on the people, there were in Egypt large areas of arable land abandoned by

67. [Jebel al-Tur in the Sinai Peninsula. (Tr.)]

68. `Abd al-Rahman ibn Ruqayah (535–605 A.H./1141–1208 A.D.).

69. Ibn `Abd al-Hakam, *op. cit.*, p. 87.

70. *Ibid.*, pp. 176–77.

their Coptic owners who had refused to pay the taxes imposed on them. When the Arabs came, other arable lands were abandoned by people for the same reason. Thus authorities gained nothing from these lands. In 109 A.H. [727 A.D.], the wali al-Walid ibn Rifā`ah presented the deepening problem of deteriorating land to the Caliph Hisham ibn `Abd al-Malek,[71] petitioning him to permit the migration of some Arab tribes to Egypt to fill the vacuum that he complained of. The wali announced that allowing Arabs to settle in these lands would not cancel the *kharaj* [one fifth of the income] by replacing it with the *`ushūriyiah* [one tenth of the income]. However, [he noted,] such a migration might lead to the prosperity of the country because these lands paid neither the *kharaj* nor the *`ushūriyiah*.

On the advice of Walid ibn Rifā`ah, the Caliph Hisham ibn `Abd al-Malek allowed three thousand members of the Qays tribe to migrate to Egypt on condition that they not reside in al-Fustāt but in al-Hūf al-Sharqī [near Bilbeis].[72] Those who stayed there became rich in a short period of time as a result of transporting goods exported to Arabia. When they informed their relatives in Arabia of their new wealth, five hundred of them rushed to join them in Egypt. Other waves of migrants from Arabia followed in search of wealth, and they settled on lands abandoned by the original inhabitants.

It is appropriate to mention that the Arabs did not go to Egypt for economic purposes only, because the wali al-Walid ibn Rifā`ah did not offer his suggestion to the caliph until after the rebellion of the people in the eastern valley [al-Hūf al-Sharqī]. The first group of immigrants settled in the city of Bilbeis, the location where the rebellion broke out.

Over time, the Arabs penetrated all parts of the country, lower, upper and middle Egypt. They married Coptic women who converted to Islam, and it became difficult to differentiate between them [the immigrant Arabs] and the natives who converted to Islam. The majority of immigrants acquired lands, which created a problem concerning the kind of taxes that these new land owners were to pay. A legislator intervened in the interest of the ruling authority, and a *fatwa* was issued to the effect that lands subject to the *kharaj* should continue to pay this tax, even after transferring its ownership to Muslim owners. The legislator's justification for this was not to sacrifice public interest for private interest.

This *fatwa* indicates that authorities exploited a mistake for their own interest by ignoring the difference between the *jizyah* which was paid in cash, and

---

71. [Umayyad caliph, 690–743 A.D. (Tr.)]

72. [A town in the Sharqiya province about 30 miles northeast of Cairo. (Tr.)]

the *kharaj* which was paid in kind. However, these two taxes were required of the Ahl al-dhimmah alone.

Although authorities were forced to exempt city dwellers who converted to Islam, they continued to collect *kharaj* from all agricultural land owners. This happened in spite of the fact that *kharaj* was nothing but *jizyah* imposed on agricultural lands, and the village populations were collectively responsible for paying it. When inhabitants of the provinces realized that they received no financial gain from converting to Islam, they hesitated in converting to the new religion, contrary to what happened among city dwellers. The orientalist Silvestre de Sacy observed that "this might be one of the reasons for the persistence of Christianity in the provinces for a longer period of time than in the cities."[73]

When it was discovered that this measure would not be sufficient to overcome the budget deficit, authorities considered increasing the *jizyah*. al-Maqrizi states that, "Mu`awiya ibn Abi Sufyan wrote to Wardan, who was in charge of collecting the *kharaj*, telling him to increase the *kharaj* required from every Copt. But Wardan asked him how he could do that because the covenant mentioned that there would be no increase in their *kharaj*. Mu`awiya fired him."[74]

Abu Yūssuf tried to justify the increase in *jizyah* and *kharaj* by saying, "`Umar ibn al-Khattab (may God be pleased with him) thought that the *kharaj* was suitable for the land at the time. When he imposed the *kharaj* he did not say that it was the responsibility of the taxpayers, nor did he say that it was mandatory for them; further it was not legal for him nor for the caliphs who would come after him to decrease or increase it."[75]

The authorities considered holding the living responsible for paying the *jizyah* of the dead. Ibn `Abd al-Hakam reported that, "Hayyan wrote to `Umar ibn `Abd al-`Aziz asking whether he should impose the *jizyah* of dead Copts upon their survivors." `Umar asked `Araq ibn Malik[76] about the matter. `Araq said, "I have never heard that they had any covenant of agreement, for they were taken by force like slaves." `Umar then wrote back to Hayyan ibn Sharih to impose the

---

73. *Droit de proprieté territoriale*, p. 185. In: *Tois memoires...*

74. *al-Khitat*, 1:79.

75. Abu Yūssuf, *op. cit.*, p. 48. al-Balladhūrī mentions that the tax levied on the city of Alexandria, which was eighteen thousand dinars, was increased during the reign of Hisham `Abd al-Malek to thirty thousand.

76. [A Muslim *'ālim* (scholar). (Tr.)]

jizyah of the dead Copts on those who were living.[77] This measure indicates, according to al-Maqrizi, that 'Umar believed both that Egypt was conquered by force [not by peace treaty] and that the *jizyah* was levied on villages. The death of some villagers would not result in the reduction of the *jizyah*, for it continued to be the same.[78]

'Umar ibn 'Abd al-'Aziz refused to follow the advice of his walis regarding the increased number of those who were converting to Islam and refusing to pay *jizyah*. When they recommended that the *jizyah* should be collected from this class of Muslims, the caliph responded, "God has sent Muhammad (peace be upon him) as a guide to the right way, not as a tax collector. Upon my life, 'Umar is unhappy that not all people will convert to Islam through him."[79]

All groups exempted from paying the *jizyah* after the conquest eventually lost this privilege. The monks in particular lost the privileges that they had enjoyed, resulting in an increase in the number of those who converted to Islam and a decrease in the number of monks. Monasteries were gradually deserted and fell into ruin.[80]

In 65 A.H. [685 A.D.], 'Abd al-'Aziz ibn Marwān was the first to levy the *jizyah* on monks at the rate of one dinar per person. He justified the measure by stating that it was not fair for the poor classes to pay taxes while monks, bishops, and patriarchs who own great wealth were exempted. When 'Abd Allah ibn 'Abd al-Malek became the wali of Egypt in 86 A.H. [705 A.D.], the Copts thought that the authorities had canceled this order. But the wali disappointed them. Thereafter, Christian historians launched an attack on him, expressing their hatred towards him.

Nevertheless, state revenues were in rapid decline in spite of the increase in taxes. Therefore, 'Ubayd Allah ibn al-Aḥdath decided to conduct an accurate land survey, including barren lands after eighty years of Arab conquest. He

---

77. Ibn 'Abd al-Hakam, *op. cit.*, p. 89.

78. *al-Khitat*, 1:77.

79. *Ibid.*, 1:78.

80. It seems that this decision was made after the monks had abused their privileges. An incident took place in 1274 A.D. [672 A.H.] when monks asked to be exempted from paying the *jizyah*. The authorities responded favorably to their request on condition that they should not give refuge to tax evaders in their monasteries and not consecrate any new monk without the permission of the Divan (see Habib al-Zayyat, *Kharaj al-Adyarah wa jizyat al-Ruhban (The kharaj of the Monasteries and the jizyah of the Monks in al-Mashriq)*, 1938, pp. 401–16.)

carried out the survey in 106 or 107 A.H. [724 or 725 A.D.] and collected for the state treasury four million dinars, despite a decline in the price of wheat.

It was later discovered that the land surveyors had not been accurate in their work. They had directed their attention to saving the state from financial ruin at the expense of the people. We learn this from reading one of the papyri in the René Papyri Collection. It states that one of the surveyors estimated a piece of land to be two hundred feddans. But the landowners, who were women, objected to this estimate, saying that they had surveyed the piece conscientiously and found that it was 139 feddans of agricultural land. After examining thoroughly the papers and documents related to this acreage, the authorities estimated it at 148 feddans only. Professor Grohmann has commented on this incident by saying, "If these mistakes appeared in the documents of large estates, what could have been the case of the small farmers who lacked the adequate means of defending themselves successfully?"[81]

In 186 A.H. [802 A.D.] during the reign of the Caliph Hārūn al-Rashīd, al-Layth ibn al-Fadl, the wali of Egypt, surveyed the lands of al-Hūf al-Sharqī [the valley to the east of the Delta]. The surveyors used a measure shorter than the qasabah[82] which raised suspicion among the people. But al-Kindī states that the wali rejected their complaint.[83] Later the wali resorted to a measure that had been imposed by the Byzantines at the end of the third century A.D., that is, the system of mandatory work for public service [liturgy].[84] This was another proof of the confusion among authorities concerning the financial situation. Based on the Arabic papyri that he studied, Grohmann observed, "The authorities followed the system of obligating people to public service, maintaining naval ships in particular. The major part of the navy depended on Egypt's revenues, and it was supplied by weapons in Egypt. Egyptian forced labor was not limited to maintaining the navy and supplying it with provisions, but was extended to the craftsmen and skilled laborers who built a palace for the caliph at Babylon and

---

81. Grohmann, *op. cit.*, 1:80.

82. [A qasabah equals 3.55 meters or 11.64 feet. (Tr.)]

83. al-Kindi, *op. cit.*, p. 140.

84. [A "liturgy" was originally any of various public services or offices imposed in rotation at Athens upon its wealthy citizens. (Tr.)]

carried out other projects outside Egypt.[85] Moreover soldiers and employees sent to work outside the country were paid from the treasury of their native country."[86]

In 256 A.H. [869 A.D.], a new official responsible for *Bayt al-Mal*,[87] called Ahmad ibn al-Muddabir, arrived in Egypt. Both Muslim and Christian historians have criticized him bitterly because of his strictness. But his policy was inevitable under the circumstances. Sawirus ibn al-Muqaff`a says about him, "He was a tough man, his actions were unbearable. Feared by everyone, no one could beat him, and he did many things that no one before him could do. He had resided in Palestine for a long time and caused its people difficulty and disaster. When our father the patriarch heard of his arrival in Egypt he was saddened. After his arrival, he doubled and tripled the *kharaj* on Muslims, Christians, and Jews to the extent that he filled the prisons all over the country [with those who could not pay the tax]. He sent his emissaries to monasteries everywhere and had them count the monks living there and demand *jizyah* and *kharaj* from them."[88] Ibn al-Muddabir also established a department for grazing lands which had not been taxed previously. He also forbade trading in these lands and levied a tax on them called *al-Mara`i* [grazing land]. This tax, referred to repeatedly in lists written on papyri, was probably levied on sheep and goats. Another tax mentioned in the papyri—without an explanation of its nature—was levied on pastures. The tax on hunting also goes back to the time of Ibn al-Muddabir.

All these taxes were entered under the name "al-Dara`ib al-Hilaliyah" (crescent taxes) because they were collected according to the lunar calendar, unlike the *kharaj* which was collected according to the solar calendar. Added to these taxes was another called "al-Sadaqah" [charity] which, as indicated in the Arabic papyri, at that time became legal compulsory charity in the form of a tax paid by both Muslims and Christians. Some fees imposed on vegetables developed into a tax. Authorities later levied taxes on palm trees and vineyards. Moreover, the population paid most of the expenses for improving agricultural lands. Craftsmen contributed to that work. While taxes were levied on industries of all kinds, we are not sure how much Ibn al-Muddabir raised them. We know only that he

---

85. Grohmann, *op. cit.*, 1:67. It is difficult to specify the period during which this system was applied and to what extent it was applied during the second century A.H.

86. *al-Khitat*, 1:314–15.

87. [The Islamic state treasury that had the *jizyah* and *kharaj* as main sources of revenue. (Tr.)]

88. Sawirus, *op. cit.*, 1:242.

reestablished the monopoly system and decreed fees on receipts, stationery and other such items.[89]

Ibn al-Muddabir was the last wali to rule Egypt for the government of Baghdad. After him came Ibn Ṭūlūn. He set out to cancel the new fees and taxes imposed by Ibn al-Muddabir which had had the worst effect on the country, even though they were well-established measures implemented by the walis in agreement with the caliphs to increase the revenues of Bayt al-Mal.

There were other injustices to which both Copts and Muslims were subjected. They faced the craving of the walis who briefly ruled Egypt and sought to get rich quick at any cost before leaving the country. The orientalist J. J. Marcel concluded that "since the wali was confident that he would be dismissed and be replaced by someone else, he took care of his personal, not the country's interests. His only concern was to get rich during his short tenure by any means in order to compensate him for his loss by dismissal. That was why every wali increased the taxes levied by his predecessors."[90]

Was it greed or intolerance?

I personally believe that the power of religious motives was a means used by the walis to acquire wealth. Undoubtedly, other reasons caused the same walis to behave differently. But one is not justified in depending only on the policy of the walis and the measures that they took in Egypt to decide whether they functioned under the influence of tolerance or fanaticism. When we speak about exceptions, particularly ʾAbd al-ʾAziz ibn Marwān, who was wali of Egypt for twenty years, we find that, although Christian historians did not forgive him for the taxes that he levied on the monks, he was a just and kind ruler. One Coptic bishop once mentioned that ʾAbd al-ʾAziz occasionally used to invite Yuhanna, the head of the bishops, to meet with him because of the friendly relations they had. The wali honored Patriarch Isaac[91] and protected him from jealous persons and back-biters.[92] This tolerance was due to the fact that ʾAbd al-ʾAziz was influenced by a Christian educator named Anistas, or Bar Jūmi. Of him, Michael

---

89. Grohmann, *op. cit.*, 1:74. He set prices for parchment and papyrus.

90. Marcel, J.J. *L'Egypte arabe*. Paris, 1872. p.p. 43–44.

91. [The forty-first Patriarch of the Copts, 690–92 A.D. (Tr.)]

92. "Vie d'Isaac, Patriarche d'Alexandrie." *Patrologia Orientalis*, vol 11. Paris: Fermin – Dirdot, 1907, pp. 377–85.

the Syrian said, "He was intelligent and well-read."[93] It is most probable that his [Christian] educator had his effect on his sympathizing with the Copts.

Christian historians, on the contrary, portray his brother `Abd Allah[94] in a terrible light because he not only levied the dinar tax on Christian men of religion but he also imprisoned the Coptic patriarch to force part of his wealth from him.[95] Sawirus ibn al-Muqaff`a says,

> "When `Abd Allah ibn `Abd al-Malek arrived in Egypt, he committed evil deeds. All the notables were apprehensive of his actions which were inspired by the devil. In those days the blessed patriarch Alexander II[96] left Alexandria for Cairo to greet him, as was the custom. When the new wali saw the patriarch, he asked who he was. He was told that he was the father and patriarch of all the Christians. He took him to one of his guards and told him, `Humiliate him in any way you want until he pays three thousand dinars.' The guard took him away and kept him for three days. When Jerja the deacon realized that the patriarch would not be released until the money was paid, he asked the guard, `Master, do you seek the life of the patriarch or the money?' He said, `the money.' The deacon said, `Release him to me for two months and I will take him to Lower Egypt to meet the notables and the Christians, and get you three thousand dinars.' He released the patriarch to him whom he accompanied on a tour of cities and villages, meeting with those who believed in Christ until he raised the money."[97]

Sawirus accused this wali of collecting two-thirds of a dinar more than what each one of the Ahl al-dhimma used to pay, describing him as one who "loved money very much."[98] al-Kindī accused him of encouraging bribery and filling his pockets with the *jizyah* money.[99] Qurrah ibn Shurayk, the successor of

---

93. *Michel le Syrien*, 2:475.

94. [`Abd Allah ibn `Abd al-Malek ibn Marwān. (Tr.)]

95. [Which was in fact the church's wealth. (Tr.)]

96. [The forty-third patriarch, 705–30 A.D. (Tr.)]

97. Sawirus, *op. cit.*, vol. 1, pt. 3, pp. 308–9, ch. 16.

98. *Ibid.*, p. 309.

99. al-Kindī, *op. cit.*, p. 59.

'Abd Allah, loved money no less than his predecessor. Sawirus recounts that, when the miserable patriarch went to congratulate Qurrah on his appointment as wali, according to custom, Qurrah arrested him and said, "You should pay me an amount of money similar to what 'Abd Allah took from you."[100] The same historian also tells us that Qurrah broke into the church at al-Fustāt, accompanied by a group of vicious people, and stood [menacingly] close to him as he sat in front of the altar during a church service.

The practice [of increasing taxes] was thus established by one of the greedy walis. Afterwards, it became impossible to prevent successive walis from emulating their predecessors. The Caliph Sulayman ibn 'Abd al-Malek [96–97 A.H./715–17 A.D.] sent 'Usama ibn Zayd to Egypt to administer the Bayt al-Mal. It seems that this man was greedier than his predecessor. Both Muslim and Christian historians tell us that he illegally confiscated property and was excessive in killing people. He brought the monks together and told them of the necessity of maintaining the tax levied on them by 'Abd al-'Aziz. He also forced them to receive from the tax collectors iron stamps with their names engraved on them, along with the date that the taxes were due, on condition that each one should carry the stamp on his finger as a ring. If a monk was caught without the ring, his hand was to be cut off.

It seems that 'Usama's order was put into effect. As for the monks who fled to monasteries, believing that they would be able to evade paying taxes with impunity, they were pursued by the police and arrested. They were executed by beheading or being beaten to death. Moreover, 'Usama issued a decree mandating that people traveling north or south on the Nile River carry stamped passes.

These measures had a debilitating impact on the psychology of the populace. However, the timely death of the caliph prevented the outbreak of revolution in the country. Thereupon, after the succession of 'Umar ibn 'Abd al-'Aziz to the caliphate [99–101 A.H./717–20 A.D.], he soon removed 'Usama and appointed Ayyūb ibn Shurhabil in his place. He charged him with calming the people and asked him to be lenient with them. The caliph also ordered him to put 'Usama under arrest, to put an iron ring around his neck, and to lock his hands and feet in wooden stocks. While in this condition, 'Usama was driven to the place where he was to be executed; but he died on the way.

'Umar ibn 'Abd al-'Aziz did something else of great importance which gained him the support and love of the people. He ordered the cancellation of the

---

100. Sawirus, *op. cit.*, p. 312.

taxes on monks and bishops.[101] But the tax was reinstated during the reign of Yazīd II [101–5 A.H./720–24 A.D.] and the Copts resumed their complaints about the injustice of the walis. During the caliphate of Hisham [105–25 A.H./724–43 A.D.], Hanzalah ibn Safwan was reappointed as wali over Egypt [119 A.H./736 A.D.]. He had filled this position during the reign of the Caliph Yazīd. Hanzalah did not follow the wise course set out by the caliph for him, and he raised taxes, levying taxes not only on people, after he had conducted a census, but also on animals. He levied a further tax on receipts [stamp tax].

Caliph Hisham pursued a wiser policy than that of his agent. He sought the support of the Copts, who had not lost their influence in the country, instead of angering them by levying new taxes. Because the Copts remained without a patriarch for some time, the caliph ordered the appointment of a religious leader for them. He also ordered that a certificate be given to everyone, in his own name, who had paid taxes in order that "no one is treated unjustly and no injustice takes place in his kingdom." Sawirus then added, "Hisham was a man who feared God through Islam and he loved all people."[102]

These events indicate that the walis' unjust treatment of the people arose principally for personal reasons. Eventually the walis found persons who emulated their behavior, such as employees who worked under them. Michael the Syrian tells us, "When al-M'amūn left Egypt, disasters befell the Egyptians. The Persians[103] entered the villages and put in shackles those who resisted, ten or twenty together, and they sent them to al-Fustāt without verifying whether they were guilty or not. Many died without committing any crime. Some of those arrested, while being led to their deaths, offered bribes to their guard to set them free. After they gave him the money, the man said, 'Wait until we meet others on our way to put them in shackles instead of you.' They met three men, a priest and two Arabs, one of whom was an imam of a mosque. The guard set free those who bribed him and he arrested those three instead."[104]

The irresponsibility of the walis towards Egypt was apparent. When conspiracies and intrigues increased at the court in Baghdad in the third century A.H. [tenth century A.D.], it was rare for a man of influence in the court to live away from it. If he was appointed as a wali over one of the provinces of the

---

101. Sawirus, *op. cit.*, p. 152.

102. Sawiris, *op. cit.*, p. 152 (Seybold edition).

103. [By the time of the Abbasid Caliph al-M'amūn (198–218 A.H./813–33 A.D.), Persians were hired in the armies of the Arab empire. (Tr.)]

104. *Michel le Syrien*, 3:77–78.

empire, he would appoint an agent to act in his name and would give him a part of the income in return for his services.

Hoarding wealth was the chief goal of the walis. Consequently, the country faced a severe economic crisis before the establishment of the Ṭūlūnid state. Crops also decreased as a result of the government's systematic exploitation of the country's resources.

In fact, the Umayyad treatment of the conquered people was, in general, better than that of the Abbasids. Often the Abbasids resorted to violence to get hold of the people's money. Most probably, their great need for money detered them from following a lenient policy. In any case, the history of the Coptic patriarchs was nothing but a long series of complaints that began with the fifty-second patriarch after St. Mark [Joseph, 831–49 A.D.]. One bishop, called Kuzman, was so desperate that he abdicated his authority to the elite of his community and held them responsible for paying the government its dues while he withdrew to a city called Demro.[105]

D. The Coptic Revolution.

The Copts realized that their optimism [for the future] was misplaced because a government cannot exist without taxes, however tolerant it might be. Their disappointment grew when they realized that the new [Arab] conqueror wanted to enjoy the fruits of his victory. It did not take them long before their eyes focused on one goal: changing their new rulers and liberating themselves from their domination.

In the beginning, the people took a neutral position on the Arab invasion. Although they sympathized with the Arabs, some Copts living in the environs of Alexandria sided with the Byzantines, and they joined their ranks when these counterattacked against the Arabs. The reason for taking sides—as mentioned above—was that ʿAmr ibn al-Āṣ responded roughly to the governor of Ikhna when the latter asked him to specify the amount of tax due to the treasury. At any rate, the Copts did not try to move against the Arabs after the murder of ʿUthmān [35 A.H./655 A.D.] and the schism which took place between the followers of ʿAli ibn Abi Talib and his enemies. The stance of the Copts has surprised orientalists. But the Coptic clergy—who were then able to start a revolution—were content under the Arab occupation, because ʿAmr had honored their patriarch in every way, offering him respect and reverence and seeking his advice and blessing. He also ordered that Christian men of religion be exempted from the *jizyah*.

---

105. [In the Gharbiyah province. (Tr.)]

When the Abbasid revolution against the Umayyads broke out, the situation in Egypt had changed completely because the [Umayyad] caliphs of Damascus had levied taxes on the men of religion and had increased taxes on the people because of their need for money. These two measures angered the people, and they revolted in 107 A.H. [725 A.D.] during the caliphate of Hisham ibn `Abd al-Malek. This reflected the frustrations of the Copts—led by their men of religion—with their rulers.

It was by divine foreordination that Marwān ibn Muhammad,[106] the last of the Umayyad caliphs, took refuge in Egypt where he persecuted the patriarch before putting him in shackles. This act was like an advance notice to all Christians to side with the Abbasids (whom Sawirus ibn al-Muqqaf`a called the Khorasanians).[107] This historian has supplied us with important information about his co-religionists. "The Christians in Egypt told the Khorasanians, `Here is our father the patriarch under arrest by the order of Marwān, and we do not know what he is going to do to him.' The Bashmūrs[108] had met the Khorasanians at Farma[109] and told them that Marwān had taken the patriarch to kill him because we [Christians] resisted him and killed his soldiers before the arrival of the Khorasanians. The people prayed to God to help the Khorasanians who decreased the *kharaj* for those who carried the sign of the cross, treating them well and doing good to them all over the country. Later the Khorasanians killed Marwān and then crucified him with his head down. The Khorasanians honored Anba Khayal and revered him greatly."[110]

Because the Abbasids were more knowledgeable than `Amr ibn al-Ās, they knew how to use those people who were ready to help them against their rulers. But history often repeats itself. The Abbasids were forced to levy exorbitant taxes. Concerning this development, Sawirus said, "In the third year of the reign of the Khorasanians, they doubled the *kharaj* on the Christians and did not fulfill their promises to them."[111] This policy resulted in five wide-spread rebellions in the country that took place between 121 A.H. [739 A.D.] and 156

---

106. [Marwān II, 127–32 A.H./744–50 A.D. (Tr.)]

107. [Khorasan was a province in northeastern Iran. (Tr.)]

108. [Copts who lived in the province of Bashmūr. (Tr.)]

109. [Farma is the key city in northeastern Egypt, also called Pelusium, whose original name was Pheromī (in Coptic). (Tr.)]

110. Sawirus, *op. cit.*, pp. 204–5 (Seabold edition).

111. *Ibid.*, p. 305.

A.H. [773 A.D.]. The largest occurred in 216 A.H. [831 A.D.] during Caliph al-M`amūn's reign, causing much bloodshed and bringing terrifying results. Many Muslims joined the Christians in their revolt.[112] The rebels chose the right time for their movement when a good number of the provinces [of the Islamic empire] were in a state of revolution. If political ambition abroad was the reason behind these other revolutions, in Egypt exorbitant taxes were the major reason, as they had been in the past. al-Maqrizi wrote concerning this matter, "In Jumada al-`Ula, 216 A.H., the Arabs and Copts revolted, dismissed the agents of the wali, and disobeyed the authorities because of the misbehavior of the representatives of the sultan; and there were wars between them and the army of al-Fustāt."[113]

The presence of the Bashmurians[114] among the rebels increased the ferocity of the fighting. An Arab writer quoted by al-Maqrizi mentions that those people were more fierce and obstinate than all other Egyptians, and they caused trouble for the authorities. Did they not resist the Arabs for seven years after the fall of Alexandria into the hands of `Amr ibn al-Ās? Were they not the first to revolt against the tax collectors?

Quatremère referred in his research[115] to an Arabic manuscript on the life of [Patriarch] Michael from which he obtained detailed information about the ability of these people to fight. This manuscript mentions that

> "the Bashmurians revolted against `Abd al-Malek ibn Marwān under the leadership of Mena ibn Bakirah. They joined the people of Shubra Sunbat, took over that region, and refused to pay taxes to the ruler and the chief tax collector. `Abd al-Malek went to quell the revolt at the head of his army, but he fled after a great battle. Then `Abd al-Malek sent an army and a fleet, but they failed drastically [to quell the revolt]. When the Caliph Marwān came to Egypt and was told what had happened, he wrote to the Bashmurians offering them general amnesty. But they rejected his offer. He then sent a strong army composed of Egyptian and

---

112. [Atiya, A.S. A History of Eastern Christianity. New York: Kraus Reprint, 1980. p.p. 85-86. (Tr.)]

113. *al-Khitat*, 1:79–89 and 1:127–28 (in the edition of 1324 A.H.).

114. These were inhabitants of Bashmūr, a land lying between Alexandria and Rashīd near lake Edko. It was characterized by swamps where bamboo was grown. Said ibn al-Bitriq claims that these inhabitants were the descendants of forty Greeks who remained in Alexandria after the Arab conquest, and their numbers increased through marriage (Ibn al-Bitriq, *op. cit.*, p. 57).

115. *Recherches critiques et historiques sur la langue et la literature de l'Égypte*, Paris, 1808, pp. 152–56.

Syrian soldiers. But the forces could not engage the rebels because they took refuge in a swampy region which would allow passage for only one person at a time. If a person slipped in the mud, he would sink into it and die. The Arab armies were able to besiege the area. But when night fell, the Bashmurians left their hiding place and walked through roads known only to them. It did not take long before they stormed the Muslims, killing all they could and taking their money and horses.

When al-Kawthar ibn al-Aswad, the commander of Marwān's forces, entered Alexandria he ordered the imprisonment of Patriarch Michael after beating him, and ordered that he be beheaded. His order was about to be carried out, and the executioner's hands were raised to fall upon the patriarch's neck, when Kawthar's heart was filled with pity for him and he told his entourage, `What shall we reap from killing this old man? I have written to the Bashmurians asking them to stop fighting us, but they have rejected my advice. Let us take him to Rashīd with us and ask him to write to these people, telling them that the ill treatment that he has suffered was due to their behavior.' While the prince was on his way to Rashīd, he learned that the city had fallen to the Bashmurians, who destroyed and burned it down after killing the Muslims who lived in it."[116]

Had the revolution broken out only in Egypt, because of taxes, the caliph would have not traveled to Egypt to quell it. But it happened at the same time that Nasr ibn Shabath declared a revolution against the caliphate. He relied on Syrians, who had remained loyal to the Umayyads, and on a fleet of military ships that had arrived in Alexandria from Spain. al-M`amūn grew very anxious and feared that the revolution would spread because the Egyptians would readily cooperate with the Umayyads who had taken refuge in Spain, in the way that they cooperated with the Abbasids against the Umayyads.

Michael the Syrian meant what he said when he wrote, "Nasr and his followers declared the revolt in Syria, and at the same time they urged the Egyptians to revolt."[117] Two men took over the revolution: Siri and Jarawi.[118] After they collected gold like stones, they started to collect the *jizyah* in their names. When they died they were succeed by their sons. "Ubeid ibn Siri reigned

---

116. *Ibid.*, pp. 152–56.

117. *Michel le Syrien*, 3:59.

118. These are al-Siri ibn al-Hakam and `Abd al-`Aziz al-Jarawī.

over al-Fustāt and Upper Egypt, and Ahmad[119] over Lower Egypt. Concerning Alexandria, people who came from Andalusia [Spain] ruled over it."[120]

Although the patriarch Yusāb[121] did his best to convince the Bashmurians not to commit acts of violence, Sawirus justifies their revolution saying,

"The Arabs treated the Bashmurians with extreme cruelty. They tied them with chains to the grain mills and beat them severely so that they would grind the grain exactly like animals. The Bashmurians were forced to sell their children [into slavery] to pay the *jizyah* and to relieve themselves from the pains of torture. When they became convinced that only their death would put an end to these injustices and realized that their region was covered with swamps—with narrow paths known only to them—and that it was impossible for the Muslim armies to penetrate those swamps, they unanimously agreed to revolt and to refuse to pay the *jizyah*. Patriarch Yusāb grieved for his people who risked annihilation because of plague, famine and war. Nevertheless, the Bashmurians were determined to continue fighting. They made their own weapons, they publicly fought the caliph, and they refused absolutely to pay the *jizyah*. They even reached a point at which they killed everyone who went to them as an intermediary between themselves and the authorities. The patriarch was deeply worried because they had gone to war against an enemy who excelled them in numbers and arms, and had willingly exposed themselves to death. He wrote them a letter trying to convince them that they would be unable to resist the caliph's military. He described the disasters that would befall them and asked them to change their minds. When he realized that his letter had not brought the desired effect, he sent them one letter after another insisting on his request. When the bishops went to deliver these letters, the Bashmurians attacked them, stripped them of their clothes, and dismissed them after heaping abuse on them. The bishops went back and told the patriarch what had happened, and he decided to leave these people to their destiny."[122]

---

119. The historian means `Ali ibn `Abd al-`Aziz al-Jarawī.

120. Sawirus mentions this incident in his history without attaching any importance to it.

121. [Fifty-second Coptic patriarch, 831–49 A.D.; see S.Y. Labib, "Yūsāb I," *The Coptic Encyclopedia*, 7:2362–63. (Tr.)]

122. Sawirus, *op. cit.*, pp. 276–77.

Caliph al-M'amūn was at that time staying in Syria. He hurried to Egypt after granting amnesty to Nasr the rebel. At the same time the Jacobite patriarch Dionysius of Tallmahrē [817–845 A.D.] was staying in Damascus. al-M'amūn sent him a message saying, "Stay here so that you can accompany us to Egypt, because we want you to go as ambassador to the Bayamay[123] [the Bashmurians] in Lower Egypt to convince them to give up fighting and to surrender."[124]

Dionysius later reported the development of events as follows:
"When we reached al-Farama, the caliph called me in and said, `I have known, Patriarch, of the rebellion of the Egyptian Christians called the Bayamay, and that they were unsettled by the disasters that befell them as a result of our first onslaught. Except for my tolerance and refusal to annihilate them, I would not send them a man of your stature. Take all the bishops of Egypt with you and go to meet with them. Negotiate with them on condition that the rebels surrender and come with me and my army to where I shall resettle them. If they refuse, I will kill them with the sword.' When I talked to the caliph at length about the Bashmurians subjecting themselves to his authority, on condition that they are left to live in their own country, he refused and said, `No, either they leave the country or expose themselves to death'."

Dionysius resumed his story.

"We found them together hiding on an island surrounded by water, with bamboo and reeds on all sides. Their leader came out to talk to us. When we blamed them for revolting and for the massacres they had committed, they blamed their rulers.[125] But when they learned of the demand to leave their country, they were very upset and pled to send a message to the caliph asking for an audience with him to tell him how much humiliation they had suffered. They said that the wali responsible for collecting the *kharaj* forced them to pay a *jizyah* that they could not afford. He imprisoned them, tied them to the mills, beat them severely, and forced them to grind the grain like animals. When their wives came

---

123. This was the name that some Christian historians, including Ibn al-Bitriq, gave the Bashmurians.

124. *Michel le Syrian*, 3:76.

125. Probably they meant the wali.

to them carrying their lunch, his servants raped them. Many of them were killed. He intended to annihilate all of them for fear that they would complain about him to the caliph. . . . When we returned to the caliph, we informed him of the injustices suffered by the Egyptians and the cruelty of the wali. After I submitted my report to him he said, `I am not responsible for the policy of my walis because I did not dictate to them the measures that they took. I never thought of overburdening the people. If I have pity for the Romans who are my enemies, how can I not sympathize with my subjects'."[126]

One Muslim historian mentions that when al-M`amūn arrived in Egypt he reprimanded and removed Essa ibn Mansūr, the wali, telling him, "These serious events were the result of your actions and the actions of your agents. You overburdened the people and hid it from me until the situation became serious and the country fell into chaos."[127]

In spite of the repeated advice of the clergy, the Bashmurians refused to surrender. al-M`amūn had no other choice but to crush them, killing a large number of them. He then called in their leaders and ordered them to evacuate the region. They told him of the cruelty of the walis and that, if they left their country, they would lose their source of income because they lived on selling papyrus and fishing. At last they carried out his orders and sailed to Antioch. Then they were sent to Baghdad.[128] There were about three thousand of them; most died on the way. Those who were captured during the fighting were taken as slaves and distributed among the Arabs. There were about five hundred of these who were sent to Damascus and sold as slaves.[129]

al-M`amūn was able to put down the revolution which had deep roots in the country. Of this al-Maqrizi said, "After these events took place, God humiliated the Copts in all the land of Egypt and broke their power. Thus not one of them was able to rebel against the sultan. The Muslims took over the villages,

---

126. *Michel le Syrien*, 3:78–9.

127. al-Kindī, *op. cit.*, p. 192.

128. The author of the *History of Patriarch Michael* wrote the following details: "al-M`amūn ordered a search for the rest of the Bashmurians and sent them to Baghdad where they were kept in prisons. Then they were released by al-M`utasim, the brother and successor of al-M`amūn. Some of them returned to Egypt, and others have remained in Baghdad until now [the time of the author] and are known as the Bashmurians. Some returned to Egypt with revolution still on their minds." See Quatremère, *op. cit.*, pp. 161–63.

129. *Michel le Syrien*, 3:83.

and the Copts resumed their conspiracies against Islam and its adherents by resorting to ploys and deception, and they succeeded in having control of the *kharaj* books."[130]

It is worth noting that, while the Bashmurians were desperately fighting their last revolution, whose serious results are noted by al-Maqrizi, the historians mention no other Coptic revolution in any other part of the country. In fact, as al-Maqrizi states, the Copts did not resort to the old method of revolution after that event, but always adopted a peaceful approach. When revolutions broke out, the Copts participated in them at the encouragement of foreign elements, whether Muslim or Bashmurian [who were a mixture of Copts and Greeks]. After the Bashmurians were wiped out, the Copts never tried to revolt.

E. The Benefits That the Copts Reaped.

The Copts monopolized administrative positions.

The events we have mentioned above do not imply that the Copts were miserable under the Arab walis. They were in fact in a better situation than they were under the Byzantines. In spite of the caliphs' efforts and their interest in applying the teachings of the Qurān, Copts not only occupied most of the administrative posts, but also sometimes had full powers. The tax and accounting system continued to be in their hands, which gave them opportunity to achieve big gains. We can safely say that the teachings of the Qurān were not applied when dealing with the Copts.

The caliphs repeatedly expressed their desire to keep the Copts out of administrative positions. They also expressed their disappointment—orally if not in writing—whenever they found them in such positions. But the political acumen of 'Amr ibn al-Ās overcame the religious fanaticism of 'Umar [the caliph]. When 'Umar ibn 'Abd al-'Aziz became caliph a century after the conquest of Egypt, he reminded the rulers of the provinces of their duties, directing a strong message to them in which he said,

> "'It is 'Umar ibn 'Abd al-'Aziz who is reading the words of God to you.'
> Here he mentioned some Quranic verses related to the dhimmis. He
> added that he had heard in the past that, when the Muslim armies
> conquered a country, the polytheists used to meet with them, and the
> faithful [Muslims] would request their assistance in administering the
> country because of their sound opinions and their knowledge of

---

130. *al-Khitat*, 1:79–80.

administrative matters and tax collection. 'But sound opinions and knowledge are not available to those who receive the rage of Allah [dhimmis]. God and his Messenger have ordered putting an end to this state of affairs. I do not like it when someone tells me that a wali has left in his position an agent who adheres to any other religion but Islam. I will remove such a wali from his position at once. It is our duty to keep the dhimmis out of such employment as it is our duty to eradicate their religions. Every wali should tell me of the situation in his *wilayah* [governorship].'"[131]

When Ayūb ibn Sharhabil received this message, he canceled the permits of the Copts to manage the financial affairs of the districts and replaced them with Muslims.[132]

However, thirty-five years had passed since the issuance of this order when the Abbasid Caliph al-Mansūr[133] issued strict orders removing the dhimmis from their positions, a sudden measure. It happened that some Muslims complained to the caliph during one of his pilgrimages, and petitioned him to protect them from the injustice of the Christians. After the caliph had permitted them to meddle in Muslim affairs, and to tell him all that they knew about the Umayyads, al-Mansūr told his private secretary: "Here is my seal. Send my order to seek out all Muslims who have knowledge of the work done by dhimmis, and write to all the walis to fire all the dhimmis from their positions." Since the private secretary was convinced that the order would not be carried out, he later told the caliph, "I did not carry out your order because I am confident that the dhimmis would conspire against us if they were fired collectively. We will make the change gradually."[134]

In fact the dhimmis were never removed from their positions as a group. On the contrary, during the caliphate of al-Mahdi they became very influential and so arrogant that the Muslims grew angry with them and protested their behavior. As a result, the caliph ordered the wali not to leave any dhimmi on his staff, and

---

131. Ibn al-Naqqash; this is the translation of the text included in *Journal Asiatique* in French. [This is the exact text in the manuscript of Ibn al-Naqqash, *op. cit.*, pp. 83–84. (Tr.)]

132. al-Kindī, *op. cit.*, p. 69.

133. [Abbasid Caliph, 136–158 A.H./754–775 A.D. (Tr.)]

134. Ibn al-Naqqash, Manuscript, p. 85.

he ordered him to cut off the hands of Muslims who might seek the assistance of a Christian clerk."[135]

The Caliph al-Mahdi, who recommended that his walis get rid of their dhimmi employees, never practiced what he preached. Christians continued to occupy administrative posts as they had in the past. The proof is in what al-M'amūn told his private secretary when he was in Egypt: "I am tired of the complaints that I receive against Christians concerning their ill-treatment of Muslims and their lack of integrity in handling financial affairs."[136] The caliphs 'Umar ibn 'Abd al-'Aziz, al-Mansūr, al-Mahdi, Harūn al-Rashīd, al-M'amūn, al-Mutawakkil, and al-Muqtadir bi-llah were satisfied by nominally removing Christians from their public positions. In fact, they left them in those positions.

Orders relating to special dress for Christians were not carried out.

'Amr permitted the Copts to dress like Muslims.[137] Afterwards, they faced no pressures concerning the matter. In fact, until 233 A.H. [848 A.D.] neither the caliph nor the wali thought of canceling permission. 'Umar ibn 'Abd al-'Aziz found it handy that the dhimmis remind his walis of 'Umar's prior covenant with them at the time he ordered their removal from their positions. Ibn al-Bitriq tells us, "The Christians continued to wear black clothes and ride horses until the days of al-Mutawakkil [232–247 A.H./847–861 A.D.]. Later this caliph wrote to all the provinces that Christians should wear al-'ayar[138] and al-ruqq'ā[139] with two patches, one on the front and another on the back, and that they should not ride horses.[140] They should also have handles on their wooden saddles, and pictures of devils [in another edition of the same source, pictures of pigs and monkeys] should be painted on the doors of their houses. The Christians were deeply hurt, and they suffered affliction and grief."[141]

---

135. *Ibid.*, pp. 85–86.

136. *Ibid.*, p. 86.

137. Rather, he did not prevent them from dressing like the Muslims.

138. [*Libas al-'ayar* was a kind of clothing which distinguished Christians from Muslims. (Tr.)]

139. [*al-ruqqā'* (pl.); *ruqq'ah* (sing.) was a multi-colored dress, as if made of patches of different colors. (Tr.)]

140. Ibn al-Bitriq, *op. cit.*, 1:59.

141. *Ibid.*, p. 63.

F. The Tendency of the Arabs to Follow a Colonial Policy.

We have explained that both Arabs and Copts were affected by financial considerations. In fact, money continued for a long time to be the dominant factor in their relationships. Gaston Wiet mentions that, "the first caliphs thought, during the first fifty years after the death of the Prophet, that they were unable to build an Islamic empire."[142] Therefore money, which the Arabs needed badly, became the heart of their policy towards conquered peoples. Their lack of experience did not enable them to follow a proper colonial policy. Moreover, internal conflicts that broke out in the new empire did not allow them to formulate a long-range policy.

The Arab empire started during the Umayyad period. When their borders became secure, the caliphs began to overlay the occupied countries with an Arabic-Islamic character. There are many examples of this. When `Amr established a criminal justice system in Egypt, he respected the Copts' needs by having them tried by justices of their own culture and religion, except in criminal cases. But as soon as Mu`awiya ibn Abi Sufyan became caliph in 60 A.H. [644 A.D.], he appointed a Muslim judge with the Coptic judge to prosecute the civil cases of the dhimmis. In 124 A.H. [745 A.D.], Hafs ibn al-Walid decided to distribute the inheritance of the dhimmis according to Islamic law, not according to their own laws.[143] `Umar ibn `Abd al-`Aziz decided that, if an Arab killed a Christian, he would not be executed but pay five thousand *zouzah* as a ransom. He also forbade the deduction of sums of money from house rents, inheritance and lands to support churches, monasteries and poor Christians.[144] These examples reflect clearly the prevailing mood during this period. This mood became stronger because the victorious Arabs wanted to show their superiority over the conquered dhimmis.

The decision that had the greatest consequences for the social life of the Copts concerned making Arabic the official language. This decision was made in 85 A.H. [705 A.D.] during the reign of `Abd Allah ibn `Abd al-Malek.[145] The Copts had begun to neglect learning the Greek and Coptic languages and had started to learn Arabic, which had become the language of business. Before that, some Arabs had taken the practical step of learning the Coptic language. al-Kindī

---

142. "L'Égypte Arabe" in *Histoire de la Nation égyptienne*, 4:47.

143. Ibn Taghribirdī. al-Nujūm al-Zahira, 1:294.

144. *Michel le Syrien*, 2:489.

145. al-Kindī, *op. cit.*, pp. 58–59.

mentions the judge Khayr ibn Na`īm [120 A.H./738 A.D.] as an example. "He listened to the Copts talking in their own language and spoke to them in Coptic. He also listened to the witnesses speaking Coptic, and he made his legal decisions based on their testimony."[146] From this example, we assume that some Arab employees learned Coptic to strengthen their relations with the people. Renaudot mentions that "when Patriarch Yusāb spoke in Coptic to the bishops, who leveled certain accusations at him, some Muslims understood what the patriarch said and interpreted it for the judge."[147]

The Arabs were concerned because of the speed with which the Copts learned the Arabic language, especially the Qurān. Arabs believed that they could force the Copts out of their jobs if they ordered them to use the language of the Qurān in official business. That was why in 235 A.H. [849 A.D.] the Caliph al-Mutawakkil issued a circular warning against hiring Christians and Jews and teaching them the Arabic language.[148] Abu al-Faraj ibn al-Jawzi added in his chronicle for the year 240 A.H. [854 A.D.] that al-Mutawakkil asked the dhimmis to teach their children the Hebrew and Syriac languages instead of Arabic.[149]

Moreover, with the increasing number of converts to Islam, the majority perceived Christians as elements of resistance in the midst of a Muslim society. Muslims also tended to consider Christians as natural allies of the Byzantine Christian empire. As a result, from time to time Christians suffered from the reactions of Arabs to this perception. Michael the Syrian ascertained that `Umar ibn `Abd al-`Aziz mistreated the Christians because his armies were forced to end the siege of Constantinople after suffering great losses.[150]

The Caliph al-Mahdi also was indignant with the Christians because some Byzantine army divisions defeated his son Harūn al-Rashīd and two of his generals. "Then al-Mahdi sent a muhtasib[151] to destroy the churches built during

---

146. *Ibid.*, p. 349, footnote.

147. Renaudot, *Historia*, p. 290.

148. *al-Khitat*, 2:494.

149. Quoted by Habib Zayyat in his article "The Title of Qadi under the Mamlukes," in *al-Mashriq*, 1938, pp. 57–59.

150. *Michel le Syrien*, 2:488.

151. ["Market inspector;" he was also in charge of enforcing public morality. (Tr.)]

the Arab rule, he ordered Christian slaves sold, and he also destroyed a large number of Jewish temples."[152]

Then came Harūn al-Rashīd who imposed a certain dress for the dhimmis because the inhabitants around the borders were spying for the Byzantine emperor Nicephorus.[153] But it seems that the measure was implemented in Baghdad only and that it did not apply to the Copts of Egypt. When the independent walis took over the rule of Egypt, they put a limit on the policy of the caliphs, and the Christians again enjoyed some tolerance for reasons that we shall mention in the next chapter.

---

152. *Michel le Syrien*, 3:3.

153. [Nicephorus I, emperor of the Eastern Empire, 802–11 A.D. (Tr.)]

Chapter 5

THE POLICY OF THE INDEPENDENT MUSLIM WALIS `PREFECTS': THE ṬŪLŪNID AND THE IKHSHĪDĪD DYNASTIES

The Ṭūlūnids[1] and the Ikhshīdīds[2] became independent in Egypt, even though they continued to be under the nominal authority of the Abbasid caliphate.[3] The orientalist C. H. Becker states that "the history of Islamic Egypt started with Ṭūlūnids. After Ahmad ibn Ṭūlūn became independent from the central government [in Baghdad], he no longer made a point of plundering the country, but rather tried to make it yield a permanent revenue and to increase the glory of his dynasty. Thus Egypt developed from being a dependency to being the center of a great empire. The government improved and general prosperity increased as it always did in times when the country had a strong government."[4]

This situation brought natural results. One conspicuous result was that the independent walis no longer relied on the caliph [in Baghdad] and they were quite ready to face his enmity. Therefore, they tried to gain the support of the people, including the Copts. However, we cannot estimate precisely the degree of tolerance of these governors. The reason is that the rule of the Ṭūlūnids and the Ikhshīdīds was very short—thirty-seven years for the Ṭūlūnids and sixty-four years for the Ikhshīdīds—and the sources available give scanty information about relations between Muslims and Copts.

Nevertheless, we know that Ibn Ṭūlūn opened his reign with a decision that was received gratefully by both Muslims and Copts: He decided to cancel all taxes imposed by the chief of the *kharaj*, Ahmad ibn al-Mudabbir, which were called *hilaliya*.[5] After Ibn Ṭūlūn dismissed him, he centralized in his own hands all civic, military, political and financial authority. The wali gave priority to canceling certain taxes and banning the violent methods of collecting them. Not surprisingly, the income from these taxes decreased by one hundred thousand dinars in the first year. But the people were pleased with the wali's decision and resumed their activities after slowing down [production] under the burden of

---

1. [The Ṭūlūnid dynasty ruled Egypt from 254 to 292 A.H. (868–905 A.D.). (Tr.)]

2. [The Ikhshīdīd dynasty ruled Egypt from 323 to 358 A.H. (935–969 A.D.). (Tr.)]

3. [The Abbasid caliphate ruled in Baghdad from 255 to 623 A.H. (869–1258 A.D.). (Tr.)]

4. Becker, C. H., article "Egypt" in *The Encyclopedia of Islam*, edited by M. Th. Houtsma and others (Leyden: E. J. Brill, and London: Luzac, 1927), 2:8.

5. [The *hilaliya* tax was collected at the first of every Arabic Hejira calendar month when a new *hilal* (crescent moon) appeared. (Tr.)]

hilaliya taxes. Some Arab historians have indicated that the income from the collected taxes that were brought to the Bayt al-Mal did not exceed 800,000 dinars at the beginning of the period while it reached 4,300,000 dinars before the death of Ahmad ibn Ṭūlūn [in 884 A.D.] whose wealth was estimated at more than ten million dinars. By and large, during this period Christians and Jews were not ill-treated. They made no specific complaints, although we know that the Coptic patriarch was imprisoned because he had not paid a fine imposed on him [and his people].

How can we explain the tolerance of Ibn Ṭūlūn toward the Ahl al-Dhimmah in light of his cruelty to the Coptic patriarch? We read in a Coptic manuscript[6] written about that date that Ibn Ṭūlūn did not treat all classes of the Egyptian people equally. He favored Turks over all other Muslims,[7] and the Melchites[8] over all other Christians. He tended to consider the patriarch of the Copts as his dangerous enemy. He took every opportunity to impose fines on him [and his followers] so that the church would remain in a state of extreme poverty.

We believe that this treatment, coupled with the Baghdad caliph's non-recognition of Ibn Ṭūlūn as a legitimate governor of Egypt, made the Coptic patriarch refuse to jeopardize his position by becoming totally loyal to Ibn Ṭūlūn. However, Christians did not complain of Ibn Ṭūlūn's treatment of them. The historian al-Balawī has reported his conversation with monks of Dayr al-Qusayr.[9] He states that they told him, "Prince Ahmad ibn Ṭūlūn often visited us and stayed in a monk's cell and spent his time meditating. He used to talk in particular to a monk called Anton."[10]

The monks of course benefited from Ibn Ṭūlūn's interest in them. When they complained to him of the heavy burden of the *jizyah*, he gave them some privileges and ordered his men to refrain from interfering in their affairs. It is

---

6. Butcher, Edith Louisa, *The Story of the Church of Egypt*, London, 1897, 1:457–58.

7. [This was because he was of Turkish origin. (Tr.)]

8. [Melchites were royalist Christians in Egypt and Syria who accepted the decrees of the Council of Chalcedon in A.D. 451 against Nestorians and Monophysites. (Tr.)]

9. [This monastery was located near the city of Helwan twenty miles south-east of Cairo. (Tr.)]

10. al-Balawī, *Sirat Ahmad ibn Ṭūlūn*, p. 118. The monk referred to was Anton Miyah Andona.

said that an officer took five hundred dinars by force from a monk who then complained to the wali. He received his money back at the wali's order.[11]

Ibn Ṭūlūn allowed Greek mercenaries to join his army and, when he fell seriously ill, he asked his people who were of various religions to pray to God to grant him recovery. Concerning this incident the historian al-Balawī relates,

"When Ibn Ṭūlūn saw that his illness was growing worse, he called in his confidants and told them not only to ask all the people to pray for him but also to request them to go to the [nearby Mokattam] mountain and pray to God—holy be his name—to bestow recovery upon him. His request spread among the people. The Muslims went out to the slope of the mountain carrying Qurāns and praying to God with great sincerity to cure him because of their love for him. When the Christians and Jews saw this, they joined the Muslims, the Christians carrying the Bible and the Jews carrying the Torah. Their voices were so loud that Ibn Ṭūlūn heard them in his palace and wept."[12]

The people's compassion increased during the reign of Khumarawayh[13] who tried to correct one of his father's mistakes as soon as he was enthroned. When Ibn Ṭūlūn died, the Coptic patriarch Michael[14] was still in prison. He had been slandered by some Copts because he had dismissed a bishop called "Saqqa" who was guilty of bad behavior and deviation from Church rules. The bishop was embittered and sought revenge against the patriarch. He accused the patriarch of amassing a large fortune. At the time, Ibn Ṭūlūn was preparing a military campaign against Syria and his treasury was almost empty. He summoned the patriarch and ordered him to deposit all his wealth [the church's property] in the state treasury. Quoting Bishop "Saqqa," Ibn Ṭūlūn said that Christian monks should not keep any money except enough for their subsistence and to clothe their bodies in compliance with their religion. The patriarch tried to prove the falsehood of what the bishop had said, but Ibn Ṭūlūn imprisoned him for a whole year. Yuhanna and Ibrahim ibn Musa, the private secretaries of Ibn Ṭūlūn, were able to gain the release of the patriarch on condition that his followers [the Copts]

---

11. al-Balawī, *op. cit.*, p. 206.

12. *Ibid.*, p. 330.

13. [Khumarawayh was the son of Ahmad ibn Ṭūlūn and ruled from 270 to 282 A.H. (884–896 A.D.). (Tr.)]

14. [56th patriarch, Khael III or Michael I (880–907 A.D.). (Tr.)]

pay a large sum of money [to the state treasury]. The patriarch was compelled to sign a pledge in which he promised to pay 20,000 dinars in two installments. With difficulty he was able to pay the first installment after he arranged for loans and sold land owned by the Church[15] because the money he had collected from the Copts was not sufficient to meet the demands of the wali. Because the patriarch was unable to pay the full amount pledged to the wali, he was sent back to prison after he had retreated to Saint Mary's Monastery adjacent to Qasr al-Sham'a in al-Fustat. He remained in prison until Ibn Tulun died. When Khumarawayh came to power he released the patriarch and exempted him from his obligations.

Khumarawayh followed the example of his father by visiting the Melchite monastery of al-Qusayr. He ordered that a reception room be built in it. Abu Salih al-'Armani[16] stated that Khumarawayh used to marvel at the mosaic work on the walls of the monastery and at the pictures on them of the Virgin Mary, the Christ and his twelve disciples.

Christian historians have never recognized the Ikhshīdīds to be as tolerant as the Tūlūnids. In fact, they accused the founder of the Ikhshīdīd dynasty, Muhammad ibn Tughj al-Ikhshīdī,[17] of persecuting the Ahl al-Dhimmah and exacting money from them, which forced them to sell lands owned by the church so that he could pay the salaries of soldiers which he had been unable to pay. As a result, they have kept silent about one of the most unusual events in the history of Islamic Egypt, the official participation of a Muslim governor in a Christian religious feast, the feast of baptism[18] celebrated by the Copts with great fanfare. al-Mas'ūdi describes the event in detail:

"I attended in the year 330 A.H. [941 A.D.] the feast of baptism in Cairo. During that time the governor of Egypt, al-Ikhshīd Muhammad ibn Turghj was in his palace, called al-Mukhtar, on al-Roda island which is surrounded by the water of the Nile. He ordered that ten thousand torches be lighted on the island and along the Nile shore of al-Fustāt. This was over and above the [number of] torches that the people had lighted in the city. Thousands of Muslims and Christians came to the

---

15. To the Jews he sold one-fourth of the churches of Alexandria, land in Cairo, and a church adjacent to the Mu'allaqah Church in Old Cairo. He also imposed an annual levy on every Copt. See Jirjis ibn al-'Amīd, *L'Histoire mahmetane*, Pierre Vattier (trans.), p. 185.

16. Abu Sāliḥ the Armenian, *The Churches and Monasteries of Egypt*, pp. 49–51.

17. [Ruled Egypt 323–334 A.H. (935–946 A.D.). (Tr.)]

18. [Celebrated every year by the Copts on January 19. (Tr.)]

Nile shore, others came in boats and others watched from their homes overlooking the river. Many on the shores of the Nile, who did not disapprove of eating and drinking in public, showed up in their gold and silver jewelry and played music to entertain themselves. It was the best evening in Cairo, and full of joy. During that evening the gates remained open and many people immersed themselves in the Nile claiming that it gave them protection from illness and prevented the spread of disease."[19]

Kafūr's[20] reign was interrupted by the wars waged on the border of Syria by the Byzantine emperor Nicephorus II Phocas.[21] While Kafūr achieved a great victory, a majority of Egyptians stiffly resented the action. And although after each battle against the Byzantines a segment of the people caused disturbances by attacking Christians and destroying their churches, the authorities did not encourage these disturbances and were quick to quell them. Gaston Wiet states, "The government had no hand in these disturbances."[22] On the contrary, to calm emotions throughout the Islamic empire the caliph in 313 A.H. [925 A.D.] issued a decree in which he declared that *jizyah* would not be imposed on bishops, monks, and poor civilians.

Unfortunately, the power of the Ikhshīdīds started to decline and [as a result] they failed to protect minorities in Syria. In spite of their assistance to the patriarch of Jerusalem against ambitious army commanders, they could not save his life.[23] The downfall of the Ikhshīdīds and the rise of the Fatimids enabled the Christians to enjoy influence and affluence for some years.

---

19. [al-Mas'ūdi, *Murūj al-Dhahab wa M`ādin al-Jawhar*, Cairo, 1927, pp. 212–13. (Tr.)]

20. [Kafūr al-Ikhshīdī ruled Egypt from 966 to 968 A.D. (Tr.)]

21. [Nicephorus II Phocas (c. 919–969 A.D.) was emperor from 963 to 969 A.D. (Tr.)]

22. *Encyclopedia of Islam*, article "Kibt," vol. 2.

23. al-Antaki, *op. cit.*, pp. 124–25.

Chapter 6

THE RISE AND FALL OF THE COPTS
DURING THE REIGN OF THE FATIMIDS

While the policy of the walis toward the Copts was based on certain rules
and exclusions or exceptions, the policy of the Fatimids,[1] which was generally
based on tolerance, underwent noticeable changes that depended on the personal
dispositions of the walis who ruled.   The Fatimids' policy fluctuated between
extreme tolerance and atrocious persecution.   After they had initiated an
unexpected tolerant period in which the Ahl al-Dhimma flourished, the Fatimids
reversed themselves. They also brought about their own final destruction.

It is no surprise that the independent [Shi'ite Fatimid] caliphate, which
had established itself in Egypt in a short period, soon exhibited tolerance: it had
strong enemies in both Byzantium and Baghdad, and could not depend on the
loyal assistance of the [local] Sunni Muslims.   At times the Ṭūlūnids and
Ikhshīdīds had followed the same policy for largely personal reasons; however, the
coming to power of the Fatimids ignited the hopes of the Copts, leading them to
reach out a helping hand.

On their arrival in Egypt, in fact, the Fatimids had immediately tried to
gain the support and respect of the Sunnites, a pragmatic move on their part. The
first *khutbah*[2] delivered by the Caliph al-Mu'izz Li-Din Allah [ruled 341–365
A.H./952–975 A.D.], and mentioned by most historians, referred to this attitude.
The caliph announced to the multitudes who received him near Alexandria: "We
have not marched to Egypt to increase the size of our kingdom or our wealth, but
we have marched here because of our belief in *jihad* and our desire to achieve
victory for the Muslims, as well as to establish rightfulness and the Sunna."[3] In
order for al-Mu'izz and his successors to realize their sacred goal, they sought the
help of Christians and Jews and those among them who had recently converted to
Islam.

The victorious [Fatimid] commander Jawhar was a Greek slave who had
been given as a gift to the Caliph al-Mu'izz; hence he was called al-Rumi [the

---

1. [The Fatimids were a Shi'ite North African dynasty that ruled Egypt 297–567
A.H./909–1171 A.D. (Tr.)]

2. [A *khutbah* is the sermon given at the Friday noon prayer in a mosque. (Tr.)]

3. al-Maqrizi, *Iti'az al-Hunafa*, p. 88. [*Sunna* refers to the ways and customs of the
Prophet Muhammad and his companions. (Tr.)]

Roman]. Concerning [the Jewish treasurer] Ya`qūb ibn Killis,[4] he had converted to Islam under circumstances that raise questions about the sincerity of his religious sentiments. Born in Baghdad, he went to Egypt during the reign of Kafūr al-Ikhshīdī. The historian Ibn al-Qalanisi describes him as intelligent and rueful. He tells us that Kafūr once said of him, "If he were a Muslim, I would have appointed him a vizier."[5] When Ya`qūb learned that he could enter a mosque on a Friday and pronounce the *shihadatayn* [the two testimonies[6]], then Ibn Hanzabah, the current vizier, decided that he should kill Ya`qūb before he became his dangerous competitor. Ibn Killis escaped to the Maghrib [Morocco] and then helped the Fatimids in their invasion of Egypt. As a result, al-Mu`izz appointed him as his chief advisor and keeper of the treasury Bayt al-Mal. When al-`Aziz came to power [365–386 A.H./975–996 A.D.], he appointed Ibn Killis as his vizier. al-`Aziz also appointed Isa ibn Nastoros, a Melchite, to be a vizier, and he appointed a Jew called Minasha as governor-general of Syria.

Later al-Hakim [386–411 A.H./996–1020 A.D.] discontinued the practice of hiring dhimmis and began to persecute them. But he never eliminated all Christian employees. When al-Mustansir became caliph [411–427 A.H./1020–1035 A.D.], he returned to the policy followed by the earlier Fatimids and sought the services of Badr al-Jamali the [formerly Christian] Armenian[7] to save his throne. Badr ruled the country in an absolute manner and appointed his son al-`Afdal Shahinshah to succeed him in the viziership. In addition, the [later] Caliph al-Hafiz Li Din Allah [525–544 A.H./1130–1149 A.D.] readily sought the help of the Christian Melchite Behram, after he bestowed the title of Sayf al-Islam[8] upon him.

The presence of Christians in high offices of the state is a sure proof of the tolerance of the Fatimids. In addition, that period in the history of Egypt teemed with events related to the Ahl al-Dhimmah; however, every caliph followed a policy different from his predecessor's. We think that it would be helpful to examine each reign independently in order to understand each stage of

---

4. [Yaqūb ibn Killis was the treasurer of al-Mu`izz and the vizier of al-`Aziz. (Tr.)]

5. [Ibn al-Qalanisi, Abu Ya'la Tarikh, Leyden: E. J. Brill, 1908, p. 32. (Tr.)]

6. [The two testimonies consist of bearing witness to the Muslim creed by stating: "There is no God but Allah, and Muhammad is his prophet." (Tr.)]

7. [Badr al-Jamali was a Christian Armenian general from Syria, later hired by the Fatimids as commander-in-chief and vizier. When he died in 487 A.H. (1094 A.D.) he was 80 years old. His son al-`Afdal was also hired by the Fatimids as a vizier after him. (Tr.)]

8. [The phrase means "the sword of Islam." (Tr.)]

this important period in the history of the Copts, and thereby reach some conclusions.

al-Mu'izz li Din Allah (358–365 A.H./969–976 A.D.).

The army commander Jawhar started to build al-Azhar Mosque, an indicator of the caliph's generosity, because he supplied it with a rich library collection and because classes on Shi'ite theology were allowed in it. Further, teachers and students of al-Azhar later received salaries from the Caliph al-'Aziz bi Allah.

al-Mu'izz clearly understood that he could not rule the country while facing a current of public hostility. Because the Shi'ites were not liked in Egypt and Syria, he tried to gain the support of the Sunnites by showing some aversion towards the dhimmis, hence his cancellation of the practice initiated by the Ikhshīdīds of attending Christian feasts. Furthermore, he forbade the Copts from collecting charitable contributions, from spraying the muddy Nile water on passers-by, and from lighting fire-works during the Coptic New Year's Eve festival [*Nawrūz*].[9] He also forbade them from erecting their tents and sailing in boats on the Nile near the nilometer, *Miqyas al-Nil*,[10] during the feast of baptism [Eid al-Ghitas], and threatened to hang anyone who did not abide by his orders. Thus Christians ceased to celebrate these feasts during his reign.[11] al-Mu'izz also released the Ikhshīdīds whom Jawhar had arrested.[12]

The authority of Ibn Killis led to a strange incident, if we can believe the reports of Christian historians. After converting to Islam, Ibn Killis wanted to belittle the importance of Christianity in the eyes of the caliph. He therefore requested that religious discussions be conducted in the caliph's presence.[13] During these discussions the caliph heard that one could move mountains by

---

9. [*Nawrūz*, or New Year's day, is Tūt 1 of the Coptic Calendar which corresponds with September 11 of the Gregorian Calendar. See Archbishop Basilios, "Nawrūz," in *The Coptic Encyclopedia* 6:178. (Tr.)]

10. [*Miqyas al-Nil* is a measuring device built in the Nile near al-Roda island, and elsewhere, to measure the rise and fall of the river, especially during the flood season. The Greeks called such a device a Nilometer. (Tr.)]

11. Ibn Iyas, *op. cit.*, 1:46–47.

12. al-Antākī, *op. cit.*, p. 139.

13. *Patrologie Orientale*, 3:384. Sawiris ibn al-Muqaffa' participated in these discussions. See Ferdinand Wüstenfeld, *Geschichte der Fatimiden Caliphen*, Hildesheim; New York: G. Olms, 1976, p. 127, and Ibn al-Rāhib, p. 133.

strong faith. He summoned Abraham the Coptic patriarch [975–78 A.D.][14] and asked him whether the Bible contained such an idea. After the patriarch answered in the affirmative, the caliph ordered him to move the mountains, otherwise he "would erase the name of Christianity from the surface of the earth."[15] When the orders of the caliph reached the Coptic monks, they were stunned and started praying and supplicating at the church of al-Mu`allaqah.[16] After three days the patriarch saw in a dream the Virgin Mary calming him. Surrounded by a large number of Copts carrying crosses and Bibles, he then hurried to a specified place where the caliph and his entourage were waiting for him.

Christian historians assure us that the miracle took place[17] and that the astonished caliph ordered all the destroyed churches to be rebuilt. He summoned the Coptic notables and the Muslim ulama[18] and ordered the Bible and the Qurān to be read in his presence. When he listened to the two texts, he ordered either the demolition of the mosque built in front of Abu Shinūda Church and the building of a church in its place, or the expansion of the church of Abu Sayfein.

Some may ask why the caliph did not take the last step and convert to Christianity. Coptic historians readily affirm that the Caliph al-Mu`izz was baptized in a place adjacent to Saint John's Church and that he abdicated in favor of his son al-`Aziz bi-`Amr Allah, spending his last days in one of the monasteries. Marcus Samaika Pasha, one of the founders of the Coptic Museum

---

14. [The 62nd patriarch, he lived during the reigns of al-Mu`izz and al-`Aziz. See S.Y. Labib, "Abraham, Saint," *The Coptic Encyclopedia*, 1:10–11. (Tr.)]

15. Abū Salih, pp. 116–17.

16. [al-Mu`allaqah Church is one of the oldest Coptic churches in old Cairo, dating perhaps to the fifth century A.D. See C. Coquin, "Church of al-Mu`allaqah," *The Coptic Encyclopedia*, 2:557–60. (Tr.)]

17. Renaudot does not believe in this miracle. He notes that al-Makīn, the Christian, and al-Maqrizi, the historian, do not refer to this incident. But the Venitian Marco Polo, who returned to his country in 1295 A.D., carried with him details related to the incident. Both Jacobites and Melchites claim that they were the agents of the miracle.

18. [*Ulama*, pl. of `alim, refers to scholars who are learned in the Islamic sciences. One goes through a long process of formal education in these sciences before being acknowledged as an `alim. (Tr.)]

in Old Cairo, has repeated this story but Ahmad Zaki Pasha[19] and Abd Allah Inan[20] have strongly objected to it.[21]

al-`Aziz bi `Amr Allah (366–386 A.H./976–996 A.D.).

All reliable historians have reported events accurately for the reign of Caliph al-`Aziz bi `Amr Allah, events that indicate his patronage of the Coptic] and Melchite Christians. Before the caliphate of al-`Aziz, people considred the wali tolerant if he gave permission to renovate a church or build a new one in return for a gift of a few hundred dinars. But during al-`Aziz's caliphate, and afterwards, we find that the authorities built churches for Christians and looked after the construction workers when necessary, and that the Christian historians praised the walis who were not unjust toward their [Christian] kinsmen. Importantly, al-`Aziz tried to eliminate social differences between Muslims and dhimmis. Considered an important turning point in the history of Islamic Egypt, the caliphate of al-`Aziz called for complete equality between the two religious groups of the country for the first time ever.

al-`Aziz had married a Coptic Melchite woman. Among her children, she gave birth to a girl whom her father called Sit al-Mulk. Her moral values were like her mother's, that is, she had great sympathy for Christians. al-`Aziz loved his wife and daughter very much and followed their advice to the extent that he issued an order which was against the law: he appointed "Arsin" and "Arestid," his in-laws, as patriarchs, one for Alexandria, the other for Antioch. Did this mean that al-`Aziz was weak? No, because his reign was distinguished by the defensive wars which he led on the eastern borders of his empire and by the establishment of an efficient administration for the country. In order for the state to meet its financial needs, the Bayt al-Mal was subjected to strict supervision. He gave employees fixed salaries and sternly forbade them from accepting bribes or gifts. He also ordered them not to expend anything except by written

---

19. [Ahmad Zaki (1866–1934) was an Egyptian historian and linguist. He edited scores of classical Arabic manuscripts. (Tr.)]

20. [Muhammad Abd Allah Inan (1896–1987?) was an Egyptian historian who specialized in Islamic history. (Tr.)]

21. No reputable historian has mentioned that al-Mu`izz converted to Christianity. As for Sa`id al-Antaki, he makes no reference to the miracle of the mountain but mentions without specific reason that the death of al-Mu`izz was kept secret for about eight months. He also mentions that one day before al-Mu`izz's death he requested that his family pledge their allegiance to his son as his successor. See al-Antaki, *op. cit.*, p. 146.

authorization.[22]   al-`Aziz established a strong army that included Turks and Africans. Further, he took part in many battles against Byzantium. Indeed, the Fatimid caliphate reached its zenith during his reign.

Muslims think that al-`Aziz made a serious mistake by depending on the dhimmis and others who were nominally Muslims. For example, Ya`qūb ibn Killis continued for fifteen years in his position at the right hand of the caliph and carried out many reforms. al-Antaki reported that when Ibn Killis died, "the caliph went to his home, prayed over him, uncovered his face and cried bitterly".[23] Ibn al-Qalanisi added that "al-`Aziz ordered Ibn Killis buried in one of his houses in Cairo under a dome which he had built for himself. He attended his funeral and closed government offices and businesses for several days."[24]

After the death of Ya`qūb, al-`Aziz began to confide in Isa ibn Nastoros, a Melchite, who soon became a vizier. He also hired Abū al-Mansūr, the Coptic physician of al-Mu`izz, for a responsible position. The caliph then began to notice that his Muslim subjects were unaccustomed to seeing Christians occupying high state positions, enjoying all sorts of respect, to the extent that those subjects expressed their indignation about such appointments. One day, while the caliph was strolling in the city, he saw the shadow of a woman[25] who was carrying a petition that said, "By [God], who dignified the Jews by [appointing] Menasha, and the Christians by [appointing] Isa ibn Nastoros, and humiliated the Muslims through you. . . ."[26]

---

22. *Encyclopedia of Islam*, article "al-Aziz bi `Amr Allah."

23. al-Antākī, *op. cit.*, p. 172.

24. Ibn al-Qalanisi, p. 32.

25. Some historians, such as Yūssūf ibn Mar`ī al-Qudsi, claimed that the person who carried the petition disappeared after delivering it. al-Makin places this incident in al-Ḥakim's reign who took revenge by burning the capital.

26. Abū Saliḥ, *op. cit.*, p. 35. [The Egyptian historian Hasan Ibrahim Hasan observed that Al-`Aziz was very sympathetic toward Christians and Jews, a characteristic that many Muslims protested. After he appointed the Christian Isa ibn Nastoros as vizier and Menasha the Jew as wali over Syria, these two men exhibited their biases towards their co-religionists and appointed many of them to government positions, resulting in protestations by Muslims. The frustration of one Muslim led him to write a complaint, hand it to a woman, and give her money to obstruct the procession of the caliph while submitting it to him. It read as follows: "By (God), who dignified (honored) the Christians by appointing Isa ibn Nastoros (as vizier) and dignified the Jews by appointing Menasha ibn Ibrahim al Farrar (as wali of Syria) and humiliated the Muslims through you, would you not look into my complaint?" See Hasan Ibrahim Hasan, *al-Faṭimmūn fī Misr* (The Fatimid in Egypt), Cairo: al-Maṭba`ah al-Amiriyah, 1932, pp. 199–200 (in Arabic). (Tr.)]

al-`Aziz wanted to alleviate the anger of the people. He therefore laid off a number of Christian employees, but later reinstated many in their positions, either because of pressure from his wife and daughter or because he found that it was impossible to do without their services. At last the discontented kept silent because they also found themselves facing an administration that was supported by a large armed force. However, the high positions held by dhimmis were rather insignificant if we compare them to their other benefits during the same period.

First, despite heavy expenses that depleted the budget because of the extravagances of the caliphs and because of the expense of arming a large number of military companies in preparation for war, `al-`Aziz did not reinstate the *hilaliya* taxes imposed by Ibn al-Mudabbir and canceled by Ibn Ṭūlūn. Consequently, the income from the *kharaj* and the *jizyah* decreased more than it had in the past. Of course, the people were very appreciative of the moderation in the imposition of taxes, as they always have been.

The Copts were very happy to see that their patriarch, Abraham, was well-respected and esteemed by the caliph during whose reign the patriarch decided for the first time to transfer the Apostolic See from Alexandria to Cairo. On his part al-`Aziz apparently allowed the patriarch to renovate old churches without seeking official permission. An incident that took place after the work of building the Saint Macarius church had begun supports this observation. Abu Salih says, "No sooner had the patriarch started the work of building the church than the Muslims attacked him. The caliph hurried to him and ordered the building work resumed. He also promised to pay for the expenses. Later the patriarch received the [needed] approval for building the church, but he accepted no money from the caliph, asking al-`Aziz not to insist on making him accept it. al-`Aziz agreed to return the money to the state treasury and ordered an army battalion to guard the building during the period of construction, and to arrest and punish anyone who might obstruct the caliph's orders. When people learned the intentions of the caliph, no one tried to interfere. Thus the building [of the church] was completed."[27]

We notice the excessive compassion of al-`Aziz for Christianity in his refusal to punish a Muslim apostate. The incident can be summarized as follows: one of the Muslim notables named Wasā'[28] converted to Christianity. Authorities arrested him and accused him of apostasy, but other notables supported him. The wife of al-`Aziz spoke on his behalf to the caliph who ordered Wasā' released

---

27. *Ibid.*, p. 35.

28. Quatremère spelled this name Vasah.

without harm. Wasā' then entered a monastery in Upper Egypt where he spent the rest of his life.

Another important incident took place during that period. If it had happened at some other time, it could have been catastrophic for the Christians. It brought results contrary to what some Muslims would have liked. According to Sa`īd ibn Yahya al-Antaki,

> "al-`Aziz planned to invade Byzantium and ordered [his vizier] Isa ibn Nastoros to prepare the navy. He decided that the navy would set sail after the Friday noon prayer. A fire broke out in the ships and burned sixteen of them. Some accused the Roman merchants, who were then bringing goods to Egypt, of arson. The people became angry and attacked the Roman merchants, killing one hundred and sixty of them. They also looted the church of Saint Michael in the Qasr al-Sham`a district. Also looted was the church of the Nestorians. Ibn Nastoros ordered the looting stopped and kept the mob from [again] attacking the Romans. He required all the looters to return everything that they had taken. He also ordered the Roman merchants whose lives were spared brought to him and compensated them for their losses. Thirty-six looters were arrested. al-Aziz commanded that one-third of them be released, one-third be beaten, and one-third be executed. al-Aziz wrote on some slips of paper the words "to be beaten," on others "to be executed," and on the rest "to be released." These paper slips were then covered by a piece of cloth. Each one of the looters picked out a slip of paper. The order was carried out according to what was written on the paper slip."[29]

These actions fed the anger of the Muslims. When al-Hakim bi `Amr Allah persecuted the Christians, it was [apparently] done with the purpose of satisfying the vengefulness that was instigated by the people. The cruelty that characterized the persecution of the Christians during al-Hakim's reign was also due to the fact that he was bloodthirsty.

al-Hakim bi-`Amr Allah (386–411 A.H./996–1020 A.D.).

While al-`Aziz bi-Allah was in Bilbeis[30] preparing for the resumption of war against Byzantium, he died in his bath. His young son from his Christian

---

29. al-Antākī, op. cit., p. 178–79.

30. [Bilbeis is a town in the Sharqiya province of Lower Egypt. (Tr.)]

wife succeeded him. He was eleven years old and was given the title of al-Hakim bi 'Amr Allah when he was enthroned.

There was no indication of the alarming catastrophic events that would spatter his reign with blood and equally terrify both Christians and Muslims. In fact, when al-Hakim reached his majority he was quick to assure all Christian employees that they would continue in their positions, following the advice of his sister Sit al-Mulk who strongly sympathized with Christians.[31]

Because al-Hakim was under age when his father died, he was put under the guardianship of Bargwan, a Slavic eunuch slave. Chaos prevailed in the country during the period of guardianship due to the conflict between the guardian and Ibn Ammar, the commander of the army who was [later] killed after Turkish forces defeated his army of North African tribesmen. Before he died, Ibn Ammar had Ibn Nastoros killed. Not long after that Bargwan was also killed. The caliph had ordered his assassination in 390 A.H. [999 A.D.] because of his haughtiness and because Bargwan had called him names.

The young caliph's order to kill Bargwan caused anxiety and restlessness among the people, who subsequently demonstrated in front of the caliphate headquarters. al-Hakim was unable to avoid the blame for the rebellion of his people except through his crying and wailing, excusing himself because of his youth and inexperience with government affairs. We may ask: was he shamed by showing weakness [when weeping], and is that why he decided to take revenge on the people? We raise this issue because we do not want to overlook it.[32] Whatever the case, we cannot put the full responsibility on him alone for the bloody events that [chiefly] involved Christians.

The fact is that some conspirators tried to eliminate the influence that the dhimmis had exercised during the reign of al-'Aziz by cultivating the vengeful, bloodthirsty attitude of the [new] caliph. It is wrong to believe that al-Hakim hated the dhimmis. How could this be in light of the fact that his parents, whom he loved dearly, were very tolerant? When al-Hakim became caliph he appointed Fahd ibn Ibrahim, a Copt, as his private secretary and placed his confidence in him, bestowing the title of *Ra 'is* [chief] on him. When Bargwan was killed, al-Hakim summoned Fahd and bestowed a robe of honor on him, telling him, "Do not be anxious about what has happened." Ibn al-Qalanisi describes what happened between al-Hakim and his private secretary:

---

31. Ibn al-Qalanisi, *op. cit.*, p. 60.

32. After al-Hakim started to preach his own divinity in 408 A.H. [1017 A.D.], the people became angry and attacked the caliph's palace. al-Hakim took revenge by burning Cairo.

"al-Hakim summoned al-Hussein bin Jawhar [the secretary] and Abu al-
'Alā' ibn Fahd ibn Ibrahim, the vizier, and asked his secretary to bring
in all the scribes of the diwans [the government department heads],
which he did. After he [the secretary] introduced them to al-Hakim, the
caliph told them, "This is Fahd. Yesterday he was the secretary of
Bargwan my slave, but today he is my vizier. Listen to him, obey him,
and let him lead you. Devote your time to your work and to guarding our
financial resources." Fahd and the department heads bowed and kissed
the floor saying, "We hear and obey our master." al-Hakim also told
Fahd, "I am thankful to you and very satisfied with you and these
servants of mine, the department heads. Recognize their rights, treat
them fairly, protect their esteem, and give a raise to him who may
deserve it because of his efficiency and honesty."[33]

In a short time Fahd became a target for conspiracies because the envious
were afraid that the confidence he gained would increase his influence and that of
the Christians. Hence they began slandering him to his master in order to weaken
his confidence in him. Further, the scribes Abu Taher and Ibn 'Addas accused
him of embezzlement. But al-Hakim was slow to heed their complaint, so they
pushed others to file similar charges against him. Although al-Hakim understood
the intent of these accusations, he ordered Fahd's assassination. He later explained
to his entourage that he had issued his order under great pressure. He then
summoned the sons of the murdered Fahd and gave them robes of honor, directing
that no one should harm them or loot their homes. By so doing, al-Hakim
challenged Abu Taher and Ibn al-'Addas who had instigated the crime. Clearly,
they had had to reach their high positions in order to carry out their designs
against Christians in Egypt and Syria. Even so, al-Hakim was forced to kill
another group of Coptic notables some time later. These Copts had sensed the
danger that was about to befall them because of the assassination of Fahd. When
the caliph ordered one of them, called Abu Najāh, to convert to Islam, he asked the
caliph to give him one day's time for a decision. He then went to his friends and
urged them to prepare for martyrdom, saying, "Christ has given us many of the
blessings of this world. He has been kind to us and he is calling us to the kingdom
of heaven."[34] From that time on, the persecution of Copts became more violent by
the day. Government employees were the first to be subjected to it. The caliph

---

33. Ibn al-Qalanisi, *op. cit.*, p. 56.

34. Renaudot, *op. cit.*, p. 395.

dismissed a large number of them and exempted only those whose services were indispensable.[35] Notably, the dismissal of the majority of employees eroded what remained of the influence of the dhimmis who had enjoyed substantial power in government departments.[36]

By 395 A.H. [1004 A.D.] persecution of Christians prevailed and al-Hakim directed his wrath against both Christians and Sunnites.[37] He ordered the former to dress in clothing that distinguished them from others. He also wrote phrases on the walls of mosques that were insulting to Abu Bakr, `Umar, Uthman, and Aisha.[38] He additionally forbade the population from eating certain foods preferred by some Arab Sunnite leaders.

In 399 A.H. [1008 A.D.] al-Hakim added new restrictions on the dress of Christians and forbade them from owning slaves and hiring Muslims. In the same year he ordered the destruction and looting of the churches in Cairo. When he heard that Christians walked around the church of the Resurrection in Jerusalem during their religious feasts, especially on Palm Sunday and Easter, he ordered the church demolished. This last action caused an uproar not only in the East but also in the West: "All Christians cried [because of that incident]".[39] This episode was surely one of the important reasons for the crusades. The story goes that the scribe who wrote the order was a Christian and he died after a few days because of his grief.

In 400 A.H. [1009 A.D.] strict orders were issued canceling Christian feasts and forbidding their celebration throughout the country. The religious endowments of the churches and monasteries were confiscated for the Bayt al-Mal. Ringing church bells was forbidden and crosses were removed from the domes and towers of churches. Christians were also forced to erase the tatoos [of Christian

---

35. al-Maqrizi reports that the Christian physician of al-Hakim reinstated many of these employees one week after they were dismissed.

36. al-Antākī, *op. cit.*, p. 185.

37. al-Hakim burned the Qurāns that were written during the period of the Sunnite rule before him.

38. [Abu Bakr was the first of the "guided caliphs"—*Rashīdūn* (11–13 A.H./632–634 A.D.), `Umar ibn al-Khattab was the second (13–23 A.H./634–644 A.D.), Uthman was the third (23–35 A.H./644–656 A.D.), and Aisha was the wife of the Prophet Muhammad. al-Hakim wrote as he did because the three caliphs were Sunnites while he was a Shi`ite follower of Imam `Ali, the fourth of the guided caliphs. (Tr.)]

39. Michaud, *op. cit.*, 1:24.

symbols] from their hands and arms.[40] In 402 A.H. [1011 A.D.] al-Hakim instructed Christians to carry wooden crosses, each measuring a dhir`ā[41] in length and weighing five pounds. al-Hakim's orders were carried out to the letter, especially among the remaining [Christian] government employees, to harass them.[42]

In [the month of] Rabī`a al-Awal[43] of 403 A.H. [1013 A.D.], an order was issued to destroy and loot the remaining churches and monasteries in Egypt, without exception. Each employee charged with the responsibility of carrying out this order had to be sure of completely destroying these buildings in the area under his jurisdiction. It is said that the number of churches and monasteries destroyed was thirty thousand. The savagery of the mob that carried out the wish of their master caused the situation to deteriorate even more. These people actually eradicated churches from the surface of the earth, and their vengefulness reached the point of digging up the bones of dead Christians to use as fuel for their public baths.[44] Later, orders were issued to donkey drivers and boatmen not to transport dhimmis.

In the end, al-Hakim gave dhimmis a choice: death or conversion. A large number of people converted to Islam to avoid further oppression. Many deserted their homes secretly and took refuge in the provinces of the Byzantine empire. Those who hid their beliefs met in private gatherings where they kept in hiding the sacred containers and paraphernalia that had escaped the confiscation, looting and plundering. al-Maqrizi reports an order that in effect exiled all Christians to lands under Byzantine rule.[45] Christians then sought clemency from al-Hakim and he allowed them to stay in Egypt.[46]

al-Antaki described an incident that took place in Cairo in 403 A.H. [1012 A.D.]:

---

40. [It appears that tattooing was a general custom among Copts. For more information, see John Carswell's *Coptic Tattoo Designs*, Beirut: The American University of Beirut, 1958. (Tr.)]

41. [A *dhir`ā* measures 58 cm. or 23.2 inches. (Tr.)]

42. al-Antākī, *op. cit.*, p. 195.

43. [The third month of the Hejira calendar. (Tr.)]

44. al-Antākī, *op. cit.*, p. 195.

45. It is possible that the Christians referred to were Melchites only. al-Antākī does not speak about the exile but refers to a secret emigration movement which was the result of a law issued by al-Ḥakim.

46. al-Maqrizi, *al-Khitat*, 2:496.

"All scribes, employees, physicians and others met with their bishops and priests and walked together to the palace of al-Ḥakim bare-headed and bare-footed.[47] They walked through the Cairo city gate wailing and weeping, asking for al-Ḥakim's forgiveness and pardon. They continued walking, sometimes kissing the ground, until they reached the palace. al-Ḥakim sent one of his entourage who received from them a paper in which they begged for al-Ḥakim's pardon and forgiveness. When he learned the contents of the paper, he asked his messenger to go back to them with a comforting answer."[48]

Since the Arab invasion of Egypt, Christians had never suffered persecution worse than that of al-Ḥakim's reign. Not one single Muslim historian has tried to justify the atrocities. But some historians, writing about the period, have tried to relieve al-Ḥakim from responsibility by reporting that he was insane. But nothing supports the view that al-Ḥakim was deranged. Perhaps he was an ill-tempered, sadistic person who found pleasure in torturing others and was quite aware of his actions, even the most grotesque ones.[49] Moreover, every order that he issued was a response to a certain [overall] idea, whether good or bad. For instance, closing all public places and forbidding women to leave their homes, as well as the insulting phrases that he wrote on the walls of the mosques [against Sunnites], were all done according to a well-designed plan.

al-Ḥakim continued to exploit the submissiveness of his people until an adventurer from Spain called Abū Rakwah, who claimed to belong to the Umayyads,[50] arrived in Egypt. He led a revolution in which a large number of people who hated the actions of al-Ḥakim followed him. As a result, al-Ḥakim, who was realistic and was able to measure [the impact of] his actions, ceased to challenge the Sunnites and stopped afflicting people. He also canceled some rituals of the [Shi`ite] Ismailis and adopted some Sunnite customs.

---

47. [These actions are expressions of sadness and humiliation. (Tr.)]

48. al-Antākī, op. cit., p. 188.

49. [For a detailed description of this ruler's irrational and contradictory actions and his mysterious disappearance, see Ibn Taghribirdi, op. cit., 4:176-96. This author quotes many other Muslim historians. (Tr.)]

50. The Umayyad dynasty ruled in Damascus from 41 to 132 A.H. [661–749 A.D.] and in Spain (al-Andalus) from 755 to 1031 A.D.

His claim of divinity was a logical result of the Ismailī Shi`ism,[51] not an aspect of lunacy. We wonder whether his assertion of divinity was the reason for the tolerance that he showed towards the end of his reign, as some orientalists have claimed. There is nothing that impels us to accept such a claim. We believe that it was a serious incident that forced him to be tolerant.

The doctrines of Ismailī Shi`īsm inspired and guided the Fatimids. Such doctrines were adopted only after al-Ḥakim had announced his [divine] call. On the other hand, four years passed between announcing his call and the procedures that al-Ḥakim took to pardon Christians. It would be understandable if al-Ḥakim pardoned and rewarded those who accepted his call. What he did however was to the contrary. He allowed dhimmis to worship in public. He even urged them to rebuild their churches and monasteries and to increase the number of their monks.

The events in the last period of his caliphate throw light on what we have said. al-Antaki reports that in 411 A.H. [1028 A.D.] Anba[52] Salmon, the head of the monastery of Ṭūr-Sinai went to al-Ḥakim and explained to him the impoverished condition of the monks of the monastery and requested the return of the religious endowments that had been confiscated. al-Ḥakim granted his request. In the same year Anba Ṣalmon sought permission to renovate the al-Qusayr Monastery and to send the monks back to pray in it. al-Ḥakim also granted this request, and a decree was issued to this effect to "Salmon ibn Ibrahim" during [the month of] Rabī`a al-Akhar[53] of 411 A.H.[54] During [the month of] Jumada al-Akhar[55] of the same year, a decree was issued permitting the rebuilding of the church of the Resurrection [in Jerusalem].

Similar orders concerning other churches and monasteries followed. The Christians seem encouraged because they filed more requests. Sa`īd al-Antākī stated,

---

51. [Ismailiya is a Shi`a sect that maintains that Isma`il ibn Ja`afar al-Sādiq was the true Imam, not Mūsa al-Kazim. For more information, see Seyyed Hossain Nasr's *Ismailī Contributions to Islamic Culture* (Tehran, 1977) and Farhand Daftary's *The Isma`ilis: Their History and Doctrines* (Cambridge: Cambridge University Press, 1990). (Tr.)]

52. [In the Coptic Church "Anba" is a title given to members of the upper hierarchy, such as bishops or patriarchs. The term is derived from the Hebrew *abba* and Coptic *apa*, "father." (Tr.)]

53. [The fourth month of the Hejira calendar. (Tr.)]

54. al-Antākī, *op. cit.*, p. 299.

55. [The sixth month of the Hejira calendar. (Tr.)]

"When al-Ḥakim became tolerant concerning the building and renovating of churches and the returning of religious endowments to these churches, a group of Christians who had converted to Islam under persecution met with him. They prostrated themselves in front of him and said, "It was not our choice nor our desire to pretend to convert to Islam. We humbly ask that you order us to return to our religion Either you agree to that, or you order us killed." He ordered them to wear their *zananeer*[56] and black clothes and to carry their crosses. Everyone of them was anxious to change his clothing."[57]

The same historian has also mentions that only a small number of people followed suit for fear that al-Hakim had set a trap, because Islam forbids apostasy. But, according to Anba Salmon, al-Hakim had confirmed his good intentions toward the Christians.

Sa'īd al-Antākī has stressed the friendly relations between al-Ḥakim and Anba Salmon. He reports that the caliph was quick to grant all of the monk's wishes and that he used to meet him daily on the desert road leading to Dayr al-Qusayr on the Mokattam hill in order to ask him about his needs. Consequently, some Muslims have slandered al-Ḥakim, claiming that he had become a disciple of Anba Salmon, especially after al-Ḥakim began to wear a monk's attire.

These details and what followed is of importance for later events. al-Antaki continues his report by saying,

"On many a day al-Hakim went to Dayr al-Qusayr to check on the construction workers, urging them to finish the construction. He had allotted an amount of money to be spent on it. He also paid the monks who were residing in that monastery and charged them with helping the construction workers. al-Hakim also used to visit monasteries adjacent to the large cemetery that the Copts had renovated. If he wanted to go up the mountain to visit Dayr al-Qusayr,[58] or any other monastery, his

---

56. [*Zananeer* (pl. of *zinnar*) were broad belts made of cloth that Christians used to wear at the time. (Tr.)]

57. al-Antākī, *op. cit.*, pp. 230–31. al-Antākī reported the contents of each order in an accurate manner.

58. It was a Melchite monastery.

entourage stayed behind at the cemetery or at the *saqiyah*[59] and al-Ḥakim went on alone."[60]

On one of his trips al-Ḥakim disappeared forever and his disappearance has remained a mystery. Was he killed at the instigation of his sister Sit al-Mulk because he had threatened to kill her for her bad behavior, as some historians have reported? al-Antaki has not ruled out the possibility that al-Ḥakim was murdered. But he did not go into detail and was content with saying that, when Sit al-Mulk learned of her brother's disappearance, she quickly ordered a search for him in Dayr al-Qusayr [lest he should be hiding in it]. The Muslim historians' version of how al-Ḥakim disappeared came late and is dubious. Abū al-Mahasen ibn Taghribirdi[61] reports that al-Ḥakim gave his mother thirty thousand dinars to insure her against poverty before he left his palace for the last time. The same report states that al-Ḥakim used to watch the stars and wait for a certain one to appear announcing the end of his life. When he saw that star on the evening of his disappearance, he announced the news in a loud voice heard by all in his entourage. He went on his usual nightly excursion after taking care of his personal affairs, as if he would never come back.[62] Sawirus ibn al-Muqaffa`,[63] who wrote his history thirty years after the death of al-Ḥakim, does not mention Sit al-Mulk, saying only that the caliph dismissed the two servants who were in his company after he ordered them to tie up the donkey. He then disappeared.[64] Some were convinced that al-Ḥakim was still alive so that, when an imposter named "Sakkin" claimed in 434 A.H. [1041 A.D.] that he was the Caliph al-Ḥakim—to whom he had a great resemblance—many in al-Fustāt believed him and followed him toward the caliph's palace shouting, "Here is al-Ḥakim."[65]

Whether al-Ḥakim was killed or simply disappeared or hid in one of the monasteries, the undeniable fact is that he had destroyed the influence of the

---

59. [*al-sāqiyah* means "the water wheel;" either there was a *saqiyah* at that location or the location carried that name because at one time in the past there had been a water wheel. (Tr.)]

60. al-Antākī, *op. cit.*, pp. 232–33.

61. Ibn Taghribirdi, *op. cit.*, 4:187.

62. Ibn Taghribirdi, *op. cit.*, 4:187.

63. [Sawirus ibn al-Muqaffa` was bishop of al-Ashmunein (fl. 955–987 A.D.). (Tr.)]

64. Silvestre de Sacy, Antoine Isaac, *Exposé de la Religion des Druzes*, Amsterdam: Adolf Hakkert, 1964, vol. 1, p. CCCXVI (reprint of 1838 edition).

65. Quatremère, *Memoires*, 2:342.

Christians in Egypt before he left his throne. From that time forward, Copts were largely disregarded and their history became a series of secondary events. Later, they gradually lost their identity through an amalgamation into the majority who looked down upon them.

al-Zahir li-`Izaz Dīn Allah (411–427 A.H./1020–1036 A.D.).

The power of Sit al-Mulk was revived after the disappearance of al-Ḥakim. She had always sympathized with the Christians and encouraged them publicly by sending gifts and donations to the Melchite bishop.[66]

After some years, in 418 A.H. [1027 A.D.], "a truce was signed with the Roman emperor[67] and al-Zahir reopened the church of the Resurrection in Jerusalem. He allowed those who had converted to Islam during the reign of al-Ḥakim to return to Christianity; and many did."[68] Thus al-Zahir accepted [this type of] apostasy and issued an official decree in which he said, "Conversion to Islam must be voluntary, not by force." According to this report al-Zahir allowed Christians to return to their original religion,[69] a unique incident in the history of Islam and the most important one in the reign of al-Zahir. Moreover, "some Christians returned from Byzantium pretending to return to Christianity after converting to Islam. No one objected to their behavior. They, and others who returned to Egypt, paid *jizyah* retroactively from the year that each one left to the year of return."[70] It was said that al-Zahir allowed the Copts to celebrate the feast of Baptism [Eid al-Ghitās] and to hold the festivities of the occasion in public.[71] It seems that, by and large, the Copts recovered some sense of confidence and security, leading Nassiri Khosrau[72] to say about his visit to Egypt in 1035 A.D.:

"I have not known a country that enjoys security and safety like Egypt. I saw a Christian who was one of the richest men in Egypt. No one knew

---

66. al-Antākī, *op. cit.*, p. 237.

67. [Constantine VIII (1025–28 A.D.). (Tr.)]

68. al-Maqrizi, *op. cit.*, 1:355.

69. al-Antākī, *op. cit.*, pp. 235–36.

70. *Ibid.*, p. 239.

71. Ibn Iyas, *op. cit.*, 1:58.

72. Nassiri Khosrau (1004–ca. 1088 A.D.) was a Persian poet, theologian and traveler who converted to Isma`ilism in his later life and served the Fatimid dynasty.

the number of ships he owned nor could anyone learn the number and value of his properties. The vizier summoned him and told him, 'The conditions this year are not good and this causes the entourage of the sultan to feel the pains of the people. Tell me how much wheat can you give us whether through purchase or loan.' The Christian answered, 'Thank God! Due to the grace of the sultan and his vizier I own a great amount of wheat. I am thus able to supply Egypt with it for six years'."[73]

Doubtless, some exaggeration exists in Khosrau's story. But lack of reference to persecution and quoting these candid words of the Copt indicate that the Christians in that era were living in peace.

al-Mustansir bi-llah (427–495 A.H./1036–1101 A.D.).

The Caliph al-Mustansir ruled the country for a very long time. He was enthroned at the age of seven, but his caliphate was not illustrious. The decline of the Fatimid dynasty, that had begun in the previous period, continued as a result of internal chaos. For example, Turkish mercenaries looted the caliph's palace. When they dispossessed him of his wealth, the caliph was forced to sleep on a straw mat in his palace that had been looted of furniture. He was in such bad straits that even his enemies felt sorry for him, and some wept for his misery.

al-Mustansir was unable to influence the flow of events. While the Turkish and black soldiers engaged in bloody and violent fighting, and starvation was so severe that people ate the carcasses of dead animals, viziers followed one another in quick succession to the seat of power. The result was the perpetuation of the chaos in which the county was submerged.

We mention these details, that may seem irrelevant to the main topic, only to explain why the caliph—who was at a loss—sent for the Armenian Badr al-Jamali. Security was maintained in the country, especially for minorities, during the reign of this vizier who had been a slave, had then converted to Islam and become a notable vizier.

Before the arrival of Badr, minorities suffered a good deal due to the bad temper of the viziers al-Yazouri and Nasr al-Dawlah. During the viziership of al-Yazouri, the interest of the Fatimids shifted to the East for good. When Tunis revolted against the caliphate of Egypt, al-Yazouri sent no army against the rebels but sought the assistance of the tribes of "Bani Hilāl" and "Bani Salim,"[74] allies of

---

73. Nassiri Khosrau, *Sepher Nameh*, pp. 155–56.

74. [Major tribes of North Africa at that time. (Tr.)]

the Fatimids. These two tribes were widely known for looting and plundering along the western borders of the Nile Delta. al-Yazouri told them, "We have left for you the governorship of Tunis. Sweep through it and destroy it."[75] The reason for his lack of action was that the Fatimids were busy helping to finance the rebellion of a Turkish commander against the caliphate in Baghdad [450 A.H./1059 A.D.], and they were less concerned about the destiny of their own country. When the rebellion against the Abbasids in Baghdad failed, al-Yazouri was dismissed.

It is obvious that under such unstable conditions the rulers of Egypt would seek the support of all classes of the Egyptian people, more than they had at any time in the past. But since the caliphate of al-Hakim the influence of the Copts had indeed diminished because, during the rule of al-Yazouri, he could express hostility towards them and take every opportunity to rob them of their money. For example, when the patriarch Christodoulus[76] was accused of encouraging the Christian king of Nubia not to fulfil his obligations towards the Fatimid caliph, al-Yazouri had the patriarch arrested without investigating the matter, and ordered him to pay one hundred dinars. When the patriarch was brought to Cairo he sent a message to Abdel Dawla, the governor of Lower Egypt, who was convinced of his innocence. Abdel Dawla met al-Yazouri "who immediately gave him his approval for the patriarch's release."[77]

Another example concerns the head of Saint Mark the disciple [of Jesus] that was kept in Alexandria in the house of Yahya ibn Zakariya. When Yahya fell seriously ill the Christians grew fearful that his property and money would be sequestered by the government in case of his death. The sacred relic would thus fall into the hands of the Muslims. The Christians were helpless, but they transferred the box, that contained the saint's head, to the house of Abū al-Fattāh the father of the historian who completed the *History of the Patriarchs*.[78] But Abū al-Fattāh had already experienced the yoke of persecution, had paid fines, and feared that the caliph would be disappointed in him. So he refused to keep the head in his custody. The head was then transferred to someone named "Sūrūr" who was living across the street from Abū al-Fattāh. When news reached the vizier, he ordered the arrest of Abū al-Fattāh and all the Copts who had

---

75. Quatremère, *op. cit.*, 2:299–300.

76. [The 66th Coptic patriarch (1046–1109 A.D.). (Tr.)]

77. Quatremère, *op. cit.*, 2:299–300.

78. [He was the father of Mawhūb ibn Mansūr ibn Mufarrij al-Iskandarani who completed the *History of the Patriarchs*, written by Sawirus ibn al-Muqaffa'. (Tr.)]

participated in transferring the box. The governor of Alexandria, Kawkab al-Dawlah, insisted that the head of Saint Mark and the ten thousand dinars that were with the head be returned to him. The accused were successful in gaining their release, except for Abū al-Fattāh who was sent to al-Fustāt where he was put in custody until he was able to pay a sum of money fixed by the governor. After three days, Abū al-Fattāh was released after paying only six hundred dinars.

Other incidents proved that al-Yazouri, the vizier, and his men had no regard for Copts. For instance, the author of the *History of the Patriarchs*[79] states:

"Aba al-Hussein al-Sayrafi, who held several positions, including that of judge of Alexandria, was at last appointed as head of the council on contracts [*Majlis al-`Ugūd*]. It happened that he passed by the city of Demro, the seat of the Coptic patriarchs. He claimed that he was not received at that city with the respect and esteem that his position deserved. He wrote the vizier a letter in which he levelled many accusations against the patriarch. In the letter he mentioned that Demro had become another Constantinople with seventeen churches, most of which were newly built. In addition, a large number of churches were newly built in villages surrounding the city. The patriarch had built himself a palace on which he had engraved writings insulting to the Islamic religion. The judge concluded the letter by suggesting to the vizier that he close all churches and order the demolition of the newly built ones. He recommended especially that the Copts be forced immediately to pay large sums of money. Based on this letter, the vizier al-Yazouri ordered the churches closed throughout Egypt. The governor of Lower Egypt, Nasr al-Dawlah carried out the order. He imprisoned the patriarch and the bishops, and then forced the Christians to pay ten thousand dinars."[80]

At times Muslims helped Copts—apparently unexpectedly because they had been hostile to Copts for a long time. We have already referred to the account of Abd al-Dawlah who released the patriarch after he was convinced of his innocence. It seems that Hisn al-Dawlah was more sympathetic with the Copts than he. When the vizier ordered the closure of the churches of Alexandria and the confiscation of all the valuables in them, imposing a fine of ten thousand

---

79. [Sawirus ibn al-Muqaffa`. (Tr.)]

80. Quatremère, *op. cit.*, 2:342–45.

dinars on the Christians, Hisn al-Dawlah contacted the compiler of the *History of the Patriarchs*, Mawhūb, and his uncle "Sadaka" who was working for him. He told them, "This message is for you. It contains instructions that I am to carry out tomorrow. Go at once and remove all the valuables from your churches."[81] A monk, as was common in such cases, betrayed the patriarch [and the others] to the vizier in order to take revenge because he had not been elevated to the rank of bishop.

The chaos that prevailed in the country after the death of al-Yazouri prevented Christians from improving their lot. The members of the Berber tribe, called al-Lawattah, took advantage of the defeat of al-Mustansir's army by forces of the Turkish commander Nasr al-Dawlah and put the patriarch Christodoulus under arrest. After torturing him, they looted his home. Abu al-Tayeb al-Zarawi rushed to see the private secretary of Nasr al-Dawlah. He begged him to negotiate with the al-Lawattah, which he did. He was able to free the patriarch after paying a ransom of three thousand dinars.[82] But this agreement did not put an end to the acts of plunder by this tribe, that swept through the Nile Delta and looted the monasteries of Wadi Habib [Habib valley], killing most of its monks and scattering those who were not killed.[83]

The situation was aggravated by starvation that spread all over the country while Nasr al-Dawlah was challenging the caliph, encouraged by his previous success and the victory that he had achieved. The caliph could do nothing but summon Badr al-Jamali. al-Jamali had been an Armenian slave of the Syrian emir Jamal al-Dawlah ibn Ammar. He was noted for his strong personality, penetrating intelligence and good administration. He depended on an Armenian force and other battalions loyal to him.

Gaston Wiet believes that Badr al-Jamali was the strongest personality in Islamic Egypt, despite his temperament which was different from that of people of the East. "He wanted to be a dictator from the beginning. When the caliph offered him the position of vizier, he dictated his conditions and accepted no discussion."[84] Badr informed the Caliph al-Mustansir that the mutiny was so widespread among the soldiers in Egypt that it would be impossible for him to enforce discipline, and that he would not obey the caliph's orders unless the caliph

---

81. *Ibid.*, 2:347–48.

82. *Ibid.*, 2:398–99.

83. *Ibid.*, 2:400.

84. G. Wiet, *Les mosques du Caire*, p. 34.

agreed to replace them with other [troops] from Syria. In this case he could insure peace and security in the country.[85] The caliph then gave him a written authorization of his appointment to the viziership, which featured the following titles: "The Most Venerated Seigneur, the Emir of the Armies, the Sword of al-Islam, the Supporter of the Imam, the Legal Guardian of the Muslim Judges and the Guide of the Heralds of the Faithful."

Badr started his work by assassinating the Turkish emirs during a banquet that he hosted in their honor. When he had cleared the path of opposition, he began working diligently to develop the resources of the country and to maintain security within and without its borders. Arab sources have not reported on his administration in detail, but they have referred to the peace, affluence, agricultural development, and increase of the annual income during his reign.

It is natural that relations between Muslims and Christians tend towards moderation under a wise government. The Christians were content under the Armenian whose rule of the country was absolute. They considered him one of them in spite of his conversion to Islam. For his part, he sympathized with them and his judgment regarding their complaints was fair.[86] They readily sought his mediation in their purely religious disputes. An incident that Father Renaudot rehearsed attests to that conclusion. He reports:

"In the year 475 A.H. [1082 A.D.] fifty-two Egyptian bishops went to Badr al-Jamali complaining about Patriarch Cyril.[87] The vizier urged them to live together amicably and to be united. He requested that they respect their religious leadership. He also advised them not to accumulate wealth and explained to them the benefits of spending their collected income on the welfare of their bishoprics. Then he ended the meeting after he gave each one of them an official order that protected him from unfair treatment."[88]

---

85. al-Maqrizi, *op. cit.*, 1:382.

86. A large number of Armenians came to Egypt during Badr al-Jamali's reign. Local authorities held a large reception for the Armenian patriarch Gregory and gave him a church in Turah [a town ten miles to the south of Cairo]. See Abū Saliḥ, *op. cit.*, p. 47.

87. [Cyril (Kyrollos) II was the 67th Coptic patriarch (1078–1092). (Tr.)]

88. Renaudot, Abbé E., *op. cit.*, pp. 457–59.

Badr al-Jamali's understanding of Christians should not be conceived of as bias or partiality. Once some Muslim merchants complained to him that Victor, bishop of Nubia, had demolished a mosque. He immediately ordered the arrest of Patriarch Christodoulus and held him responsible. Renaudot also reported that Badr al-Jamali issued a decree in 479 A.H. [1086 A.D.] ordering Christians and Jews to wear a black belt and to pay an additional tax of one and one-third dinars for each individual.[89] In fact, this tax was a traditional method of filling the state coffers.

When Badr al-Jamali died in 487 A.H. [1094 A.D.], the caliph immediately appointed al-`Afdal, the son of the deceased, as vizier; he in turn chose the title of Shahinshah. The caliph died a few months after the death of Badr. The first crusade broke out during Shahinshah's tenure. We shall turn to this war in the next chapter.

Badr and his son succeeded in consolidating the Armenian influence in Egypt. That influence was to last until the time of Behram, the Christian vizier of al-Hafiz Li Din Allah [525–544 A.H./1131–1149 A.D.], who succeeded the Caliph al-`Amir bi Aḥkām Allah.

al-Āmir bi Aḥkām Allah (495–525 A.H./1101–1131 A.D.).

al-`Amir was the third Fatimid caliph to be enthroned at a young age. He was five years old when his father died. When al-`Afdal, and al-M`amūn after him, refused to relinquish their absolute authority, al-`Amir grasped the first opportunity in 519 A.H. [1125 A.D.]—at the age of twenty-nine—to gain authority by refusing to appoint a vizier to succeed al-M`amūn. He appointed only two chief officers: Ja`afar ibn Abd al-Moneim and Abu Y`aqūb Ibrahim al-Samiri, under the supervision of a Coptic monk called Ibn Abu al-Najāh.[90] Abu al-Najāh was excessive in his partiality towards Christians, at the expense of Muslims.[91] al-Qalqashandi has mentioned some details that indicate that the Copts had quickly forgotten the reasons that had led to their persecution during the reign of al-Hakim bi `Amr Allah. The author of *Ṣubh al-`Asha* states:

"In the days of al-`Amir bi Aḥkām Allah the Fatimid in Egypt, the Christians became aggressive and some became traitors, because they

---

89. *Ibid.*

90. He was Ghalib Abi al-Najah who was killed during the reign of al-Ḥakim bi-`Amr Allah.

91. al-Maqrizi, *op. cit.*, 2:291.

tried to hurt the Muslims in a variety of ways. The caliph used one of them called "the Monk" [al-Rahib] who carried the titles "The Father Saint, the Spiritual, the Precious Father of the Fathers and the Sword of the Chiefs, the Leader of Christianity and the Master of the Patriarchate, the Favorite Companion of God and his Chosen, and the Thirteenth of the Disciples [of Christ]." The cursed "al-Rahib" seized the wealth of a great number of the Egyptians: scribes, governors, soldiers, workers and merchants. His hand reached all classes of people. Some chief scribes tried to scare him by reminding him of his creator, his resurrector and his reckoner [God], and they warned him against the evil results of his deeds, advising him to abandon those that might cause his ruin. A group of the Egyptian scribes and Copts were once in his presence and he addressed the group saying, "We are the owners of this country, its land and taxes. The Muslims seized it from us and have ruled it and taken control of it by force. Whatever we do to the Muslims is in return for what they have done to us. It is nothing compared to those whom they killed of our leaders and kings in the days of their conquest. All the money that we take from the Muslims, their kings and their successors is legitimate and it is a payment that they owe us. We do them a favor if we keep some money from them." The Christians and hypocrites who were listening expressed their appreciation for what they heard; and they repeated it."[92]

While we cannot prove the validity of the story, we can be sure that Ibn Abu al-Najāh was hated by the people. He was assassinated in 523 A.H. [1129 A.D.]. The caliph, who loved his people, was assassinated the following year.

How can we explain the return to religious tolerance during the reign of al-ʿAmir bi Ahkām Allah? Gaston Wiet comments:

"There are several hypotheses related to the matter: Perhaps a king of holy unity, like the one that comes after national catastrophes, arose among the people of Egypt. A catastrophe caused by starvation fell upon the Egyptians during the reign of al-Mustansir. We should not forget that commerce and agriculture were mostly in the hands of Christians. We can also assume that the Ismaʿīli Shiʿism which had spread since the reign of al-Mūstʿalī[93] angered many Muslims and made them avoid

---

92. al-Qalqashandi, op. cit., 13:369–70.

93. [al-Mūstʿalī reigned 487–495 A.H. (1094–1101 A.D.). (Tr.)]

contact with their government. As a result of this, the viziers of al-`Amir followed a balanced policy and found among Christians the support they lacked from others."[94]

We have noted that the policy of Badr al-Jamali and al-`Afdal Shahinshah brimmed with sympathy for the Christians. It was also probable that al`Amir issued a decree—to soothe Muslim public opinion—ordering the governors of the provinces not to exempt the dhimmis from *jizyah*, even if a dhimmi was a notable among his own people, and not to allow a dhimmi to send his *jizyah* through someone else, even if he was a notable or a chief among his co-religionists. The decree also ordered all dhimmis without exception to pay the *jizyah*.[95]

Except for two important sentences contained in this decree it would have been of no historical value. During the Fatimid period the Christians employed certain means by which to pay the *jizyah* in order to maintain their dignity. Sometimes they were relieved of paying the tax altogether. Can one imagine that a vizier, who controlled the affairs of the entire Fatimid empire, had to pay his *jizyah* in person? Doing this would have belittled him in the eyes of his subordinates. The document mentioned by Ibn al-Naqqash throws light on a part of Islamic history that has not been clear.

It is unusual that al-`Amir became known for his inclination to visit monasteries. He built sitting rooms adjacent to them where he used to spend long hours.[96] Muslims blamed al-`Amir for, among other things, his neglect of holy war and his [flawed] campaign during his reign against the crusaders that resulted in the Europeans taking over a large segment of the coast of Syria and other fortified locations.[97]

al-Hafiz li-Dīn Allah (525–544 A.H./1131–1149 A.D.).

The sad end of al-`Amir did not keep his successor and cousin, al-Hafiz li-Dīn Allah, from appointing an Armenian Christian called Behram [as vizier]. Commenting on this appointment, the historian Yūssūf ibn Mir`ī observes:

---

94. G. Wiet, *Materiaux pour un Corpus inscriptionum Arabicarum, Memoires 2*, Cairo: Institut français d'Archéologie orientale, 1930.

95. Ibn al-Naqqash, Manuscript, p. 95B.

96. Abū Salih mentions that al-`Amir built a sitting room with a large dome in al-Nahiya Monastery (*op. cit.*, p. 62).

97. al-Maqrizi, *op. cit.*, 2:291.

"The people reluctantly accepted that appointment which contradicted common practice and good taste. Some members of al-Hafiz's entourage protested his action and told him that a Christian should not be appointed as vizier because it was the duty of the vizier to accompany the caliph at Friday prayers [at the mosque]. But al-Hafiz insisted on his appointment and decided that the chief judge would act for Behram on that occasion."[98]

The Copts were unhappy with Behram's cabinet because they feared the increase in the number of Armenians in Egypt. In fact, not only did the vizier bring his relatives to Egypt and appoint them to important positions and give them high salaries, but he also encouraged more than thirty thousand Armenians to immigrate to Egypt. "In addition to the concern and jealousy of the Copts, the Muslims were surprised and resentful of the increasing Christian influence, as numerous churches and monasteries were built, to the extent that Muslims became worried about the future of the Islamic religion."[99] When Radwan took over [as vizier] from Behram, he successfully gained the support of the mobs by playing on their religious sentiments. Concerning this development, al-Maqrizi states that Radwan "inflicted punishment and humiliation on the Christians and the people thanked him for it."[100] He dismissed Christian employees, especially those appointed by Behram. He tried to gain absolute authority, but al-Hafiz did not allow it. After al-Hafiz challenged [Radwan's position] by receiving Behram at his headquarters, [Radwan] incited his soldiers against [Behram]. When Behram's situation worsened, he was forced to Aswan where he spent the rest of his days in a nearby monastery. With his departure the Armenian influence was effectively eliminated from Egypt.

The last of the Fatimid Caliphs (544–567 A.H./1149–1171 A.D.).

The importance of the Fatimid caliphs arises from their direct connection with the crusades. The day that Caliph al-`Adid li-Dīn Allah sought the help of the armies of Nūr al-Dīn[101] [of Aleppo] to save him from the crusaders was the day that he condemned the rule of his dynasty to termination.

---

98. "Passe-Temps," *Revue d'Égypte*, June 1895.

99. G. Wiet, *L'Égypte arabe*, p. 275.

100. al-Maqrizi, *op. cit.*, 1:357.

101. [Nūr al-Dīn was ruler of Syria from 1146 to 1174 A.D. (Tr.)]

The Fatimid Caliphs and the Christian Feasts.

Not only did the Fatimid caliphs appoint dhimmis to leading positions in the state but they also revived the practice that Muhammad al-Ikhshīdī started of participating in Christian feasts. But the Ikhshīdīds involved themselves on a personal basis while the Fatimids imparted an official dimension to their participation. They did not attend these religious feasts in their personal capacities, but the state itself celebrated them.

We have described above Eid al-Ghiṭās [the feast of Baptism] according to al-Mas'ūdi. When al-Mu'izz came to power he canceled this celebration. But al-'Aziz soon reinstated it and conducted it with great festivity. In 388 A.H. at the beginning of al-Hakim's reign, al-Maqrizi reports—based on al-Misbahi's account—that the authorities continued to celebrate the feast with the same splendor under the leadership of Fahd ibn Ibrahim, the private secretary of Bergwan the vizier. In 401 A.H., al-Hakim canceled the celebration when he started his noted movement of persecuting Christians. But when al-Zahir succeeded him, he renewed permission for celebrating the feast in 405 A.H. He even half-heartedly participated in the celebration. al-Maqrizi reports:

> "The emir al-Mu'aminīn [the prince of the Faithful] al-Zahir li-'Izāz Dīn Allah, the son of al-Hakim, went to the palace of his grandfather al-'Azīz bi-Allah to look on the al-Ghiṭās festival with his harem. It was announced that Muslims should not join the Christians when they dipped into the water of the river Nile at night. [Even so,] the caliph ordered that torches be lit at night, and there were a great many of them. The monks and priests carried crosses and candles, and prayed and sang hymns for a long time until they dipped into the Nile."[102]

The Melchites and Copts celebrated the feast together. The Melchites started their celebration from the church of Saint Michael in Qasr al-Sham'a. When they arrived at the Nile shore, the bishop gave a sermon in Arabic and asked God to bestow his blessings on the caliph and his entourage. Then they returned to their church along the same route, carrying candles and crosses, where they concluded their prayers.[103]

---

102. al-Maqrizi, *op. cit.*, 1:295–96.

103. al-Antākī, *op. cit.*, p. 196. This historian mentions that al-Hakim had attended the celebration several times in disguise.

"Ibn Iyas has reported some unusual details about the feast: He relates that the Nile was full of ships and boats carrying the notables and the general public of Muslims and Christians. At night the ships were decorated with kerosene lamps and candles that were also set along the Nile shore between Cairo and al-Roda [Island][104]. During the evening there were more than one thousand torches, one thousand lamps; and the notables of the Copts went on board the ships. Great sums of money were spent on food and drink, and the people publicly drank liquor. Entertainers of all sorts gathered together and people enjoyed themselves beyond all limits. No shop, street or market was closed on that evening. After dinner Christians and Muslims alike dipped into the water of the Nile. They claimed that whoever dipped into the water that night would be safe from weaknesses of the body during that year."[105]

There was another feast of similar importance, *Nawrūz*,[106] the Coptic New Year's day. Respected Muslim historians have complained that on that occasion the Copts were excessive in enjoying the freedom granted to them and that [their behavior] was extremely harmful to the morale [of the people]. When al-Maqrizi describes the Nawrūz in 517 A.H. [1123 A.D.], during the caliphate of al-`Amir, he notes that "the caliph's embroidered attire arrived from Alexandria along with gilded fly swatters and silk clothes. He distributed men's and women's uniforms and other valuable things, as well as [decorated] paper related to celebrations. There were watermelons and tangerines, and pudding made of chicken meat, lamb, and beef with bread. The scribe brought out the inventory register that contained a list of donations of valuables, paper and uniforms of all sorts to be distributed on the Nawrūz that cost four thousand dinars and fifteen thousand silver dirhams."[107] al-Maqzizi added that the markets were usually closed on that occasion and almost no one walked in the streets. Money was donated as gifts to government employees, their wives and children.

Christmas was the third feast celebrated with great fanfare during the reign of the Fatimids. "It was the custom that the Fatimid state distribute jars full of candy made in Cairo, baskets full of fish, and boxes full of raw sugar and

---

104. [al-Roda is an island in the Nile near Cairo. (Tr.)]

105. A similar account was written by al-Maqrizī, *op. cit.*, 1:296.

106. [This festival falls on the first day of the first month, Tūt, of the Coptic calendar. (Tr.)]

107. al-Maqrizi, *op. cit.*, 1:493.

120

pastries and sesame blocks. The receivers of these state gifts were the high officials, soldiers and scribes, according to lists that specified who received them."[108] al-Maqrizi also said,

> "We attended Christmas in Cairo and throughout Egypt. It was a splendid feast during which people bought colored candles and beautiful statues that cost a lot of money. People from high and low social classes bought these things for their children and relatives. In the markets and in many stores were hung beautiful lanterns for which the people competed in raising their prices."[109]

There was another feast during which the celebrants behaved improperly. It was Eid al-Shahid [the feast of the Martyr] that was canceled during the Mamlūk reign. During this feast the finger of a [deceased] saint was dipped into the water of the Nile. The people believed that the Nile flood would not take place unless the finger of that saint was dipped into the water of the river. Historians assure us that the farmers in Shubra [north of Cairo] depended on selling liquor during the feast to pay their taxes. On the occasion of that feast, the Fatimid governments used to mint 500 gold dinars that were distributed to government department heads.

It was the Christian custom in Akhmim[110] on Eid al-Zaytunah [Palm Sunday] for priests and deacons to carry frankincense-burning censers, crosses, Bibles and lighted candles, and to go to the judge's house and the houses of the Muslim notables. In front of their doors, they would burn incense, read a chapter from the Bible and sing a song in praise of the owner of the house. When the Ayyubids came to power they abolished all such customs.

* * * * * * * *

We have mentioned various events related to relations between Copts and Muslims during the period [of the Fatimids] and have explained their importance. But we do not know [precisely] how to uncover the reasons behind the policy of this or that Fatimid caliph. There is another point that is significant for our work: the Fatimid regime functioned to a great extent like Freemasonry does nowadays.

---

108. *Ibid.*, 1:494; see *Patrologia Orientalis*, vol. 10, fasc. 4, p. 322.

109. al-Maqrizi, *op. cit.*, 1:494.

110. [Akhmim is a city in the province of Suhag in Upper Egypt. (Tr.)]

The [intimate] followers of the Fatimids were informed of the secrets of their rituals little by little. They also met in lodges according to their ranks. There would have been—as in the case of Freemasonry—a certain terminology used. Some terms were known to all members, others only to the leaders. It is taken for granted that we do not know the terms used by the Fatimids, which remain unknown. For this reason some aspects of Fatimid politics will remain obscure. We cannot be sure whether al-'Aziz, or al-Hakim, or their successors were inspired by the orders of their "grand lodges," or whether they acted according to their own tendencies or in the interests of the country.

The Fatimids—who were foreigners in Egypt—tried to achieve national unity and sincere cooperation among all Muslims, as the announcements of al-Mu'izz and his army commander clearly indicate. But it seems that early on the successors of al-Mu'izz shifted away from a policy of *rapproachment* towards the Sunnites after they had unsuccessfully tried to achieve national unity. Because they had a large army under their command composed of people from North Africa, later reinforced by Turkish and black African elements, they preferred to win the support of the dhimmis who were still rich and influential—before the arrival of the Fatimids—because they belonged to the educated class in control of the government machinery. This observation should not be overlooked because the history of the Fatimids indicates that they were ambitious. As rulers of Muslim Egypt they, unlike others, publicly severed their relationship with the Abbasid caliphate [in Baghdad] and declared their political and religious sovereignty. Each ruler of that dynasty wanted to expand the empire, and to immortalize his reign by building a splendid mosque or a magnificent palace. Each of them led a life of luxury and opulence. If with al-Maqrizi we were to calculate the Caliph al-Mustansir's wealth, or the wealth of the Fatimid coffers and works of art looted by the rebels, we would feel as if we were reading "One thousand and one nights."

For such reasons, the Fatimids were badly in need of money, that is, they needed a disciplined administration on which they could depend made up of efficient and loyal employees who collected taxes on time and did their best to develop the economic resources of the country. The Copts were quite ready and able to play that role.

When the Fatimids lost hope of attracting the Sunnites to their side because of their lack of enthusiasm, they sensed the loyalty of the Christians who were both efficient at accounting and tax collecting, and skillful at manufacturing. They wanted to repay the good deeds of the Copts by showing them unlimited tolerance.

There is another point that still causes concern. When al-Mu'izz (the first Fatimid caliph) died, rumors accompanied his death. The Coptic historians picked up these rumors, adding that the caliph abdicated after converting to Christianity. On the other hand, al-'Aziz's tolerance towards the Christians reached a point that was surprising at the time. As for al-Hakim, he vanished after he had been visiting with monks and had renovated several monasteries and churches during the last months of his caliphate. Then came al-Zahir who issued a decree allowing [a form of] apostasy, followed by al-Mustansir who appointed a [formerly Christian] Armenian vizier Badr al-Jamali. As for al-'Amir, he visited monasteries, decorating some of them, and neglected fighting the crusaders. Then came al-Hafiz who endangered his own life to protect Behram, his Christian vizier. Can we be sure that the extreme tolerance of the [Fatimid] dynasty was a response only to the loyalty of the Christians to it?

The Copts of the era achieved fame, wealth, authority and favored positions until popular resentment caused a decline in their influence. The reason for this was that the [Christian] religious minority exploited the confidence of the caliphs to ensure the maximum tolerance toward the dhimmis while [at the same time] they were indifferent if not hostile towards the religious majority [the Sunnites].

Based on the book entitled *Qanūn Diwan al-Rasa'il* [The Law of the Diwan, The Administrative Offices of the Government][111] by Ibn al-Sayrafi, we are able to understand how government departments functioned. For example, he mentions that [standard] remarks were written on the different "complaints" or petitions: "to be presented" [was written] on some, and "to be presented again" [was written] on most. They were [essentially] meaningless remarks and usually resulted in returning the petitions to their signers. If the [signers] renewed their petitions, the same remarks were written on them. The remark "there is no way to do that" was commonly used. Even if a Christian wrote a petition to convert to Islam or a Muslim wanted to build a mosque at his own expense on a piece of land that had no owner, the person would receive the same remark, "there is no way to do that." No decision was made concerning a document unless it related to collecting *jizyah* from the dhimmis or to building churches or to similar requests, because some of those who had to sign were Christians.[112]

---

111. [The purpose of writing this book, according to its author (p. 7), was "to have standard regulations for the selection of employees in that diwan, whether they are hired in junior or senior positions." See Ibn al-Sayrafi, Abu al-Qasim 'Ali ibn Munjib (d. 542. A.H.), *al-Isharah ila man Nala al-Wizarah*, edited by 'Abd Allah Mukhlis (Cairo: Institut français d'Archéologie orièntale, 1924). (Tr.)]

112. Ibn al-Sayrafi, *al-Isharah*, pp. 150–51.

It is no surprise that the Copts were hoping at that time to regain the influence that they had enjoyed before the Arabs conquered Egypt. When al-Hakim persecuted them, they thought of the low level of degradation that they had reached and were sorry for [the loss of] the high prestige that they had attained before they descended into the depth of darkness.

Chapter 7

THE ATTITUDE OF THE CRUSADERS
TOWARDS THE (EASTERN) CHRISTIANS;
THE POLICY OF SALAH AL-DĪN AND
THE AYYUBIDS TOWARD THE COPTS

The sheer size of the crusaders' preparations for war, as well as their repeated attacks, undoubtedly indicates that the crusades were an attempt to eradicate the influence of Islam from the East. The initial war was waged to take the protection of the Holy Sepulchre out of the hands of the caliphs. But it did not take long before it turned into general fighting between the armies of Islam and the armies of Christianity, between Muslim East and Christian West.

When discussing the Islamic conquest, we have tried to define the position of the conqueror and that of the peoples threatened by the invasion. We shall also try to define the policy of the invading crusaders towards the Christians of Egypt and the attitudes of those Christians towards them. Yet, the documents that we have had access to were few because the Christians of the East, especially in Egypt, had lost their influence, as we have noted. Hence, there is a lack of interest on the part of historians of the crusades, whether eastern or western, in the fate of religious minorities. They are mentioned only coincidentally. We must therefore follow a deductive method in our study, utilizing the small number of documents available to us in an attempt to give an accurate account.

The Ignorance and Roughness of the Crusaders.

The crusaders were horsemen who had no fear of death. They excelled in the arts of dueling and fighting. They depended on their courage and strength to seize an enemy and overcome him. Because of their pride and arrogance they disdained peaceful and diplomatic means to achieve their goals. The historian Michaud has said, "Because of their roughness, the barons and noblemen were ignorant of words expressing human rights, and their knowledge was limited to battlefields, which was the policy of the princes and states of that time."[1]

Michaud relates an old story which reveals the mentality of the horsemen of the middle ages:

---

1. Michaud, M., *Histoire des Croisades*, 1:41.

"While a number of French princes were offering their respects to Emperor Alexius[2] at a reception in his honor, Count Robert de Paris sat beside the emperor. Baldwin of Hainaut[3] held [the count] by his arm and said, 'You should know that one should respect the customs of the country one is visiting.' Robert answered, 'Really! How can this peasant [emperor] sit down while a large number of great commanders stand up?' The emperor wanted to know what was going on and, when the noblemen were leaving, he asked Robert to stay. He asked him about his origin and country. He answered, 'I am a French descendent of the oldest nobility, and I know but one thing. Adjacent to every church there is a field to which anyone who wants to show his courage should go. I went there several times but no one dared to fight me'."[4]

The crusaders put themselves in critical situations because they conducted their dangerous venture by depending only on the sword. While enthusiasm led to [the recruitment of] large numbers of soldiers, the armies moved without precautions. In fact, they were preceded by a large number of unarmed pilgrims, who were led by the preaching of Peter the Hermit and by their fanaticism, facing death with gratification. The Turks annihilated them all.

When the armies of the barons departed for the East, their soldiers numbered about half a million. But they lacked discipline and had no skilled commanders. Disputes often erupted among them and each party tended to act according to its whims. As a result, the army faced serious troubles and heavy losses despite the superiority of its forces over the defending Muslim forces. Moreover, the clothing of the soldiers was too heavy for the warm weather of Palestine. Further, they brought no armament that was required to press the sieges, and they thwarted their military operations by [accepting] an army of women that slowed their movements, delayed progress and consumed supplies.

The crusaders were unaware of the character of the countries that they invaded, and most of the time they sought no help from guides or scouts. There is a story, whose source is unknown, that a native called "Qara Qoush"[5] was the one who brought to Philip August's attention the fact that Egypt was the key to Syria. Afterwards, the crusaders repeatedly attacked the Nile valley in order to

---

2. [Alexius I Comnenus was the emperor of Constantinople (1048–1118). (Tr.)]

3. [Baldwin became emperor of Constantinople and lived 1048–1118 A.D. (Tr.)]

4. *Ibid.*, 1:116.

5. [This may be a fictitious name. (Tr.)]

prevent Arab [counter] attacks and to take over a country famous for its fertile land.[6] When the crusaders invaded Egypt, they knew nothing about the Nile flood and its results. So they proceeded without paying attention until the time of the opening of the dams and the overflowing of the canals and waterways. With water surrounding their armies, they were forced to surrender. They were also ignorant of the political system of the country so that they called the vizier al-`Afdal Shahinshah "Malck Babylon" [King of Babylon].[7]

Moreover their lack of diplomatic experience was more troublesome for them than their lack of military readiness. For instance, they took up arms to save the Byzantine Emperor Alexius[8] from Ottoman peril. But they forgot to obtain assurances from him. When they arrived at the shores of the Bosphorus, they soon lost patience over his indecisive policy. They did not even take the precaution of signing an agreement with the Byzantine Empire, to arrange their movements in its lands, until the third crusade.

The crusaders were ignorant of the Byzantines, who were known for their trickery and cleverness in the art of diplomacy and who considered the European peoples to be barbarians. They were also planning to rid themselves of the crusaders, after they secured themselves from the threat of the Muslims, and to reap the fruit of their victories. When they realized that the forces of the West were not enough to repel the danger to their empire, they rushed to pacify the two fighting parties. Isaac[9] the Angel signed two treaties at the same time, the first with Frederick II[10] and the second with Salāh al-Din al-Ayyubi [Saladin][11].

How can one expect that military men, whose keenest interest is in competing on the battlefield, solve the complicated riddles of politics or grasp offers to sign treaties of alliance presented to them by other people, such as the Tatars? Were they able to understand that the Muslim East was not united when they went into it [on the first crusade]? How could they understand, with their ignorance of the religion of Islam, that there were two caliphates, both still powerful, competing for the dominance of the Muslim world? (The first was in

---

6. Ryme, A., *L'Égypt française*, Paris: Collection l'Universe pittoresque, p. 7.

7. Michaud, *op. cit.*, 1:507.

8. [Alexius I Comnenus became emperor of Constantinople (1048–1118 A.D.). (Tr.)]

9. [Isaac II Angelus was emperor of the East (1185–1204 A.D.). (Tr.)]

10. [Frederick II was emperor of the Holy Roman Empire and King of Sicily 1194–1250 A.D. (Tr.)]

11. [1169–1193 A.D. (Tr.)]

Egypt, the Fatimid Shi`ite caliphate, and the second was the Sunnite `Abbasid caliphate in Baghdad.)

However, without much effort the crusaders would have prevailed in victory if they had only the Arabs to fight. The Turks, who came from Asia, interfered by supporting the faltering power of the caliphs, thus helping Islam to predominate. Even then, when the Turks sided with the `Abbasids, they brought on themselves not only the enmity of the crusaders but also that of the Fatimids and the Syrian provinces which found opportunity in the chaos to declare their independence.

The Fatimids did what the crusaders never expected. They sent a delegation to sign a treaty of alliance with them. The Fatimid delegation came to Antioch which the crusaders held under siege. Robert Le Moine[12] reports an interesting story about the meeting:

> "The Christian soldiers tried to hide from the Muslims the fact that they suffered misery and affliction. They dressed in their best clothes and carried their most beautiful arms. The commanders of the army received the Egyptian delegation in a beautiful tent. The delegation candidly told the crusaders that the caliph had never thought of making an alliance with Christians. But the victories of the crusaders over the Turks, the worst enemies of the descendants of `Ali ibn Abi Taleb[13], had made the caliph believe that God had sent them to Asia as punishment against the Turks and as an indicator of his justice."

The Egyptian caliph was ready to accept the victorious Christians [as allies] and to enter Palestine and Syria at the head of his armies. When he learned that all the crusaders wanted was Jerusalem, he promised to renovate and open the churches for service, and to open the gates of the holy city for all pilgrims on condition that they come to the city unarmed, and not stay in it more than one month.

It is possible to consider the offer made by the vizier al-`Afdal Shahinshah on other bases. First, the Fatimids were especially interested in securing the eastern borders of Egypt by regaining Palestine from the Turks. Second, the influence of the religious minorities, including the Armenian influence in Egypt, was then strong because the caliph's authority was nil. It is

---

12. Michaud, *op. cit.*, 1:156.

13. [The Shi`ites. (Tr.)]

thus not improbable that the Fatimids, whose tolerance included appointing Christians to the vizierate, sought a military alliance with the [crusading] Christians to save their collapsing throne. Nevertheless, the crusaders were incapable of following a wide-ranging policy. Astonishingly, they responded harshly [to the Fatimid offer] by saying:

> "We have not come to Asia to be subjected to the orders of Muslims or to accept their favors. Moreover, we have not forgotten the insults of the Egyptians to western pilgrims and we still remember that Christians during al-Hakim's reign were delivered to the executioners, and their churches were destroyed, especially the church of the Resurrection. Christians want to guard Jerusalem by themselves and to have control of it. Go and tell the one who sent you that he should choose between peace and war, and tell him that the Christians camping in front of Antioch are not afraid of the peoples of Egypt, Ethiopia or Baghdad [Iraq]. They also do not ally themselves except with countries which respect the just laws and the banners of Jesus Christ."[14]

It is surprising that, despite the harsh response, the negotiation was not discontinued, and a Christian delegation accompanied the Muslim ambassadors back to Egypt. The treaty suggested by Egypt to the crusaders was nothing compared to what the Tatars later suggested to King Louis IX[15]. In fact a large number of Tatars were converted to Christianity through the influence of the Nestorian priests and the Christian wife of Genghis-Khan[16] who demanded that her husband be tolerant with her co-religionists and asked him to ally himself with the crusaders. If such an alliance had been established, the Turks would have not resisted such allied forces for long. But the crusaders turned their back on this offer that could have strengthened the Eastern Latin Empire, which was then collapsing. They thus tended to add to the number of their enemies as well as the hatred of their allies [against themselves]. Thus we find them, during the second

---

14. Michaud, *op. cit.*, 1:157.

15. [Louis IX was king of France, 1226–1270, and led a crusade against Egypt in 1248. (Tr.)]

16. [Mongul conqueror, 1163–1227 A.D. (Tr.)]

Crusade[17], turning against the wali of Damascus, their natural ally because he was the enemy of the Turks, instead of attacking Nur al-Din's[18] forces.

While we do not intend to examine details of the crusades, our goal of reviewing these events is to indicate that the crusaders were unprepared—militarily and politically—to enter upon their broad venture. The historian René Grousset has stated that "the barons went too far into the vast and complex Islamic world without being prepared. They had to haphazardly create institutions of state, to follow a steady policy towards the natives, and to create an administrative system that fit into the environment."[19] "Haphazard" is the best word to use in this situation because the crusaders had not prepared any plan in advance, and circumstances dictated the positions that they took. They had not thought of seeking the cooperation of the Christians of the East before they started their crusade. For our study, we shall limit ourselves to the relation between the crusaders and the religious minorities, the issue that concerns us here.

The Crusaders and the Eastern Christians.

It is not possible to study the position of the Eastern Christians vis à vis the crusaders in a thorough way. We should not differentiate merely between Jacobites [Monophysites] and Melchites, but between Jacobites [Monophysites] and all other Christian communities in the East because the Syrian Jacobites, who out of fear took refuge in Egypt when the crusaders approached Syria, did not stay long before returning to their country after the situation in Jerusalem stabilized."[20] It is not difficult to understand the reason behind this. At the beginning of the tenth century A.D., the Byzantines, under the leadership of Nicephorus Phocas and his vice-commander Zimisces, swept through the provinces of Sicily, northern Syria and Lebanon where the Fatimids' influence ended. For one hundred and fifteen years the Byzantines kept a large part of the lands that they had occupied before they gradually replaced Muslim elements with Christian ones. It happened that fifteen years before the crusaders appeared on the scene the Turkic tribes,

---

17. [The second crusade took place from 1147 to 1149 A.D. and was unsuccessful from the European viewpoint. (Tr.)]

18. [Nūr al-Dīn Mahmūd Zangī was ruler of Aleppo (541–569 A.H./1146–1174 A.D.). (Tr.)]

19. Grousset, *op. cit.*, 1:313.

20. Martin, Abbé, "Les premieres princes croises et les Syriens jacobites de Jerusalem," *Journal Asiatique* (Nov.–Dec. 1886).

under the leadership Tughril Beg,[21] took away these lands from the Byzantines. It was natural that the Christian peoples in Armenia, Asia Minor and Syria rush to receive the crusaders, particularly because they had come to the East seeking the religious goal of liberating Jerusalem, the object of veneration of all Christians, in response to the call of Emperor Alexius I Comnenus.

The Armenians were the first to help the crusaders while they were crossing Asia Minor. Michaud reports, "Baldwin was not in need of guides in a country where the people had offered to help."[22] The enthusiastic people of Raha elected Baldwin their king. When he went to Ruha, its bishop and twelve of its elite went to see him and spoke to him about the wealth of Jordan, inciting him to invade it.

The Lebanese followed the example of the Armenians. They helped the invaders and became their best helpers.[23] At the time, there was in Beirut a large number of Jacobite [Monophysite] and Melchite Christians. All were eager to help the crusaders, even marrying them; thus the number of European families increased. They came to constitute the majority of the physicians and pharmacists in the army and camps of the crusaders. Moreover, they did the translation work in different government offices."[24]

The crusaders were pleased with the attitude adopted by these people. They found in them loyal allies in the heart of the Islamic empire. At any rate, the crusaders showed sympathy equally to all the Christians. They had only one enemy: the Muslims.

The Jacobite bishop Michel le Syrien wrote about this matter. "When the crusaders crossed the sea, they got together and pledged to God that, if they conquered Jerusalem, they would live in peace with all the Christian denominations and distribute churches and monasteries among all of them."[25] But the euphoria of victory made the crusaders forget some of their promises. "When the crusaders occupied Antioch they dismissed the adherents of the Greek orthodox faith from their large churches, as well as their bishops, and they

---

21. [Tughril Beg was the first sultan of the Seljuk Turks (988–1063 A.D.). (Tr.)]

22. Michaud, *op. cit.*, 1:136.

23. Grousset, *op. cit.*, 1:142.

24. H. Lammens, "La vie à Beyrouth sous le regne des croises," in *al-Machriq* (1933), p. 721.

25. Michel le Syrien, *op. cit.*, 3:183.

appointed a patriarch and several Latin[26] bishops."[27] Matthew of Edessa confirms this story, and he accuses the victorious Latins of taking over the Armenian, Greek, Syrian and Georgian[28] monasteries, which were later returned to them. After noting this situation, Michel le Syrien describes relations between the Christians of the East and West.

> "There were Latin Bishops in Antioch and Jerusalem after the crusaders had occupied the two cities. But our [eastern] bishops lived among them without being discriminated against or insulted by anyone. The Europeans caused no problem concerning the beliefs of any Christians, nor did they try to impose a single solution to achieve the unity of all those who believed in Christianity. They considered anyone who believed in the cross a Christian without investigation or examination."[29]

There is another indicator that shows the crusaders' toleration of eastern Christians, the letter sent by their leaders to Urban, the [Latin] Pope[30] inviting him to visit Jerusalem. In the letter they said, "We have defeated the Turks and the pagans, but we cannot use violence against the atheists of the Greeks, Armenians, Syriacs and Jacobites [Monophysites]. . . . Come and destroy all atheism using your unparalleled influence."[31]

Moreover, after the massacres that caused the Muslim population to evacuate Jerusalem, Baldwin decided to settle eastern Christians in it. He allowed the Syrians and the Greeks living in Jordan to settle in Jerusalem, disregarding the doctrines they believed in. Mutual understanding was almost complete between Christians of the East and West, with the exception of Egypt.

On the other hand, the Muslim traveler Ibn Jubayer,[32] known for his dislike of the Christians, acknowledged that the crusaders treated Muslims well.

---

26. ["Latin" refers to Catholics of the Latin rite. (Tr.)]

27. Michel le Syrien, *op.cit.*, 3:191.

28. Quoted in Grousset, *op. cit.*, 1:312.

29. Michel le Syrien, *op. cit.*, 3:222.

30. [Urban II was pope (1088–99) during the first crusade. (Tr.)]

31. Michaud, *op. cit.*, 1:150.

32. [Muhammad ibn Ahmad ibn Jubayr was an Arab traveler and chronicler (1145–1217 A.D.). (Tr.)]

He said, "The Muslims are living in good conditions under the crusaders; may God protect us from civil strife [*fitnah*]."[33]

We still have to examine the position of the Copts in Egypt. It seems that the lack of documents and the confusion of the Melchite with Coptic Christians in the historians' stories will hinder us from reaching a clear view concerning this issue. However, one of the crusaders' decisions concerning the Copts throws some light on the matter. When the crusaders occupied Jerusalem, they prevented Egyptian Christians from completing their pilgrimage to the city, claiming that they were atheists [heretics]. One Coptic historian complained of this treatment: "The sadness of the Jacobites [Monophysites] was not less than that of the Muslims." He added, "Who has the right to prevent Coptic Christians from making the pilgrimage to Jerusalem or coming near it? The crusaders hate us as if we had deviated from the true faith."[34]

We have mentioned before that the crusaders showed no prejudice towards other Christian denominations. Why did they show prejudice only towards Egyptians? Did they detect the rancor of the Copts against the Melchites? This rancor, that started with Dioscorus[35] and lasted until the nineteenth century, makes us inclined us to believe that the Egyptian Copts felt uncomfortable with the presence of Catholic armies in the East.[36] But, did this attitude relieve them from harassment by their Muslim [countrymen]?

When the first crusade started, history recorded no anti-Coptic incidents, in spite of the participation of the Fatimid armies in defending Jerusalem, which they had taken away from the Turks before the crusaders appeared. That was because al-'Afdal Shahinshah ibn Badr al-Jamali was ruling the country under the Fatimids.

When the crusaders learned their way to Egypt, they repeatedly attacked it. During that era, the influence of the Fatimids was on the decline. Their caliphs were so weak that they were subjected to the rule of their ministers until al-'Adid[37] sought the help Nūr al-Dīn. Suddenly, his deputy, Salāh al-Dīn,

---

33. *Travels of Ibn Jubayr*, 2nd ed., Leiden, 1907, p. 329.

34. Renaudot, *op. cit.*, p. 479.

35. [Dioscorus was bishop of Hermopolis. He died in 403 A.D. (Tr.)]

36. [After the sixth crusade, Melkites were not allowed to renovate their churches. In contrast to the Jacobites, who enjoyed some easement related to their way of living, the Melkites were forced to conform to certain demeaning laws. (Tr.)]

37. [al-'Ādid was the last Fatimid caliph (555–67 A.H./1160–1171 A.D.). (Tr.)]

invaded the Nile Valley with his Kurdish army, expelling both the Fatimids and crusaders.

The *History of the Patriarchs* [by Sawirus] explains that, during the period of chaos that followed the expulsion of the Fatimids, the Kurds reinstated the special laws related to the dress of the dhimmis, they stained the churches with mud and broke the crosses. The number of Christians who converted to Islam during that period is an indicator that persecution took place.[38]

We wonder whether Salāḥ al-Dīn was the same leader who became known in the West for tolerance toward his Christian subjects. This has been the western view until today, stressing his respect for his European enemies. But such a view lacks proof. When Ahmad Zaki Pasha[39] wanted to show the religious tolerance of the founder of the Ayyubid dynasty [Salāḥ al-Dīn], he said that the Copts of Egypt had spied for Salāḥ al-Dīn. But this observation supports our view that the Copts hated the westerners.

We should not forget that Salad al-Dīn issued a decree preventing dhimmis from being appointed to state positions on the same day that Caliph al-ʿAdid appointed him a minister, succeeding Shirkūh.[40] Because Salāḥ al-Dīn was religious, he did not breach his principles. He followed the example of his older brother Nūr al-Dīn, who once told the ʿAbbasid caliph, "'The Muslims have ruled for five hundred years and have not mistreated the Christians. Now that all these years have passed, Christians should not stay in the Islamic empire. He who does not convert to Islam should be killed.' The caliph responded saying, 'You have not understood the sayings of the Prophet [Muhammad]. God has not ordered us to kill those who have done no wrong.'"[41]

We are not sure whether Salāḥ al-Dīn was a fanatic or persecuted Christians, but we believe that he had no liking for them, despite employing a number of Christian administrators, none of whom received any special treatment. Reinaud has described Salāḥ al-Dīn thusly:

---

38. Renaudot, *op. cit.*, p. 540.

39. Ahmad Zaki, "Coupe magique dédiée à Salaheddine," in *Majallat al-Majmʿa al-Ilmī al-Misrī*(1916).

40. [Abū al-Harith Asad al-Dīn Shirkūh (d. 1169) was the uncle of Salāḥ al Dīn and one of the army commanders of al-ʿAdid, the last Fatimid caliph. He became the vizier of al-ʿAdid and was succeeded by his nephew Salāḥ al-Dīn. (Tr.)]

41. Michel le Syrien, *op. cit.*, 3:343–45.

"His rule was torn between two emotions: ambition and his hatred for Christians. It is strange that he did not hate Christians as individuals but as a nation. No sooner had he defeated them than he changed his position toward them. The proof is that he was not satisfied with being tolerant toward the Copts of Egypt, whose number was then rather large. But he observed their covenant and employed some of them in his service."[42]

It was from Salāh al-Dīn's position on the Christians after his conquest of Jerusalem that Reinaud formed his opinion of him.

The conditions for surrender specified that only European Christians were considered prisoners of war and they had to pay a war ransom if they wanted to go free. Ibn al-ʿAthīr,[43] who witnessed the crusades, added:

"The Europeans living in Jerusalem started to sell what they were unable to carry away of their possessions, valuables and property. They sold these things at very low prices to the merchants, who were relatives of Salāh al-Dīn's soldiers, and to the native Christians of Jerusalem who were not Europeans. The native Christians had asked Salāh al-Dīn to allow them to stay in their home in return for [paying] the *jizyah*, which he approved. Thus they stayed and bought the possessions of the Europeans."[44]

The tolerance of Salāh al-Dīn toward the eastern Christians was due to the fact they had facilitated his conquest of Jerusalem through their persistent persuasion of the crusaders to surrender the city. Because their number exceeded that of the crusaders they succeeded.[45]

Briefly speaking, Salāh al-Dīn refused to acknowledge the rights acquired by Christians during the Fatimid reign. It is possible that removing the dhimmis from their positions, as Gaston Wiet indicates, was a sort of purging of the

---

42. Reinaud, Joseph Toussaint, *Notice sur la vie de Saladin*, pp. 36–37.

43. [Izz al-Din ibn al-Athīr (555–630 A.H./1160–1233 A.D.) was an Arab historian. (Tr.)]

44. Ibn al-Athīr, *al-Kamel fi al-Tarikh,* Cairo: al-Azhar Printing House (1301 A.H.), 2:552.

45. Renaudot, *op. cit.*, p. 545.

Fatimids more than an expression of hatred for Christians.[46] But Salāḥ al-Dīn did not hesitate to cancel the participation of the caliphs in Christian feasts, a tradition that had become firmly established in the country.[47] However, the Copts viewed the sultan as a just and kind ruler because his power had shielded them from tribulation and had stopped acts of destruction. Without Salāḥ al-Dīn, chaos would have continued in the country. The Copts were also happy that Salāḥ al-Dīn canceled the *hilaliyah* taxes which had been reinstated by the Fatimid caliphs.

After the death of Salāḥ al-Dīn, the Ayyubids faced two strong crusades against Egypt, the crusade led by Jean de Brienne[48] and that led by Louis IX. When Jean de Brienne landed on the Damietta shore and occupied the city, the Egyptian authorities were worried. They tried to learn whether the Christians in Egypt would welcome the Europeans the way that the Armenians and Syrians had. They also tried to learn whether it would be wise to prevent any collaboration that could bring serious consequences for the Muslims. The situation was complicated by the fact that Damietta had a large number of Melchite Christians. The proof is that al-Antakī referred to the existence of a special bishop for that city during the reign of al-Zahir li-Dīn Allah.[49]

The worry of the Egyptian authorities was alone sufficient to cause disturbances in Cairo. The whole population was shocked and panicked. Rumors were spread about the position of the Christians, and they became the subjects of suspicion. Many people became [openly] hostile to them. The sultan issued orders to mobilize half the population of Cairo, whether they were willing or reluctant to fight the crusaders. Additional taxes were levied on the Christians living in Cairo, and on all the rich people as well.

The government thus seized the opportunity, born of panic throughout the country, to refill its coffers, which were empty because of the war. What deserves mention here is the method followed by government officials to wring as much

---

46. *First Encyclopedia of Islam*, vol. 4, article "Kibt."

47. Emile Amélineau said, "Although the Ayyubid rule was not cruel to the Christians, compared to other rules, one notices that the condition of the Copts changed from what it had been during the walis' reign, such as that of ʿAbd al-ʿAzīz ibn Marwān. Amélineau retold a Coptic historian's account about a Coptic merchant, named Hanna, who married a Muslim woman. When he repented of his action, he wanted to become a martyr, and so he brought the wrath of a mob against himself. The Coptic historian ended his story by saying, "Pray for us, thou great martyr, because you know what hard times the Copts are living in." In "Deux documents coptes," *Majallat al-Majmʿa al-Ilmī al-Misrī* (1885).

48. [King of Hungary who led the fifth crusade, 1217–21. (Tr.)]

49. al-Antakī, *op. cit.*, p. 237.

money as possible from the Christians without resorting to violence. Renaudot offers interesting details about the situation:

> "The ruler of Egypt, after consulting with his legal advisers, summoned the Coptic, Melchite and Jacobite priests and told them, `Go with the Muslims.' To increase his intimidation he added, `Go with the Muslims to the war. But no sooner will you arrive than they kill you and no one would blame them under the present circumstances.' He was referring to the Melchites whom Muslims blamed for their resemblance to the Europeans because of emulating their customs and hair styles, and not circumcising their children, and in other things. The priests were terrified of what they heard and one of them quickly said, `We have one thousand dinars.' The ruler said, `Well, go and bring this sum of money.' Then it was said to the Coptic priests, `These people are not of your stature. Each one of you is equal to twenty-four of them. But if we assume that each one of you is equal to only ten of them, you should pay us ten thousand dinars.' Finally it was agreed that [the Copts] pay three thousand dinars only. Seals were [then] put on the Mu`allaqah[50] church [of the Copts], the Melchite church and the Jewish temple."[51]

Renaudot added that soldiers from Cairo looted the churches of the Copts and the Melchites on their way to Damietta. The sultan ordered the demolition of St. Mark's Church in Alexandria, claiming that it overlooked the port and that, if the Europeans captured it, they would be able to install weapons in it and control the gulf. The Christians tried in vain to pay two thousand dinars to save the church, but it was completely destroyed.

It seems that persecution became violent, as the historian Coulbeaux says in his book on the history of Ethiopia,[52] because in 1218 A.D. the Nagashi Labilela welcomed ten thousand Copts who had escaped the vengeful actions of the Muslims. But there was no justification for persecution because there is not one single Arabic document which refers to Christian assistance to the crusaders. The

---

50. [The church of the Holy Virgin, known as the "Hanging Church" (al-Mu`allaqah) is still standing on the same site in Old Cairo. For a description and history of this church, see Charlambia Coquin, "Church of al-Mu`allaqah," in *The Coptic Encyclopedia*, 8 volumes, New York: Macmillan, 1991, 2:557–60. (Tr.)]

51. Renaudot, *op. cit.*, p. 572.

52. Coulbeaux, Jean Baptiste, *Histoire, politique et religieuse d'Abyssinie depuis les temps les plus reculés, jusqu'à l'avenement de Menelick II*, Paris: Geuthner, 1929, pp. 256–57.

mere appearance of the crusaders was sufficient cause for suspicion on the part of the Muslims. This happened in all the countries where the crusaders appeared.

King al-Kāmil,[53] who succeeded his father king al-'Ādil, showed much sympathy toward the Christians. A Franciscan story claims that he even spent the later part of his life in a monastery, something we consider improbable. It seems that the threat of the Tatars' coming from the east influenced his policy towards the crusaders. It is mentioned in a Christian document that he forbade [his subjects from] calling the Christians names or insulting them, even by gestures.[54] He threatened those who did not abide by his orders with severe punishment. However, he failed to prevent the Bedouins from mistreating the Christians after he had ordered the Bedouins to sweep across the areas adjacent to Damietta.[55]

The crusade lost its religious character during the reigns of Frederick II and al-Malik al-Kāmil, after the German emperor made peace with the Muslim king who surrendered Jerusalem without a fight. But during the reign of Louis IX the crusade became a war of annihilation. al-Maqrizi quotes a letter that Louis IX sent to al-Malik al-Salih,[56] which reads:

"It is not unknown to you that I am the guardian of the nation of Christ. It is additionally not unknown to me that you are the guardian of the nation of Muhammad. It is also not hidden from you we have the people of Andalusia, and they deliver money and gifts to us. We drive them like cattle, and kill their men and make their women widows, and capture their daughters and sons, and make their homes empty. I have explained enough to you to make you understand, and have always given you advice. If you were to take all kinds of oaths, and bring to me all the priests and monks, and burn candles in front of me as a sign of your submission to the cross, I should reach out to you and kill you, [even] where you are best defended. Either the country becomes mine, as a gift in my hands, or it becomes yours, and I am defeated and you have the upper hand. I have told you and warned you about the soldiers under my command who cover the valley and the mountain and are innumerable and have been sent to you carrying swords that will determine your fate."[57]

---

53. [al-Malik al-Kāmil (615–635 A.H./1218–1238 A.D.) succeeded his father al-Malik al-'Ādil I (596–615 A.H./1200–1218 A.D.). Both belong to the Ayyubid dynasty of Egypt. (Tr.)]

54. Mentioned in Michaud, *op. cit.*, 2:425.

55. *Ibid.*, 2:240.

56. al-Malik al-Salih Najm al-Din Ayyub of Egypt (637–647 A.H./1240–1249 A.D.).

57. al-Maqrizi, *al-Khitat*, 1:219.

The response of al-Malik al-Salih to this letter was just as arrogant. He said,

"I have received your letter in which you confidently threaten [us] with your armies and your numerous heroes. We are true fighters. As soon as one of us is killed, we immediately replace him. No tyrant has attacked us without being destroyed. If you, the arrogant, saw the edges of our swords, and how prodigious our wars are, and how we have conquered your fortresses and shores, and how we have destroyed your towns and cities, you would have bitten your fingers in repentance. You will surely make a mistake someday, making a wrong judgement. 'The wrong doers will soon know the place whither they will return.'[58] When you read my letter, you will find its beginning to be that of Surat al-Nahl[59] which says, 'The decree of Allah is at hand, so seek ye not to hasten it.' When you reach its end, you will find yourself at the end of Surat Sād which says, 'And you will witness the fulfillment of its warnings after a while.'[60] We go back to God's saying: 'He who is the most truthful.' 'Many a small party has triumphed over a large party by Allah's command; Allah is indeed with the steadfast.'[61] We also remind you of what the wisemen said: 'The tyrant will be destroyed.' Your tyranny will destroy you and will make you fall in tribulation. Greetings!"[62]

It is most probable that the exchange of these messages had its effect on the position of the rulers of the Christians in Egypt. But history does not inform us about this point. However, we can present details about events in Damietta, thanks to a report written by Comte du Champaign about the campaign[63]. While Louis IX was preparing to besiege Damietta, the Muslims killed all the Christians in the city without exception. The next day the crusaders found Damietta an empty city. The Christians who had escaped the city and were saved from being

---

58. Qurān: al-Shulara, ch. 26, verse 227.

59. Qurān: Surat al-Nahl, ch. 16, verse 2.

60. Qurān: Surat Sād, ch. 38, verse 89.

61. Qurān: Surat al-Baqarah, ch. 2, verse 250.

62. al-Khitat, p. 219.

63. Michaud, op. cit., 3:122.

killed returned to the city and killed the Muslims who were unable to join the retreating Muslim army because of sickness or old age. These Christians rushed to welcome [the crusaders,] who treated them as brothers, and joined their victory procession.

Was there in Cairo a spy network working for the crusaders? Islamic history mentions only a single case, that of [the Christian] Abi al-Faḍā`il ibn Dukhan about whom Ibn al-Naqqash wrote:

> "He was the most influential of all government officials. He was the eyesore of Islam and the abscess which distorted the face of religion. He was so influential that once he sent to a Christian, who had converted to Islam, an order signed by the sultan urging him to return to Christianity. He regularly corresponded with the Europeans telling them about what was happening among the Muslims, the rulers and the elite [`ayan]. The ambassadors of the Europeans and Christians always frequented his office where he received them in a friendly manner and dealt with their business before others' business."[64]

Did some Muslims convert to Christianity during the crusades? Some western historians have alluded to this. In one work, a crusader was quoted as saying, "We have some eastern faithfuls on whom we can depend. They know every nook and cranny of the country, and the dangers that we may be exposed to, and they were baptized into the true faith."[65] We do not know whether the writer was referring to members of the Coptic community who rejoined the Catholic church or to Muslims who had converted to Christianity.

It is amazing that, after the disaster which befell the armies of Louis IX, completely destroying them, a number of crusaders were so disturbed and panicked that they began to doubt their faith. And when they were given the choice between converting to Islam and death, they unhesitatingly converted to Islam.

Nevertheless, the crusades had a disastrous impact. If relations between [Christian] East and West were [generally] characterized by mutual understanding and respect, there is no doubt that the wars created a huge gap between Islam and Christianity.

The Copts of Egypt considered the defeat of the Europeans as God's new punishment for adherents to the church of Rome. In spite of the persecutions that

---

64. Ibn al-Naqqash, manuscript leaf 96B–97A. A French translation appears in *Journal Asiatique* (1851).

65. Michaud, *op. cit.*, 3:464.

they suffered, they continued to be the main force on which the highest ranking Muslim rulers depended.

Chapter 8

THE TRIBULATION OF CHRISTIANITY UNDER THE MAMLUKS

The story of the crusades helps one to understand more clearly the decline of the Copts after the persecutions of al-Ḥakim bi-ʾAmr Allah. This condition continued through the reigns of the Mamluk and Turkish sultans who exhibited no [special] interest in the [Coptic] minority. The sultans considered Copts an integral part of the nation because they rendered valuable services related to tax collection. Moreover the rulers were capable of fleecing money from the minority without fearing a revolutionary movement. In fact, they shaped the destiny of the Copts according to their own whims and those of the general populace.

Some Coptic secretaries were able to occupy high positions in the state. But people used to express their anger when they saw a Copt with influence, as if it were unacceptable that a small religious minority had any rights [to high positions]. But a Copt was able to advance in such a situation because his Muslim counterpart "at that time" did not have the necessary qualifications, or [seemingly] did not want to seek the qualifications, to collect taxes. Aside from this particular job the Copt felt that he was unwanted. Thus the Coptic community became a group for training specialists in taxes and financial affairs.

The condition of the Copt did not change during the six centuries preceding Muhammad ʾAli. Nothing important happened except a few acts of accidental persecution, affecting his effaced life which had one goal: to continue in the only kind of work allowed him by the civil authorities. This work, tax collecting, was the basis of his existence and his only hope to accumulate wealth.

Concerning Muslim-Coptic relations during that long period, we shall limit ourselves to mentioning some scattered, unrelated incidents, following the method of the Arab historians in reporting events, adding details about a few important ones.

While Louis IX was evacuating the remains of his defeated army from Egypt, the Baḥrī Mamluk dynasty[1] took over the Egyptian throne. The responsibility laid upon the shoulders of the new dynasty was not light. It had to liquidate the Latin state in the East and prepare to face the threat of the Mongol invasion. We should give deserved recognition to Egypt, which saved the Islamic

---

1. [The Baḥrī Mamluk dynasty, 1250–1382 A.D., was followed by the Burjī Mamluk dynasty, 1382–1517 A.D. (Tr.)]

world from the [threatening] catastrophe, thanks to the courage of al-Malik al-Muzzafar Quttuz[2] and his Mamluks.

In praise of al-Malik al-Zahir Baybars I,[3] the successor of Quttuz, an Arab said, "One day he was in Egypt, on another day in Hijaz [Arabian peninsula], on a third day in Damascus and on a fourth day in Aleppo." The costs of war were enormous,[4] and the kings of the dynasty lived luxuriantly in their private lives, hence their continuing need for money. Besides regular and additional taxes, they unhesitatingly usurped the money of the dhimmis.

It is worth noting that the Melchites were favored over the Copts [and Monophysites] because the West had not forgotten the services rendered by the Melchites during the crusades. As trade relations between Muslims and Christians developed and flourished, the western countries were able to pressure the Muslim countries whenever the Melchites were exposed to persecution. It was rare for Muslim countries to disregard those "warnings." For their part, the Copts remained isolated from the rest of the world. From time to time the kings of Ethiopia threatened the Mamluks of Egypt in an effort to make them more tolerant. We have devoted a chapter to these foreign interferences. Let us return to internal affairs.

We first notice an important matter. Sultan Aybak,[5] the first to rule in the Bahri Mamluk dynasty, hired a Copt named Sharf al-Din Abu Said Hebat Allah and granted him substantial authority.[6] We should wonder, after the chaos and disturbances that the European armies caused in the country and after the resulting afflictions that the Christians suffered, how the people in power could think of appointing a Coptic minister in Egypt. But al-Maqrizi, who reports the

---

2. [Quṭuz ruled 657–658 A.H./1259–1260 A.D. (Tr.)]

3. [Baybars I ruled 658–676 A.H./1260–1277 A.D. (Tr.)]

4. Heyd, W., *Histoire du Commerce du Levant au Moyen-Age*, Reprint, Amsterdam: Adolf M. Hakkert, 1959, 1:386 (originally published by Harrassowitz, Leipzig, 1885–1886). Heyd says, "While the religious war was raging, the East found European merchants who supplied the Egyptians with war materiel which was immediately used against the crusaders. Financial interests ruled supreme."

5. [Aybak ruled 648–655 A.H./1250–1257 A.D. (Tr.)]

6. al-Maqrizi, *al-Khitat*, 2:90. It seems that this Copt had converted to Islam and gained the confidence of the last Ayyubid sultan. It did not take long before Quṭuz ordered him crossed at the [Cairo] city gate of al-Qal`ah [the Citadel].

incident, added that this minister levied new taxes called "The Rights of the Sultan." The people were hurt by these taxes.[7]

When the sultan found that his coffers were empty, and wanted to increase his income and reform the finances of the country, he immediately sought the help of a professional in financial affairs, and that professional was none other than a Copt. However, Baybars the First resorted to a quick means in 663 A.H. [1265 A.D.] to achieve the same ends, if we can believe the Christian historian al-Muffadal ibn Abi al-Fada`il[8] who wrote,

"When the sultan returned from Syria, he ordered that the Christians and Jews be arrested. Without exception all of them were arrested. A fire of wood was made in a pit on the [grounds of the] Citadel[9] that had been built as a home for al-Malik al-Said.[10] The sultan wanted them burned in it. But al-Habīs al-Rahib ransomed them by paying five hundred thousand dinars. They then had to pay fifty thousand dinars every year. This al-Habīs was first a secretary in the court secretariat, then he became a monk in the mountains of Helwan.[11] It was said that he found a treasure in a cave that belonged to al-Hakim al-`Ubiedy,[12] one of the `Abbasid caliphs. When he obtained this wealth, he helped the poor and the disadvantaged of all religions. When Sultan al-Zahir[13] heard about him, he summoned him and ordered him to hand over the money. He told the sultan, 'If the sultan is asking me for money to be paid directly to him, I say "no." But he can get this money through those who cannot pay the ransom that he has requested from them. I shall give the money

---

7. *al-Khitat*, 2:237.

8. The crusades cost Egypt exorbitant sums of money. As an example, al-Maqrizi reports that the bridge built in Damietta to prevent the western fleet from entering the Nile [after they had cut the chains that had stopped them from sailing into the port] cost 70,000 dinars. See *al-Khitat*, 1:216.

9. [The Citadel, which overlooks the east side of Cairo, was at one time one of the strongest fortresses in the Muslim world. Its construction was begun in 1176 A.D. by the order of Salāh al-Dīn and completed in 1207 A.D. by the vizier Bahā' al-Dīn Qaraqūsh. It played an important role in the history of Egypt until the reign of Muhammad `Ali (1805–1841). (Tr.)]

10. al-Sultan al-Malik al-Said Naser al-Din Muhammad, (676-678 AH / 1277-1279 AD).

11. [A city south-east of Cairo. (Tr.)]

12. [al-Hakim II ruled 741–753 A.H./1341–1352 A.D. From 659–923 A.H./1261–1517 A.D. the `Abbasid caliphs resided in Cairo, following the conquest of Baghdad in 1258 A.D. (Tr.)]

13. [al-Zahir Jaqmaq ruled 842–857 A.H./1438–1453 A.D. (Tr.)]

to those people to help them free themselves [financially] from you. Do not be in a hurry. After this meeting, he ransomed those who were in the sultan's custody, using the money demanded from the Christians. He went to the prisons and released those who had debts to pay, but were unable to do so, whether the debts were large or small. He went to Upper Egypt and paid the money due from the dhimmis to the sultan. He also went to Alexandria where he astonished its people [by his generosity]. It was said that when they calculated the money received by Bayt al-Mal in two years from him it amounted to six hundred thousand dinars, in addition to what he gave to people secretly and paid as ransom for detainees."[14]

This story, told by Christian historians, suggests that Baybars I wanted to usurp the treasure of the monk by intimidating the Christians. As told by al-Maqrizi, the story differs somewhat from that of al-Muffadal. al-Maqrizi said,

"Fires burned repeatedly in Cairo and Fustāt during the absence of the sultan. It was rumored that these were the acts of Christians. The fires caused the people great affliction. Oil and matches were found at some places where fires had broken out. As a result, the sultan ordered the arrest of Christians and Jews. He reprimanded them for these incidents, which abrogated their [prior] covenant, and he condemned them to death by burning. He collected a great number of them in the Citadel. Stalks and weeds were brought to make a fire, and he ordered them to be thrown into it. The people pleaded for his forgiveness and asked for mercy. The prince Faris al-Din Aqatay, the commander of the army, mediated their release on condition that they assume the financial responsibility for what had been burned down, and pay fifty thousand dinars to Bayt al-Mal. The sultan released them. The patriarch took charge of collecting the money, and they committed themselves not to repeat these abominable actions and not to go beyond the limits agreed on for dhimmis. They were then released."[15]

In 678 A.H. [1279 A.D.] all Christians working for the department of war were dismissed and replaced by Muslims. On the same day that the authorities

---

14. Blochet, "Chronique de Muffadal ibn Abi al-Fada'il," in *Patrologia Orientalis*, 12:477–79.

15. al-Maqrizi, *al-Suluk fi M'arifat al-Mulūk*. Cairo: Dar al-Kutub, 1939. 1:535.

carried out this order, the monastery of Deir al-Khandaq, that stood outside Cairo near the city gate "Bab al-Futuh," was demolished. Not one stone remained in place. A large number of people participated in its destruction.

All indicators show that Sultan Qalawūn[16] and his son al-Ashraf Khalil[17] reinstated the Christians in their jobs after Qalawūn had [initially] dismissed them. al-Maqrizi says that these Christians had been treating Muslims disdainfully. They wanted to show their importance by wearing expensive clothes. It is recounted[18] that a Christian called "`Ayin al-Ghazal" by chance met "the middleman in charge of the granary owned by the sultan in the streets of Old Cairo, in 682 A.H. The middleman dismounted from his donkey and kissed the feet of the scribe who started calling him names and threatening him because of overdue money that remained from the price of the grain owned by the emir and which he had to repay. The middleman apologized and tried to calm him. But this angered the scribe all the more, and he ordered his valet to tie the middleman hand and foot and pull him through the street, with people everywhere, until he reached the mosque of Ahmad ibn Tulūn accompanied by a large crowd. Everyone in the crowd asked him to let the middleman go, but he refused. Then the crowd attacked him and pulled him off the back of his donkey and released the middleman. At that point they were near the house of the emir for whom the scribe worked. The scribe sent his servant to seek help from whomever was there. The servant returned with some of the servants and employees of the emir and they saved him from the people. They even arrested some to punish them. The people shouted that it was not legal. They went quickly and stood beneath the Citadel and shouted, `May God give victory to the sultan.' The sultan sent his guards to learn what was happening. They returned and told him about how the Christian scribe had been cruel to the middleman and what happened afterwards. The sultan summoned `Ayin al-Ghazal and asked the crowd to bring some Christians to him. He called in Emir Badr al-Dīn Baydara and Emir Singer al-Shujā`ī[19] and ordered them to bring to him all the [assembled] Christians and kill them. But they talked to him until the situation calmed down. They then sent town criers into Cairo and Old Cairo saying that no Christian or Jew would be allowed to work for an emir. The sultan also ordered all the emirs to invite the Christian scribes who were working for them to convert to Islam. Anyone who refused was

---

16. [Qalawūn reigned 678–689 A.H./1280–1290 A.D. (Tr.)]

17. [He ruled 689–693 A.H./1290–1294 A.D. (Tr.)]

18. [According to al-Maqrizi this incident took place in 682 A.H./1283 A.D. (Tr.)]

19. [The emirs were vice-sultans. (Tr.)]

to be executed by the sword and anyone who converted was to be kept in the service. The vice-sultan was also ordered to review the case of all the employees of the diwān[20] of the sultan and to apply the same measure to them. The order was delivered to the diwān, but only after all the Christian employees had escaped. The mobs then attacked their homes and looted them. Looting spread to all the homes of Christians and Jews. Some of their women were taken as captives, others were killed by the mob.

"The sultan and his vice-sultan Emir Baydara had to deal with the mob. They sent the wali of Cairo to call in the streets that anyone who looted the house of a Christian would be hanged. Some members of the mob were arrested, and were shamed in the streets of Cairo [by tashhīr[21]] after they had been beaten. As a result the mob stopped looting, [but only] after they looted the Mu`allaqah church in old Cairo and killed some Christians in it. The vice-sultan summoned a large number of Christians who were scribes of the sultan and the emirs, and had them meet with the sultan, [but only] at a distance from him. The sultan ordered al-Shujā`ī and the emir Jandar to take their [scribal] equipment, go to [the market] Suq al-Khayl near the Citadel, dig a large ditch, throw the scribes into it, and burn them. Emir Baydara tried to intercede with the sultan, but he refused, saying, `I do not want an office full of Christians in my state.' But Baydara succeeded in convincing him to let those who would convert Islam stay in their jobs and those who refused be executed. All converted to Islam."[22] Their conversion did not please al-Maqrizi who reported, "The humiliated among them became haughty because of their conversion. Then they humiliated the Muslims, treating them unjustly and arrogantly, which their Christianity [ideally] did not allow them to do."[23] Even such situations did not discourage Muslims from treating the dhimmis cruelly. They also took revenge on Christians whenever European sea pirates attacked the Egyptian coast."[24]

---

20. [Diwāns were government departments. (Tr.)]

21. [*Yushahhir* (verb) and *tashhīr* (noun) refer to a process in which a criminal is forced to ride a donkey with his face toward the back, and callers walk in front of the donkey ringing bells, announcing the crimes of the person. The procession goes from one street to another; then the criminal is returned to the prison. (Tr.)]

22. *al-Khitat*, 2:497-98.

23. *Ibid.*, 2:498.

24. Michaud, *Histoires des Croisades*, 3:365.

In [the month of] Rajab 700 A.H. [1301 A.D.] an unusual tragedy took place in Cairo. During that month the vizier of the sultan of the Maghreb [Morocco] arrived while on his pilgrimage [to Mecca].

"One day while he was riding near the Citadel, he saw a man on a horse wearing a white turban and a new cloak. A group of men were following him begging him and kissing his feet while he turned his face in the other direction, rebuffing them. [The vizier] asked his own servants to keep them away from [the man]. Some of the people told the vizier, 'Oh sheikh, by the life of your young children, look into our case.' This [plea] made the man more arrogant and haughty. The Moroccan sympathized with them, and was about to talk to the man when someone told him, 'By the way, he is a Christian.' The Moroccan vizier grew angry and was about to kill him. But he changed his mind and went to the Citadel."[25]

The historian continue the story saying that the Moroccan vizier met with al-Malik al-Nasir Muhammad ibn Qalawūn[26] and his vice-sultan Emir Salar. The vice-sultan spoke with him and with the emir Baybars al-Jashankir concerning the Jews and Christians. The Moroccan vizier said that [in Morocco] they lived in humiliation and lowliness, and that none of them could ride horses or get a job in government departments. He also criticized the conditions of the Christians and Jews of Egypt because of their splendid clothes and because they rode horses and mules, and were hired for government posts, holding authority over Muslims. The vizier also said that their covenant had ended in 600 A.H.[27] His statements had an effect on the officials, especially Emir Baybars al-Jashankir. He ordered that no Christians or Jews be hired in government departments or by the emirs. He also ordered that Christians change their turbans. They had to wear blue turbans and *zananir* [wide waist belts]. The Jews had to wear yellow turbans and abide by 'Umar's covenant."[28]

---

25. *al-Khitat*, 2:498–99.

26. [al-Nasir Muhammad ibn Qalawūn; the Bahrī Mamluk sultan's first reign was 693–694 A.H./1294–1295 A.D., his second reign 698–708 A.H./1299–1309 A.D., and his third reign 709–741 A.H./1309–1340 A.D. (Tr.)]

27. Historians have not explained what the vizier meant by this statement. Perhaps he meant that the Europeans' attack on Egypt made the Muslims feel that they were not obliged to observe previous agreements with Christians.

28. *al-Khitat*, 2:498.

Muslim historians also mention that the churches in Cairo were closed for several days. Abu al-Fada`il notes that, although these churches were closed for a short time, the monasteries in the suburbs of Cairo and the churches in the provinces were not affected.[29] But if we look to Alexandria we find that immediately after receiving the orders the authorities started destroying the churches and homes of Christians.

In 702 A.H. [1303 A.D.] al-Malik al-Nasir Muhammad ibn Qalawūn and Emir Baybars al-Jashankir canceled the Feast of the Martyr.[30] We have spoken of this feast in connection with the Fatimid period. Ibn Iyas gives us more details. Each year on the 8th of the Coptic month of Bashans [May 15], the Copts took out the finger of one of their martyrs from a box kept in the church of Shubra[31] and dipped it in the water of the Nile. The Christians celebrated this occasion with great festivity. They came from all over the country to visit the church at Shubra. A large number of male and female dancers used to take part in these festivities. Thousands of people gathered at the spot, spending lots of money on entertainment, committing ill-deeds and drinking to the point of drunkenness. Many people even became victims of murder and assassination because there were neither policemen nor a governor present to prevent such crimes.

I have previously mentioned that the people of Cairo had participated in this festival for a long time. It is said that during the three days of the festival five thousand dinars worth of wine was sold.

"The farmers of Shubra depended on the wine they sold during the Feast of the Martyr to pay their *kharaj* [tax]. All the Copts liked this festival. One of the Copts, a man named al-Taj ibn Sa`id al-Dawlah, was a scribe in the service of Emir Baybars. He had a strong influence on the emir

---

29. One supposes that the measures referred to were to be applied in both Egypt and Syria. But two cities were exempted, Karak and Shūbākh, because the Christians in these two Syrian cities constituted a majority. This shows that the relatively small number of the Copts permitted their persecution.

30. [The Feast of the Martyr (`Eid al-Shahīd) is a Coptic feast celebrated on May 15, the traditional date of the martyrdom of St. Mark. See Aziz S. Atiya, "Martyr, Feast of the," in *The Coptic Encyclopedia*, 5:1547–548. (Tr.)]

31. [Shubra is one of the northern districts of Cairo. (Tr.)]

and full control of his affairs, because the Turkish kings and emirs of Egypt were submissive to their Coptic scribes."[32]

The Copts persuaded al-Taj ibn Sa`id to talk to his employer Emir Baybars about the problem that he had created. He convinced the emir that canceling the festival would negatively affect the taxes of the district of Shubra because most of the taxes came out of the festival's activities.

The festival was discontinued until 738 A.H. [1338 A.D.] when an unusual event resulted in the resumption of the celebration of the Feast of the Martyr. The emirs Yalbugha al-Yahyawi and Altanbugha al-Maridini asked the sultan to allow them to go hunting for a period of time. The sultan was unhappy about their request because he loved them and even shamelessly boasted of his love for them. And he wanted to dissuade them from traveling. He told them, "We shall resume the celebration of the Feast of the Martyr. Your looking on it will be more entertaining to you than going hunting."[33]

But in 755 A.H. [1354 A.D.][34] Muslims attacked the Christians, and the Coptic church at Shubra was destroyed. The finger of the martyr, that had been kept in a box, was taken away and brought to al-Malek al-Salih.[35] It was burned in front of the king in the square of Qal`at al-Jabal and its ashes were scattered in the sea so that the Christians could never get it back. The Feast of the Martyr has been abolished since that day.[36] Let us return to our original topic following this digression.

The year 720 A.H. [1320 A.D.] was disastrous for the Copts. What happened is not accurately known, but at a signal the people attacked Copts all over Egypt, which makes us think that the movement had been pre-planned for a long time. At the beginning, al-Nasir Muhammad ibn Qalawun[37] did not sense the dangers of an action pre-planned in secrecy. When the movement gained

---

32. *al-Khitat*, 1:69. The Copts were reinstated in their jobs two years after the visit of the Moroccan vizier.

33. *Ibid.*

34. [Ibn Iyas recorded this incident among the events of the year 760 A.H. (1358 A.D.). (Tr.)]

35. [This Burji Mamluk sultan ruled 752–755 A.H./1351–54 A.D. (Tr.)]

36. al-Maqrizi did not try to hide the the matter and mentioned all of the unfortunate events without taking sides; see *al-Khitat*, 2:512.

37. [This was the third reign of this sultan (709–741 A.H./1309–1340 A.D.). (Tr.)]

momentum, he was forced to do as the mobs did, persecute the Christians. al-Maqrizi rehearses these persecutions in detail.[38] He relates that,

"when al-Malik al-Nasir Muhammad built al-Mahari square near al-Sib`ā bridge in 720 A.H., he also planned a cattle barn near the al-Ṭibarsy mosque. He ordered that a mound of dirt on the spot be removed to build the barn. He channeled the Nile water to the place, which later became known as the Nassiriyya [man-made] lake. The digging of the lake started at the end of [the month of] Rabi`a al-Awal,[39] 721 A.H. When the excavators neared al-Zuhrī church, which had many Christians inside and was surrounded by other churches in a place called Hikr Aqbagha, they kept digging, passing around the Zuhrī church until it stood in the center of what would be the Nassiriya lake. The digging was continued until the church stood alone. The diggers wanted the church to fall down without they themselves destroying it. The servants of the emirs and others who were digging requested that the emirs demolish the church; but they disregarded their request until Friday, the 9th of Rabi`a al-`Akhar.[40] At the prayer time [in the mosques] on that day, the digging was at a halt. Without permission from the sultan, a large mob gathered and shouted, `Allah Akbar, God is the Greatest.' Then they used tools to demolish the Zuhrī church until it became a heap of rubble. They killed all the Christians who happened to be inside and looted everything in it. They also demolished the church of Bo Mena in the Hamr`ā district which Christians had venerated for a very long time. The church accommodated several Christians, who had lived in seclusion within it, while other Christians supplied them with provisions. The church had also received votive offerings, and many donations. Thus in the church there was money, gold, and so on. The mobs climbed the fence and opened the church doors. They took away money, clothes and jars of wine. It was terrible.

"After destroying the church in al-Hamr`ā the mobs moved to two more churches in another area called al-Sab`a Siqāyāt. One of the churches was called the church of al-Banāt [church of the girls] that accommodated Christian nuns and a number of monks [sic]. They broke

---

38. The description of the following events is from al-Maqrizi, *al-Khitat*, 2:512–16.

39. [Third month of the Islamic Hejira calendar. (Tr.)]

40. [Fourth month of the Islamic Hejira calendar. (Tr.)]

into the doors of the two churches and took girls as captives [there were more than sixty of them]. They took their clothes and looted everything that their hands could reach, demolishing both churches while the [larger Muslim] populace was performing Friday prayers. When the people left the mosques they beheld wide-spread destruction accompanied by dust, smoke, and people in wild confusion carrying off their booty. People made analogies between that day and the day of resurrection.[41]

"The news travelled fast to al-Remalah near Qal`at al-Jabal. The sultan heard loud noises, startling him. He sent his guards to see what was happening. When he was told, he was very disturbed and expressed anger at the mobs because of they dared to act without consulting with him. He ordered Emīr Ayd-ghamash Amir Akhūr to ride with the *aushaqiya*[42] to put an end to the disturbances and to arrest the perpetrators. While Ayd-ghamash was preparing to depart, news came from Cairo that mobs had rebelled there and destroyed a church in Harat al-Rūm,[43] and another in Harat Zuwaylah.[44] Other news came from Old Cairo that mobs had mobilized in large numbers and moved towards the Mu`allaqah church in Qasr al-Sham`a. The Christians barricaded themselves within the church while the attack was in progress.

"The sultan became infuriated and was about to go by himself to punish the mobs, but changed his mind when the emir Ayd-ghamash returned. The sultan accompanied four of his emirs to Old Cairo. The emirs Baybars al-Hajib[45] and al-Mass al-Hajib went to where the digging was taking place and Emir Teenal went to Cairo. Each one of the emirs headed a large number of soldiers. The sultan ordered them to kill as many of the mob as they could, not sparing anyone. Cairo and Old Cairo were chaotic. Looters were able to escape and the emirs unable to catch up with them, except those who could not move as a result of being drunk on the wine that they had stolen from the churches. Emir Ayd-ghamash

---

41. [To Arabs a day of tragic events, catastrophe or chaos is compared to the day of resurrection. (Tr.)]

42. [A military group in the service of the sultan, usually in charge of horses. (Tr.)]

43. [The district in Cairo where Europeans, Armenians and Greeks lived at the time. (Tr.)]

44. [A district in Cairo. (Tr.)]

45. [A *hajib* was an emir whose job was to coordinate relations between the emirs and the soldiers, to judge among them in consultation with the sultan, and to be the liaison between the sultan and the soldiers when they paraded. (Tr.)]

went to Old Cairo. The wali of Cairo had already gone to the Mu'allaqah church to expel from the al-Mu'allaqah alley those who went there for looting. The mobs threw stones at him and he had to flee for his life. Arriving later, Ayd-ghamash and his followers pulled out their swords to assault the mob. But there were so many people that he feared the results of any attack, and he abandoned the idea. Instead he ordered his soldiers to frighten the people without spilling their blood. His street caller declared that anyone who stood still would be killed. The crowd escaped and dispersed. Ayd-ghamash remained there until the afternoon call for prayer, fearing the return of the crowd. He ordered the wali of Old Cairo to stay there overnight with his troops, and he left fifty of the *aushaqiyah* with him. As for Emir al-Mass, he went to the churches in al-Hamr'ā and those of al-Zuhrī to protect them, but he found them heaps of rubble with not a single wall standing. He and the other emirs carried the news to the sultan whose anger was heightened; but they [eventually] calmed him.

"The destruction of the churches was astonishing. When the people at the mosque of Qal'at al-Jabal ended their Friday prayers, an agitated man stood up, as if he had suddenly falled victim to an unexpected fever, yelling in the center of the mosque, 'Demolish the church in the Qal'ah! Destroy it!' He continued yelling until he became deranged. The sultan and the emirs were led to wonder at his pronouncements. The sultan ordered the chief of the army and his private secretary to investigate the matter.

"The people left the mosque for the Ruins of the Tatar, a place near the Qal'ah, finding a church that had been recently built. They destroyed it. No sooner had they finished than news about [the disturbances at] al-Hamra and the Cairo churches arrived. The sultan was very astonished at the behavior of the *faqīr*[46] [the agitated man]. He wanted to summon him, but no one could find him. Coincidentally, on the same day when people were at the al-Azhar mosque for Friday prayers, another *faqīr* was moved, then stood and recited the call to prayer before the preacher could speak, shouting, 'Destroy the churches of tyranny and polytheists. Yes, Allah Akbar [God is the greatest]. Triumph and victory for God.' He shouted loudly again and again. The people watched him in astonishment. They did not understand his

46. [*Faqīr* or *fakīr* was a poor ascetic man who was sometimes considered a dervish wonderworker. (Tr.)]

behavior and differed in their explanations. Some thought him mad, others said that his behavior was the result of a certain incident. When the preacher took the pulpit, the man stopped shouting. When he was sought after the prayers, he had disappeared. When the people left the mosque, they saw looters carrying wood from the churches and clothes that belonged to Christians and other booty. Inquiring about the matter they were told that the sultan had ordered the destruction of the churches. The people [at first] believed that what was said was true, but after a while they realized that the sultan had not issued such orders. A church in Harat al-Rūm, another in Buduqaniyīn[47] and two churches in Harat Zuwaylah were destroyed that day in Cairo.

"On the third Sunday after that Friday when the churches were destroyed in Cairo and Old Cairo, news came from Emir Badr al-Din Baylbak al-Muhsini, the wali of Alexandria, that on Friday, the 9th of Rabi`a al-`Akhar, after prayers, there was confusion among the people and they left the mosque. They heard someone shouting, 'The churches have been destroyed.' The wali moved immediately to investigate the matter. He learned that four churches had become heaps of rubble. A note came from the wali of the province al-Buhayrah stating that two churches in Damanhūr had been destroyed while people were at Friday prayers. There was great wonder as a result, and on Friday the 16th of Rabi`a al-`Akhar news came from Qūs[48] that, on Friday the 9th of Rabi`a al-`Akhar, when people had finished their prayers, a *faqīr* stood up in the mosque and addressed the people saying, 'O faqīrs, go out to destroy the churches.' He went out in a group of people who found that the destruction of the churches had begun. Six churches in Qūs and its environs were destroyed at the same time. From Upper and Lower Egypt news came of many churches and monasteries destroyed on that day, including Qūs, Alexandria and Damietta. The sultan grew more furious at the mobs and feared the worst. The emirs calmed him saying, 'This matter is not within the power of human beings to do. If the sultan himself had wanted this matter to happen as it did, he could not have done it. This is the will of God (May He be praised) because He knew of

---

47. [A district in Cairo. (Tr.)]

48. [A city in the Qena province of Upper Egypt. (Tr.)]

154

the corruption of the Christians and their excessive arrogance. What has happened was retribution and torture for them.'[49]

"The mobs became fearful of the sultan because they heard of his threats to kill them. A number of the riffraff and the rabble escaped. al-Qadi Fakhr al-Din, the chief of the army, tried to dissuade [the sultan] from taking revenge on the mobs, while Karim al-Din al-Kabir, the superintendent of the sultan's estate, persuaded him to do just that. The sultan sent Karim al-Din al-Kabir to Alexandria to collect taxes and to learn which churches had been destroyed there.

"One month had passed after the destruction of the churches when fires broke out in Cairo and Old Cairo. These fires were much more disastrous than the destruction of the churches. Fire broke out in a section of the al-Shawayeen district of Cairo on Saturday, the 10th of Jumada al-'Ula, spreading through that section until the end of Sunday. Much was destroyed. When the fire died down, another started in Harat al-Daylam in the 'Arisa lane near the living quarters of Karim al-Din, the superintendent of the estate of the sultan. When the sultan heard about the fire, he was alarmed because his grain stores were located there. He ordered some emirs to put out the fire. They collected people to assist. The disaster was at its worst from Monday night to Tuesday night. The fire continued [unabated] and the emirs and the people failed to extinguish it because it had spread to many places. Further, the wind was strong enough to blow branches off of the palm trees and to sink ships. People grew afraid that all Cairo would be destroyed by the fire. They climbed the mosque minarets. The faqīrs and the pious gathered and prayed, 'Allah Akbar' [God is the Greatest]. People shouted and cried. The sultan went to the top of his palace, but he could not keep his balance because of the strength of the wind.

"No sooner had the fire been put out and the grain transferred to another place than a fire broke out in al-Zahir,[50] outside Bab Zuwaylah, which had one hundred and twenty houses. A strong wind was also blowing. The private secretary of the sultan and the wali of Cairo went to oversee putting out the fire. They demolished several houses [in order to prevent the spread of the fire] before the fire was extinguished. On the next day, a fire broke out in the house of Emir Slar

---

49. al-Khitat, 2:513.

50. [A district of Cairo. (Tr.)]

155

in Bayn al-Qasrayn[51] and others started in Harat al-Rūm and in other locales. No day passed without a fire somewhere. As people became aware of what was happening, they thought that these were the acts of Christians. Fires could be seen from the tops of the minarets, from the walls of the mosques and schools. An investigation of the matter determined that the fires were caused by cloths soaked in oil, gasoline or tar.

"On the night of Friday the 15th of Jumada al-`Ula, two monks were arrested while leaving the school of al-Kahariya after dinner time. The school had been set on fire and the monks had the smell of sulphur on their hands. They were taken to Emir `Alam al-Din al-Khazin, the wali of Cairo, who informed the sultan of the incident. The sultan ordered them punished. When the sultan came down [to the city] from the Citadel, he found that some common people had caught a Christian dressed as a Muslim at al-Zahir mosque carrying rags soaked with tar and oil in the shape of a cake. He had thrown one of the rags near the pulpit and waited until smoke came out of it. He then tried to escape from the mosque. A person had secretly kept an eye on him without the Christian noticing his presence. He arrested the Christian and people gathered around. They dragged him to the house of the wali. He was punished by Emir Rukn al-Din Baybars al-Hajib. The man confessed that a group of Christians had agreed to distribute oil among certain of their followers. He was one of those who had received oil and was ordered to put it next to the pulpit of al-Zahir mosque. The two monks were [also] punished, confessing that they were residents of al-Baghl monastery and had set fire to the places in Cairo mentioned above because of their zeal and rancor against the Muslims that had resulted from the destruction of the churches. They also stated that a group of Christians had contributed a large sum of money to set the fires.

"It happened that the superintendent of the estate of the sultan, Karim al-Din, arrived in Cairo from Alexandria. The sultan informed him of the arrest of the Christians. He said, 'The Christians have a patriarch with whom they can consult and who knows their affairs.' The sultan ordered the patriarch to be summoned to Karim al-Din's home to talk with him about the fires and the confession of the Christians who had started them. The patriarch came, [but only] that night under the protection of the wali of Cairo for fear of the mobs. When he entered the

---

51. [A district in Cairo. (Tr.)]

house of Karim al-Din in Harat al-Daylam, the three arrested Christians were brought to him from the wali's custody. In the presence of the wali and the patriarch, they told Karim al-Din everything that they had already confessed doing. The patriarch cried when he heard their confession and said, 'These are the riffraff of the Christians who wanted to respond to the riffraff of the Muslims' destruction of the churches.' The patriarch left Karim al-Din's house with honor and respect. He found at the outside door that Karim al-Din had prepared a mule for him to ride. The neighbors decided that it was too much [to honor and respect the patriarch] and they unanimously expressed their opposition to Karim al-Din. Except for the protection of the wali, the patriarch would have perished. Next morning Karim al-Din rode to the Citadel as usual. When he was in the street, the crowds shouted at him saying, 'Judge, you are not allowed to protect the Christians after they have burned down the houses of Muslims, after which you allowed them to ride mules.'[52] He was very disappointed; then he met with the sultan. He belittled the Christians held under arrest, describing them as low and ignorant. The sultan ordered their punishment to be severe. The wali carried out the order and punished them severely, eliciting a confession that fourteen monks in the monastery of al-Baghl had conspired to burn the houses of Muslims. One of the monks knew how to make gasoline. They had divided Cairo and Old Cairo into sectors and assigned eight of them to Cairo and six to Old Cairo. The monastery of al-Baghl was attacked by the authorities and all its residents arrested. Four of the monks were burned alive in the Ibn Tulūn Mosque square, on a Friday, a large crowd looking on. After the incident, the mobs were encouraged to attack Christians, beat them and take their clothes. The situation deteriorated and the crowds grew in number. The sultan became infuriated and planned to punish the crowds.

"It happened that while he was going down from the Citadel to the Midan al-Kabir [the big square] on Saturday, he saw a multitude filling the streets shouting, 'May God give victory to Islam. May God give victory to Muhammad ibn Abdullah.' At the moment Karim al-Din was passing by in his official dress. The people threw stones at him shouting, 'You protect Christians and ally yourself with them.' They cursed him and called him names. He had no choice but to return to the sultan who was in the square. The shouting and uproar of the mob

---

52. [This was a sign of respect and honor. (Tr.)]

became so loud that it reached the sultan. When Karim al-Din informed him about what had happened to him, the sultan was furious and thereupon consulted with his emirs. He said to Emir al-Mass, his private secretary, `Go with four of the emirs and attack the crowds with swords in the area between Bab Zuwaylah and Bab al-Nasr.[53] Do not spare anyone.' He also said to the wali of Cairo, `Go to Bab al-Lūq and to Bab al-Bahr.[54] Allow no one to escape arrest and bring those whom you arrest to the Citadel. And unless you bring to me those who stoned my assistant—Karim al-Din—I swear that I will hang you instead of them.' By sunset he brought about two hundred men whom he had arrested. The sultan divided them into groups. The first was to be hanged, the second group was to be struck by the sword at the waist [*tuwasat*[55]], and a third group was to have their hands cut off. The arrested men shouted in unison, `O, sultan, you cannot do this. We are not those who threw the stones.' Then the sultan instructed the wali, `Take a group of them and set up stakes in the area between Bab Zuwaylah and the Citadel in [the market] Suq al-Khayl, and suspend them by their hands from the stakes.' The next day, Sunday, all were hung on the stakes from Bab Zuwaylah to Suq al-Khayl. The sultan sat `at the window'[56] and had brought to him a group of those arrested by the wali. He ordered the hands and feet of three of them cut off [in his presence]. The emirs were unable to talk to him because of his anger. At this point Karim al-Din stepped forward, uncovered his head and kissed the floor asking for forgiveness which the sultan granted.[57]

"When the sultan left the window, news came of fires in the area of the Ibn Tulūn mosque, in Qal`at al-Jabal and in the house of Emir Rukn al-Din al-`Ahmady. On the morning that these fires broke out, three Christians were arrested carrying wicks soaked with oil. They were brought to the sultan and confessed that they had set the fires. When the sultan went to the square as usual, he found twenty thousand people

---

53. [Districts of Cairo. (Tr.)]

54. [Districts of Cairo. (Tr.)]

55. [*al-Tawseet* refers to a blow to a criminal's mid-section (*wasat*) by a sword; see al-Maqrizi, *al-Suluk*, 1:404, footnote 1. (Tr.)]

56. [Through the window the sultan could see what was going on outside without himself being seen. (Tr.)]

57. *al-Khitat*, 2:516.

carrying pieces of blue cloth with crosses on them. When they saw him they shouted in unison, `There is no religion but Islam. May God give victory to the religion of Muhammad ibn Abdullah. O King al-Nasir, O sultan of Islam, support us against the infidels. Do not support the Christians.' The place shook with their loud voices and God filled the hearts of the sultan and the emirs with terror. The sultan, overwhelmed by his [fearful] thoughts, continued until he reached the square, while the mobs still shouted. He found it wise to be complaisant toward the crowd, and he ordered his private secretary to send street callers to tell the people, `He who finds a Christian is free to kill him or take his money.' On hearing the call, the mobs shouted and roared, `May God give you victory.' And they supplicated blessings for him.

"Christians at the time used to wear white turbans. The street callers were sent into the streets of Cairo and Old Cairo shouting, `Anyone who finds a Christian with a white turban is free to take his money or his life. Anyone who finds a Christian on the back of a riding beast is free to take his money or kill him.'

"The sultan [also] forbade the emirs from hiring Christians, who were thereupon dismissed from their jobs at the sultan's diwān. The sultan also sent word to all other [government] departments to dismiss all Christian *mubashirīn*.[58] The attacks of the Muslims against Christians increased to the extent that Christians ceased to walk in the streets and many of them converted to Islam. Jews were spared during the period. If a Christian wanted to leave his home, he had to borrow the yellow turban of a Jew and wear it in order to be safe from the mob in the streets."

Finally, "people were informed of the return of peace, and were invited to view the sultan's procession on his way to the square. They had been afraid because of their excessive fighting against the Christians and their excesses in injuring them. As a result of the call, however, they felt safe and went to the square where they expressed their good wishes for the sultan saying, `May God give you victory, O sultan of the world. We have peace together. We have peace together.' The sultan was pleased and smiled when he heard them."[59]

---

58. [Administrative employees were called *mubashirīn* (pl.), *mubashir* (singular). (Tr.)]

59. [*al-Khitat*, 2:516–17. (Tr.)]

al-Maqrizi then inventoried the losses which had resulted from the catastrophe. He said that fifty-four churches had been destroyed, over and above several monasteries that were completely destroyed. Many people had been killed and an uncalculated amount of money was wasted.

From these events one can reach some conclusions. We need not refer to the position of the sultan Muhammad ibn Qalawūn who was sympathetic toward Christians and wanted to protect them, but later was forced to go along with the angry mobs. We also need not praise the wisdom of the authorities and the hatred of violence within the Muslim and Christian leadership.

Undoubtedly, this movement was secretly planned by religious factions that resented the continuing Christian influence in the country. On the other hand the acts of revenge carried out by Copts were planned secretly by an extremist group which thought that by committing these acts it could convince the majority [of the Mulims] to be moderate in their treatment [of Christians]. The patriarch's protest against the terrorist acts is an indicator that these acts were detested by most Copts. However, the authorities' interference saved the Copts again from a terrible catastrophe.

In 728 A.H. [1328 A.D.],

"the Christians petitioned the sultan al-Malik al-Nasir Muhammad ibn Qalawūn asking his permission to rebuild [in Old Cairo] the church of Saint Barbara,[60] which he allowed. They rebuilt it better than it had been. As a result, a group of Muslims were angry and they complained to the sultan that the Christians had added a new building to the church. The sultan ordered Emir `Alam al-Din Singer al-Khazin, the wali of Cairo, to demolish what had been added to the church. He went there, and many people gathered around the church. They destroyed the whole of it in a short time and built a pulpit on its site where they called for prayer and read the Qurān. It was not possible to oppose them for fear of rioting. This was very hard on the Christians, who complained to the qadi[61] Karim al-Din, the trustee of the estate of the sultan. He shook with

---

60. [The church of Saint Barbara, or Sitt Barbara, is one of the oldest churches in Old Cairo. It was dedicated to St. Barbara as early as the 8th century A.D. For details, see Peter Grossmann, "Babylon," in *The Coptic Encyclopaedia*, 2:318–19, and Murād Kamil, *Coptic Egypt*, Cairo: Le Scribe égyptien, 1968, pp. 133–34. (Tr.)]

61. [A *qādī* is a judge. (Tr.)]

anger at the thought of [the violation of] the religion of his ancestors.[62] He persuaded the sultan to order the demolition of the pulpit. It was demolished in a heap of rubble, and the problem was over."[63]

After some years a Christian was "accused" of being the grandson of a man who had converted to Islam. The qadi ruled that this Christian should convert to Islam, and he ordered him imprisoned to force him to do so. Many Christians went to see the sultan and were able to secure the release of the man in the dark of night. On the day after, a mob went to the residence of the qadi whom the governor had summoned to reprimand him strongly for the procedure that he had followed. But the mob openly supported the qadi's position. Shops were closed and the mob stoned the house of the governor until he was forced to leave the city. Then the mob went to the church in that location, destroyed it and burned the crosses and the icons in it. They also desecrated the tombs by taking out the corpses and throwing them into a fire. After doing that, the mob attacked the Christians living in the district. Meanwhile the governor complained to the qadi about the violent actions against the Christians that then resulted in chaos in the country and caused the sultan to lose one of his sources of revenue, amounting to 500,000 dinars.[64]

In 755 A.H. [1354 A.D.], "lists of the religious endowments of the churches and monasteries were submitted to Emir Targhatmash by the diwān of the Ethiopians. These endowments consisted of twenty-five thousand feddans[65] in the hands of Christians. When Emir Targhatmash heard about this, he became angry and went to the Citadel to consult with the sultan about the matter. The sultan ordered the land of the Christians confiscated, and he issued decrees donating the land to the emirs, in addition to their feudal estates. The sultan also decreed the destruction of churches and monasteries [in Ethiopia]."[66]

At this point we may ask: What were the events that led to these severe measures against the Christians? History does not explain these events. It is possible that the treasury was out of money, and it is possible that the sultan wanted to pacify the Muslims in order to prevent another rebellion.

---

62. [It seems that Karim al-Din was a convert to Islam. (Tr.)]

63. *al-Khitat*, 2:511.

64. Quatremère, *Memoires*, 2:251–52.

65. [A feddan is an Egyptian unit of area equivalent to 1.038 acres. (Tr.)]

66. Ibn Iyas, *op. cit.*, 1:206.

It seems that under the conditions the Christians lost their patience and abandoned their impassiveness, moving to destroy the properties of the Muslims and burning down their mosques, thus exposing themselves to martyrdom. al-Maqrizi has reported some cases of persons who reached such a level of despair. In 754 A.H. [1353 A.D.] an isolated incident took place in which a Christian from the town of al-Tūr, who was a clerk in one of the diwāns, went to Cairo and stood to give a speech against the Muslim religion. When he was brought to the qadi for interrogation, he stated, "My goal is to gain the honor of martyrdom." In 791 A.H. [1388 A.D.] a group of men and women came to Cairo and publicly announced that they had converted back to Christianity, saying, "We have come here to repent of the sins that we have committed, offering our lives on the altar of sacrifice to receive the grace of our Lord Jesus Christ." They were all beheaded. In 795 A.H. [1392 A.D.] four monks in Jerusalem publicly challenged some Muslim fuqah`ā and they spoke disgracefully about Islam. They were burned alive.[67] However, these incidents that were expressions of indignation by Christians were not repeated and had no [general] affect on the people.

In 787 A.H. [1385 A.D.],

"Sultan al-Malek al-Zahir Barqūq decreed the abolishment of the customs observed on the [feast] day of Nawrūz. He sent his secretaries with a group of Mamluks, who were in his service, and the chief of police. They made a tour of the places of celebration and the streets. Whomever they found celebrating the feast was punished by being struck with hammers. They cut off the hands of others. They were so vigilant in their efforts that the celebration was totally abolished in Cairo. They even threatened to hang anyone who celebrated this feast, leading the people to abandon the practice ever after."[68]

---

67. Quatremère, *op. cit.*, 2:251, 257.

68. Ibn Iyas, *op. cit.*, 1:263–64.

In 803 A.H. [1400 A.D.] Emir Yalbugha al-Salmi[69] destroyed the church near Shubra al-Khaymah[70] along with more than forty thousand jars of wine. He intended to persecute the Christians, but the other emirs obstructed his efforts.[71]

In 818 A.H. [1415 A.D.] Emir Sayf al-Din wanted to impose a fine on Christians, but higher authorities opposed him. He angrily went to the district where wine was sold and ordered several thousand jars of wine to be spilt; and he took money from Christians by force.[72]

In 822 A.H. [1419 A.D.] Christians and Jews were forced to wear [clothing with] tight sleeves, and shorter turbans. They were also obliged to hang small bells around their necks when they entered public baths. Their wives were ordered to wear yellow dresses. In the same year Christians were criticized for not observing the new laws regulating dress. After long discussions it was decided that offenders should be dismissed from government service. The private secretary of the Christian minister Abu al-Fada'il was imprisoned, whipped and paraded in the streets of Cairo, followed by a *muhtasib*[73] shouting at the top of his voice, "This is how we treat [offending] Christians who hold jobs in the government departments of the sultan." After this incident no Christian dared to seek any official position.[74]

Among other things, Christians were forbidden from riding mules in Cairo. But they were permitted to do so outside Cairo, in the fashion that women did.[75] This forced some to convert to Islam to escape humiliation. Thus their conversion allowed them to move from the depths of humiliation to the paradise of honor and veneration, riding horses instead of mules. [After their conversion,] they looked down upon Muslims, and enjoyed the flattery from them and the seeking of their good offices.[76]

---

69. For the history of this emir see *al-Khitat*, 2:291–93.

70. [A district in the north of Cairo. (Tr.)]

71. *al-Khitat*, 2:292.

72. Quatremère, *op. cit.*, 2:258–59.

73. [A market inspector who was also in charge of enforcing public morality. (Tr.)]

74. Quatremère, *op. cit.*, 2:460–62.

75. [By riding the donkey with both legs on one side. (Tr.)]

76. al-Maqrizi complained bitterly about attempts by the authorities to convert Christians to Islam [by force].

In 846 A.H. [1442 A.D.], "what befell the Christians and Jews in terms of humiliation, disgrace and degradation was beyond description."[77] This was because of the innovations that the Melchites had secretly introduced into their churches. "The sultan ordered a meeting held to which were summoned the four qadis,[78] other Muslim sheikhs and high officials of state, the Coptic patriarch John, the Melchite patriarch Philotheus, Farag Allah representing the Karaites,[79] Abdul Latif representing the Rabbinists,[80] and Ibrahim the chief of the Samaritans.[81] They were asked about the covenant that had been written for their ancestors, but they did not know it. The discussion in the meeting focused on their duties and ended by renewing the covenant according to the one authored by the 'Emir of the Faithful,' 'Umar ibn al-Khattab."[82]

During 849 and 850 A.H. [1445–1446 A.D.] some churches were destroyed and their rubble was sent to the authorities. al-Sakhawi reported that in 852 A.H. no church escaped damage.

We have mentioned these prominent events of the era to show the extent of the deterioration of the Coptic community and how Muslims worked to weaken Coptic influence in the country. On the other hand we have noticed the critical situation in which the sultans found themselves, protecting the chicken that laid golden eggs (in fact the production of the chicken was very weak). The sultans could not do without the services of the Copts; hence their attempt to put limits on the angry mobs.

---

77. al-Sakhawi, *al-Tibre al-Masbūk fi Dhayl al-Sulūk*, Boulaq edition, p. 36.

78. [They represented the four major schools of Islamic law: the Shafi'i, Maliki, Hanbali, and Hanafi all of which are Sunni. See al-Sakhawi, *op. cit.*, pp. 39–40. (Tr.)]

79. [Karaites form a small Jewish sect that rejects rabbinic laws and the Talmud, basing its tenets on the Scriptures. Karaism was founded in Baghdad about 765 A.D. by Anan ben David. (Tr.)]

80. [Rabbinism refers to the teachings and traditions of the rabbis. Later rabbis adhered to the Talmud and rabbinic law, in distinction from the Karaites who rejected such views. (Tr.)]

81. [Samaritans constitute a waning sect centered in the Holy Land whose worship is centralized at Mount Gerizim near ancient Shechem. Their scriptures are limited to the Pentateuch. (Tr.)]

82. al-Sakhawi, *op. cit.*, p. 40.

Chapter 9

THE COPTS IN THE SERVICE OF THE MAMLUK BEYS:
THEIR CONDITION BEFORE THE FRENCH CAMPAIGN

Sultan Selim I[1] entered Egypt in 923 A.H. [1517 A.D.] after defeating the forces of Tumān Bey.[2] Ibn Iyas describes this conquest in a detailed and interesting manner. But he mentions the Copts only once, while talking about transferring some craftsmen, whom the sultan had selected, to Asitana [Turkey]. Ibn Iyas recounts that the conqueror took with him a group of Samaritan Jews and Christians, and he reports their names. Among them was the Melchite patriarch of Alexandria.[3]

The same source records an incident four years later which shows that justice in Egypt under Ottoman rule had not changed from its normal course.

"When Sultan Suleyman[4] was victorious in his war against the Europeans, and the news reached Egypt, there were celebrations in Cairo for seven consecutive days. It happened that three Christian tax collectors went to the home of al-Qāḍī Bishr to observe the celebrations. They became roaring drunk and misbehaved badly. al-Qāḍī Bishr advised them not to act so, but they refused to listen to him and continued to misbehave. He then called them names and they responded by calling him names. It is said that they reviled the religion of Islam. al-Qāḍī Bishr summoned some officers who arrested them and took them to the school of al-Ṣālihiya where the four qadis gathered on Friday before prayer time. When the chief qadi of the Maliki school, Mohi al-Din al-Damiry, asked about the case, he was informed of what the Christians had done to al-Qāḍī Bishr, who was of the Hanafi school. The Maliki qadi did not want to have the Christians executed, saying, 'They should

---

1. . [Ottoman Turkish sultan, 918–926 A.H. (1512–1520 A.D.). (Tr.)]

2. [The thirty-seventh and last Mamluk sultan was al-Malik al-Ashraf Ṭuman Bey (d. 922 A.H./1517 A.D.). (Tr.)]

3. Ibn Iyas, *op. cit.*, 3:139.

4. [Suleyman I Qanūnī (the Magnificent) ruled 926–974 A.H. (1520–1566 A.D.). (Tr.)]

be subjected to *al-Hadd*[5] and *al-T'azīr*;[6] they were drunk.' The rest of the qadis concurred with him. When al-Qāḍī Bishr heard the decision, he criticized the qadis and called the chief Maliki qadi names. A large crowd gathered at the school of al-Ṣāliḥiya and were on the verge of throwing stones at the qadis. Then the *inkishariyah*[7] soldiers arrested the Christians and dragged them out of the school where they cut them to pieces with axes. The mob gathered at the door of the school, collected the corpses of the Christians and set fire to them by collecting the shades of nearby stores, piling them on the corpses, and igniting them. They were burned to ashes."[8]

Ibn Iyas has also reported a similar incident that took place in 928 A.H. [1521 A.D.], illustrating that Coptic administrative employees were still enjoying substantial influence. They were able, if necessary, to defend the interests of their co-religionists. It happened that

"a group of Christians were drinking in a house near the al-Maqsi mosque near al-Khalīj.[9] When they became excessively drunk, they caused a lot of noise and their drunkenness became public. At the time, the son of Sheikh Muhammad ibn Anān was staying in the mosque. He was annoyed by the noise. He sent someone to ask them to stop the racket. He was harsh to them, saying, 'Are you not ashamed of yourselves, making noise while Sheikh ibn Anān is close by?' They responded by cursing Sheikh ibn Anān. Then the sheikh went to complain about these Christians to the chief of the emirs who ordered them arrested. All but one escaped. The chief emir decreed that he be

---

5. [*Hadd*, in Islamic law, expresses the punishments whose limits have been defined by the Prophet Muhammad either in the Qurān or the Hadith. (Tr.)]

6. [*T'azir* (from 'azara, "to censure or repel") refers to the discretionary correction which is administered by the qāḍī for offences for which *hadd* or "fixed punishment" has not been established. (Tr.)]

7. [*Inkishariya* was a brigade of Christian young men in the Ottoman army recruited for the sultan's service from the Christian cities under his authority. They were brought up with total loyalty to him. They had substantial authority during the 17th and 18th centuries. Sultan Mahmūd II eliminated the *Inkishariyah* brigade for good in a massacre which took place in Istanbul in 1826. (Tr.)]

8. Ibn Iyas, *op. cit.*, 3:268–69.

9. [al-Khalīj is a section of the Nile near the Roda district of Cairo. (Tr.)]

burned alive. When the Christian saw the seriousness of the situation, he converted to Islam for fear of being burned. They made him wear a white turban.[10] When this happened, the rest of the Christians grew fearful and took refuge at the home of Yunis the Christian."[11] Ibn Iyas said about Yunis that Khayer Bey had "appointed him the spokesman for all government departments, and the Muslims were at his service and under his control."[12]

The major historic event during the Ottoman rule, however, was undoubtedly the attempt of the Copts to come to terms with the Catholic Church, which had appeared to show no interest in dealing with the separation between it and the Copts, because it was unable to do so. But its interest in the fortunes of the Jacobites in Egypt never flagged. An attempt was made to reconcile Copts and Catholics, however, in the time of Patriarch Cyril III,[13] during the Ayyubid period, but without success.

In 1439 A.D., at the ecumenical council in Florence, where the Byzantines and Latins reunited after their schism, the Egyptian church wanted to be represented [after almost a millennium of separation].[14] Then after more than a century, in 1560 A.D., two Coptic priests went to Rome carrying a petition that expressed the desire of their church leaders that all the Coptic people return to the domain of the Catholic Church and submit to the authority of the pope of Rome, the representative of Christ. Pope Pius IV[15] responded positively to their request. He ordered two Jesuit priests, Christophorus Rodriguez and Giambattista Eliano,[16] to travel to Egypt to talk to the Coptic patriarch about his intentions. The two Jesuits went to Egypt and conducted talks with two members of the Coptic church

---

10. [White turbans were allowed for Muslims only. (Tr.)]

11. Ibn Iyas, *op. cit.*, 3:310–311.

12. *Ibid*, 3:315.

13. [The 75th Coptic Patriarch, Cyril III, 1235–43 A.D. (Tr.)]

14. Without trying to establish a relationship between these two incidents, we note that for the first time treaties were signed between Ethiopia and Europe in 1429 and in 1442. Ethiopia also requested the right to have a representative in the council of Florence.

15. [Pius IV, John Angelo de Medici, was pope 1559–1565 A.D. (Tr.)]

16. [Vincent Frederick, "Eliano, Giambattista," *The Coptic Encyclopedia*, 3:952. (Tr.)]

appointed by Patriarch Gabriel.[17] But the negotiations broke down. The Coptic negotiators acknowledged that in the letter sent to the Pope of Rome the Copts had used certain titles for him, such as "Father of Fathers," "Shepherd of Shepherds," and "Chief of All Churches," [but only] out of veneration. They added that it was the custom to write letters to friends in this manner. They also insisted that every patriarch had full authority over his church following the council of Chalcedon[18] and that several independent patriarchs should be appointed.

Twenty years after this attempt, in 1582 A.D., the Copts resumed their endeavor with the [Roman] Apostolic See and requested the dispatching of Father Giambattista Eliano (who was then in Syria) to see for himself their good intentions and to give him strong proof of their good faith and submission. The pope of Rome ordered Eliano to travel to Cairo where he met with the Copts and their patriarch [Gabriel VII]. An agreement was about to be reached when the patriarch suddenly died. The Catholics claimed that he was poisoned. However, the meetings were closed upon the death of the patriarch and the representative of the pope was arrested as a foreign spy. The pope had to pay a ransom of five thousand dinars to free his representative and enable him to return to his country.

Relations were reconsidered in 1597 when the Coptic patriarch Gabriel VIII[19] sent two representatives with a statement of faith bearing his signature. He mentioned in his statement that he had an unshakable belief in the laws issued by the council of Nicea[20] and the law of the council of Constantinople.[21] He also acknowledged that no one outside the Catholic church could achieve eternal life. But the patriarch's statement did not refer to decisions made at the council of Chalcedon [against the Monophysites]. Because he could not obtain everything that he wanted at one time, he had decided to keep silent on this matter.

While the two Coptic representatives were in Rome, the patriarch sent them the following instructions: "Do not have interpreters except those from Lebanon who are Maronites. They are our relatives and they know our language

---

17. [Patriarch Gabriel VII was the 95th Coptic patriarch, presiding more than 40 years (1525–1568). (Tr.)]

18. [The ecumenical council held in Chalcedon in 451 declared Monophysitism heretical. (Tr.)]

19. [The 97th Coptic patriarch, 1586–1601 A.D. As a young cleric, he had opposed accommodation between the two churches; see Khalil Samir, "Gabriel VII," *The Coptic Encyclopedia* 4:1134, and "Gabriel VII", *The Coptic Encyclopedia*, 4:1135. (Tr.)]

20. [The first of the ecumenical councils, it was held in Nicea in 325 A.D. (Tr.)]

21. [An ecumenical council held in Constantinople in 381 A.D. (Tr.)]

and our friends. You also should kiss the hands of his holiness the pope, and ask his grace and generosity in granting a charitable gift every year [to the Copts] by arranging a regular donation, because we are facing very hard times. Our churches, monasteries, our poor and disadvantaged, our widows and orphans, those who are imprisoned or in iron because of not paying taxes, and others are facing extremely hard times. You, my sons, know this better than I do. It is part of your job to inform his holiness the pope about this [set of circumstances]. Jesus Christ has given him authority over all Christians and he is their father, and ours too. Since he is our father, he should help us in our crisis." The pope sent some assistance for which he was thanked.[22]

This document reveals some of the intentions of the Copts. There was a strong relationship between financial and religious affairs. The Copts might also have hoped that a strengthened Europe would interfere on their behalf, as it had for the Melchites, if they joined the ranks of the Catholics. But there is no known document that would support this speculation. The harmony between the Coptic church and Rome lasted one and one-half centuries. Renaudot claims that the harmony ended because the Coptic church was in need of the support of the Turkish pashas.[23]

Other than this incident, we note that nothing serious occurred in the history of the Copts during the seventeenth and eighteenth centuries, with the exception of fines imposed haphazardly on Coptic churches that were ordered closed until people paid the levied taxes.

Egypt was relatively peaceful and affluent during the reign of `Ali Bey.[24] Then chaos erupted and the Copts were indirectly persecuted. When Qabatān Hassan Pasha arrived in Egypt in 1200 A.H. [1785 A.D.] to confirm the sovereignty of the *Sublime Porte* over Egypt, he refused to leave the country until he had filled his pockets with money. In doing so, he took some severe measures against the Christians. al-Jabartī[25] reported that the street callers told Christians not to ride on animals, not to hire Muslims, and not to buy slave girls or slaves in

---

22. Anton Rabat, "The Pope Clement VIII and the Coptic Patriarch Gabriel," in *al-Mashriq* [a series of articles], 1907–1914.

23. *Historia Patriarcharum Alexandrinorum Jacobitarum*, Paris 1713.

24. [`Ali Bey al-Kabīr (the Great) ruled 1728–1773 A.D. He was one of the last great Mamluks who largely succeeded in gaining Egypt's independence from the Ottoman sultan's rule. (Tr.)]

25. [`Abd al-Rahmān al-Jabartī (1754–1825) was an Egyptian historian whose book *Ajā'ib al-`Athār fi al-Trajim wa al-Akhbār* is considered to be an important source of information on the history of Egypt. (Tr.)]

general. If a Christian had some slaves, he should sell them or free them. Christians should also abide by their special dress—the wide waist belt and the special shirt [that distinguished them from Muslims]. For the purpose of collecting money, Qabaṭān Hassan Pasha sent to the judge an order to find out what Mu'alim Ibrahim al-Jawharī[26] had endowed to the monasteries and churches from his lands, revenues and properties. The next day, the street callers told the Christian community to feel safe, and orders were issued to the crowds and lower class people not to hurt them. al-Jabartī also reported that Christians and Jews were ordered to change their names from those of the [biblical] prophets, such as Abraham, Moses, Esau, Joseph and Isaac. They were also ordered to release their slaves. If they did not do so, they were threatened with a search of their homes and residences. They made a compromise with the authorities by paying some money. Hence they gained [a partial] pardon by being allowed to sell their slaves and keep their money, which they deposited with some of their Muslim friends.

After two days of such events, Christians and Jews were ordered to bring their slaves out immediately. Soldiers attacked the homes of Christians to force the slaves out. Many [of the slaves] were brought to Qabaṭān Pasha and were sold at an auction. Most of them were bought by soldiers who resold them to other people at a profit.

Qabaṭān also levied seventy five thousand riyals as taxes on the houses of Christians. He ordered an inventory made of all houses and properties of Christians and ordered lists made of all these items. He then imposed annual fees on these properties. The lists also had to reflect the changes in ownership of the properties. Five hundred kees[27] were levied as individual taxes, which had a disastrous impact on the poor. He levied an additional one dinar *jizyah* on every dhimmi, of all classes, in addition to the *jizyah* already levied by the diwān.

Qabaṭān Pasha also arrested a monk and took from him a box full of the Christians' deposits. He arrested Mu'alim Wasif, a famous tax collector, and imprisoned and beat him, demanding money from him. Wasif had learned the revenues and expenditures of the state and had copies of the state accounting books. He had mastered every detail of the state financial affairs; nothing escaped his memory. And he knew Turkish. Also arrested were some women relatives of Mu'alim Ibrahim al-Jawharī. These women were at the home of Hassan Agha, the

---

26. [Ibrahim al-Jawharī (d. 1209 A.H./1794 A.D.) was the Coptic "Chief of all the Scribes of Egypt" of 'Ali Bey al-Kabīr and his successors. Owing to his good relations with the authorities, he built and renovated many churches and gave many endowments to Coptic churches and monasteries. See Harald Motzki, "Ibrāhīm al-Jawharī," *The Coptic Encyclopedia*, 4:1274. (Tr.)]

27. [Each kees contained about 500 dinars. (Tr.)]

manager of `Ali Bey. They revealed the existence of hiding places where gold, silver plates and cups, horse saddles and other things could be found.[28]

After Qabaṭān Pasha left, `Abdy Pash and Ismail Bey shared the rule of Egypt. The Copts were again subjected to persecution. al-Jabartī reports, "`Abdy Pash and Ismail Bey went to visit al-Shaykh al-Bakri on the occasion of the birthday of the Prophet [Muhammad]. After they sat down the pasha looked in the direction of Harat al-Nasara[29] and asked who lived there. When he was told that the residents were Christians, he directed that their houses be destroyed. He also ordered Christians not to ride donkeys. They sought conciliation with him, which was achieved by their paying thirty five thousand riyals. The Syrian Christians had to pay seventeen thousand of the amount and the rest was paid by the Coptic scribes."[30]

Despite all this, Father Berna, a Jesuit, wrote to Father Florio in 1711 saying, "Egypt is the only country in the Islamic empire where Christianity is practiced more freely than in any other country. That is why a large number of Christians from other countries take refuge in it."[31] This notice causes us to have second thoughts about the condition of the Copts before the French campaign.

The Copts before the French Campaign.

Many important changes took place during the nineteenth century. How did the Copts react to these changes? How important were the Copts numerically? How was their morale? We base the answers to such questions on the published stories of travelers and journals of consuls.

Generally speaking, the Copts left a bad impression on foreigners. By that time, their influence had declined and their number dwindled. They had no influence, except in Cairo and Alexandria where they worked as craftsmen and accountants, and in Upper Egypt around the city of Assuit and to the south in the direction of Aswan. In these places far away from the capital, anti-Coptic feelings were less violent. Hence the Copts lived in relative peace in these regions.

---

28. al-Jabartī, *op. cit.*, 2:108–139. These events and many more, which rehearse the injustices committed by the Turkish Qabaṭān Hassan Pasha against Christians, are detailed by al-Jabartī under the heading "The events of the year 1200 A.H./1785 A.D."

29. [An area where only Christians lived. (Tr.)]

30. al-Jabartī, *op. cit.*, 2:154.

31. [*Lettres edifiantes et curieuses, ecrites des missions etrangeres*, Lyon, France: J. Vernarel, 1819, 14 volumes. The letters were collected by C. le Gobien, et al., and first published in Paris, 1702–1776. A new edition and rearrangement was edited by Y. M. M. T. de Querbeuf (Paris, 1780–1783). The citation is from vol. 5, p. 226. (Tr.)]

At the beginning of the nineteenth century there were about one hundred and fifty thousand Copts among a population of three million. In Cairo there were ten thousand Copts. Some Christian statistics mention that six hundred thousand individuals were making contributions to the patriarch at the [time of the] Muslim conquest, and that this number had declined to between ten and fifteen thousand individuals when Father Vansleb visited Egypt in 1671 A.D.[32] Moreover, Niebuhr mentions that in 1760 there were twelve bishops, most of whom were in Upper Egypt, while there had been seventy at the time of the Muslim conquest.[33]

The number of monks had grown very small. They were distributed among four or five monasteries, such as the monastery of Saint Macarius and that of Saint Anthony, all of which were in a deplorable state. The priests—all of whom were married—were more interested in their material needs than their religious duties. Ignorance prevailed among them to the extent that it was difficult to elect a patriarch from among them.[34] But we cannot deny them some piety. However, they believed that religion was nothing but saying prayers and observing the many days of fasting.

If foreigners considered the Copts "ignorant and uncivilized,"[35] their excuse was that the appearance of the Copts, which reflected humility and poverty, inspired spite for them. On the part of the Muslim historians during the Mamluk period, they ignored this minority, which was [actually] indispensable to them, in spite of the inconvenience that they caused and in spite of their weakened, suffering condition.

The Copts became tax collectors or scribes, [often] exposed to persecution and insult. Vansleb wrote,

"We state that there is no religious minority in Egypt exposed to persecution like the Coptic community. This was because there was no one among them who could gain the respect of the Turks by his knowledge, or arouse their fear because of his power. The Turks considered them the scum of the earth and of less status than the Jews. They mistreated them whenever they liked, and closed their churches and

---

32. Vansleb, *Nouvelle relation*, pp. 298–99.

33. *Voyage en Arabie.* Father Berna wrote to Father Florio on July 20, 1711, saying, "The hierarchy consists of eleven or twelve bishops."

34. Thevenot, *Relation*, p. 501.

35. *Ibid.*

houses whenever they wanted for the most trivial and unfair reasons, in order to usurp their money."[36]

Nevertheless, the administrative posts that the Mamluks were obliged to award to Copts gave them opportunity to take revenge on their masters for their injustices and to amass wealth quickly. Moreover, the deterioration of the Copts took place in phases. It started before the Arab conquest, during the Roman and Byzantine periods. This observation shows that Copts had grown accustomed to this kind of life over a long period and that they had become content with their modest life. Further, they did not complain because they believed that they were the inteligensia that the country could not do without, especially their knowledge and experience in the world of business—if the country wanted to have a good administration. On the other hand, Muslims were in no better condition than Copts under the rule of the Mamluk beys.

The best proof of the contentment of Copts with their situation is that they never thought of emigration [except during the reign of al-Hakim and Muhammad Ibn Qalawūn[37]] because they were very attached to their country. The French consul Du Mayée wrote about this saying,

"In September 1699 I received an order from the king of France to select Coptic children to send to France to bring them up in the occidental manner. The Coptic priests tried to convince some rich people to send their children. But they were no more successful with them than they were with the poor, whatever the number of their children might be. Some parents withdrew their children from missionary schools and went without financial assistance, in spite of their great need for it, because of their fear that their children would be taken away from them against their will. This indicates how much they love their country and how attached they are to it." Du Mayée commented [further] on this incident by saying, "The Copts believe that their country is matchless, and they are right. Who can criticize them for their love of a country which foreigners describe as paradise on earth."[38]

---

36. Vansleb, *op. cit.*, pp. 298–99.

37. [The modern immigration of Copts to western countries and Australia began largely after Nasser's 1952 revolution. See Atiya, *History of Eastern Christianity*, pp. 166a–166g. (Tr.)]

38. Du Mayée, *Description de l'Égypte*, 2:134–35.

If we disregard the amount of money that was usurped from the Copts, we note that they were [effectively] living in isolation. They enjoyed relative peace, especially in the provinces. It is true that some western travelers spoke indignantly about the restrictions imposed upon Christians (for instance, their dress). They also noted that it was forbidden for non-Muslims to ride horses. However, these regulations were implemented in large cities only, and nowhere else. Other than these matters, one could not distinguish between Copts and other Egyptians. Thevenot wrote, "The Christians, whether Europeans or others, were not allowed to ride horses in the cities. But they were able to do so in the countryside if they wanted."[39]

We should not forget that educated Copts, such as Mu`alim Rizq, the manager of `Ali Bey's affairs and his private secretary, enjoyed wide-range authority and prestigious status with their rulers. There was also Mu`alim Ibrahim al-Jawharī who died in 1209 A.H. [1794 A.D.] and whom al-Jabartī distinguished from other Christians by including him in his obituaries of famous men. Muslim historians [generally] had no interest in reporting the death of a Christian, however high his status might be. The following is what al-Jabartī said in his obituary about al-Jawharī:

"The dhimmi Mu`alim Ibrahim al-Jawharī has died. He was the chief of the Coptic scribes. He reached a degree of greatness and influence and fame for a very long time in the Egyptian state, which no one in his community had been able to attain before him, as far as we know. He began his career during the tenure of Mu`alim Rizq, the scribe of `Ali Bey al-Kabīr. When `Ali Bey died and Ibrahim Bey took over, he assigned al-Jawharī all the [same] responsibilities. He became the reference [point] in all state affairs. He had full control of the state books, the revenues and the expenditures of the state, and all the scribes and financial officers. He was one of the leading political personalities of the world and one of its most shrewd politicians. Nothing escaped his memory. He was affable with everyone. He favored some people, gave away gifts to others and thereby consoled them. He did everything that attracted people to him and made them like him. He used to send substantial gifts and candles to the emirs. When Ramadan[40] started, he used to send candles, gifts of rice, sugar and clothes to most of the state

---

39. Thevenot, *op. cit.*, p. 508.

40. [Ramadan is the Muslim month of fasting. (Tr.)]

174

officials. During his life, the churches and the monasteries flourished. He established great endowments of land to support the churches and monasteries. He also arranged annual charitable gifts for them. Ibrahim Bey was saddened at his death, and he went to Qasr al-`Aini to participate in his funeral."[41]

Coptic managers in general, however, did not enjoy authority like that of al-Jawharī, and their sole goal was to accumulate wealth. "They became disinterested in what promoted the interest of their country. Their love of money and their miserliness made them stay away from the sciences and arts, for they had no incentive to excel at these activities."[42]

---

41. al-Jabartī, *op. cit.*, 2:262.

42. Du Mayée, *op. cit.*, 14:299. This was the case then, reflecting the general conditions current in Egyptian society.

Chapter 10

THE ISLAMIC POLICY OF NAPOLEON
AND THE POSITION OF THE FRENCH TOWARD THE COPTS

The French campaign in Egypt is important for several reasons. It was the first attempt by a non-Muslim country to invade Egypt following the crusades. It was also the first time after the Arab conquest that Egypt was ruled by a Christian country. It was also the first time following the advent of Islam that European Christians tried to cooperate with Egyptian Muslims.

For these reasons the French campaign also has an important place in the history of Muslim-Coptic relations. Further, the two [Egyptian] communities faced a new problem: What was their position from the viewpoint of the invader?

Bonaparte,[1] Defender of Islam.

On June 28, 1798, before the French forces landed on the Egyptian shore, [British] Admiral Nelson arrived in Alexandria. He was looking for Bonaparte's fleet. When he did not find it there, he tried to warn the Egyptians against a sudden attack. But they refused to listen because they had never trusted foreigners, and they asked him to leave the city.

Bonaparte knew that his own fleet would be received with animosity when it arrived at Alexandria. But he had great confidence in his new policy that he thought would remove the long-standing obstacles between the Muslim East and Christian West. From the viewpoint of the [ruling] Mamluks, the French campaign against Egypt was a resumption of the attempts by Baldwin, Amaury, Jean de Brienne, and Louis IX to eradicate Islam. At the very least it was a raid by European pirates on a larger scale.[2]

Bonaparte advanced to the walls of Alexandria, claiming to be the defender of Islam and even one of its heroes. He declared, "We are not polytheists of the primitive ages who have come to fight your faith. We acknowledge that your faith is superior. We shall convert to your religion when the [appropriate] time comes and the wise French will become true believers."[3]

---

1. [Napoleon I, emperor of France, 1769–1821. (Tr.)]

2. Niebuhr, the traveler, says that the people of Damietta are distinguished from all other Egyptians by their intense hatred of Christians. It would be the memory of the crusades that inspired this hatred.

3. From a message to the wali of Aleppo, dated September 1798. The documents of the French campaign were published in several sources. We shall not here mention the source but only the

(continued...)

Bonaparte attached little importance to the peoples' attempts to repel the French invasion or to their disbelief in his eloquent speeches, even though he had great hopes that they would sooner or later listen to his cry. Until then, he spared no effort in showing them his sympathy and loyalty. Francis Charles-Roux wrote,

> "No European colonizer has ever gone to Muslim countries as full of tolerance, respect and compassion as Bonaparte. He particularly never considered conducting missionary work in support of Christianity. He avoided any religious designs that might hurt Islam. No other European invader came with a benevolent attitude like that of Bonaparte, nor could he have made any more candid and public announcements [than he did], nor could he have offered [more] convincing proofs of what he said."[4]

Before the French forces disembarked on Egypt's shore on July 1st, Bonaparte's first declaration was,

> "The people with whom we are going to live are Muslim. They first believe that, `There is no God but Allah and Muhammad is his messenger.' Do not argue with them about that. Deal with them as you have dealt with Jews and Italians, and respect the men of religion as you respect rabbis and bishops. Towards the mosques and towards the religious feasts prescribed by the Qurān show the same tolerance that you show towards monasteries and temples, and the religions of Moses and Christ."

Because the French revolution had distanced the French from religion, Bonaparte was anxious to advise his men to show respect for Muslims. But his proclamation to the Egyptian people was [even] clearer because it revealed his real intentions and his future policy toward them, features that lasted during his stay among them. Bonaparte said in his proclamation to the Muslims,

> "To the sheikhs, judges, chiefs, imams and the elite of the country: Tell your nation that the French are also sincere Muslims. The proof is that they went to great Rome and destroyed the throne of the pope who has always urged Christians to fight Islam. Then they went to Malta and

---

3(...continued)
date of the document.

4. Charles-Raux, F., *Bonaparte, gouveneur d'Égypt*, p. 76.

177

expelled the Hospitallers[5] who claimed that God had asked them to fight the Muslims. Nevertheless, the French were at all times loving and loyal to the Ottoman sultan and were the enemies of his enemies. May God perpetuate his reign."

When the French commander conquered the country, he eagerly fulfilled his promises. Within one month of his landing in Alexandria, he ordered the celebration of the birth of the Prophet Muhammad in the magnificent manner described by the historian A. Rhyme, a contemporary of the campaign. He gave the following insightful portrayal of the event:

> "Bonaparte was robed in a beautiful oriental dress, with a turban on his head and slippers. All his officers and commanders accompanied him to the main mosque where about one hundred sheikhs were gathered. Bonaparte sat with them on pillows spread on the floor. He folded his arms and began to recite poems that recounted the life story of the Prophet from his birth until his death, beating his chest as they did and moving his head, [gestures] that attracted the attention of the men who admired his piety."[6]

Since Bonaparte wanted to publicize his position, he wrote to General Marmon on August 28, 1798, saying,

> "On my behalf meet Sheikh al-Misiri and tell him how we celebrated the birth of the Prophet. Tell him that in Cairo I meet with the chief judges and the prominent members of the community three or four times every ten days and that I am more convinced than any one else of the purity and sacredness of the religion of Islam."

On the same day he wrote directly to the same sheikhs saying, "I hope the time will soon come when I can bring together the wise and educated elements of the country and establish a permanent [governmental] system based on the principles of the Qurān which are the only and true ones that can make humanity happy."

---

5. [Hospitallers were members of a religious order—later military—established in Jerusalem in the 12th century. See "Hospitallers," in *The Oxford Dictionary of the Christian Church*, 2nd ed., F. L, Cross and E. A. Livingstone (eds.), pp. 669–70. (Tr.)]

6. Rhyme, A., *L'Égypte francaise*, p. 64.

Was Bonaparte sincere in his expressions? Although in our view political considerations dictated his position, we should not exclude the possibility that the East had a profound influence on him and that he harbored great respect for Islam. Therefore he did not tire of meeting with the ulama who were comfortable holding religious debates in his presence, although the French invader was viewed by them with suspicion and to them he was nothing but a polytheist. They admired his keen intelligence and hoped that some day he might join them in raising the banner of Islam.

Bonaparte fell into the net that he himself spread out. Did he not tell his entourage one day of his intentions to dress in oriental clothes and that he might convert to Islam? Since Bonaparte had no religion and did not believe in the existence of God, it is not thought that his possible conversion to Islam would have caused him any anxiety. In addition, his conversion would serve his political goals. But his commanders considered the idea foolish and later opposed it openly.

Bonaparte temporarily postponed carrying out his [announced] intention. He reconsidered it seriously after his defeat at Acre. When he returned from Syria he announced to certain people that "he was receiving lessons in the Qurān and had started to understand and love it." He added that he "intended to build a large mosque, then convert to Islam." At this point he was resuming his discussions with the ulama, asking them about the characteristics of the true Muslim. He presented the question to them very candidly and wanted an accurate answer. Because he doubted the feelings of his soldiers, he asked himself whether his conversion to Islam alone would result in the political coup that he hoped for. However, the consequences of the conversion of General Abd Allah Menou to Islam discouraged Napoleon from doing the same.   The French fleet was sunk [by the British] at Abu Qīr[7] and nothing of [Bonaparte's] support remained except his thousands of soldiers. When transportation lines were cut between himself and France and he lost hope of receiving assistance, he could only hope—and it was a distant hope—in his ability to win the support of the people [of Egypt], most of whom were Muslims who harbored a hatred for him. But [in a different vein] how did Napoleon deal with the Copts [in particular] and the Christians in general?

Bonaparte Sacrifices the Copts to Support Islam.

Since Bonaparte was influenced by the principles of equality and fraternity, he refused to allow a segment of the Egyptian people to fall under the

---

7. [The first Abu Qīr battle between the British fleet and the French fleet, which was landing at Abu Qīr near Alexandria, took place on August 1, 1798.]

yoke of persecution and to be held back from living freely. Thibaudeau observed that "although Bonaparte wanted to show the Muslims his inclination towards Islam, he did not turn from protecting other creeds."[8]

Nevertheless, he withheld giving Copts total freedom, especially freedom of religion. In one instance, when Copts requested that he abolish the restrictions imposed by the Mamluks on their religious practices, he responded to Mu`alim al-Jawharī in a letter dated December 7, 1798, saying,

> "I have received the message sent to me by the Coptic nation. It is my pleasure to protect this nation which from now on will never be subjected to disrespect. When time permits, which is not far away, I may allow this nation to practice its religion in public, as is the case in Europe, where everyone practices his own religion."

He then added, "I will severely punish the villages where any Copts may be killed during revolutions, and you can tell the members of your sect that I allow them to carry arms, ride mules and horses, to wear turbans on their heads and to dress as they may like."[9]

This message from Bonaparte is considered the only practical measure that benefited the Copts. Bonaparte, however, went back on his promises to them sooner than they might have thought. al-Jabartī stated that "the Christians of al-Shām resumed their old customs of wearing black and blue turbans and abandoned the wearing of white turbans, as well as colored kashmirī shawls, because the French forbade them from doing so. They also declared at the beginning of [the month of] Ramadan that the Christians of the country should not eat or drink in public or in the markets, and they should not smoke in public."[10] al-Jabartī also retold the following story:

> "A *faqīh* [sheikh] was passing by and saw a Christian smoking [during Ramadan]. He scolded him and the Christian responded harshly. The sheikh dismounted from his riding animal and beat the Christian. People gathered around them and the district governor took the case to the governor-general who asked the Christians who were present with him about their customs during Ramadan. They informed him that when

---

8. Thibaudeau, Antoine Claire, *Histoire de la Campaigne d'Égypte*, nouvelle edition, 2:71.

9. *Ibid.*, 2:7.

10. al-Jabartī, *op. cit.*, 3:45.

Ramadan began they never ate or drank in public in the presence of Muslims. He ordered the Christian to be beaten and the sheikh to be released."[11]

The animosity of Bonaparte towards Copts did not result in persecution, even though he had no sympathy for them. Nicola al-Turk[12] stated that [in a move directed principally against the Coptic minority]

"General Bonaparte requested a loan of two hundred thousand francs from the Muslim spice merchants and a loan of two hundred thousand francs from the Coptic scribes and tax collectors in the provinces; he also requested one hundred thousand francs from the merchants of Bilād al-Shām."[13]

During Bonaparte's hegemony in Egypt the Copts suffered one disappointment after another. It is true that he sought their assistance in collecting taxes, as the Mamluks had before him. But he [apparently] took this action reluctantly because [occasionally] he spoke very harshly about them: "They are the hated thieves in the country, but we should care for them because they alone know the general principles of managing the country."

For this reason, when Bonaparte appointed Muʿalim Jirjis al-Jawharī[14] as chief administrator and gave him authority over all other employees, he was careful to appoint a French official with al-Jawharī to keep an eye on him. From that moment on, Bonaparte looked for the first opportunity to get rid of al-Jawharī. When the French general left Egypt, he sent a letter dated August 22, 1799, to [his successor] General Kleber[15] telling him candidly, "I was determined, if events took

---

11. *Ibid.*

12. [Nicola Yusuf al-Turk (1763–1828) was a Lebanese Catholic of Greek origin. He was an eye-witness of many events of the French campaign which he has detailed in his book *Mudhakirat Nicola Turk* (Cairo: Institut francais d'Archéologie orientale, 1950) (in Arabic). (Tr.)]

13. *Ibid.*, p. 28. [At the time Bilād al-Shām included Syria, Lebanon and Palestine under the Ottoman rule. (Tr.)]

14. [Jirgis al-Jawharī was a brother of Ibrahim al-Jawharī. He succeeded to the job of chief scribe and tax collector after the death of his brother. He served Ibrahim Bey, then later served under Napoleon and Muhammad ʿAli. He died in 1816 A.D. See Harald Motzki, "Jirjis al-Jawharī," *The Coptic Encyclopedia*, 4:1332–34. (Tr.)]

15. [Jean Baptist Kleber, 1753–1800. (Tr.)]

their normal course, to set up a new tax system which would allow us to do without the services of the Copts."

Finally, although Bonaparte needed to increase the numbers in his army, he never thought of seeking the assistance of the Copts who [in any event] had shown no enthusiasm for being drafted into the army. The Coptic Legion was not formed—as we shall explain later—until General Kleber took charge and under circumstances totally beyond the control of the Copts.

By doing away with the services of the Copts, Bonaparte hoped to have virtual control over taxes. On the other hand, he particularly wanted to please the Muslims. On many occasions he wrote to his commanders telling them, "Whatever you do, be sure that the Christians are on your side. However, do not hesitate to give priority to Muslims over Copts." Bonaparte repeated this statement to General Kleber before the left for France. When Bonaparte achieved victory over the Ottoman forces at Ābu Qīr and wanted to assure the notables and the ulama of his good intentions, he publicly declared,

> "Yes, I hate the Christians. I have crushed their religion and destroyed their churches and killed their priests and smashed their crosses and denied their faith. Even so, I see that they rejoice when I rejoice and feel pain when I feel pain. Is it reasonable to convert again to Christianity? What shall I gain from this?"

The Muslims' Position.

Based on the evidence that we have previously referred to, we can be sure that Bonaparte tried by word and deed to gain the support of Muslims. He did not reach the point of persecuting Christians to achieve his goal, but he showed the latter no sign of sympathy. However, Bonaparte was unsuccessful in eliminating the hatred in the hearts of Muslims towards him, [chiefly] because of his presence among them, despite his showing encouraging signs [of converting]. He felt that the people were reluctant to be governed by him and were waiting for an opportunity to get rid of him. When al-Jabartī spoke about the visits of the French commanders to the elite on the occasions of Muslim feasts, he candidly observed that the notables received them with bogus warmth.

The first Cairo rebellion[16] tore down the curtain behind which the farce of French-Muslim cooperation had been hiding. The conspiracy was planned in al-Azhar [University] only a short time before Bonaparte had shown his extreme sympathy with Islam. "On Sunday the 20th of Rubi`a al-Akhar, a minor sheikh

---

16. [The first Cairo rebellion took place on October 21, 1798. (Tr.)]

of al-Azhar went into the city's streets calling out that everyone who believes in one God should go to al-Azhar because, on that day, we should express our anger against the disbelievers [the French]"[17] The French were surprised by the attack on them while they were walking unarmed in the streets of the capital. The mobs then killed those Muslims and Christians who had cooperated with the French.

When Bonaparte decided to be lenient with the rebels, no one trusted him. When some Christians wanted to be compensated for their damaged homes, the Muslims refused to likewise petition because of their strong belief that no one would listen to their complaint, as al-Jabartī has noted. After some weeks, when the people learned that the Ottoman forces had occupied the fortress at Abu Qīr, "they rejoiced, and cursed the Christians publicly."[18] But General Bonaparte was victorious over the Ottomans and returned to Cairo. The notables, the ulama and the members of the diwān (consultative council)[19] had to go to his residence to congratulate him on his happy return. For a second time Bonaparte noticed their sadness and disappointment. But he did not want to take revenge or change his policy towards them. He continued the same policy that he had followed after the [first] Cairo rebellion. However, he blamed them privately for their position saying, "Oh ulama and notables! I wonder about your sadness at my victory. You have not appreciated my position toward you until now, even though I have repeatedly said that I am a Muslim, that I believe that there is no god but Allah, and that I revere the Prophet and like the Muslims."

This illustrates that the relationship with the occupier was warm in appearance only. Although Bonaparte continued to show friendship toward Muslims, he failed to convince them of his good intentions and of the importance of power to maintain public order. The Egyptians considered him an infidel leading an army of infidels, and believed that his presence in Egypt encouraged Christians at the expense of Muslims. Nevertheless, until the last minute Bonaparte hoped to be able to change the people's animosity towards him. His insistence deserves admiration, although his commanders suppressed their anger

---

17. al-Turk, *Mudhakirat*, p. 28.

18. al-Jabartī, *op. cit.*, 3:75.

19. [Established by Napoleon, the diwān was made up of Muslim ulama and other notables. (Tr.)]

183

at his policy. When General Kleber received authority, he readily favored the Christians and allowed General Mu`allim Y`aqub[20] to form "the Coptic Legion."

Before we discuss this legion, which has been criticized by some Egyptian historians and has been subjected to unfounded accusations, it would be appropriate to review the position of the Copts from the French viewpoint.

The Position of the Copts.

The Egyptian Muslim believed that the Copt, who had been mistreated and humiliated by the Mamluks, was influenced by the presence of Christian armies in the land of Egypt and was ready to join them. Therefore, when the French fleet reached the waters of Alexandria, the French and Copts continued to be distrusted by Egyptian [Muslim] authorities. As a result, they were exposed to acts of violence.

The authorities had ordered some resident French people not to leave their homes [when the French reached Alexandria]; others had been arrested in the Citadel. It is said that Murad Bey had decided to behead them, but he postponed carrying out his plan until after his hoped for victory [over the French] on the advice of Carlo Rosti, the Austrian Consul. The Copts expected the same fate, but the pasha[21] interceded on their behalf and saved them from sure death. Nicola al-Turk stated,

> "The vizier and Sheikh al-Balad Ibrahim Bey[22] said that it was impossible to agree to such a decision or opinion because the Copts were the subjects of the high highness, the sultan, who enjoyed victory, glory and authority. Daily, the vizier and sheikh al-balad sent Selim Agha [the chief of *inkishariya*] to the Christians to assure them of their safety and of the safety of their shops and possessions. He sent street callers in all

---

20. [Mu`allim Y`aqūb (Jacob) (1745–1801) was a Coptic merchant and businessman turned soldier in Murad Bey's army. After Murad's defeat, he was attached to General Desaix in Upper Egypt. He showed such devoted loyalty to Desaix and to the French, and rendered such good service, that he was later appointed general and given the command of a "Coptic legion." He embarked with the French army when it evacuated Egypt and died on board ship. See Anwar Louca, "Ya`qūb, General," *The Coptic Encyclopedia*, 7:2349–52. (Tr.)]

21. [Pasha was the title of the Turkish wali at the time. (Tr.)]

22. [In Egypt the title Sheikh al-Balad ordinarily denoted a village elder or mayor. However, the Sheikh al-Balad of Cairo was the "head of the country," the acknowledged head of the Mamluk beys. At the time of the French invasion the title was borne by Ibrahim Bey. (Tr.)]

directions into the city to urge people to maintain the safety of the [sultan's] subjects and not to antagonize them."[23]

al-Jabartī adds that,

"the Mamluk emirs searched the stores of Europeans for arms and other things. They also searched the homes of Christians [Syrians, Copts and Armenians] as well as their churches and monasteries for arms. The common people were not satisfied and wanted to kill the Christians and Jews but the rulers prevented them. Without [such protection] they would have been killed during the time of upheaval."[24]

In the position of the Copts was there anything that justified the vengeful spirit [on the part of the Muslims]? The answer is no. It is possible that the Copts found in the arrival of the French, their co-religionists, something that might ameliorate their situation. But their position from [the standpoint of] the Europeans during the past [crusades] and the documents related to the French campaign in Egypt bear no assurance that the Copts tried to help the invaders.

Can we hold the passiveness of the Copts in times of danger against them? More to the point, were they able to do anything after the authorities disarmed them? I believe that the Christians were too weak to make any decision [to rebel] and were subjected to the authority of the majority. They considered themselves cooperative with their Muslim compatriots during the fighting [against the French invaders].

The victory of the French and the flight of the Mamluks had no affect on the behavior of the Copts. When Richardot, one of the French officers in the campaign, described the victorious French army as it entered Cairo, he acknowledged that "the victorious army's entrance into the modern capital of ancient Egypt attracted no attention. The population of the city did not care about it, and people did not go out in the streets—where one could [hardly] find groups of men or even children. Briefly speaking, the public showed no interest in the event."[25]

It is known that Bonaparte took the initiative and summoned Mu'allim Jirgis al-Jawharī who introduced to him the Coptic notables. Naturally the Copts

23. al-Turk, *op. cit.*, p. 13.

24. al-Jabartī, *op. cit.*, 3:7.

25. Richardot, *Noveaux memoires*, pp. 59–60.

seized this opportunity to express their obedience and submissiveness to the man who sat upon the wreckage of the Mamluks and who had established himself as the ruler of the country. The members of the Coptic delegation were robed in formal dress with sleeves embroidered in gold and ornamented with small golden flowers, and had kashmirī turbans as headdresses. They expressed to Bonaparte their absolute loyalty."[26]

The Muslims became worried as a result of the Copts' actions, and al-Jabartī accused the Copts openly of cooperating with the French. He also pilloried the Syrian and Greek women who visited the harem of the Mamluk beys in order to intimidate them into paying the taxes levied by the French. He also took sides against Coptic administrative employees who collected the taxes "as if they were high officials," that is, by whipping people to force them to pay. He finally said that the Copts, Syrians, Greeks, and Jews became unbearable because they rode horses and carried arms.[27]

We have previously mentioned that Bonaparte treated the Copts unkindly and that they received no favorable treatment until after General Kleber had received authority and the people of Cairo had revolted against the French for the second time. Following the assassination of the new commander [Kleber], all state of emergency measures were abolished.

When the rebels in Cairo had requested assurance for their safety, Kleber had granted it. But afterwards he overburdened the people with taxes. He summoned the ulama and the notables and spoke to them in intimidating and threatening words and described them as evil, ungrateful men. He also informed them that he would levy an additional tax on all the people except the Christian dhimmis.[28]

This measure, which well suits Kleber's toughness, was considered unwise because it created a schism between the Muslim, the enemy of the French, and the Copt his co-religionist. Besides this, the Christians who were mistreated during the first and second Cairo revolutions[29] thought that, after Kleber's victory

---

26. Homsy, G., *Le General Jacob et l`Expedition de Bonaparte en Égypte*, p. 42.

27. [al-Jabartī, *op. cit.*; included in the events of Sh`abān 1213 A.H. (January 1799 A.D.). (Tr.)]

28. al-Turk, *op. cit.*, pp. 89–90.

29. [The second Cairo revolution against the French took place on March 20, 1800. It was put down by General Kleber. He was assassinated on June 14, 1800, by a Syrian Muslim student of al-Azhar. (Tr.)]

on the plain of `Ayn Shams[30] [over the Turks] and his suppression of the revolution, the rule of the French had been consolidated for good and that they would be its prime beneficiaries, without competition. Taking advantage of their closeness to the occupier, they became arrogant and defiant. al-Jabartī reported that

"the Copts and the Christians of Bilad al-Shām [Syrian Christians] were arrogant and insolent to Muslims and took revenge on them, revealing their spite and allowing no room for reconciliation. They spoke openly of the end both of the Muslim religion and of the days of the monotheists. The French ordered that mules be collected and they strictly forbade Muslims from riding them, except five Muslim ulama: al-Sharkawi, al-Mahdi, al-Fayumi, al-Amir, and Ibn Muharam.[31] Christian translators and other Christians were then allowed to ride mules."[32]

When Sulayman al-Halabi assassinated General Kleber, the desire for revenge suddenly seized the French soldiers. Nicola al-Turk stated that they had intended to annihilate the entire population of Cairo, Muslim and Christian.

Menou[33] succeeded General Kleber. Because Menou was a good administrator, he expressed suspicion toward the Coptic chief tax collector. Since the French [generally] did not like the Copts, the latter suffered innumerable afflictions, and the tax collectors were put under strict supervision. "The French severely punished the Coptic tax collectors who embezzled money. They were waiting for an opportunity to discharge any disloyal employees. And in the month of vendémiaire of the ninth year of the French revolution [October 1800], Esteve accused the Copts of embezzling 1,293,143 pounds from the taxpayers. Menou ordered the arrest of Antoun Aboutakia, the chief tax collector, and fined him 750,000 pounds to make up for the loss [in state revenues]."[34]

---

30. [To the east of Cairo. (Tr.)]

31. [These were the leading sheikhs of al-Azhar and members of the diwān.]

32. al-Jabartī, op. cit., 3:113.

33. [Jacques Français Menou, a general (1750–1810), succeeded Kleber after his assassination (June 1800). He converted to Islam to marry a Muslim Mamluk woman and took the name "Abd Allah." He had to leave Egypt on June 17, 1801 with the French forces, accompanied by his wife Zubaydah and their son Sulayman. (Tr.)]

34. Rigault, Le general Abd Allah Menou, p. 118.

Concerning the reorganization of the Egyptian administration, we also read in clause number four of the order dated 10 vendémiaire of the tenth year of the French revolution [October 1800] the following:

"The Copts are nothing but a minority hated by the Muslims and they have brought this hatred against themselves. We should ensure justice and freedom for them, but it is not wise—and even dangerous—to be allied with them and to grant them privileges. Therefore their leaders and those of the Greek and Syrian communities will attend the meetings of the diwān [only] on a consultative basis."

Menou worked to achieve Bonaparte's objective of depriving the Coptic administrative employees of their privileges. He actually eliminated the positions of tax collectors (*mubashireen*) in the new administrative system, with the exception of the position of Mu`allim Y`aqūb: "Because of his confirmed efficiency and loyalty to the French, he would stay in the diwān as a consultant to the director of the general revenues. He was asked to introduce to General Esteve the sheikhs who would collect the taxes and who would carry the title *mubashir*. He was also to introduce to him the Copts who would work under the supervision of these sheikhs."

Menou wrote to General Mu`allim Y`aqūb explaining why he had made this decision: "You know that I have little confidence in a large number of your Coptic compatriots. You should supervise them very carefully because they are not comfortable with the administrative procedures that I have set up, which aim at a reorganization that they dislike."[35]

The Copts in return accused the French of trying to get rid of them in order to embezzle money from the public treasury. In general, the tough measures directed against them made them wish that the French would evacuate Egypt. They were aware that their Muslim compatriots would try to take revenge on them if the French departed. But they chose the lesser of two evils, preferring to suffer at the hands of the Muslims for a period of time than to be deprived of their jobs forever.

General Y`aqūb and the Formation of the Coptic Legion.

The military cooperation of the Copts with the occupier is one of the points that needs clarification. Some national writers have thought that the question of Mu`allim Y`aqūb is clear: he was a traitor who cooperated with the

---

35. A letter dated March 12, 1801.

French and contributed to the humiliation of the Egyptian people. Even Coptic writers have not tried to differentiate between the position of Mu`allim Y`aqūb and that of the rest of the Copts. One writer tried to cover up the problem [by not discussing it] which doubled the Copts' guilt in the eyes of the people.[36]

The historian George Duane has concluded that Y`aqūb aimed at achieving Egypt's independence. He based his observation on a conversation between Captain Joseph Edmonds, General Y`aqūb, and his friend Laskaris on board the ship Palace on their way to France. The Egyptian historian Shafik Gharbal has supported this view.[37] Salama Musa, an Egyptian writer, depended on these sources [alone] when he wrote a series of articles in *Misr*, a Coptic newspaper, glorifying the actions of General Y`aqūb whom he considered the first to raise his voice in Egypt as well as in Europe demanding the freedom and independence of Egypt.[38]

I personally think that all the interpretations of the Y`aqūb affair are wrong and that General Y`aqūb denied his homeland, if not by word, then by deed, from the moment he formed the Coptic legion. For its part, the Coptic community was cool toward the actions of the general.

But this does not mean that Y`aqūb was a traitor,[39] because at the time there was no defined Egyptian nationality. How can we blame him for his position if the Ottomans sought his help when the French withdrew? If we want to understand the psychology of the man we should review his actions before the French occupation.

Y`aqūb was intelligent and physically strong. He was known to be a seasoned horseman. He occupied the position of *mubashir* like many of his co-religionists. But he was not as quiescent as they were because, long before the arrival of the French, he joined the army of Ibrahim Bey and Murad Bey in the big battle between the Mamluk and Qabaṭān Pasha armies.[40] The beys thanked him

---

36. Sharabim, *al-Kafī fi Tarikh Misr al-Qadīm wa al-Hadith*, Cairo, 1898 (in Arabic). 4 volumes.

37. Ghorbal, *General Yaqūb wa al-Faris Laskaris*, Cairo, 1932.

38. The *Misr* newspaper issue is dated November 26, 1946.

39. Ahmad Hafiz Awad supports our view in his book *Fath Misr al-Hadithah* (Cairo: Matb`at Misr, 1925).

40. [The battle took place at `Ayn Shams, east of Cairo, in 1200 A.H. (1780 A.D.) between the Turkish forces, led by Qabaṭān Pasha on one side, and the forces of Murad Bey and Ibrahim Bey, the Mamluk leaders. (Tr.)]

for his courage and showered him with gifts. By 1798 Y`aqūb had become a rich notable, respected and revered by all around him.

When Jirjis al-Jawharī introduced him to General Poussielgue,[41] the latter wrote to Bonaparte saying, "al-Jawhari says that you will not find a man more protective of our interests than he is and that he puts his head in your hands, hoping that you would order it chopped off if Mu`allim Y`aqūb were to show any sign of treason."[42]

I feel that Y`aqūb the soldier admired the strength of those young [French] soldiers who conquered the Mamluks of Murad Bey and Ibrahim Bey, who had had the reputation of being invincible. It is known that Y`aqūb was loyal to his superiors to the extent of self-denial. The Mamluks had been his superiors of yesterday, but today the French were his superiors.

General Y`aqūb was attached directly as an administrator to the force of General Desaix who admired the young commander for his extraordinary courage and military skill. As a result, Y`aqūb exchanged the ink pad that was fixed to his waist belt for a sword with which he faced battle and exposed himself to death more than a hundred times. He considered himself one of Bonaparte's soldiers, and gradually put behind him his Egyptian Coptic origin.

When Desaix joined Bonaparte in France, Y`aqūb settled in Cairo where he supplied useful information to the French. But the smell of powder quickly attracted him. When the rebels in the second Cairo revolution besieged him [and his comrades], he proved his skill more than once, putting him in a position to ask for Kleber's approval to form a Coptic legion under his leadership. Kleber granted his request as well as the rank of *agha*.[43] Y`aqūb was very pleased and wanted to express his gratitude not only by forming the legion but also by supplying it with arms at his own expense. The legion included eight hundred men and is described by al-Jabartī as follows:

> "When Y`aqūb the Copt joined the French and was appointed military commander of the Copts, he recruited young Copts, had them shave, and dressed them in uniforms like those of the French soldiers. What distinguished the Copts from the French was the cap they wore on their

---

41. [The administrator general of finances for the French army. (Tr.)]

42. A letter dated August 2, 1798.

43. [An *agha* was an Ottoman officer whose title can be translated as "chief" or "master." It was used for medium-level and some high-level officials of the Janissary Corps, the sultan's palace service, as well as for local officials. (Tr.)]

heads which resembled the [French] hat but with a piece of black sheep skin attached to it. The cap looked extremely ugly above their ugly faces and black skin and their bodies which smelled bad."[44]

al-Jabartī's prejudice against the legion reveals the hostile feelings of some contemporaries towards it.[45] But the Copts were not the first to supply men to the French army. Omar al-Qalqaji preceded them.

"He mediated with the Moroccans of the al-Fahameen district of Cairo and recruited many of them and others, introducing them to the French commander who selected the young and the strong among them. [The French commander] supplied them with arms and equipment, and organized them in military fashion, appointing Omar as their commander. The Moroccan troops resided in a building at Bab Sa`ada.[46] A French group used to visit this building daily to teach the Moroccans the French military tactics, laws and signals. The teacher stood in front of the students who stood in a line holding their rifles, and he issued orders to them in their language."[47]

After the Moroccans, the Mamluks joined the French; the Copts were the last to join the army. However, in contrast to the Moroccans, their effort was very limited. The Copts did not even participate in the battles that preceded the surrender of the French armies. Their legion remained in its camp in Cairo. The members of the legion even thought of disbanding. In fact, while Y`aqūb was preparing to sail to France his troops deserted despite pressure from him.

A man does not leave his country in search of adventure, except for strong reasons. The Copts never knew the reason for their being drafted. But Y`aqūb was aware of what he was doing. He [effectively] forgot his fatherland and dedicated himself to the service of his new masters after the happy days of his cooperation with General Desaix. But how could he secure their respect for himself while he was an administrative employee? This consideration was

---

44. al-Jabartī, *op. cit.*, 3:162.

45. [One published work which reflects the hostile feelings of some Muslim writers is *Mu`allim Y`aqūb* by Ahmad al-Sawī (Cairo: Dar al-Fikr, 1986). In the book, the author has made several prejudicial statements against General Yaqūb and Christians in general. (Tr.)]

46. [A Cairo district at the time. (Tr.)]

47. [al-Jabartī, *op. cit.*, 3:28. (Tr.)]

[probably] the reason that he joined the army, and his heroic deeds helped him to gain the confidence of the French. Ten days before the evacuation of the French army he was granted the rank of general, receiving a letter from Bonaparte that expressed his sincere thanks for his services to France. This appreciation led him to turn down the Ottoman grand vizier's offer to give him security and reinstate him in his previous job. As for Jirgis al-Jawharī, he accepted the offer of the grand vizier and resumed his activities as a tax collector under the Ottomans because of the absence of a comraderie between himself and the French, in contrast with Mu`allim Y`aqūb who had grown attached to general Desaix and who openly showed affection for him. When Desaix was killed on the European battlefield, his soldiers in Egypt mourned him. "Mu`allim Y`aqūb attended [the memorial] in his magnificent military uniform, surrounded by his honor guard and a unit of his soldiers. His sadness exceeded any limit. When the French thought of establishing a monument for Desaix, Y`aqūb rushed a letter to General Menou saying, `O Desaix! A monument will be established for you in France. Y`aqūb whom you liked and who pampered you more than himself will pay one–third of the cost of the monument, whatever it might be. Thus the coming generations will know that Y`aqūb, who fought by your side, deserved your respect. Alas! he gave you his affection long ago.'"

These feelings were not common among Copts of those days. Y`aqūb was thus unique among his people. His aim, like that of Desaix, was to gain honor on the battlefield. But he fell ill of an unknown disease on board a ship carrying him to France, and he died shortly afterward. His last words were not about Egypt, nor about his family, nor about the members of his legion who had followed him. While he was in the throes of death he asked General Belliard,[48] who was beside his bed, to do him the favor of burying him in Desaix's tomb. But his wish went unfulfilled because he died on ship and his body was buried at sea.

The Copts after the French Evacuation.

The French tried to ensure the safety of the Christians and Muslims who had helped them when they signed the treaty concerning their evacuation. In the twelfth clause of the treaty, they included a condition that everyone living in Egypt—of whatever nationality—had had the right to join the French army without his family being exposed to persecution or his property being sequestered. Clause number thirteen stipulated that those who lived in Egypt—of whatever religion—would not be persecuted nor their property sequestered due to any

---

48. [Augustin-Daniel Belliard, French count and general (1769–1832). (Tr.)]

relationship to the French during their occupation of Egypt, and that they should follow the laws of the country from that time on.

Despite these two clear clauses, the Egyptians made excessive demands on the French during their evacuation, then they turned against their fellow Egyptian Christians. Neither the procedures followed by policemen nor the pronouncements of the wali quenched the fire of revenge which had been blazing in the hearts of the people for a long time.

Lessons from the French Campaign.

The French occupation of Egypt lasted less than three years, but it was a period full of events and lessons. Bonaparte came to Egypt full of positive feelings towards Muslims. He wanted to show them favor above and beyond the Christians. But the Muslims doubted [the sincerity of] his intentions and came to hate him in the end. They forgot the pronouncements of Bonaparte which overflowed with sympathy toward Islam, and they always remembered the French invading the court of al-Azhar where the rebels of Cairo sought shelter.

The feelings of the Christians appear more complex. Some, like the Greeks, Syrians, and the European community in Cairo, welcomed the foreign occupation of Egypt, while others like the Copts suppressed their feelings, refraining from expressing their hostility as when the crusaders landed on the Egyptian shores. The reason for this response was that Bonaparte's campaign bore no religious imprint. They welcomed the French, hoping that they would elevate their status. But when they realized that the occupier wanted to deprive them of their traditional jobs, they hoped for the return of their Turkish superiors.

No one has described the feelings towards the French like Bonaparte himself. He said on Saint Helena [Island] in the presence of Las Cases,

> "I had such control over my soldiers that it would have been sufficient to issue a regular daily order to make them convert to Islam. The people would have been pleased with this action. Even the Christians themselves might have found this action the best solution for their problem. They would have supported my order because of their belief that I could not have done better for ourselves and them."[49]

---

49. [Las Cases was one of Napoleon's friends who voluntarily accompanied him into his exile on St. Helena Island. See Albert Carr, *Napoleon Speaks* (New York: Viking Press, 1941), pp. 351–52, 354, 365–66, 378–79. (Tr.)]

Briefly speaking, Copts wished that the foreigners, who brought them no benefits, would leave because their presence increased the hatred of Muslims toward them.

We can deduce three important results from the [French] campaign. First, the disdain of Muslims for Copts made mutual understanding very difficult between the two groups. Second, the presence of a Christian occupying force in Egypt hurt relations between Copts and Muslims, even though the [occupying] nation sympathized with the majority populace. Third, the Copts who were persecuted and disdained by the Mamluks welcomed the European Christian nations on condition that these nations avoid matters of religion.

Chapter 11

THE TOLERANCE OF MUHAMMAD 'ALI'S DYNASTY AND THE ACKNOWLEDGEMENT OF LEGAL EQUALITY AMONG MUSLIMS AND COPTS

In the chaotic early nineteenth century, no one imagined that an Albanian officer, who had recently come into the country, would be able—by his own will—to change laws that had been enacted generations previously and had defined the social status of dhimmis in the Muslim world. It was also difficult to imagine that an obscure ruler, subject to the sovereignty of the [Turkish] sultan, would inaugurate a daring reform movement that would teach the sultan and the rest of the world an exemplary lesson in tolerance.

Some may say that Muhammad 'Ali followed such a policy because of his strong desire to please foreigners and because he was careful to create an atmosphere suitable for mutual cooperation. Such cooperation was necessary for many reasons. For the sake of argument, let us assume the validity of this view. Yet, why was he also tolerant toward his Christian subjects? What compelled him to behave so? It is certain that the foreigners did not disdain the Copts, nor was it the *Sublime Porte*[1] that caused a revolution in the empire against intolerance towards dhimmis.

When the walis of modern Egypt planned their national policies, they did not confuse the Copts with Christians from the west. And the Copts themselves did not want their destiny tied to that of foreigners, [chiefly] because they distrusted them. In the middle of the nineteenth century, new trends appeared that led to the final destruction of the old social systems, trends that were largely due to the royal family's policy and its influence. This slow but sure development was successful, owing to the cooperation of the royal family with influential persons. We have to define the role of each party before we study the official decrees that mandated political and social equality among all segments of the Egyptian population.

Tolerance of the Royal Family.

Muhammad 'Ali clearly created a new social atmosphere in Egypt. Because his successors were deeply influenced by his spirit, they [generally] followed a policy that increased the prestige of Egypt in the eyes of western

---

1. [The phrase means "sublime gate" and refers to the gate of the sultan's palace where justice was administered. In this context it means the government of the Ottoman empire. (Tr.)]

nations. We cannot enumerate the royal family's positive actions in this connection because there were so many, in contrast to previous historical periods.

The services of Muhammad ʿAli to his family were notable [precisely] because he came to power during an extremely chaotic period. During that era, the coffers of the Egyptian treasury were empty, expenses were high, and the religious minority was exposed to persecution by rulers. Muhammad ʿAli was greater [than his predecessors] because he was the first Muslim ruler who followed a truly religiously tolerant policy. As for Sultan Mahmūd II,[2] who was installed on the throne of the Ottoman empire in 1808, he emulated Muhammad ʿAli in words, but not deeds. In 1830 he made the following statement: "I want no discrimination among my people who belong to different races and religions. They should have no differences except in the way that they pray in their respective temples."[3]

After the death of Mahmūd II, and immediately following the ascendancy of his son Abdulmecid, a decree embodying these principles was proclaimed by Mustafa Reshid Pasha. The Hatt-i Şerif Gülhane, or "Noble Rescript of the Rose Chamber," was based on western notions of human rights,[4] but was [purposely] written in vague terms. After another seventeen years, the Europeans extracted from the Turkish sultan a promise [concerning equality and justice for religious minorities] that was reflected in the imperial decree of 1856.[5]

During the same period, under the supervision of her walis, Egypt was moving rapidly towards political and social equality among her people. Credit for this should be given to the strong will and determination of the founder of the royal family [Muhammad ʿAli].

When the French evacuated Egypt, they had left behind the Copts, who were powerless, and the Muslims, who were in a state of excitement. Copts were accused of cooperating with the Christian foreigners, although the Copts—as we explained—had not wanted foreigners among them and had wished that they would leave. But the Muslims, who had suffered because of French actions of

---

2. [Mahmūd II was the Turkish sultan from 1808 to 1839. (Tr.)]

3. [This is quoted in Envar Karal's paper "Non-Muslim representatives in the first constitutional assembly," in *Christians and Jews in the Ottoman Empire*, Benjamin Braude and Bernard Lewis, eds., New York: Holmes & Meier, 1982, 1:388. (Tr.)]

4. [I have slightly expanded the author's statements about these fermans. See Karal, *op. cit.*, pp. 388–89. (Tr.)]

5. [The *Hatt-i Hümayun* ("Imperial Rescript") of 1856 made explicit the provisions of the earlier decree: that Ottoman citizens, regardless of religion, would be accepted into government service and were free to enroll in both military and civilian state schools. See Karal, *op. cit.*, pp. 388–89. (Tr.)]

suppression during the two Cairo revolts, tried to take revenge on Christians by defaming them, by imposing fines on them, and by condemning some of their notables to death. Therefore, it is not surprising that, at a time of misery in their history, the Copts momentarily looked to foreigners [for assistance]. Mr. William Hamilton, the British navy commander, wrote from Athens in July 1809: "The Copts are favorably disposed towards the English. They are at this moment quite ready to accept the British government's demands."[6]

When the British turned their backs on the [Copts'] overtures, the Copts turned to the French. In a report to Bonaparte dated January 1803, General Sibastiani wrote that "the Coptic *mubashir* has suggested that he correspond with me to inform me of important events in Egypt and Syria. He has offered his and his people's services in case we are interested in the East. All indications show that he is very loyal to us, but I have answered him that I have received no instructions concerning this matter."[7]

Muhammad `Ali exhibited no favorable disposition toward the Copts until he had ensured state security. Because paying his soldiers and foiling the conspiracies of his enemies were his first priorities, he first followed the traditional method of imposing fines on the Copts who had succeeded in diverting attention away from themselves during the battles between the Turks and the Mamluks, among the Mamluks themselves, and had then succeeded in being appointed as *mubashireen* and becoming rich.

When Muhammad `Ali became firmly established, he abandoned the old-fashioned methods of governing. From the moment that he decided to hire Egyptians and depend on them, he concurrently eliminated the discrimination between Copts and Muslims because both were able to render him important service. He also found no reason to look down on Copts, because people need to be respected if they are to carry out their duties satisfactorily. The contents of the following memo is the best proof of the good intentions of Muhammad `Ali. It states, "Yusūf the dhimmi works in the armory in the service of the state. We have written him this memo that is issued by our office and delivered to him so that he not be exposed to remarks concerning his clothes."[8]

---

6. The British documents were published by Mr. Douin under the title *L'Angleterre et l'Égypt*, Cairo: The Egyptian Royal Geographical Society, 1929, p. 408.

7. French document in *L'Égypte de 1802 à 1804*, p. 11.

8. Yacoub Artin Pacha, "Un tezkere divani de 1222 de L'Hégire," in *Majallat al'M`ahad al-Ilmī al-Misrī*, Alexandria, 1894.

The order was unambiguous. Because the question of clothes was still as pressing at the beginning of the nineteenth century as it was when the Islamic invasion began, the Muslims were angry at the [revolutionary] position of Muhammad 'Ali. This is proven by an order issued in 1817 A.D. [1233 A.H.], referred to by al-Jabarti:

"An order to the Copts and Greeks to adhere to their blue and black clothes: They are not to have white turbans as head dresses because they have universally exceeded their limits. As head dresses, they may use expensive and colorful kashmiri shawls. They may ride amblers, mules and horses, with valets running before them carrying sticks and urging people out of their way. When they carry arms, groups of them are to go out in the open air and set up a target to shoot at with their guns."[9] But al-Jabarti doubted that the order would be carried out, and added, "What a good thing it would be if this order became permanent."[10]

From another point of view, Muhammad 'Ali did not prevent the Copts from practicing their religion, nor did he reject their requests to build or renovate churches. The manuscript collection in the Abdin Palace contains a large number of orders related to churches. They took the following format: "Order to [name of official] concerning permitting the Copts to renovate the church, helping them to accomplish that, and not obstructing them from it."[11] During Sa'id Pasha's[12] and Khedive Isma'il's[13] reigns, the number of orders related to churches grew, and the rulers themselves demanded expeditious action in carrying out those orders.[14]

During the Mamluk period, Copts had faced many difficulties in obtaining permits for pilgrimages to the Holy Land. But thereafter they were able to make pilgrimages every year under the protection of the authorities. The first relevant document goes back to 1241 A.H. [1825 A.D.], before the invasion of

---

9. al-Jabarti, *op. cit.*, 4:288.

10. [*Ibid.* (Tr.)]

11. Abdin Palace Archives, register no. 728 ("Turkish"), the Khedive Diwan, 7 Muharram 1235 A.H. [1819 A.D.].

12. [Sa'id Pasha was khedive of Egypt from 1854 to 1863. (Tr.)]

13. [Isma'il Pasha was khedive of Egypt from 1863 to 1879. (Tr.)]

14. Abdin Archives, order dated 18 Ramadan 1271 [1854 A.D.], register no. 1882, p. 426.

Syria by Ibrahim Pasha.[15] In this document, Muhammad `Ali recommended Copts, who wanted to make a pilgrimage to Jerusalem, to the commander of Gaza and ordered him not to allow anyone to interfere in their affairs.[16] Documents dated to 1827 and 1828 A.D. were addressed to the commanders of Gaza and Jerusalem. The pasha [or wali] requested protection from them for the Coptic monks and visitors who used to go to Jerusalem annually carrying boxes of candles to their church in Jerusalem. They were also to sustain and welcome them on their arrival in Gaza and Jerusalem.[17] Muhammad `Ali, a Muslim ruler, even granted some Coptic employees the title of "bey" and took Copts as his advisers.

Muhammad `Ali not only created an atmosphere of tolerance and improved the condition of Copts, but he occasionally took their side. In 1230 A.H. [1814 A.D.], during the mutiny by the Cairo garrison, Christians took refuge in their districts behind barricades, closed the street gates, and carried guns because great terror had taken hold of them. "And the pasha supplied them [the Christians] with powder and war equipment. They sought permission from Katekhda Bey[18] to block some lanes from where they might be attacked. Thus he protected them."[19]

In 1845 a quarrel erupted between a Muslim donkey driver and a Coptic farmer who called the donkey driver names. The latter complained to the authorities. The governor of Damietta ordered that the Copt be given five hundred lashes and paraded in the Christian district to humiliate him in public. When Muhammad `Ali heard of the incident, he sent one of his senior officers who sentenced the governor of Damietta to five years in the prison of the Abu Qīr citadel and fined him a large sum of money.[20]

---

15. [Ibrahim Pasha was the son of Muhammad `Ali. (Tr.)]

16. Abdin Palace Archives, register no. 19 ("Turkish"), dated 12 Sh`abān 1241 [1825 A.D.].

17. Abdin Archives, register no. 740 ("Turkish"), p. 4, dated 15 Sh`abān 1243 A.H., and, register no. 739, p. 56. dated 13 Ramadan 1244 A.H.

18. [Katekhda Bey is the title of Muhammad `Ali Pasha's deputy. The name of the deputy at the time was Laz Bey. See al-Jabartī, op. cit., 7:341, Cairo, 1967. (Tr.)]

19. al-Jabartī. op. cit., 4:226.

20. Paton, A. A., *A History of the Egyptian Revolution from the Period of the Mamlukes to the Death of Mohammed Ali, from Arab and European Memoirs, Oral Tradition and Local Research*. 2 vols. London: Trubner & Co., 1870, 2:236–37. [Paton related the story as follows: "On the day of the festival of the birth of the prophet, a poor old Copt, with a white beard, who worked in a rice threshing mill, fell into a dispute with a Moslem ass driver; and, after exchanging words, the ass

(continued...)

Besides this, the bishop of the Catholic Copts made a statement to Dr. J. Bowring to the effect that he used to move freely in the city, with a cross hung on his chest where all could see it, and no one tried to insult or humiliate him. He added that all Copts could practice their religion with complete freedom.[21]

The authorities used to respect Christianity. In 1225 A.H. [1810 A.D.], Muhammad `Ali, like Ibn Tulūn before him, ordered that people offer prayers to raise the water level of the Nile. "The Coptic Christians went out for this purpose and gathered on al-Roda [Island][22] with their priests and monks. They were riding horses, amblers, mules and donkeys decorated impressively, accompanied by a group from the entourage of the pasha carrying sticks decorated with silver."[23]

It is natural that those who had their own way of understanding things were uncomfortable with the change in how Christians were treated. al-Jabartī, who expressed to some extent the religious feelings of his co-religionists, has conveyed the stinging complaints of the people.

"They wrote messages to the leading multazimīn[24] saying that the effandina [the pasha or wali] had been informed about the injustice that the Copts had committed against the nultazimīn and the exorbitant interest that they had charged them. He [the pasha] was disappointed at this. `You are requested to come four days from now and to calculate

---

20(...continued)
driver went to the governor and complained that the Copt had turned the prophet and his religion into ridicule. Ali Bey caused the man to be brought to the court of justice, and, on this worthless testimony, he was condemned to receive 500 blows of the bastinado. After the man had received several hundred additional blows, a cross was tied on his back, and he was paraded on a buffalo through the town. The procession was then led through the Christian quarter. A shawl placed around the neck of the wretched man, and held on each side, hindered him from falling, for he was now more dead than alive; and at one place near the shore, boiling pitch was thrown on him by a boat calker, amid the applause of the mob. Mohammed Ali, on hearing of this event, sent to Damietta one of his chief officers, who condemned Ali Bey to five years' imprisonment in the fortress of Aboukir, as well as to pay a heavy fine. The Pasha also pensioned the unhappy wretch who had been the object of this outrage. Whatever defects might exist in the agricultural administration of Mohammed Ali, his punishment of fanatic violence was prompt and salutary." (Tr.)]

21. Bowring, J., *Report on Egypt and Candia*, p. 149.

22. [al-Roda is an island in the Nile across the river from Giza. The Nilometer was in Roda. (Tr.)]

23. al-Jabartī, *op. cit.*, 4:121–22.

24. [*Multazimīn* (sing. *multazim*): The holder of an *Iltizam*, which was an Ottoman system of tax-farming, paid fixed fees to the government for the right to collect taxes. This was usually applied to rural peasants, but could also be applied against urban taxes. (Tr.)]

your interest, so that you receive your reimbursement. The *effandina* is not pleased with injustice.' The papers carried the signature of the *defterdar*.[25] Many of the simple-minded people were pleased to hear about his [message] and they sent out rumors to the effect that stakes had been erected in front of the Shubra palace to impale Mu'allim Ghali and other notables of the Copts."[26]

Can one understand from this that Muhammad 'Ali was uninterested in religious affairs? No, because he rewarded converts to Islam by giving them money, appointing them to government jobs, and so on.[27] And he punished publicly those Muslims who apostatized.[28] But he did not attach the same importance to the [religious] differences which were deeply rooted in the old, fraying customs.

Despite the clear signs of tolerance that characterized Muhammad 'Ali's era, Christians were still unable to claim that they were equal to Muslims. Muhammad 'Ali urged the governor of Cairo, Colonel Sayf [later Sulayman Pasha[29]], to convert to Islam because a non-Muslim was not allowed to be army commander. Undoubtedly the governor knew that the time had not yet come to set aside old customs. al-Jabartī informs us that when Muhammad 'Ali eulogized a Christian *mubashir*, called Abboud, whom "the pasha liked and trusted, he had not appointed him to be the head of the department of finance out of fear of criticism."[30]

This outright confession defines accurately the position of the wali concerning the dhimmis. We should also note that even Muhammad 'Ali did not

---

25. [*Defterdar* is a Turkish word that refers to the director of the financial administration of a province. (Tr.)]

26. al-Jabartī, *op. cit.*, 4:221.

27. We mention here the order dated 1 Shawwal 1241 A.H. [1825 A.D.]: "Register no. 57, Turkish second grade officials [*saniya*], p. 34," and the order dated 7 Dhi al-Q'ida 1241 A.H.: "Register no. 21, Turkish first grade officials [*ma'iya*], p. 84."

28. W. E. Lane has noted that he met a Muslim woman in the street in Cairo who had apostatized and married a Christian. She had been condemned to death by drowning (*Manners and Customs of the Modern Egyptians*, p. 126).

29. [Sulayman Pasha al-Faransawī (1788–1860) was a French soldier who had joined the Egyptian army in 1819 as a trainer. It was he who established the first military school in Egypt at the request of Muhammad 'Ali. He converted to Islam and in time became the chief of staff of the Egyptian army, under the name Sulayman al-Faransawī. (Tr.)]

30. al-Jabartī, *op. cit.*, 4:303.

consider Copts anything but excellent *mubashireen* and *muhasibeen* [accountants]. He did not try to draft them into the regular army. However, the disinterest of the Copts in military service was apparent, and their hatred of life in military camps did not need to be proved. Nor did he offer them modern education. We note that the first educational mission [from Egypt] to France did not include Copts, although it included a number of other Christians [Melchites].

Briefly speaking, there is agreement among historians of this period that relations between Muslims and Copts were clearly better. But they have criticized the government for not acknowledging publicly the equality between Christianity and Islam sooner.

Foreign historians have described the reign of `Abbās Pasha[31] as regressive. The fact is that `Abbās Pasha I was anti-European more than anti-Christian. Although he laid off a large number of French employees, he appointed two ministers of foreign affairs of Armenian origin, Aram Bey and Estifan Bey. He also did not consider getting rid of the Coptic *mubashireen*. Some European historians have explained his hatred of Europeans by relating it to his distaste for Christians. But we have found no order issued by `Abbās Pasha that is antagonistic to Christians.

Credit for bringing Christians, especially Copts, into the mainstream of the Egyptian populace goes to Sa`īd Pasha[32] and Khedive Isma`īl. Sa`īd wanted the people to participate in government. He specifically wanted to lay the Turks off from civil and military jobs. His nationalistic speech to Egyptian officers near the end of his tenure had a great effect upon them. It is said that the speech led to their revolution under `Urabī Pasha.[33]

It was natural that Sa`īd maintain the tolerant spirit created by Muhammad `Ali towards Christians. He even eliminated the last hurdle in their way of being integrated into the main stream of the nation by his decree that accepted Christians into the army and applied the military service laws to them. He believed that if Christians carried arms in defence of their country, and were entrusted with the same responsibilities as Muslims, they would gain the same privileges enjoyed by their countrymen. The royal decree of [the month of] Jumada al-`Ula in 1272 A.H. [January 1856] stated that, in accord with the principle of equality, the sons of the Coptic notables would be called to arms on

---

31. [`Abbās Pasha ruled from 1848 to 1854. (Tr.)]

32. [Sā`id Pasha, 1854-1863. (Tr.)]

33. [Ahmad `Urabī Pasha was the leader of the 1881–82 rebellion which was put down by the British in 1882, thus inaugurating their occupation of Egypt which lasted until 1954. (Tr.)]

an equal footing with the sons of Muslim notables.[34] But the Copts, because authorities had exempted them from military service for generations, considered this measure to be a devious action that aimed at persecuting them. They readily complained to members of the British community, that is, to Protestant missionaries approved by the Coptic patriarch. These missionaries tried to exert pressure on the wali to exempt Copts from military service. The details of the problem were recounted by two contemporary English historians.[35] They state that the [military] draft was a tool for persecuting Christians who would then be exposed to all kinds of harassment after being drafted. They added that the intention was to force them to convert to Islam because being a Muslim was essential for promotion in the army. Patriarch Cyril IV,[36] nicknamed the legislator, sought the mediation of some British who succeeded in convincing Sa`īd to exempt Copts from the draft. But it seems that the patriarch paid dearly for his action because, it was rumored, it was by poisoning that he died shortly after that. In addition, Sa`īd laid off a large number of Coptic employees.

With the sources available at present, it is difficult to confirm or deny this account. That Copts suffered some injustices is probable since Muslims were not accustomed to considering Copts their equals, especially in the army. However, it is a fact that Copts became integrated in the army during the reign of Isma`īl. Although it is not difficult to prove the distaste of both Muslims and Copts for military service, both parties understood that they were equally subject to the draft. While the French writer Gabriel Charmes was talking to Khedive Isma`īl in the Abdin Palace, a squadron of palace guards passed by in front of the palace. Isma`īl told his interlocutor, "Look at this squadron. It includes Arabs and Copts, Muslims and Christians. They are walking in one line. I assure you that there is not one among them who cares for his neighbor's religion, and equality among them is complete."[37]

It was Sa`īd Pasha who first drafted Christians into the army on his own, before the sultan of Turkey accepted the demands of foreign states to issue his

---

34. Abdin Archives, register no. 505 ("Turkish"), no. 21.

35. Butcher, E. L., *The Story of the Church of Egypt*, London: Smith, Elder, Co., 1897. 2 vols., and Montague Fowler, *Christian Egypt, Past, Present, and Future*, London: Church Newspaper Co., 1901.

36. [Cyril IV (1854–61) was the 110th Coptic patriarch. (Tr.)]

37. Charmes, Gabriel, *Cinq mois au Caire et dans la Basse Égypte*. Paris: G. Charpentier, 1880, p. 162.

decree dated February 18, 1856.[38] Egypt was thus unaffected by the reform movement in Turkey, anticipating the issuance of orders from Istanbul to do the same.

After explaining certain points related to the drafting of Copts, we should exonerate Sa'īd Pasha from accusations of fanaticism. Have we not seen that during his reign some employees tried to strengthen their ties with him by not allowing the festivities which accompanied the conversion of a Copt to Islam? The wali wrote the following to the governor of Jirja concerning the matter:

"I have learned that because of the conversion of a Copt from Suhāj to Islam some people, along with some youngsters, gathered together and met with the qadi [judge]. They then accompanied the convert and paraded him through the streets and market places in a demonstration that expressed their pride in his conversion. Since this action disappointed both Copts and foreigners [Europeans] you are requested as soon as you receive this message to disperse the demonstration in order to reassure them. You are also requested to fire the mayor of the town because he allowed such a thing to happen. Although we appreciate you taking these measures, you should follow the instructions that require informing us in case such events take place in the future."[39]

In addition, Sa'īd Pasha was the one who alleviated the *jizyah* imposed on dhimmis in his royal decree of December 1855.[40] The historian Paul Merruau said,

"The distinctions created by Islam among different groups of people were actually eliminated after Sa'īd came to power. His tolerance was reflected in a series of actions that may take a long time to enumerate. He appointed a Christian as governor of the Sudan.[41] This was one of the measures that characterized his reign, forming a new step towards a tolerance that aimed at benefiting the country by employing all qualified

---

38. [The decree concerned the rights of religions minorities in the Ottoman empire. (Tr.)]

39. Abdin Archives, register no. 530 ("Turkish"), p. 8: a royal decree dated 15 Shawal [1279 A. H./1862 A.D.].

40. We shall study the problem of the *jizyah* later on.

41. The fact is that he appointed Arakil Bey as governor of Mus'awa [on the Red Sea], not of all the Sudan.

people of whatever religion. We would add to this that Sa'īd Pasha permitted the Egyptian Christian soldiers to practice their religion in public."[42]

Concerning Khedive Isma'īl, who was educated in Vienna and Paris, he found on his return to his country that the atmosphere was favorable for following a policy of tolerance on a large scale. Like his predecessors, he wanted to follow a policy that would prevent religious affairs from causing friction between the two communities [Muslims and Christians]. It was in response to a question from a high official that he clarified his plan in the royal decree issued when he came to power. In that communication dated Muharram 10, 1280 A.H. [1863 A.D.], he said:

> "Khalil Awad al-Hāwī, of al-Salmiyah, who is a Copt, has applied to abandon his Christian religion and convert to Islam, willingly and without pressure. In this case you should call a Coptic priest and some Coptic mayors, and have Khalil Awad al-Hāwī make his pronouncement in their presence to the effect that he is willing to convert to Islam without being pressured by anyone, in order that this matter not be a subject of complaint later on. After his pronouncement in front of them, they should approve his pronouncement which has to be kept in the archives of the governorate."[43]

Such well-defined procedures had not been followed earlier in Egypt. Procedures in such cases were very simple.

In addition, relations between the khedive and the Coptic patriarch were excellent. Qallīnī Fahmī Pasha mentions the following incident in his memoires:

> "When a redesigning of the streets of Cairo was being planned and Clott Bey street was to be opened, it was found that, in order for that street to be straight, it would cut through the Coptic church. Anba Demetrius, the patriarch[44] at the time, was offered a new and better church as well as a

---

42. Merruau, *L'Égypte Comtemporaine de Mehamet Ali à Sa'id Pacha*, Paris: Didied, 1858, pp. 43–44. [This work appeared in several editions. (Tr.)]

43. Abdin Archives, register no. 530 ("Turkish"), dated 20 Muharram 1280 A.H. [1863 A.D.].

44. [Demetrius II was the 111th Coptic patriarch, 1862–70. (Tr.)]

new and better building for the patriarchate, to be built by the government in return for his approval allowing the street to be built straight."

The patriarch responded by saying, "I regard it as an evil portent to destroy a church in order to make a road. I also find it improper for his highness the khedive to agree to this project." When the khedive was informed of the patriarch's statement, he said, "Let the patriarch's will be [respected] and let the church stand where it is."[45]

For the first time in history we find a Muslim ruler who morally and financially supported sectarian education. In his royal decree sent to the ministry of finance, the khedive granted financial aid to the Coptic Orthodox schools.

> "Because of information that we have about the good efforts of the Coptic patriarchate in establishing schools and training teachers to teach children what they need to know of various subjects and foreign languages, it deserves our thanks. In order to help it to do that, and to widen the circle of education taking place in its schools, we are permitted to generously give to the patriarchate as charity one thousand-five-hundred feddans of neglected and abandoned public land in the provinces which belong to the state."[46]

The khedive believed that Copts, as Egyptians, could stand on equal footing with Muslims. [On the other hand,] he was not pleased with those converted by the English and protestant missionaries. He even took the unusual step of giving the Coptic patriarch Demetrius a steamship in which to travel throughout the country to urge Copts to remain within the Coptic church.[47]

Later on, Isma'il publicly and officially acknowledged the equality between Copts and Muslims by allowing Copts to run for elections to the consultative council[48] and by appointing Coptic judges to the courts. When

---

45. Qallīnī Fahmī, *Mudhakkitat Qallīnī Fahmī*, Minia, Egypt: Matb'at Ṣadiq, 1951, 2:34.

46. Abdin Archives, register no. 1919 ("Arabic decrees"), dated 21 Rajab 1283 A.H. [November 30, 1866].

47. Qallīnī Fahmī, *Memoires*, 1:29.

48. [Also called the legislative assembly, "Majlis Shura al-Qawanīn," it was established in 1866. (Tr.)]

Khedive Isma'īl spoke to Nubār Pasha[49] about the election of consultative council representatives, he told him, "We also have Copts among the elected representatives. We have opened the doors for Muslims and Copts equally."[50] The law of 1866, which established the consultative council, did not distinguish between Muslims and Christians. The second article said, "Every person who is twenty-five or more can run, on condition that he is honest and sincere and the government has evidence that he was born in this country." In addition, because in its beginning the consultative council sought Khedive Isma'il's advice, the representatives unanimously agreed, when they discussed the education policy of the government, that government schools should accept the children of Muslims and Copts without distinction. One of the Muslim members [Muhammad Shawarbi] said on that occasion, "The Copts are the children of this country; therefore, if they desire to be enrolled, they should be enrolled in the schools of the provinces and not be excluded."[51]

We should never forget that Khedive Isma'īl was the first Muslim ruler to request the title of "pasha" for a Christian.[52] After the death of this sovereign, the Copts used to say that their condition under his rule was better than their condition under the British occupation. They also noted that, during the reign of Isma'īl, there were large numbers of them holding high offices. [For instance,] Wasif Azmī Pasha held a very important position. He was the chief of protocol [at the royal palace]. Although some have denied such claims, saying that the Copts held lesser positions than those mentioned, the Copts at least affirmed the extreme tolerance of the khedive. The French delegate to the Egyptian government, Sachot, wrote the following to Duruy, the French minister of education:

"The people of Egypt are not only Muslims! It is well-known that not a small number of them are Christian Copts. I take this opportunity to laud the religious tolerance prevailing all over the country, which hovers over

---

49. [Nubār Pasha (1825–99) was the adviser and foreign minister of Isma'īl Pasha, and later became prime minister. (Tr.)]

50. Abdin Archives, ("European section"), letter dated November 18, 1866, register no. 2/34.

51. al-Waqā'a al-Misriya, issue no. 49, dated the 16th of Sa'abān 1283 A.H. [1866 A.D.] (minutes of the meeting of the 28th of Rajab 1283).

52. This was for Nubār Pasha (1825–1899).

everyone without exception and honors the laws of the country and the good qualities of its people."[53]

The best evaluation of the situation was expressed by Isma'īl Pasha himself. He once said to Gabriel Charmes, "The Christians in Turkey live in an atmosphere of tolerance mixed with disdain, while in Egypt they live in an atmosphere of tolerance mixed with respect."[54]

The successors of Isma'īl held to this policy, and the minority considered their stay at the helm of the state as a safeguard for themselves [that would ensure their well-being]. At any rate, towards the end of the reign of Isma'īl a new force appeared on the scene, public opinion. At the time, national affairs came to be discussed heatedly in the press, at public meetings and in the consultative council. Although the executive authority was in control of all matters of importance to the state, frequently it had to consider this new force.

Now that we have explained the position of the rulers, it is appropriate to follow up on the reaction of public opinion.

Public Opinion and the Notables vis-à-vis the New Policy of the Rulers.

Throughout this chapter we have referred to al-Jabartī's criticisms of the procedures followed by Muhammad 'Ali in the interest of the Copts. We have also mentioned that [the character of] the available documents would not allow us to report only these criticisms. The travelers who spoke of the tolerance of Muhammad 'Ali used to note the situation without saying whether the majority had become accustomed to [the new] tolerance.

It is unreasonable to expect an immediate change in the mentality of people, or at least in the mentality of the enlightened class, following the order of Muhammad 'Ali. But based on some evidence, we can ascertain that relations between the two communities were clearly improved, and the principle of political and social equality gradually became familiar. Lady Duff Gordon once wrote,

"The people of Bibbeh,[55] most of whom are Muslims, elected Jirjis the Copt as the mayor of that town. . But what impressed me was the spirit of tolerance which I found everywhere. It seems that Muslims and Copts

---

53. Sachot, C., *Rapport adresseé à S. E. M. Victor Durny*, Paris, June 1869.

54. Charmes, *op. cit.*, p. 162. A large number of Copts settled in the Sudan during this period and made big fortunes. But al-Mahdi's revolution caused them irreparable damage.

55. [Bibbeh, or Beba, is a city in Upper Egypt. (Tr.)]

are perfectly on good terms. In Bibbeh, there are thirteen Coptic families among a very large number of Muslims, despite this the people elected Jirjis as their mayor. Some were kissing his hand in humility while we were passing in the village streets."[56]

What attracts one's attention is the presence of Christian premiers, such as Nubār Pasha and Boutros Ghali Pasha,[57] serving as representatives of the khedive at the celebration of the *mahmal*.[58] Judge Van Bemmelen said that the financial crisis which took place in the country before the dethroning of Isma'īl strengthened relations between the two communities. From the first day, the Egyptians—Muslims and Copts alike—shouldered the burden that had resulted from the non-payment of their exorbitant taxes. The brotherly feelings among the members of the two communities became stronger.[59]

The first test of this solidarity was 'Urābī Pasha's revolution[60] which broke out [in an effort] to terminate the control of the Circasian officers, to get rid of foreign controllers, and to elevate the Egyptian elements [within the government and army]. Did those hard times not offer a good opportunity for both Muslims and Copts to show their solidarity and cooperation? All observers agree in lauding the spirit of cooperation that had begun to spread before the bloody

---

56. [The exact words of Lady Duff Gordon are on p. 56 of the English edition, *Letters from Egypt 1862–69*, New York: Praeger, 1969: "The thing that strikes me most is the tolerant spirit that I see everywhere. They say, 'Ah! It is your custom,' and express no sort of condemnation, and Muslims and Christians appear perfectly good friends, as my story of Bibbeh goes to prove. I have yet to see the much-talked-of fanaticism, at present I have not met with a symptom of it. There were thirteen Copt families at Bibbeh and considerable Muslim population, who had elected Girgis their headman and kissed his hand very heartily as our procession moved through the streets. Omar said he was a very good man and much liked." The author Tagher has depended on the French edition. (Tr.)]

57. [Boutros Ghali (1846–1910) became finance minister in 1893, foreign affairs minister in 1894, and prime minister in 1908. He was assassinated by a young Muslim fanatic in 1910. For further information, see Doris Behrens-Abuseif, "Boutros Ghali," *The Coptic Encyclopedia*, 2:415–16. (Tr.)]

58. [*Mahmal* (lit. "litter") was a richly decorated camel litter of the kind that would normally carry an important personage who accompanied the yearly pilgrim caravan to Mecca from Cairo, and later from Damascus as well. The *mahmal* was an emblem of the state and its rulers. Princes sent it as a token to represent them at the standing on the day of 'arafāt during the pilgrimage. See Cyril Glassé, *The Concise Encyclopedia of Islam*, p. 247. (Tr.)]

59. Van Bemmelen, Pieter, *L'Égypte et l'Europe*, Leiden: E. J. Brill, 1882–84, 1:26.

60. [Ahmad 'Urābī Pasha (1841–1911) was the leader of the 'Urābī revolution of the Egyptian army against the khedive in 1881–82. (Tr.)]

events of June and July of 1882,[61] and had started even before the dethroning of Isma'īl in 1879. The petition that was submitted to the khedive requesting the removal of Rivers Wilson[62] and the formation of a national government, and calling for the consultative council to meet, was signed by army officers, notables, the Sheikh al-Islam [Sheikh al-Azhar], and the Coptic patriarch. Wilfred Scawen Blunt who witnessed these events unhesitatingly declared that relations between Muslims and Copts were never better than at that time.[63] But the presence of 'Urābī Pasha at the head of the rebels; the letter he sent to Gladstone[64] when the English were threatening Alexandria, warning of declaring *jihad* based on the Prophet Muhammad's instructions; the fall of the first British bomb on Alexandria;[65] and the supplying of arms to members of foreign communities to be used against Egyptians—all these factors affected the course of events. The demonstrators and the retreating forces [of 'Urābī] often confused foreigners with native Christians. Later 'Urābī accused the authorities of inciting the rebels to attack the Christian minority in order to degrade the 'Urābī movement which was directed against the khedive. It was rumored that Khedive Isma'īl moved the public [against Christians] and ordered and supported the killing of all Christians.[66] Whether these rumors were true or false, we cannot use them in our study except as indicators that some people were then trying to revive old views that were on their way out.

---

61. [For a detailed report of the events of June and July of 1882, whose origins go back as early as July 1879, see P. J. Vatikiotis, *The History of Egypt*, Baltimore: John Hopkins University Press, 1985, pp. 141–66. (Tr.)]

62. [Sir Rivers Wilson was a member of the commission of enquiry established by Khedive Isma'īl in January 1878 and became a cabinet minister in the cabinet formed by crown prince Tawfīq Pasha on March 10, 1879. See Vatikiotis, *op. cit.*, pp. 130, 133, 138–39. (Tr.)]

63. [Blunt, Wilfred Scawen, *Secret History of the English Occupation of Egypt*, New York: Alfred Knopf, 1922, p. 126. His exact words are, "The feeling at Cairo between native Christian and native Mohammedan was altogether friendly. The Copts were as a rule wholly with the revolution and their Patriarch was on the best terms with the ministry of which Butros Pasha was a prominent and respected member." (Tr.)]

64. [William Ewart Gladstone (1809–1898) was the British cabinet minister for colonial affairs during whose tenure England invaded Egypt (1882) and forced it to evacuate the Sudan in 1884–85. (Tr.)]

65. 'Urābī Pasha protested to M. Gregory, the correspondent of the London *Times*, against accusing him of fanaticism. But Mr. Blunt had noticed that the Egyptian leader had given his movement a deeper religious character than the sheikh of al-Azhar had done.

66. [But Isma'īl was not in power when the 'Urābī revolution broke out. He was in exile in Italy from 1879 to 1885. Could he have done this from exile? (Tr.)]

210

The rebellion of the Egyptian officers was followed by the British occupation, in other words, a Christian state occupying a Muslim country. During the occupation, the Copts held a conference in Assiut and submitted several requests in the name of the Coptic community.[67]

Some people began to talk about treason and the Christian minority attempting to exploit the presence of an European country for its own interests. The moderates were sorry for what the Copts had done in Assiut and said that they felt prey to a British conspiracy that aimed at dividing the country in order to rule it. However, there was no treason of any kind because the Copts, who hated the foreigners, were uncomfortable with the coming of the British. Lord Cromer himself tacitly acknowledged this.[68] Neither was there a conspiracy because the British themselves were surprised at the conference. Qallīnī Fahmī Pasha, who witnessed these events, ascertained that the one who had suggested the idea of a conference was Khedive Abbās II who wanted to cause trouble for the occupier.

The convening of the Assiut conference during the British occupation was just a coincidence because the Copts would never have hesitated to express their dissatisfaction with the progress of education in Egypt at the time. Why? Before we answer this question, we should go back to follow the sequence of events.

Egypt was then a relatively rich country undergoing a modernization process to make use of the qualifications of educated young people. Until the time

---

67. [The Coptic conference was held in Assiut, Upper Egypt, on March 6–8, 1911, a year after the assassination of the Coptic prime minister Boutros Ghali. The conference was held in spite of the opposition of the Coptic patriarch and many other Coptic notables. Many Coptic politicians were in attendance. The discussions in the conference resulted in a petition detailing Coptic demands that was presented to the khedive and the British. The demands were not new. The petition asked for better representation, equal access to civil service positions, designation of Sunday as a holiday, equal access to state education and the introduction of Christian religious instruction in state schools. See B. L. Carter, *The Copts in Egyptian Politics*, London: Croom Helm, 1986, pp. 13–14, 25, 51; and Samira Bahr, *Copts in Egyptian Politics* ("al-Aqbāṭ fi al-Ḥayāt al-Siyasiyah al-Misriyah"), Cairo: Anglo Bookshop, 1979, pp. 59–67 (in Arabic).

The Muslim response to the Coptic congress was to hold the Islamic [Egyptian] congress in Heliopolis April 29–May 4, 1911, under the sponsorship of Muhammad Riyād Pasha, the prime minister at the time, and the Ummah and National parties. The congress's organizing committee reported its conclusions that the Copts were planning to form "a separate nation for themselves" and that their grievances were unfounded. In a speech in May 1980, President Anwar Sadat repeated what was said in that congress when he accused the Coptic patriarch of instigating religious strife and planning a separate state for Copts, and ordered him put under house arrest in a desert monastery. See President Sadat's speech delivered on the occasion of the tenth anniversary of the Corrective Revolution, May 14, 1980, Cairo: State Information Service, 1980; and Samirah Bahr, "Egyptian Conference of Heliopolis," *The Coptic Encyclopedia*, 3:948, and "Coptic Congress of Asyūt," *Ibid.*, 2:602–3. (Tr.)]

68. Lord Cromer, *Modern Egypt*, 2:210.

of Tawfīq Pasha[69] the country needed employees to run its affairs because students, who had graduated from the schools established by Muhammad 'Ali and improved by Ismā'īl, were not enough to meet the needs of the country. There were enough jobs for all graduates and no one objected to the right of anyone else to hold a job. Thus the Copts were in a position to manage the finances of the country alone, without a partner.

But the debts contracted by Ismā'īl Pasha created a serious financial crisis. The repayment of these debts exhausted government revenues. It was natural that the government could not support a large army or keep needed employees. The khedive laid off hundreds of army officers. For the students' part, they dropped out [of school] before completing their education in order to get government jobs, and found difficulties.

Besides, since the Islamic invasion, Copts had been able to monopolize the financial management of the country, thanks to their personal method of accounting which they kept secret among themselves. The duke d'Harcourt stated that:

"their unique calculating genius made them use figures according to methods that they had learned since childhood, making very complex calculations based on 1/24, 1/3, 1/4, 1/2, 1/24 out of 1/24. It is difficult for us to follow their method of calculation because they conduct it with great speed, using certain ambiguous abbreviations which are recorded on paper. Undoubtedly we can reach the accurate solution faster than they do by using the methods of calculation followed in Europe. But because their methods are based on measurements in use in the country and because they do not use the decimal fraction system, their speed in their calculations exceeds ours. Due to these complex methods of calculation known to them alone, the Arabs [Muslims] have become dependent on them. Although the Copts have had to acknowledge the supremacy of the Europeans, they continue to have the upper hand in the eyes of the Muslim nationals."[70]

The education inspector at the time, Dor Bey, once believed that he might discover in the Coptic schools a special curriculum for teaching mathematics. But he later stated that:

---

69. [Tawfiq Pasha was khedive of Egypt, 1879–92. (Tr.)]

70. d'Harcourt, *L'Égypte et les Égyptiens*, pp. 57–58.

"there is nothing of the sort. The Coptic children have acquired a skill in arithmetic through practical exercises when accompanying their fathers to government offices, sitting by their side or at their feet, and beginning to practice those methods. Later they entered the government service, [initially] without pay."[71]

These remarks were valid until the time of the British occupation. When the British started to reform governmental ways of doing business, they prevented the children from accompanying their parents to their offices, became strict about hiring graduates and, when the [British] spread education among the people, the Copts felt that they were going to lose their privilege of managing the financial affairs of the country which had enabled them, until that time, to lead an affluent life. The Egyptian writer Tawfīq Habīb offers the same explanation in the introduction to his report about the Assiut conference.

> "The rulers used to devote public positions to certain groups of people, either out of necessity or personal preference. For example, we have found that all rulers and walis before Muhammad 'Ali, and even he himself and some of his successors, had given Copts most government jobs in Cairo and the provinces. They also gave the Turks the military and leadership positions. If you read the Muslim historians you rarely find a Muslim name in government posts, except in Islamic legal positions."[72]

The writer also quotes Lord Cromer who said, "When England occupied Egypt, all the Egyptian interests were in the hands of the Copts."[73] The occupation

---

71. Dor, *L'Enseignment en Égypte*, p. 183.

72. Tawfīq Habīb, *Report on Assiut Coptic Conference*, Cairo, 1911, p. 2 (in Arabic).

73. Cromer, *op. cit.*, 2:210. Cromer's statement is as follows: "When the English took Egyptian affairs in hand, the accountants in the employment of the Egyptian government were almost exclusively Copts. Their system of accounts was archaic. Moreover, it was well-nigh incomprehensible to any but themselves. All tendencies in the direction of reform were resisted, partly from conservatism, and partly from instincts of self-preservation, for it was clear that if the system were simplified to such an extent as to be comprehensible to the uninitiated, the monopoly, which the copts had heretofore enjoyed, would be endangered. Finding that he could not untie the knot, the Englishman, with characteristic energy, cut it. The Coptic system of accounts had manifestly to be abolished, and as the Copts either could not or would not assist in the work of abolition, they had to give way to other agents. In the early days of the English occupation a good many Syrians, therefore, took the places of Copts. The reform was necessary, but it naturally caused much dissatisfaction amongst the Coptic community."

helped Syrian Christians and Muslims and prepared them to take over clerical and accounting positions and others which had been a monopoly for the Copts. The British occupation eliminated the monopoly of the Copts on some positions."

It was not the British occupation that eliminated the Copts' monopoly on accounting positions, due to their ancient methods. What in fact eliminated the monopoly was the introduction of new methods. To quote P. N. Hamont, "The Copts in fact rejected every system that would help to facilitate administrative work. They lived in chaos and benefitted from disorder."[74]

No one can blame them for defending their only source of livelihood—according to their own belief—in every possible way. But one can blame them for maintaining their archaic way of thinking in an age of progress and civilization. We refer to an official document that reveals the intention of Muhammad ʿAli to appoint a French expert to reorganize the finances of the country following the assassination of Muʿallim Ghali.[75]

In fact the Copts were more concerned about their future than their present condition following the British occupation. They were not right when they complained to Lord Cromer and when they held the conference in Assiut to exchange ideas about their fears. The surest proof for what we say are the statistics that Sir Eldon Gorst,[76] the British high commissioner, sent to his government in his report of 1911.[77] The statistics indicate that the Copts, who comprised not more than 10% of the population, held 45.32% of all government jobs and earned 40% of the salaries, while the Muslims' share was 44% and foreigners' was 6%.

Was the employment problem the only reason for the dissatisfaction of the Copts? No, because one cannot discount the psychological factor. If we look deeper into the matter, we realize that the anger of the Copts was to a great extent similar to the anger of ʿUrābī Pasha and his companions. Judge Van Bemmelen analyzed accurately ʿUrābī's position. We would not be incorrect if we equated the dissatisfaction of the Copts to the reasons for the dissatisfaction which led to ʿUrābī's revolution. Van Bemmelen wrote,

---

74. Hamont, *L'Égypte sous la direction de Mohamed Ali*, 1:343.

75. An order of Muhammad ʿAli to Ibrahim Pasha dated 15 Shʿabān 1237 A.H. (May 7, 1822). See Georges Talamas, *Recueil de la Correspondance de Mohamed Aly, Kedive d'Égypte*, Cairo, 1913, p. 33.

76. [British high commissioner of Egypt (1908–1911). (Tr.)]

77. [The report was dated March 25, 1911. The full text of this report can be found in Kyriakos Mikhail, *Copts and Muslims under British Rule*, London: Smith & Elder, 1911, ch. 5. (Tr.)]

"In spite of the progress achieved by the Egyptians,[78] they were less satisfied than they had been in the past. What has happened to them is what happens to an unjustly treated people whose conditions improve and their shackles are removed; the result is that the people grumble instead of being grateful. In fact, in this case we feel our severe pains, and the yoke which we still carry, and we become very eager to possess the things of which we have gained a small part. We used to submit in the past out of habit to the unavoidable and to our predestined fate. But if experience indicates that we can free ourselves from these restrictions, we would impatiently seek complete and urgent freedom. While we did not have the courage in the past to demand anything, our courage increases by achieving our demands, and our desire becomes stronger as related to what we dare to demand."[79]

The Copts did not express their discontent before 1908 when their notables submitted a petition to Mustafa Fahmī Pasha[80] and Lord Cromer in which they requested complete equality as it related to being appointed to administrative jobs, closing the courts on Sunday, appointing an additional member to the consultative council, and teaching Christianity to Christian students in government schools.

The authorities responded favorably to the second and third requests, and entertained the other two requests in their discussions. The newspapers *al-Mu'ayyad*, led by Sheikh 'Ali Yusūf, and *al-Liwā'*, the national party newspaper, welcomed the step towards social equality. But *al-Liwā'* published an article by Sheikh Abdul Aziz Jawīsh, entitled "Islam is a Stranger in its Home," that ignited a heated controversy between Islamic and Coptic newspapers.[81]

During that period Mustafa Fahmī Pasha resigned as prime minister and was replaced by Boutros Ghali Pasha on November 13, 1908. We need only say

---

78. Replace the word "Egyptians" with the word "Copts."

79. Van Bemmelen, *op. cit.*, 2:226.

80. [He was prime minister during the reigns of the khedives Tawfīq and Abbās II. Fahmī was a strong supporter of British interests in Egypt. He died in 1914. (Tr.)]

81. [For the text of Jawīsh's article and the furor that it caused among Copts, see Muhammad S. Kilanī, *al-Adab al-Qibtī*, Cairo: al-Dar al-Qawmiyah, 1966, ch. 5, pp. 70–119. This section of the book reports carefully about Muslim–Coptic relations as reflected in the Egyptian press between 1906 and 1911. (Tr.)]

that the new prime minister was coolly received. Muhammad Farīd Bey[82] made a sarcastic remark in one of his [newspaper] articles that Boutros Ghali Pasha was the only minister who had no college degree and concluded by saying that the new prime minister would be evaluated in the light of his actions.

The Copts were happy with the appointment of Boutros Ghali Pasha as prime minister and stopped grumbling, setting great hopes on his appointment. One Copt who visited the new prime minister told him, "God willing, you will look into our old requests and help us to gain equality during your tenure." But Boutros Ghali Pasha, a seasoned politician who was more concerned about the interests of the Coptic community than anyone else, interrupted him by saying, "I do not intend to interfere in this matter. Avoid hoping too much at present."

But Boutros Ghali Pasha signed the Sudan Agreement[83] with the British. As a result, he was assassinated by a young member of the national party. We can imagine the anger and frustration of the Copts over the incident. The most moderate among them were ready to agree to the most extreme suggestions.

A young orator had appeared some years before on the political scene. He had studied in universities in Egypt and France, and he foresaw the dangers that would result from the antagonism between the two communities. Because he was a sincere nationalist, he realized that the time had passed for religious controversies. The Egyptian nation had also sensed during the British occupation that it was not wise to engage in useless arguments that might divert the attention of public opinion from important matters. The populace also realized [generally] that antagonism between Muslims and Copts would only invite the occupying power to become more firmly established.

The young man was Mustafa Kamil, founder of the national party.[84] He was the first to bring Muslims and Copts together under the banner of nationalism.

---

82. [An Egyptian national party leader (1868–1919), Farīd became head of the national party after Mustafa Kamil's death in 1908, over the objections of Kamil's family. His attacks on the Copts and his support for Turkey were not well received domestically. It was a member of Muhammad Farīd's party, "Ibrahim al-Wirdani" who assassinated Boutros Ghali the prime minister in 1910. Farīd was sentenced to six months imprisonment for publishing seditious material, and he subsequently left Egypt. (Tr.)]

83. [The author refers to the Anglo-Egyptian Condominium Agreement of 1899 which outlined the administration of the Sudan. According to this agreement the Sudan was nominally under Egyptian sovereignty and was run virtually as a British colony. (Tr.)]

84. [Mustafa Kamil (1874–1908) was a leader of the modern Egyptian nationalist movement. He was a noted orator and founded the national party which under his leadership adopted pan-Islamic and pro-Turkish policies. After Kamil's break with the khedive in 1904, his main political dream was to win Egypt's independence from all forms of foreign control. (Tr.)]

He recruited to his movement a large number of Coptic notables, among whom were Wisa Wasif and Marcos Hanna Pasha who later played very important political roles. We quote the following two sentences from speeches of Mustafa Kamil: "The Muslims and Copts are one and the same people who are tied together by national customs, morals and livelihood, and they can never be separated."[85] "Copts are our partners in our fatherland."

When Mustafa Kamil died in his prime, all Egypt mourned him, The following words of Marcos Hanna Pasha sample what was said in eulogizing him:

> "The [one who is] mourned outlined a national unity and showed us the road to fraternity and liberty. Young Egyptians know that they are young Egyptians and their chief duty is serving Egypt and Egyptians, without discrimination. This is the edifice and work of Mustafa Kamil. It is time for us to reap the fruits of his work because national unity is the first step towards achieving freedom and independence."[86]

But there was a point in the national party's program that dampened the Copts' enthusiasm for it. Mustafa Kamil persisted in his support of the [religious] rights of Muslims alone because he believed in an official religion of the state. He also could not hide his interest in reviving the policy of pan-Islamism. Therefore the Copts could not approve all points of his political program.

At any rate, the relations between the Copts and Muhammad Farīd Bey, the successor of Mustafa Kamil, soon deteriorated. Muhammad Farīd was a sincere patriot but lacked flexibility. Consequently, he lost the support of the Copts for his party. He received the appointment of Boutros Ghali Pasha with coolness and, upon the assassination of the latter, said nothing that expressed his sorrow. When he lost all hope of gaining the support of the Copts he viciously attacked them. He later retreated when he learned that the murderer [of Boutros Ghali] had acted out of political and not religious impulses. But the Copts were unwilling to accept this interpretation and denounced the policy of the national party, requesting that their co-religionists boycott the party's activities.

Under these circumstances, had the Assiut congress ignited the desire [of Muslims] to seek revenge? Because of this likelihood, a large number of Coptic notables disapproved of the convening of the congress. They were led by the Coptic patriarch and Wasif Ghali Pasha, the son of Boutros Ghali. Wasif Ghali

---

85. [Excerpt from a speech delivered in Alexadria on June 8, 1897. (Tr.)]

86. [Excerpted from a speech eulogizing Mustafa Kamil that was also quoted in Fathī Radwān's "Mustafa Kamil," *Dar al-Ma`ārif*, 1974 (Iqr`a, 390, Dec. 1974), pp. 257–58. (Tr.)]

wrote on January 23, 1911, in the French newspaper *La Reform*, that mutual understanding among the two communities could be complete, and he issued a call for national unity in facing the future.

Concerning the demands agreed to in the Assiut congress, they were no different from those submitted to Mustafa Fahmī Pasha and Lord Cromer. Those demands had included (1) Sunday holiday, (2) equality in employment, (3) representation of Christians in the parliamentary organizations, (4) education in the provinces [5% tax would support Coptic schools in the provinces], and (5) equal spending from the state treasury on all Egyptian public services.

The Islamic congress held in Heliopolis at the behest of Sir Eldon Gorst, and under the sponsorship of Riad Pasha, protested the attempt of the Copts "to divide the Egyptian nation as one political unit into two religious groups, a Muslim majority and a Coptic minority."[87]

The conferees played the tune of political unity in the nation and were thus able to overcome their adversaries [the Copts]. The report of the organizing committee of the conference reads:

> "This division [into religious factions] results in dividing the political organization along religious lines, i.e., dividing the organizations into parts with different natures. Every nation has an official religion [established church] that is both necessary and constitutes one of its characteristics. The religion of any nation is the religion of its government, the religion of the majority. It is incomprehensible that a nation would have more than one official religion. Therefore it is meaningless to acknowledge the existence of religious minorities that work in the field of politics as such and thereby gain public rights beyond practicing its religion according to the principle of freedom of religion. How can we accept that a religious minority as such participate in public affairs and have its own special goals, as if it were a political minority? We cannot accept that [arrangement] unless the nation has two religions at one time and religion becomes the basis of public interests. It is wrong to recognize that the nation as a political unit consists of religious groups."[88]

---

87. The conference proceedings, Cairo: N.P., 1911, p. 5 (in Arabic).

88. [Minutes of the proceedings of the First Egyptian Conference assembled at Heliopolis April 29–May 4, 1911, Alexandria, 1911, pp. 5–6 (in Arabic). This same text was quoted by B. L. Carter, *op. cit.*, p. 14, as follows: "The principle is found that every country should have an established
(continued...)

We need not mention the responses of the Heliopolis conference to the demands of the Assiut meeting since we have mentioned the principles followed by the Islamic conference. The vehemence of the arguments between the two groups dissipated after the Heliopolis conference. Although both parties were not satisfied, they tried to put the past behind them.

It did not take long before the peace conference held in Paris[89] acknowledged the rights of Britain in Egypt. In its wake, all the Egyptian nationalists moved to protest the acknowledgement. At this point Sa`ad Zaghlul,[90] leader of the nationalist movement, realized that it was dangerous to alienate the Copts from participating in a movement whose success depended on the unity of the nation. He often stated that Egypt was for Muslims as well as Copts, and all enjoyed equally the same freedoms and rights. Significantly, while Mustafa Kamil had been an Egyptian nationalist who called for pan-Islamism, Sa`ad Zaghlūl was simply an Egyptian nationalist. It is not surprising, then, that Copts enthusiastically joined Sa`ad Zaghlūl's movement. We can be sure that they complemented their Muslim compatriots in their nationalistic feelings and had the realization of national hopes as their goal. About this movement, the Egyptian historian M. Sabry said:

"The Copts, according to the *Morning Post* of April 9, 1919, were more royalist than the king. They were the most enthusiastic people in defending nationalistic ideals, and they were the first to die for independence. Coptic priests were calling for love from the pulpits and in the mosques and in al-Azhar itself. The sheikhs and the ulama were giving speeches in the churches. It was most impressive to see flags with

---

88(...continued)
church and that such a religion will be that of the government or the majority. . . . That a state should have more than one religion is perfectly unthinkable and it would be absurd to admit that religious minorities can exist animated by political ambitions towards the exercising of public rights other than those of an essentially religious nature that are guaranteed by freedom of worship. The religion of the Egyptian people is Islam. For Islam is both the religion of the government and that of the majority." (Tr.)]

89. [The conference of Paris was the meeting for framing the treaties which ended WW I, held in Paris 1919–1920. (Tr.)]

90. [Sa`ad Zaghlūl (1854–1927) was the founder of the *Wafd* party and leader of the 1919 revolution. He served as prime minister from Jan. 1934 to Nov. 1924. (Tr.)]

the crescent embracing the cross. These events constituted a political as well as a religious revolution."[91]

The Legal Recognition of Political and Social Equality.

It is an absolute fact that Muhammad `Ali created a new social atmosphere. His successors [largely] followed his lead and completed the work that he had begun. This tolerance did not take long to be reflected in an individual's public life and to affect the laws of the country. Thus the principle of complete equality between Muslims and non-Muslims achieved victory within less than a century.

The first legal aspect of this principle [of tolerance] was the abolishing of the *jizyah* imposed upon dhimmis. Muhammad `Ali had never intended to abolish the *jizyah*, because it was a source of income for the treasury, despite the Gülhane decree of 1839 which included the abolition of this tax. This decree remained merely a piece of paper throughout the Ottoman empire. However, the *jizyah* which the Copts paid in the era of Muhammad `Ali was nothing compared to the salaries that they received from the jobs they held in the government. Taking the fiscal year 1832 A.D./1249 A.H. as an example, we find that the *jizyah* paid by Copts was 600 *keyse*[92] [3,000 Egyptian Pounds] while they received salaries of twenty-thousand *keyse* [100,000 Egyptian Pounds].[93]

On the other hand, when Muhammad `Ali continued collecting the *jizyah*, his goal was to increase the revenues of the state and not to humiliate his dhimmi subjects. Nevertheless, Muhammad `Ali was the first Muslim ruler who publicly opened the door of favoritism not only for notables but also for individuals of the general public who had rendered significant services to him. Thus, when he appointed one hundred Copts, who had proved to be efficient, to work in the shipyard of Alexandria, he ordered their exemption from paying the *jizyah*. The decree issued on the 22nd of Rabi`a al-`Akhar 1252 A.H. [May 1836] read, "This decree mandates abiding by the rules concerning specifying the salary and the

---

91. Sabry, M., *La Revolution égyptienne d'aprés des documents authortiques*, Paris; J. Vrin, 1919–21. 1:38.

92. [*Keyse* is a Turkish word meaning a small bag, a purse containing the sum of money of 500 piasters. (Tr.)]

93. Bowring, *op. cit.*, pp. 44–45.

rank of the Copts who are drafted to serve the government, who should be taken care of, and whose welfare should be ensured according to this decree."[94]

The *jizyah* was abolished for good by Sa`īd Pasha in 1272 A.H. [1855 A.D.]. It is understood that a decree was issued before that date which showed that Sa`īd Pasha had never been strict in collecting this tax. For he relinquished collecting an unpaid fifteen thousand pounds.[95] The decree of 21 Safar 1272 A.H. [1855 A.D.] expressed the desire of the wali [that a tax collector] be friendly with the dhimmis who were under his care. The decree also abolished the *jizyah*,[96] and the matter was not brought up again during the reign of Isma`īl.

It was natural, after the restrictions of *jizyah* and attire were dropped, that the dhimmis were gradually dealt with on an equal footing with Muslims. In fact, when the khedives introduced the constitutional system in Egypt they had to consider the dhimmis as an integral part of the state, and had to recognize that their rights and privileges were similar to those of the Muslims.

The fifth article of the political program created by W. S. Blunt and published by the London *Times* on January 1, 1882, says,

> "The National Party is a political not a religious party. It consists of men who belong to different religions and sects. Most of them are Muslims because ninety percent of the Egyptians are Muslims. All Christians and Jews and everyone who tills the land of Egypt and speaks its language is a member of that party which does not consider religious differences, and knows that all are brothers and are equal in their political and legal rights."

Other constitutions were clearer and more candid concerning this matter. For example, (1) there was a reform proposal submitted by the Association of the Egyptian Young Men in 1879 to his highness Tawfīq Pasha the khedive of Egypt. This project suggested a "complete equality among all Egyptians before the law,

---

94. Abdin Archives, register no. 74 ("Turkish"), document no. 910: a letter from Muhammad `Ali to Habib Effendi, dated 22 Rabi`a al-Thani 1252. The Copts had specialized in ship-building for a long time previous. Abdul Aziz Ibn Marwān (65–86 A.H./685–705 A.D.) sent three-thousand Copts to do such work in Tunis. [For additional information see "Ummayad Fleet." *The Coptic Encyclopedia*, 7:2286. (Tr.)]

95. Abdin Archives, register no. 1880 ("Arabic"), document no. 57: royal decree to the minister of finance, dated 29 Rabi`a al-Thani 1271 A.H. [1854 A.D.].

96. Abdin Archives, register no. 1883, document no. 8: a royal decree, dated 21 Safar 1272 A.H. [1855 A.D.].

and that they are all entitled to hold all positions in the government without discrimination because of national origin."[97] (2) A project to produce an Egyptian constitution [it was widely believed to have been written by Lord Cromer] was dated in 1908 and suggested that "all the subjects of the khedive are Egyptians regardless of their religion or creed."[98] (3) The electoral and statute law enacted July 21, 1913, however, reflected the restlessness that had prevailed since convening the Assiut and Heliopolis conferences. The law mandated the appointment of four Coptic members of parliament among the fifteen appointed members. Lord Kitchener[99] wrote to his government on July 6, 1913, and commented on this provision: "Mandating the representation of minorities is a sure proof that the government desires granting all the social groups this kind of representation which is their absolute right."

Some members of the committee formed to draft the general principles of the 1922 constitution raised the problem of relative representation of all religious denominations. The supporters of this view were confident that, if they ensured the permanent representation of religious minorities in the national assembly, it would be a way of preventing the British from interfering in the internal affairs of Egypt by claiming that they had to protect minorities. This would also maintain the regulations of the statute laws [already] in effect [since 1913]. Although some Muslim and Coptic members supported the principle, the majority strongly opposed it and it was dropped. Qallīnī Fahmī Pasha tells us in his memoires that King Fouad strongly opposed relative representation based on religion, despite being religiously tolerant all his life. He believed that this method of representation would perpetuate the old schisms that would result in weakening the national unity.

However, the 1922 constitution stipulated that all Egyptians are equal regardless of their religion or beliefs. It also stipulated their freedom to practice their religion and to accept appointment to government positions, and so on. It became traditional that a Coptic minister be appointed to the cabinet.[100] Thus,

---

97. A booklet published in Alexandria, pp. 33–34. N.D., N.P.

98. [The project was called *Project for an Egyptian Constitution*, but the author Tagher does not identify it further by mentioning a source. (Tr.)]

99. [Horatio Hubert Kitchener, an Earl (1850–1916), was high commissioner in Egypt from 1911 to 1914. (Tr.)]

100. [President Hosni Mubarak has appointed three Coptic ministers to the present Egyptian cabinet (1991). (Tr.)]

after efforts that lasted for a century, the constitution came to crown the works of the dynasty of Muhammad ` Ali.

Chapter 12

THE ODYSSEY OF THE COPTS

The Role of the Coptic Patriarch under Islamic Rule.

Just after the splendid welcome that the Coptic patriarch received from his followers, following the Arab invasion of Egypt, he became a source of concern to `Amr ibn al-`Āṣ, and all other walis after him. They recognized the extent of the authority of this religious leader and they immediately put him under close supervision, requesting that he submit to the legitimate authority [of the state]. In other words, they prevented him from pursuing any measure, even in the religious arena, without their permission.

The rulers first tried to establish the practice of approving the election of the patriarch and they ordered him to register his name in the diwan[1] before he undertook his job. [In one instance,] a Catholic deacon called Jirjis was able to be elected to the patriarchal throne during `Abd al-Aziz ibn Marwān's reign, an action done with the support of some bishops from Alexandria. But the Copts objected to the validity of his election because he was not elected on a Sunday. `Abd al-Aziz took an interest in the problem and immediately sent soldiers to keep order. He then invited the two conflicting parties to appear before him.[2] `Abd al-Aziz grew especially concerned when he had arrived in Alexandria [for the hearing]. The new patriarch did not welcome him, using the pretense that the wali's arrival time had not been announced. [The historian] Sawirus accuses the Melchites of causing `Abd al-Aziz's anger. In any event, the latter delivered the patriarch to his soldiers and ordered them not to release him until he paid a fine of one hundred thousand dinars.[3] In the aftermath, the wali sought always to put the patriarch at his beck and call and to have him in his retinue on all his journeys. It is said that `Abd al-Aziz ordered that a church be built in Helwan so that he could closely monitor the patriarch's movements.[4]

This practice developed into law by 184 A.H. [779 A.D.]. Sawiris ibn al-Muqaffa` recounts that after the bishops in Alexandria had convened a council [in that year] and selected a candidate for the position of patriarch, they returned to Cairo to meet the wali. When he saw them he asked, "What do you need?" Anba

---

1. [Diwan (or divan) is the state council, the royal court. (Tr.)]

2. Sawirus, *op. cit.*, p. 130.

3. *Ibid.*, p. 126.

4. Amélineau, É., "Vie d'Isaac," *Journal Asiatique*, 1885.

Michael told him, "We want to inform your highness that our religious leader has passed away and we want to appoint another to replace him to manage the affairs of the church and the people." When the wali asked them about the name of the candidate, they said, "Morcos." The wali then directed that the name be registered in the diwan and gave them permission to elect him in the place of the former patriarch Yuhanna. The name of the wali was al-Layth ibn Fadl. The biographies of the patriarchs describe him as being king to the Copts and also rehearse the first visit of a Coptic patriarch to the civil authority as follows: "The patriarch Anba Morcos came to Fustāt to greet the wali. When he arrived in Misr, Father Michael the [local] bishop, and the Copts were informed of his arrival. They went out to receive him, carrying Bibles, crosses and incense burners. They received him with great joy, praising God and reading homilies. They kept saying, 'yes, it is wonderful that you have come to us, Morcos, son of Morcos.' Afterwards he went home to rest because it was late. The next day the patriarch, Bishop Michael and the rest of the bishops gathered together to have an audience with the wali. When they reached his residence they sought permission to enter, and he invited them in. When the patriarch entered, he greeted the wali and wished him a long life. The wali asked him to be seated and spoke to him as an equal."[5]

The patriarchs had thought that, after the Arab invasion, they could continue their religious relations with monophysites living abroad. During the reign of 'Abd al-Aziz ibn Marwān it happened that the patriarch wrote to the kings of Ethiopia and Nubia [who were both Christian and belonged to the Coptic patriarchate of Alexandria] urging them to make peace and to settle the disputes between them. Spies reported this incident to the wali who became so angry that he ordered the execution of the patriarch. But the Coptic scribes—who at that time had control of the administration of the country—sought to prevent such a catastrophe. They immediately wrote letters, which were completely different from those given to the delegates traveling to Ethiopia, and withdrew the ones written by the patriarch. Then they informed the wali of the arrival of the delegates with the letters that they were to carry to Ethiopia. 'Abd al-Aziz summoned them immediately and seized the letters that they were carrying. When he read the letters, he found no mention of what was told to him, that is, no call for peace directed to the two Christian kings. His anger dissipated and he allowed the patriarch to return to Alexandria.[6]

---

5. Sawirus, *op. cit.*, pp. 238–39.

6. Ibn al-Rahib, op. cit. pp. 122–23.

In 71 A.H. [691 A.D.] patriarch Sam'ān received a messenger from India[7] who asked that he appoint a bishop and a priest. Because the patriarch knew the attitudes of the wali, he held off responding to the request until he had obtained permission from the government. But the messenger could not wait, and he directed his request to a bishop who granted his wish. This action led to the worst of results, as historians have noted.[8] Moreover, the position of the patriarch remained vacant for three years after the death of Patriarch Sam'ān.

The power of the patriarch was gradually diminished by the consolidation of the Arab empire. This religious leader became a mere tool in the hands of the rulers who used him according to their personal wishes, despite the titles that were given him by the Fatimid walis or Mamlūk sultans. In fact, the patriarch did not enjoy the supreme position in the Coptic community, a status reserved for the Copt in charge of the financial affairs of the state, particularly the one who enjoyed the confidence of the rulers.

Toward the end of the nineteenth century, this status difference between the two [the leading religious and civil personalities] was the cause behind a serious clash between patriarch Cyril V and a group of notables led by Boutros Ghali Pasha, then the leader of the Coptic community. The patriarch was opposed to a reform movement spearheaded by the Tawfīq society[9] that aimed at introducing modern methods of teaching into Coptic schools. Boutros Pasha succeeded in securing the khedive's permission to exile the patriarch. Despite the great respect that Copts had for their religious leader, they were not much moved when they saw the venerable old man on his way into exile under police escort.

However, we cannot deny the important role played by the Coptic patriarch following the Arab invasion. We shall discuss later his various endeavors in the interest of Muslim Egypt. It is worth mentioning that the Mamlūk emirs sought his assistance in collecting taxes owed by Copts. It seems that he did a good job and that [through the years] the rulers were satisfied with his efforts.[10]

---

7. The Ethiopians who lived in Palestine were known as Indians, which is not a clear term. See Kammerer, *La Mer Rouge*, vol.1, 3rd part, pp. 273–74.

8. [The most serious result was that the rulers tightened censorship over the Coptic patriarch in his relationship with his fellow monophysites. (Tr.)]

9. [See Fuad Megally and Sulaymān Nāsīm, "Benevolent Societies, Coptic," in *The Coptic Encyclopedia*, 2:374–75. (Tr.)]

10. `Ali Mubarak, *al-Khitat al-Tawfiqiyah*, Bulaq, 6:83.

The Spiritual Condition of Copts under Muslim Rule.

We previously observed that before the Arab invasion the Copts used religious means to achieve their goals. But the Arab presence, the spread of Islam in Egypt, the isolation of the Copts, the ignorance of the clergy, and their lack of interest in civil education were factors that weakened the position of Christianity with the passing of time.

The patriarch Dionysius, who accompanied Caliph al-M`amūn on his trip to Egypt during the Bashmuric revolts, described the slipping conditions of Egyptian Christianity:

> "We saw customs that did not agree with virtue and contradicted the virtues of [the patriarchs] Cyril, Dioscorus and Timothy who had established the laws of the Egyptian church. First, the Copts, especially their monks, have stopped studying the sacred books and thus receive no benefit from them. The most pious monks perform manual labor and memorize some paragraphs from their religious books. Those who intend to be promoted to the rank of bishop do not take the trouble to educate themselves but care only for collecting money to buy their ranks. Because paying a certain sum of money [is the accepted means of obtaining office], no one is able to fill such a position who has distinguished himself by his knowledge and good behavior. When we started blaming [Coptic] officials for their attitudes, the patriarch of Alexandria declared, `We follow this path because of the debts laid upon the church of Alexandria. Except for the money that comes from this source we would have defaulted.'"[11]

This was the condition of the Coptic church after only two centuries of the Arab presence. It is true that some monks tried to reform both the system and the hearts [of the people]. Some became famous for the religious and scientific books that they authored. But they were a small minority of whom their compatriots were not proud. Moreover, their works were void of originality and novelty.

The patriarchs of Alexandria [under Islamic rule] followed one after the other without adding any important chapters to their history. The peace or chaos of their eras depended on the rulers' satisfaction or dissatisfaction with them, and on the level of tranquility in the country. None of them tried to imbue a new spirit into the church which was gradually fading away. For their part, the historians

---

11. Michel le Syrien, *op. cit.*, 1:80.

who contributed to the *History of the Patriarchs* focused chiefly on the financial problems that occupied the Copts.

In addition, following the time of the Mamlūk persecution of the Copts, long periods of time would elapse before the election of a new patriarch.[12] This situation became more serious after the Turkish occupation of Egypt. But the public did not seem to care about such delays. During the reign of the Fatimids, it even happened that the layman Auram was elected patriarch, demonstrating that a layman could be selected because of a lack of candidates of religious stature. One's belief in Christianity seemed superficial. Because religious education was non-existent, the clergy became ignorant of the basics of religion. The patriarch used to discourage his followers [from learning and progressing] instead of encouraging them. This was because living in peace was his first and only priority. The Coptic *Synaxarion* mentions that,

> "once two bishops ill-treated their flock and [the patriarch] Anba Yu'annis reprimanded them, more than once, requesting that they treat the people courteously. But they did not take his advice and he paid no more attention to them. Then the people appealed to him for help saying, 'If you impose these two bishops on us, we will convert to another religion.' The patriarch unexpectedly called all the bishops of the country to a meeting where he dissociated himself from the responsibility of punishing those two bishops."[13] During the reign of al-Malik al-Kāmel[14] a Christian merchant called Hanna converted to Islam to marry a Muslim woman. But he repented of his action and decided to become a martyr. He was advised to visit the patriarch to receive his advice and follow it. But he responded by saying, "I am afraid that the patriarch will make me fear death."[15]

The conditions of the bishops and priests were even worse. Because their need for money was greater than that of the patriarch, they became money lovers. In 830 A.D., the position of the patriarch remained vacant for a long time after the

---

12. `Ali Mubarak, *op. cit.*, 6:83–84.

13. Basset, René, *Le Synaxaire Arabe Jacobite*, Paris: Fimin-Didot, 1905–29. 6 vols.

14. [Ayyubid sultan, 634–35 A.H./1237–38 A.D. (Tr.)]

15. Amélineau, "Un Document copte du XVIIIe Siecle," *Journal Asiatique*, 1897.

death of Patriarch Sam`ān.[16] At the time a man who was married and employed appeared on the scene. He gave donations to the bishops and they agreed with some notables of Alexandria to elect him as patriarch.[17] There is a further proof of their love of money. There was a bishop living in Upper Egypt in the eighteenth century who asked the French traveler and priest "Sicar" to teach him the alchemy skill of making gold.[18]

For their part, the people continued to affiliate themselves secretly with the pharaonic spiritual heritage. They had inherited from the pharaohs both customs and a language, and they wanted to honor what remained of their ancient monuments. The traveler Norden wrote that,

> "the ancient and modern Egyptians—pagans, Christians and Muslims who believe in myths—have learned how to combine the rituals of different religions. It is no wonder that we find among them those who esteem highly the pyramids and sphinx, even hiding their inner, overwhelming feelings towards them. Some people have reached the point of holding religious observances honoring these monuments. Thus they have stirred up the anger of the Muslims who have openly expressed their enmity towards worshipping idols."[19]

Norden's statement explains what al-Maqrizi has related in his history about the reason for destroying the face of the Sphinx. "There was a person called Sheikh Ṣā`im al-Dahr who tried in 780 A.H. [1378 A.D.] to change certain things that he considered to be reprehensible actions. He went to the pyramids area and disfigured the face of the sphinx."[20]

But we should not blame the Copts alone because the decadence involved all Christians of the Middle East. It is worth mentioning that in the seventeenth century the members of the Melchite community in Aleppo misinterpreted Christian doctrines to the extent that they officially sanctioned plural marriage, on condition that marrying a second wife would not be official until after the couple

---

16. [Simon II died in 830 A.D. (Tr.)]

17. Basset, *op. cit.*

18. *Lettres edifiantes et curieuses,* 5:28.

19. Norden, Frederik Ludvig, *Voyage en Egypte et en Nubie,* Copenhagen: De l'Imprimerie de la Maison royale des Orphelins, 1755.

20. *al-Khitat,* 1:123.

had had marital relations for two years. Marrying a third wife would not become official until after the couple had had marital relations for five years.[21]

The Influence of Islam on the Copts and Their Customs.

Lord Cromer, who was in control of Egypt for some time, observed in 1908, "There is a seemingly big difference between the Muslims and the Copts but in reality this difference is very insignificant. Necessity mandates that a minority is influenced by the majority. That is why in India the Muslims were influenced by Brahmanism to some extent, while the Hindus who are a majority by 5 to 1 did not take anything from the Muslims. We can apply this principle to the Copts of Egypt. The Muslims of this country were never influenced by the Copt while the Copt was influenced by his Muslim compatriot without being aware of it."[22]

Lord Cromer's remark about Egypt is totally wrong. Islam came to Egypt only to find Egyptian nationals who were most devoted to the traditions of their forefathers and who retained some customs, beliefs and myths which were [even] sacred to ancient Egyptians. In fact, the traditions of Egyptian Muslims are not totally free from pharaonic influences, while Islam has saturated the Coptic minority with its spirit, a minority that has continued to adhere to Christianity.

What the Copts Have Taken from Islam.

When Egyptian Christianity severed its relations with the Greco-Roman world, long before the Arab invasion of Egypt, it lost much of its attractiveness and power. It seems that the rise of no new religion during that period was the reason for the lack of change in the doctrines of Christianity. What supports this idea is the fact that, when the Arabs invaded Egypt, the Egyptian Christians—who were martyred in defence of a religious principal that they did not fully comprehend—did not hesitate to divert from the plain Christian doctrines.

Sawirus ibn al-Muqaff a tells us that in 76 A.H. [695 A.D.], during Patriarch Sam`ān's[23] tenure, some who claimed to be Christians deserted their wives and pressured the clergy to give them permission to remarry. When their requests were denied, they complained to the wali saying that the clergy had pushed them to commit the sin of adultery by denying their requests. The disappointed wali summoned sixty-four bishops without indicating the reason for

---

21. al-Zayyat, Habib, "The Sins of the Catholic Melkites of Aleppo in the Seventeenth Century," in *al-Mashriq*, 1938, p. 36 (in Arabic).

22. Cromer, *op. cit.*, 2:203

23. [Simon I, 692–700 A.D. (Tr.)]

this call.[24] The narrator of the account has not told us what happened in the meeting. But we know that divorce—which was officially forbidden by the Egyptian church—was practiced publicly. Even the church acknowledged it, particularly when the Copts' condition deteriorated under Ottoman rule. The French traveler D. Jauna recounted in 1795 A.D. that "the practice of divorce is not limited to Muslims but is also common among Copts who have neglected the reasons mentioned in the Bible about [forbidding it except for adultery]. For the patriarch to approve divorce, it is sufficient only that one tells the patriarch that he is not satisfied with his wife and that the wife tells him she is not living in harmony with her husband. If he were to turn down their divorce, they would carry it out in spite of him. The patriarch has never refused such requests because, by his disapproval, he would lose the payment that was usually given him if he approved the hateful separation which is emulated by members of other Christian groups."[25]

During the rule of the Mamlūks, history has given us examples of notable Christians whose marriage to two women at the same time was acknowledged by religious authorities. Those notables did not even take the trouble of abrogating their first marriage, especially if they owned a number of slaves and slave girls like their [Mamlūk] masters. There is no better proof of this than Mu'allim Ghali who, despite being a Catholic, owned sixty white, black and Abyssinian slave girls who were discovered when Muhammad `Ali ordered a search of his house.[26]

We do not know exactly when Egyptian Christians started keeping slaves. According to what historians have told us, they began this practice rather early. During the tenure of Patriarch Philotheus and the Fatimid caliphate of al-Aziz most Egyptian notables owned slave girls, of whom they owned large numbers.[27] Stochove, who visited Egypt in 1621, observed that Christians had the right of buying slave girls without restrictions.[28] Other travelers have mentioned this fact. From the accounts of al-Jabartī, we also know through the actions of Qabatan Hassan Pasha that Copts were excessive in practicing their right to own slave girls.

24. *History of the Patriarchs,* p. 135.

25. Jauna, D., *Histoire Général,* 2:1333–34.

26. al-Jabartī, *op. cit.,* 4:135.

27. al-Sakhawi, *al-Tibr al-Masbūk,* p. 385.

28. Stochove, Vince de, *Voyage du Levant,* 2nd revised edition, Brussels: H.A. Velpius, 1650, p. 432.

Scholars with the French campaign reported that "the Christians of Egypt have the right to own slaves. This right is not enjoyed by other Christians in any other part of the Ottoman empire. Even so, their right is restricted. They are not allowed to own male slaves. All they can do is buy children and release them when they reach puberty. [On the other hand,] they are allowed to own an unlimited number of women. This is why you find at least a slave girl or two owned by every family to do housework."[29]

In another vein, Copts ceased to speak their own language. Consequently, the strongest support of the Coptic character collapsed. They did not learn Arabic merely to conduct business. They went much further, completely abandoning the Coptic language and replacing it with the language of their rulers. They also adapted the etiquette, manners and other modes of behavior of Muslims. It is worth noting that the work of the Christian historian al-Makin,[30] which goes back to the thirteenth century A.D., is filled with Muslim religious terms such as, "Bism Allah al-Rahmān al-Rahīm" [In the name of God, the most Merciful and Compassionate]. al-Makin's work is even influenced substantially by a Muslim spirit, which led the orientalist Vattier, who translated the account, to say, "One characteristic of al-Makin is that he writes so sympathetically about whatever he discusses in his book that, if he mentions something about Islam, we believe that he is a Muslim, if he speaks about the Jacobites [Copts], we believe that he is a Jacobite [Copt], and if he speaks about the Catholics, we imagine that he is a Catholic."[31]

In the message that Patriarch Gabriel VIII[32] sent to Pope Clement VIII[33] in 1601 concerning the unity of the Egyptian and Catholic churches, he readily used the phrase that Muslims cherish [Bism Allah al-Rahmān al-Rahīm]. But he changed the term al-Rahmān to al-Ra'ūf ["Compassionate"].[34] The use of such religious terms was due to the use of the Arabic language by the Copts, although

---

29. *Description de l'Égypte*, 2nd edition, 1st part, p. 29.

30. [al-Makin ibn al-Suqa'ī (fl. 1250 A.D.) was a tax official in 658 A.H. (*a mustawfi*, one who makes the rules and regulations for collecting taxes). He was asked to convert to Islam, which he did. See *al-Khitat*, 4:403. (Tr.)]

31. Vattier, *La chronique d'Elmacin*, p. 15.

32. [Gabriel VIII was the 97th Coptic patriarch, 1587–1603. (Tr.)]

33. [Clement was pope of Rome, 1592–1605 A.D. (Tr.)]

34. *Majallat al-Majm'a al-Ilmi al-Misri*, 1904.

this [process] took place gradually. The proof is that Sawirus ibn al-Muqaff a, who was a contemporary of the Fatimids, never used such terms.

One of the customs that Copts adopted from Muslims at an early stage was the circumcision of children, which Christianity had abolished and which had not been practiced in Egypt prior to the Arab invasion. Later, one of the patriarchs forced his people to practice circumcision. He even gave it priority over baptism. And in 1120 A.D. Patriarch Macarius[35] instituted this practice by ordering children to be circumcised before baptism.[36] Patriarch John VI[37] [in 1208 A.D.] went beyond this by making the circumcision of children mandatory. He also abolished "the confession."[38] al-Maqrizi says that the Copts were more concerned with circumcision than the Melchites.

The veil was also adopted by Christian women in Egypt. "The Copts did not allow their wives to appear unveiled in front of the men of religion. Even the patriarch himself could not meet an unveiled woman unless her husband allowed her to do so."[39] Coptic women would also sit together in the churches, segregated from men by solid partitions.

With the exception of the crosses that decorated churches and the prayers performed within them, we notice that the churches accommodated people more interested in emulating Muslim practices than their own. In a protestant account written just one century ago, we find minute details related to this matter. The account says that Coptic men of religion advised believers to pray in their homes seven times every day.[40] Some Copts used to wash their hands and faces, and sometimes their feet, before beginning their prayers, in the same manner as Muslims. They also said their prayers with their faces turned toward the east.[41]

---

35. [Macarius II was the Coptic patriarch from 1102 to 1128. (Tr.)]

36. Ibn al-Rahib, *op. cit.*, p. 139.

37. [John VI (Yuhanna) was the Coptic patriarch from 1189 to 1216. (Tr.)]

38. Ibn al-Rahib, *op. cit.*, p. 141.

39. *Description de l'Égypte*, vol. 18, part 1, p. 19.

40. Muslims pray only five times every day.

41. *Journal of a Deputation to the East*, 1849, 1:20.

There are details more curious than these that we have just mentioned. They are recorded in Clot Bey's book[42] and in the travels of Mr. Belloc. They say, "The Copts remove their shoes before they enter their churches, like the Muslims."[43] There is another similarity in the behavior of Muslims and Copts: the Copts' fascination with pilgrimage to the Church of the Holy Sepulchre in Jerusalem to obtain the title of *hajj* [pilgrim]. When they travel to Jerusalem, they surround the event with the same fanfare that Muslims are accustomed to on similar occasions. Further, they go on pilgrimage in large caravans. al-Jabartī has narrated an interesting account of a pilgrimage of Christians. We are aware that only tolerant walis permitted Christians to visit Jerusalem and that the Mamlūks often did not allow them to make the trip. Recording events of 1166 A.H. [1704–1705 A.D.], al-Jabartī wrote: "About that time, the Copts intended to make a pilgrimage to Jerusalem. Their leader then was `Nawrūz,' the secretary of Radwan Katekhda [the deputy of the wali]. Nawrūz spoke to Sheikh Abdallah al-Shabrawi about the Copts' pilgrimage plans and gave him a gift of a thousand dinars. al-Shabrawi wrote him a *fatwa* [religious opinion by a Muslim `alim] and gave him a statement in which he indicated that the Ahl al-Dhimma should not be prevented from practicing their religion and visiting [their holy places]. As soon as the Christians received the fatwa, they began preparation for the trip. Then they departed with pageantry and pomp on horses and in *takhtirewāns*[44] that carried their women and children, accompanied by drums and single-pipe woodwind instruments resembling the oboe. At a place called Qubbat al-Izab they set up a show. They brought along some Arabs to guard them, giving them money, robes of honor, dresses and gifts. The event became widely known in the country and people came to consider it reprehensible. Sheikh Abdallah al-Shabrawi went to visit Sheikh al-Bakri when `Ali Effendi, al-Bakri's brother, was sick. When al-Shabrawi met with `Ali Effendi, the latter reprimanded him by saying, `Oh Sheikh

---

42. [Clot Bey (Antoine Barthelemy Clot), 1793–1868, was one of the European experts recruited by Muhammad `Ali. Clot Bey established the first Egyptian medical school. He also laid the foundations for public health services in the Qasr al-Aini hospital which is still in business. His book is *Aperçu général sur l'Égypt*, Paris: Fortin, Masson, 1840, 2 vols. (Tr.)]

43. Belloc, *Le pays des Pharaos*, Paris, 1800, 4:416. Belloc copied the material for his travels from Clot Bey. We should indicate here that Coptic monks remove their shoes when they pray according to the teachings of the Bible [see Exodus 3:5]. But the Copts at the time meant to emulate the Muslims. Nowadays they do not follow this custom.

44. [A Turkish word from *takht* which means any raised structure used for sitting or reclining, such as a bench, sofa, stage, or especially a sovereign's throne. *Takhtirewān* is the reputed flying throne of Solomon. In this context it refers to a camel with a structure, such as a small tent on its back, for carrying women and children in such processions. (Tr.)]

al-Islam, what have you done? How can you agree and issue a religious opinion for the Christians, allowing them to do what they have done because they bribed you and gave you gifts?' al-Shabrawi denied [his actions] and 'Ali continued, 'Yes, they gave you one thousand [dinars] in a bribe, plus a gift. They now have a precedent, and will go next year and do more than they have this year. They may even have a *mahmal*,[45] and people will speak of the hajj of the Christians and the hajj of Muslims. It will become a *sunna* [custom] for which you will be responsible on the day of resurrection.' At this point the sheikh left full of rancor, and he encouraged a mob to attack the Christians and loot what they were carrying with them. The mob was joined by a group of ascetics [*mujawrin*[46]] from al-Azhar. Together they threw stones at them and beat them with canes and sticks used to beat animals. They looted everything that they had and disgraced them by hanging bells around their necks. They also plundered the nearby church in Demerdash.[47] The Christians suffered greatly because they lost everything."[48]

Marriage rituals of Copts resembled those of Muslims. A girl was secluded when she reached the age of puberty. A young man who wanted to marry had to entrust one of his women relatives to look for a bride for him. If an agreement was reached [between two families], a priest wrote the marriage contract and performed the marriage ceremony. If the bridegroom promised a dowry, he had to pay half of it in advance, like the Muslims.[49] St. John the traveler recounts that, during the reign of Muhammad 'Ali, Coptic priests encouraged *mut'ah* marriage[50] which was known among Muslim tribes, especially

45. [*Mahmal* is a richly decorated litter sent by Muslim rulers to Mecca as an emblem of their independence at the time of the hajj. The speaker did not like the possibility of equality between Muslims and Christians in celebrating their religious activities. (Tr.)]

46. [Ascetics who retire to the al-Azhar mosque. (Tr.)]

47. [A district in Cairo. (Tr.)]

48. al-Jabarti, *op. cit.*, 1:188; pp. 85 86 in the 1959 edition.

49. Michaud and Poujoulat, *Correspondance d'Orient*, 7:79.

50. [Mut'ah is usufruct marriage, temporary marriage, a custom still followed by some Muslims. There is no consensus among Muslim thinkers about the legality of this kind of marriage in Islam. While many Shi'ite scholars consider it legal, many Sunnite scholars consider it illegal. See *Dictionary of Islam* under "Mut'ah," p. 424, and "Mut'a" in the *Encyclopaedia of Islam*. (Tr.)]

Shi`ites.[51] The Copts have even abstained from eating pork [which is strictly forbidden in Islam].[52]

What Muslims Have Borrowed from Copts.

We have previously referred to Coptic customs that were adopted by Egyptian Muslims alone. The most important of these customs, which has persisted until today, is that of hiring mourners [naddabāt][53] at funerals. This custom, inherited by Copts from the pharaohs, did not cross the borders of Egypt. The French noticed that Copts were more excessive in expressing their sadness than Muslims.[54] If we talk about what Muslims have borrowed from the Copts, we mean to review superstitions that originated in ancient times. We shall not discuss these customs at length. It is sufficient to refer to a relatively recent event mentioned by Thévenot. It indicates that belief in superstitions was widespread and common, to the extent that Muslims readily sought the blessings of unknown spirits and believed in superstitions that did not exist except in the imagination of Christians. Thévenot reports,

"There existed near Old Cairo, on the Nile shore, a large cemetery in which a large number of corpses were buried. The inhabitants of Cairo—Copts, Greeks, Turks and Moroccans—strongly believed that on the Wednesdays, Thursdays, and Good Fridays [before Easter], according to the ancient calendar, the dead were resurrected. The dead did not take a walk the cemetery, as we might have thought, but their bones came out of the ground on [each of] those three days and returned at the end of the day. I went to the cemetery and was surprised to see that there was a very large crowd, as if it were a market place. The Turks went to that cemetery in a procession, carrying their banners, to where one of their sheikhs was buried, for they believe that his bones come out every year

---

51. St. John, *op. cit.*, 2:382–84.

52. Sonnini, *Voyage du Levant*, ch. 28. See also Leeder's *Modern Sons of the Pharaohs*, p. 284, who says, "The patriarch who was enthroned in the patriarchate before Cyril V refused to eat with lady Duff Gordon and he hated the protestants `who eat meat all the year round like dogs.'"

53. [They are also called `addadāt, women who are hired to enumerate the good qualities of the deceased at his funeral. (Tr.)]

54. *Description de l'Égypte*, 2nd ed., vol. 18, 1st part, p. 19.

from its tomb like the bones of all the other dead. There they prayed in a very pious manner."[55]

Another traveler called Niebuhr personally witnessed the superstitions related to ghosts among the inhabitants of the Nile valley who occupy a part of Damietta. He reports, "This was the first time that I noticed this kind of superstition among Muslims. In Arabia they do not know ghosts, nor do they talk about them."[56]

Did such influences have a lasting effect on Muslims? Although Muslims adopted some customs that go back to the time of the pharaohs, they did not yield to the influence of Coptic beliefs. Was this also the case with the Copts? Yes, they tended to emulate Muslims outwardly, before and after converting to Islam. There were no real distinguishing marks that separated them from the majority. As long as they continued to be Christians, their outward behavior revealed no deviation from their beliefs. We cannot deny the Copts their strong attachment to their religion and their loyalty to the teachings of their church. They asked for no more serious a favor than a license to build or renovate a church. This was what the famous Mu`allim Ibrahim al-Jawhari[57] did after he rendered invaluable service to the sultan's sister during her passage through Egypt on her way to Mecca [on pilgrimage]: he asked the sultan's favor in issuing a *firman*[58] to build a church in

---

55. Thévenot, *Voyage en Égypte*, p. 275. [The following is the text as it appeared in the English edition of Thévenot's work: "Upon the Riverside near old *Caire*, there is a great burying-place, where many dead Bodies are Interred: all the Inhabitants of *Caire*, not only *Cophtes* and *Greeks*, but also Turks and Moors are fully perswaded that on Holy *Wednesday*, *Thursday*, and *Friday*, (according to their account, who follow the old Calendar) the dead rise there; not that the dead People walk up and down the Churchyard; but that during these three days, their Bones come out of the Ground, and then when they are over, return to their Graves again. I went to that Burying-place on the Holy *Friday* of the Greeks and other Christians, who follow the old Calendar, that I might see what Ground they had for this stupid Belief, and I was astonished to find as many People there as if it had been at a Fair, for all both small and great in *Caire* flock thither, and the Turks go in procession with all their Banners, because they have a *Sheikh* Interred there, whose Bones (as they say) come out every year, and take the Air with the rest; and there they say their Prayers with great Devotion." See *The Travels of Monsieur de Thévenot into the Levant*, In three parts, newly done out of French, Licensed Dec. 2, 1686, London: II. Clark, St. Paul's Church Yard, 1607, part 1, ch. XIII, p. 145. (Tr.)]

56. Niebuhr, *Voyage en Arabie*, 1:45.

57. [See Harald Motzki, "Ibrāhīm al-Jawharī" (d. 1795), *The Coptic Encyclopedia*, 4:1274. (Tr.)]

58. [An Ottoman royal decree. (Tr.)]

Azbakiyah and to exempt the monks from paying the *jizyah*.[59] He also seized the opportunity afforded by the good feelings of the sultan towards him, asking permission to renovate the monasteries and churches.[60]

We conclude this discussion by quoting Lord Cromer, "The only difference between the Copt and the Muslims is the first is an Egyptian who worships God in a Christian Church while the other is an Egyptian who worships God in a Muslim Mosque."[61]

The Competition between Melchites and Copts.

We have previously referred to the competition between the Melchites and Copts which started after the council of Chalcedon [451 A.D.] and continued throughout the Islamic era, with very serious consequences. As a result, we cannot avoid discussing it here.

The authority of the Coptic patriarch continued to be substantial, both inside and outside Egypt, in spite of the restrictions designed to limit his activities. Although the wali abstained from interfering in internal affairs between Copts—purely religious affairs—he had to interfere at the behest of the Copts themselves, especially after the conspiracies of the Melchites. Of this Michael the Syrian said,

> "When the wicked Greeks [the Melchites] were unable to hurt the Copts, as they had in the past, they did not cease trying to do so. In Antioch and Cairo they appointed patriarchs of their own to spread chaos among the Syrians, Egyptians and Armenians, like a snake whose head is severed but its tail is still moving. In Syria, Armenia, Palestine and Egypt, the Melchite patriarch and bishops did their best to spread chaos among the nationals of these countries and, when it was feasible, among the Nubians and Ethiopians, in addition to the patriarch and bishops of our denomination [of monophysites]."[62]

Copts sought the help of the wali in personal matters. For instance, we see a priest who complains to the wali that he was not promoted to the rank of

---

59. *al-Khitat al-Tawfiqiyah*, 6:72.

60. *Ibid.*, 6:85.

61. Cromer, E. B., *Modern Egypt*, 2:206.

62. Michel le Syrien, *op. cit.*, 3:22.

bishop, and tells him of the existence of a hidden treasure. We find another priest who travels to Damascus and claims in front of the caliph that he is able to fill the empty coffers of the state with the gold of the Coptic patriarch who, by following certain chemical processes, has made the gold himself, to ornament his churches with precious utensils.[63] The *History of the Patriarchs* repeats similar stories, but there is no need to discuss the subject at length, especially since most of these cases are exceptional. We cannot deny that the desire to take revenge created serious precedents. However, if we want to be accurate, we should say that [in general] the Melchites, not the Copts, incited the Muslim walis to interfere in purely religious affairs.

The Melchites were favored by the Byzantine authorities because of their loyalty. And they did not readily submit to the Arab rule. The dignity that `Amr ibn al-'As bestowed on the Coptic patriarch Benjamin, and his confiscation of most churches and monasteries of the Melchites in favor of the Copts, intensified the Melchites' desire to take revenge.

The differences between the two groups increased with the consolidation of Arab rule in Egypt. The Copts were extremely happy to be rid of the Greeks. They were no longer obliged to seek help from Byzantium. If Nubia and Ethiopia disappointed them by not sending aid in times of crisis, the Copts kept to themselves and tried to pacify their rulers toward themselves. In contrast, the Melchites did not cease even for one day to look to Byzantium. Events that occurred on the Bosphorus were of equal interest to them as those that occurred on the banks of the Nile. For this reason, when Said ibn al-Bitriq wrote his history he gave the Byzantine and Egyptian events the same care while his antagonist, Sawirus ibn al-Muqqaf a, paid no attention to events except those that occurred within the Egyptian borders, neglecting those beyond.

However, the Melchites did not publicly oppose the Arab rule. In fact, they tried to create mutual understanding between themselves and the new occupier. To achieve their goal, they pursued the objective of assisting the Arabs to tighten their control over the Copts. They thus killed two birds with one stone, gaining the favor of the victors and weakening the influence of the Copts at the same time.

They began their efforts right after the fall of Alexandria. John of Nikiou reports, "Menas, the atheist, collected 32,057 pieces of gold and delivered them

---

63. Sawirus, *op. cit.*, pp. 219–20.

to the Ishmaelites[64] (sic), while the fine that ʿAmr imposed on the city was only 22,000 pieces."[65]

We also read in the Coptic *Synaxarion* that Patriarch Aghato "suffered many hardships because of his honesty. During his time a man called Taudasius, who was a Melchite, went to Damascus and offered Caliph Yazid ibn Muʿawiyah[66] much money in return for a decree appointing him wali over the provinces of Alexandria, al-Buhayra, and Maryūt [Mareotis]. When he returned, he imposed the *jizyah* on the patriarch and his disciples [thirty-six dinars on each annually]. He also imposed on him the annual payment of all expenses of the ships of the fleet every year, about seven thousand dinars yearly. Because of the man's evil doings, his co-religionists boycotted him because they hated what he had done to the Coptic patriarch. He did not even allow the patriarch to leave his cell and issued an order saying, ʿAnyone who finds the patriarch in street must kill him.' The patriarch remained in his cell until that hypocrite perished."[67] The Copts did not accept defeat. One of them, who was chief adviser to Qurra ibn Sharīk,[68] succeeded in convincing Ibn Sharīk to impose a double tax on the Melchites.[69]

Undoubtedly the Melchites continued to feel influential because, during the reign of ʿAbd al-Aziz ibn Marwān, they thought of electing one of their number as patriarch and imposing his authority on both groups. Moreover, when al-Walid said, "I would not allow a patriarch to be in the front line [of advisers] during my tenure,"[70] there was a doctor in Alexandria named Anobis, a Roman Chalcedonian [Melchite], who, when he found his way to the emir, asked him to order his appointment as patriarch of Alexandria. And the emir granted his request. There was also a scribe called Anastasius in Alexandria who paid the

---

64. [He meant the Muslims who are believed to be the descendants of Ishmael, son of Abraham. (Tr.)]

65. John of Nikiou, *op. cit.*, p. 585.

66. Yazid I was an Ummayād caliph (60–64 A.H./679–83 A.D.).

67. John of Nikiou, *op. cit.*, p. 341.

68. [Umayyād walī of Egypt, 90–96 A.H. (708–14 A.D.). (Tr.)]

69. Sawirus, *op. cit.*, p. 150.

70. *Ibid.*

emir one thousand dinars and was appointed the assistant Chalcedonian patriarch in Alexandria.[71]

It also happens that the favorite wife of Haroun al-Rashid was successfully treated by the Melchite patriarch of Alexandria when she was ill. The caliph gave him a large sum of money as a gift and issued a decree according to which he should regain all the churches that had been confiscated in the interest of the Copts. The patriarch thereupon returned to Alexandria and reacquired the churches.[72]

The caliphs exploited the rancorous feelings of the two groups. They had members of one group carry out the orders that they issued against the other group. When the Caliph al-Ma'mūn ordered the removal of "the pillars and marble from all the [Coptic] churches, the one who convinced the caliph to issue the order was an opponent, a hateful Nestorian named Lazarus. When he returned to Egypt, his co-religionists [the Chalcedonians] living in Alexandria welcomed him."[73] During the tenure of Caliph Abdul Allah ibn Marwan, the Mechites and Copts requested the intercession of a Muslim judge concerning the problem of the ownership of one of the churches.

It is natural that the Arab rulers did not resent these renewed conflicts because they offered an opportunity to interfere in affairs in which they had at first refused to interfere. Further, they expressed their anxiety about the close relations between the Melchites and Byzantium, and between them and the Catholic countries of Europe. al-Qalqashandī has preserved the texts of some very important documents related to this matter. These documents deal with the protocol of the induction of the Melchite and Coptic patriarchs in Alexandria. In their decrees, the rulers requested that the Melchite patriarch prevent his followers, who were living in the coastal areas, from establishing any clandestine relations with foreigners who came to Egypt. The decree concerning the induction of the Coptic patriarch does not mention anything related to this matter, but refers to the patriarch's relationship with Ethiopia.[74]

To understand the relations between Copts and Melchites, we recount a story that indicates the degree of hatred that separated the two groups. The story concerns the reformer Marcus ibn Kunbur. We need not dwell long on this

71. *Ibid.*

72. Ibn al-Bitriq, *op. cit.*, p. 52.

73. Sawirus, *op. cit.*, pp. 286–87.

74. al-Qalqashandī, *Subh al-'Asha*, Dar al-Kutub ed., 2:392–405.

account, which has been related in detail by Abu Salih al-Armani. We need only say that the reforms suggested by Marcus to the Coptic patriarch that would reconcile the two groups led to his excommunication. Marcus suggested that Copts be allowed to grow their hair long and that circumcision be prohibited. He also recommended that the confession [of sins] be made secret. When the schism became serious, Marcus sought the help of the sultan. But the Coptic patriarch came out victorious because the Melchites were then weak. The Coptic *mubashireen* [administrators] took revenge by doubling the *jizyah* on cities that followed Marcus ibn Kunbur. Their revenge, however, only served the interests of the Egyptian treasury.

The history of the Melchites has been shrouded in obscurity throughout the Ottoman period. They were left to themselves, living in poverty and ignorance following the fall of Constantinople to the Turks in 1453 A.D. At the beginning of the eighteenth century, there were only twenty Melchites in Cairo, one for every 500 Copts. They numbered about one hundred in Alexandria. There were also some Melchite families living in the port cities of Rosetta, Damietta and Suez. Even so, they were not powerless. The sultan occasionally approved the appointment of a Melchite patriarch for the [Coptic] see of Alexandria. It is difficult to know exactly how many Melchites continued to be loyal to Rome and how many joined themselves to Byzantium. However, the concern of the European [Catholic] nations for the welfare of the Egyptian Melchites indicates that some of them had renewed their ties to the papacy of Rome. But the popes of Rome were also concerned about the circumstances of the Copts who turned their hatred against the Europeans after the demise of the Melchites.

The Hatred of Copts for Europeans.

The Catholic church did not lose hope of bringing the Copts of Egypt within its sphere of influence, even after the failure of the attempt aimed at unifying the two churches. The founder of the Franciscan order, Francis of Assisi, laid the foundations for such unity. But the fruits of his efforts were modest, even though by 1731 A.D. Catholic missionaries had come to own nine monasteries in Upper Egypt.[75]

Both Muslims and Copts learned that it was in their interest to encourage these monasteries, in spite of their hatred for the Europeans. Niebuhr the traveler wrote that "Cairo did not have European merchants [at the time], but it had priests

---

75. Butcher, Edith Louise, *Story of the Church of Egypt*, 2:341–45.

attached to Catholic missions, among whom were Jesuits,[76] Capuchins,[77] cordiliers,[78] and propagators.[79] These monks were enthusiastic missionaries and they sometimes succeeded, in their own way, in converting some Christians to Roman Catholicism. The [Turkish] authorities approved their actions, exploiting the conflicts between those who converted to Catholicism and the members of their original church. The pasha [the Turkish wali] not only imposed fines on each of the conflicting parties but he also demanded large sums of money from the monks of each group."[80]

The preceding is what the protestant traveler Niebuhr observed. Likewise, the view of the French consul, a Catholic, is no less sarcastic. "When converts were criticized for their apostasy, they used to say, `No money, no church' [mafīsh fulūs, mafīsh kanisah]. I saw here the church of the fathers of the holy land full of new apostates who were the poorest of the poor in Egypt. Their abject poverty brought them under the will of anyone who would help them."[81] Writing after the French consul, the Italian traveler Sonnini related that,

> "the word Ifranj [Arabic for Franks] is hated by upper [class] Egyptians, a hatred rooted in the attitude of the Copts towards them. It was painful for Copts to meet Italian [Catholic] missionaries who had come to Egypt especially for the purpose of criticizing their doctrine, while accusing them of atheism and mercilessly declaring them to be doomed dogs."[82]

---

76. [Jesuits, or Society of Jesus, was the name given in 1540 to a brotherhood founded in 1534 by the Spanish Catholic priest Ignatius of Loyola (1491–1556). (Tr.)]

77. [Capuchins were a reformed branch of the Franciscan order. Founded in 1526 by a Franciscan monk of the austere type, named Matteo di Bassi, and sanctioned as a separate congregation by a bull of Pope Clement VII in 1528, these monks wore a long pointed cawl following the garb of St. Francis. (Tr.)]

78. [Cordiliers are members of the religious order of St. Francis of Assisi (Franciscans). Their name is derived from the cord with three knots wrapped around their waists. (Tr.)]

79. [Propagators were propagators of the Catholic faith. Their organization was called "Propaganda," the sacred organization for the propagation of faith. This organization was responsible for the direction and administration of Roman Catholic missionary activity. It was created in 1622 by Pope Gregory XV. (Tr.)]

80. Niebuhr, op. cit., 1:104.

81. Description de l'Égypte, 2:66.

82. Sonnini, Voyage du Levant, ch. 49.

What caused such rancor? [In their minds,] Copts had linked Franks [Europeans] and Melchites because westerners were, until the secession of Martin Luther from the Catholic Church, followers of Rome. It was natural that Copts consider westerners to be allies of the Melchites and hence their enemies. We do not know on what basis the King of Portugal wrote to Cardinal Ximénès that "the Christians under the rule of the sultan of Egypt are quite ready to join our ranks once they see the flash of our arms."[83]

The Jesuit Father Bernat, who studied these matters closely, wrote to Father Fleurian that "God's graces should fall upon us in order to alleviate the obstacles that seem to prevent Copts from joining the Catholic Church for good. The first of these obstacles is their deeply rooted hatred of Europeans."[84] In fact, the hatred that they harbored for westerners was connected to their hatred for Catholics. Niebuhr refers to that feeling in very clear terms when he says,

> "The hatred of the Copts for the church of Rome cannot be erased. The Coptic priests carefully hide the Coptic books because they are afraid, as they claim, that Catholics will take them and republish them in Europe, after they falsify their texts. If we can convince these priests that we are not followers of the pope of Rome and if we can relieve them from the pressure of their poverty by giving them donations, we shall be able to obtain copies of their buried books."[85]

Without attempting an in-depth study, we consider these simple written confessions, that depend on observation alone, as the best proof for the existence of these feelings [of distrust]. Furthermore, we cannot find an indication of any desire on their part, at any time, to seek understanding, nor any inclination to make an effort to narrow the gap between their differing views. Never did they look to the West, in spite of al-Ḥakim ibn Amr Allah's persecution and destruction of their churches, and their suffering injustices during the reign of Sultan Muhammad ibn Qalawūn, and their exposure to insults and injuries during the reign of the Mamlūks. If they [genuinely] sought to follow Rome in the sixteenth century, it was not based on faith but on their need for money.

---

83. Mentioned by the philosopher Leibnitz in his report to King Louis XIV of France. [For more information on Leibnitz's report see *Encyclopaedia Brittanica* under "Leibnitz, Gottfried Wilhelm, 1646–1716. (Tr.)]

84. *Lettres edifiantes*, 5:225.

85. Niebuhr, *op. cit.*, 1:107–8.

Before the French campaign of 1798, when the minister of war of King Louis XVI of France wanted to study the feasibility of invading Egypt, he sent detailed questions concerning this issue to Baron De Tott[86] who was living in Egypt at the time. [In his reply,] he completely neglected the matter of any assistance that the Copts of Egypt could have offered. The reason for this omission could have been because of the Copts' small numbers and their impotence. But in [his reply to] the twenty-eighth question he alluded to the situation of the Jews when he was asked, "Can you make the Jews living in Lower Egypt become interested in our cause?"[87] It is clear that the French government welcomed internal cooperation, but it understood that the Copts would withhold such collaboration.

The reports of the consular agents include reference to the hatred of Copts toward Europeans. Consul Du Mayée wrote concerning this matter, "The hatred of this people for us is so strong that, when one of them wants to insult someone else, he describes him as *Ifrinji* [French].[88] This is their way of expressing their extreme contempt for someone."[89] Actually the Copts suppressed their real feelings towards Bonaparte before they showed their animosity towards him. For their part, French administrators did not conceal their contempt for Copts [from the outset].

As the power of the Europeans increased in the country, the Copts' hatred for them also increased. Many foreigners, both travelers and residents, spoke of this hatred. Rifaud, who had good knowledge of the internal affairs of Egypt, used to advise his compatriots to be cautious, saying, "The Copts harbor intense hatred for all other Christians, and foreigners should stay away from them. If it is necessary to deal with them, it should be done in a very discreet manner."[90] The Englishman John Durban noticed that the effect of missionaries on the natives was insignificant.[91] Charles Didier went beyond that when he stated, "The Copts do not prefer their European co-religionists to the Muslims. It is said that if a new Crusader war broke out between the Muslims and Christians, the Copts would join

---

86. [De Tott (1733–1793) was a French baron and negotiator. (Tr.)]

87. F. Charles-Roux, "Le projet français de la conquête de le Égypte sous le regne de Louis XVI," in *Manshurat al-Majm`a al-Ilmī al-Misrī*, Alexandria, 14:57.

88. [Or as *khawaja*, a foreigner. (Tr.)]

89. *Description de l'Égypte*, 2:67–68.

90. Rifaud, J. J., *Tableau de l'Égypte et de la Nubie*, p. 98.

91. Durban, John P., *Observations in the East*, 1:67.

the ranks of the former."[92] Isambert, in his "Travel Guide," mentions that the hatred of Copts for foreigners largely exceeds the hatred that Muslims feel for unbelievers.[93]

The hatred of Copts for those who converted to Catholicism was more intense. Sonnini noticed this when he wrote,

"The Copts belong to a sect that the Roman church accuses of atheism. I often went to visit their notables among whom I had the pleasure of meeting an Egyptian priest who had spent fifteen years in a monastery in Rome. He spoke Latin and Italian with some fluency. I found pleasure in conversing with a man whom I considered European. He told me that Egyptians who follow the Latin church are ill-treated by their compatriots who are branded [by Catholics] as followers of atheism."[94]

The Copts in whom Muhammad `Ali confided were Catholics. The most influential among them, Mu`allim Ghali, had to defend himself against a number of conspiracies. al-Jabartī recounts one of these conspiracies.

"In 1231 A.H. [1815 A.D.] a group of Copts betrayed Ghali to the deputy of the wali, and informed him that if Ghali were to submit his accounts he would have a deficit of thirty thousand kees.[95] The deputy told them that, if Ghali did not have a deficit, they would have to pay the same amount of money to the treasury. They agreed. Then the deputy reported the incident to the pasha [Muhammad `Ali]. The pasha ordered the arrest of Ghali, his brother, and his estate manager. Ghali was also fired and ordered to pay back an old debt of six thousand kees, as well as settling his other accounts. Then he summoned his accusers and appointed them in the place of Ghali and his assistants."[96]

Before and during Muhammad `Ali's reign we notice a significant difference in the position of the two groups. In the seventeenth century, while the

---

92. [Didier, Charles, *Les Nuits du Caire*. (Tr.)]

93. Isambert, *Orient*, pp. 182–84.

94. Sonnini, *op. cit.*, ch. 43.

95. [A kees contains 500 piasters. (Tr.)]

96. al-Jabartī, *op. cit.*, 4:242.

Copts and their patriarch continued to be hostile to foreigners, the Catholic Copts sought the protection of the republic of Venice. In 1866, they sought the protection of Austria. Therefore, when in Egypt, the consul of Austria did not hesitate to request that the Egyptian government exempt Catholic Copts from litigation in the national courts, even though the government did not grant his request.

On the other hand, while a large number of travelers complained of the difficulty of visiting the Coptic monasteries, the Catholic Copts continued to enjoy friendly relations with the Latins [European Catholics] in the religious field. For example, when Father De Geramb went to Egypt, the Catholic Coptic bishop received him cordially.[97] And when the archbishop of the holy lands went to Egypt on a pastoral tour, the Catholic Coptic bishop received him in Boulaq.[98]

Undoubtedly, the spirit of tolerance initiated in Egypt by Muhammad ʿAli bore fruit later on. The monasteries opened their doors to foreign visitors, even to Catholic monks who were permitted to study the manuscripts deposited in the monasteries. In 1894 the patriarch, who had harbored animosity toward foreigners in the past, cordially received Cardinal Langenieux, the papal representative to the holy synod that was held in Jerusalem.

> "[The patriarch] met him on the first day of his visit and, when the cardinal returned the visit the next day in the church of St. Mark, the patriarch dressed in his religious attire and ordered the church bells rung as if he were celebrating the visit of a person of higher rank. People later talked about the unity between the two churches."[99]

Relations between World Christianity and Christian Egypt under Islamic Rule.

The role that the patriarch played and the daily interactions between Melchites and Copts convince us that the [European] Christian countries did not completely ignore the religious minorities in Egypt. In fact, after Islam prevailed in the East, Christians living in the occupied countries instinctively tried to maintain a spiritual bond with the major Christian countries. While the Melchites

---

97. *Pelerinage en Terre Sainte*, 3:159–60.

98. *Ibid.*

99. Malosse, L., *Impressions d'Égypte*, pp. 271–72.

turned towards Byzantium, Copts turned particularly towards Nubia and Ethiopia, because the latter was the well-fortified fortress that the Arabs could not invade.[100]

Relations between the Copts and Nubia and Ethiopia were natural because the patriarch of Alexandria was the spiritual leader of these countries. Furthermore, the almost daily decline in the patriarch's authority [in Egypt] did not diminish the respect that he enjoyed in Ethiopia. We know how the negus [Ethiopian emperor] overlooked the patriarch's [declining] prestige and respectfully asked the Egyptian [religious] authorities to send him a bishop. Ibn Fadl Allah al-'Umarī[101] describes how the rulers of Ethiopia received the person who was a delegate of the Coptic patriarch. He reports that,

> "the statesmen, the priests and the notables received him at the boundary of the country carrying incense burners. When the delegate arrived in Amhara, the negus received him personally and abstained from using royal decrees from that moment until the Sunday after the arrival of the delegate. Then the negus, the clergy and the statesmen held a meeting in the church courtyard to listen to the [patriarch's] message. The negus listened to the message while standing."[102]

Ibn Fadl Allah al-'Umarī wrote these lines during the reign of the Mamlūks, during a period when the prestige of the Coptic patriarch was shaky, which makes one ask about the reason for the respect of a king of vast authority towards a person who lived most of the time in material and moral misery. The best possible answer to this is found in the history of Ibn Fadl Allah al-'Umarī. He said that the Christian Copts believed that the ceremony of baptism is of no value unless approved by the patriarch of Alexandria. Therefore the negus had to seek the appointment of a bishop who would represent the patriarch in Ethiopia. The sending of a letter to the patriarch for this purpose was demeaning to the negus, but it was unavoidable.

Relations between the Christians of Egypt and their African neighbors continued after the Arab invasion. They were even strengthened because, during

---

100. There is no written proof that Copts ever sought the help of the emperor of Ethiopia [the negus]. The rulers severely punished Copts who were accused of secretly contacting Ethiopia.

101. [Ibn Fadl Allah al-Umarī, Ahmad ibn Yahaya (1301–1349 A.D.), was the author of *Masālik al-Absār fi Mamalik al-Amsār*, published in Cairo in 1985. (Tr.)]

102. This text was not published in Arabic, but was translated by Gaudefroy-Demombynes in his book *L'Afrique moins l'Égypte*. A new edition of al-Umarī's book, published in Cairo in 1985, contains this text on p. 76. (Tr.)]

any persecution of the Copts or in responding to any measure taken against the prestige of the patriarch, the king of Nubia and the emperor of Ethiopia would take the opportunity to interfere in Egypt's affairs. For their part, the Arab walis did not hesitate to seek the patriarch's mediation in securing their southern borders. However, the relationship between the patriarch and the Christian kings caused anxiety among the Muslim rulers, especially soon after the conquest, to the extent that the arrival of an Ethiopian priest to request the appointment of a bishop was sufficient reason to arouse fears among administrators.[103]

Ethiopia attached no great importance to the situation of the Coptic church before the thirteenth century A.D. To be sure, there had been regular contacts between them before that date for one specific reason, the appointment of the bishop (Abūna) of Ethiopia.[104] This state of affairs was due to the fact that the location of Nubia between Ethiopia and Egypt enabled Nubia to play the role of the prime defender of Egyptian Christianity (on the southern border).

Actually, the kings of Nubia [once] ordered their armies to cross the Egyptian border as vengeance for the insult that befell the patriarch Michael I.[105] This [act of support] was the first and most important action of solidarity among the Christians. Sawirus ibn al-Muqqaf'a enthusiastically described this event:

"When King Kiriakos learned that 'Abd Allah ibn Marwān had sent the patriarch to prison, he marched from Nubia towards Egypt with a great army of one hundred thousand horsemen on one hundred thousand horses and one hundred thousand camels. An eyewitness has told us that the horses fought with their front and hind feet, just like the horsemen riding on their backs. The horses were short like donkeys. When they approached Egypt to take over, they camped near the lake now called Birkat al-Habash and looted and killed people, taking Muslims as captives. They did the same to the Muslims of Upper Egypt. Before his arrival, the Nubian king had sent to Egypt a messenger, named al-Abrakhs, to 'Abd al-Malik ibn Marwān demanding the release of the patriarch. But 'Abd al-Malik arrested and imprisoned him with the patriarch. When he learned of the arrival of the Nubian king in Egypt,

---

103. See details in chapter three of this book.

104. [Abūna, or Abun, is the highest spiritual leader of the Ethiopian Orthodox Church. The term signifies "our father" and is applied to bishops, archbishops and patriarchs. See Bariu Tafla, "Abun," The Coptic Encyclopedia, 1:30–31. (Tr.)]

105. ['Abd Allah ibn 'Abd al-Malik ibn Marwān was wali of Egypt in 87 A.H./706 A.D. during the Umayyād caliphate of al-Walīd ibn 'Abd al-Malik (86–96 A.H./705–715 A.D.). (Tr.)]

he grew fearful because he could not fight him. Consequently, he released the messenger al-Abrakhs after firmly agreeing with him that he would make the king and his army return to their country and not advance on his castles and besiege them. The Muslims, in fact, used to smuggle Nubians to Egypt to sell them [as slaves]. The king returned to his country, [but only] after he looted much from the Muslims."[106]

The Copts continued to seek the help of Nubia as long as Nubia continued to be Christian. During the famine that occurred in Egypt during the reign of the Fatimid Caliph al-Mustansir bi-Allah, the Christians sought the help of King George of Nubia.[107]

Relations between [Muslim] Egypt and [Christian] Ethiopia did not reach a crisis point despite indicators [of hostility] that characterized these relations. There were many reasons why Egypt and Ethiopia did not go to war, including the long distance that separates them, the many natural obstacles that exist between them, and the internal rebellions and external dangers that threatened the two countries. While they did not want to go to war, they never tried to achieve mutual understanding or pursue a friendly, working relationship.[108]

Ethiopia needed the good will of Egypt and Egypt needed the good will of Ethiopia. We should not forget that the bishop of Ethiopia was appointed by the patriarch of Alexandria who in turn was subject to the authority of the Muslim wali of Egypt. Hence, the negus did not want war between the two countries, particularly because his subjects went on pilgrimages [through Egypt] to Jerusalem where a special residence was built for them. And they wanted to make the journey in peace.

In Egypt's view, Ethiopia was considered an uncomfortable neighbor, even a very dangerous one if ruled by a strong administration. Egypt also knew that the negus had control of some Islamic tribes and that he would take revenge on the tribes if the Coptic minority in the Nile valley were persecuted. Egypt also

---

106. Sawirus, *op. cit.*, p. 185.

107. [King George III was enthroned in 1079 A.D. after his uncle, King Solomon (Salamūn) decided to dedicate himself to the monastic life. See Giovanni Vantini, *Christianity in the Sudan*, Bologna, Italy: Publishers EMI, 1981, pp. 126–29. (Tr.)]

108. We have depended in this research on available sources, especially Gaston Wiet's paper, "Relations between Egypt and Ethiopia during the Reign of the Mamluk Sultans," in *Majallat Jam'iyyat al-Athar*, vol. 9, Alexandria, Egypt.

knew that [at least one important] source[109] of the Nile originated in the upper reaches of the Ethiopian plateau and there was fear that these sources might be cut off or diverted.

The possibility of diverting the course of the Nile had caused Egyptians anxiety for a very long time. Kammerer notes that,

> "the Muslims were terrified for generations because of their neighbors' conspiracies to deprive them of the water of the Nile. They are still terrified at this possibility. Since they are rightly convinced that Egypt cannot live without the Nile, they have supposed that it was quite possible to change the course of the River Nile, but they are wrong about that."[110]

The crusaders were no less convinced than the Egyptians. When they thought of involving Ethiopia in their wars against Islam, this potential weapon was not far from their planning. When the Mamlūk sultans discovered a conspiracy to work toward this goal, they forbade foreign travelers from entering Ethiopia [through Egypt] because they believed that the travelers would go to Ethiopia to urge the negus to change the course of the Nile. Western historians believed in the feasibility of this project. We read in the travelogue of Gilbert de Lanoy (1422 A.D.) the following statement: "The Sultan does not allow any Christian to go to India via the Red Sea nor via the River Nile, to meet with Father Yuhanna [the negus at the time] for fear that the Christians might join hands with him to deprive them of the river's water or to commit some other hostile act. The sultan believed that the Christians in Ethiopia, as well as Father Yuhanna, were his enemies. The sultan could not change the course of the Nile, but Father Yuhanna could do so at any time. That he had not yet done so was due to the large number of Christians living in Egypt and the possibility of their starving."[111] Ten years later the traveler Bertrandon de la Broquière repeated these pretexts.[112]

---

109. [The Blue Nile. (Tr.)]

110. In 1429 A.D. [832 A.H.] the negus commissioned a Muslim merchant named `Ali Tibrizi to contact the kings of Europe, but he was arrested in Alexandria and executed. (It is now possible to change the course of any river.)

111. Kammerer, A., *La Mer rouge*, vol. 1, 3rd part, p. 296.

112. *Ibid.*, p. 311

Around 1450 A.D. the king of Aragon[113] requested that the negus destroy Egypt by cutting off the water of the Nile.[114] In his book on Egypt, Vansleb expressed his belief that it was possible to change the course of the Nile. He referred to letters that the negus had sent to the sultans of Egypt threatening to change the course of the Nile if they mistreated the Copts.[115] The traveler Savary, who visited Egypt in the eighteenth century, believed that this phenomenon could come true.[116] The Coptic patriarch repeatedly played the role of mediator and his strong influence in the court of the negus insured his success.

The first time that the patriarch was asked to mediate came during the reign of the Fatimid Caliph al-Mustansir bi-Allah.[117] The caliph ordered the patriarch to go meet the negus and to tell him that the water level of the Nile was dropping, threatening harm to the population of Egypt. The caliph sent valuable gifts to the negus with the patriarch. al-Maqrizi reports that,

> "the negus ordered a dam opened to allow the water to run to the land of Egypt, which caused the water level in the Nile to rise three dhirā'[118] overnight. The increase continued until all the land of Egypt was cultivated and watered. When the patriarch returned to Egypt, al-Mustansir rewarded and honored him."[119]

On other occasions the patriarch was known to use his influence in the best interest of Egypt and Islam. Ibn Fadl Allah al-`Umarī recounts that `Abd Allah al-Zayla`ī, the Muslim head of an Ethiopian delegation, went to Egypt between 1332 and 1338 A.D. and asked the sultan to send the patriarch with a request that the negus stop persecuting Muslims and confiscating their sacred lands. The sultan commissioned that a diplomatic message be written by the

---

113. [Aragon is the name of both a region and an ancient kingdom that lies northeast of Spain. (Tr.)]

114. Kammerer, *op. cit.*, p. 300.

115. Vansleb, *op. cit.*, p. 60.

116. *Lettres sur l'Égypte*, 2:86.

117. [al-Mustansir bi-Allah was a Fatimid caliph (427–487 A.H./1036–1094 A.D.). (Tr.)]

118. [A *dhirā* is a linear measure that equals 58 cm. (Tr.)]

119. *al-Khitat*, 2:496.

patriarch to the negus that criticized such actions and urged him to prevent anyone from committing them. Ibn Fadl Allah adds that the letter brought results.[120]

The ambassadorial role of the patriarch did not prevent leaders of the two countries from contacting each other directly. But most delegates sent by the negus had one of two purposes, either to request the appointment of a new bishop or to petition for assistance in facilitating the journey of Ethiopian pilgrims to Jerusalem. Under normal circumstances the typical text of a letter was as follows: "Would the sultan be so kind as to order the patriarch to ordain a bishop for us who is pious and who does not like gold or silver." On such occasions, and writing with proper respect, the negus took opportunity to magnify his material [and military] strength to the sultan. The sultan understood the purpose of the negus, and responded by giving him an exaggerated accounting of the forces and arms under his command.

The Ethiopian delegation would always carry gifts to the sultan. Such gifts usually included slaves, instruments, and arms plated with gold. If the sultan noticed that the gift was of less value than he expected, he would quickly reprimand the chief delegate. It happened in 922 A.H. [1516 A.D.] that Sultan Qansuwa al-Ghūri estimated the value of the gifts that he received from the [Ethiopian] delegation at five thousand dinars or less. After the sultan examined the gift, he reprimanded the person who delivered it and brought to him a list of the previous gifts from Ethiopian kings to his predecessors, such as al-Ashraf Barsbay,[121] al-Zahir Jaqmaq,[122] al-Ashraf Qaytbay,[123] and others. With this list he even submitted the dates that these gifts had been delivered to the rulers of Egypt.[124]

The numbers in any delegation were large because they included pilgrims going to Jerusalem. The historian Ibn Iyās has described how this delegation was received [in 922 A.H./1516 A.D.].

---

120. *Ibid.*

121. [al-Ashraf Barsbay was the Mamlūk sultan from 872 to 901 A.H. (1468–1496 A.D.). (Tr.)]

122. [al-Zahir Jaqmaq was the Mamlūk sultan from 842 to 857 A.H. (1438–1453 A.D.). (Tr.)]

123. [al-Ashraf Qaytbay was the Mamlūk sultan from 825 to 841 A.H. (1422–1437 A.D.). (Tr.)]

124. Ibn Iyās, *op. cit.*, 3:7.

"The total number of Ethiopians who came to Egypt was about 600 persons. They were accompanied by the Coptic patriarch who was dressed in a blue silk robe. Their notables came to the meeting riding horses, while others came on foot. They ascended to the Citadel through [the gate] `Sullam al-Madraj'[125] with the patriarch leading the group. When they reached [the gate] Bab al-Hūsh,[126] they wanted to sit in the presence of the sultan on the iron chairs that they had carried with them. But the heads of the sultan's guards[127] prevented them from doing so. A similar incident occurred during the reign of al-Ashraf Qaytbay in which [Christian notables] were not allowed to sit down in the presence of the sultan. When they left the meeting, they were accompanied by the wali, the *mahmandar*,[128] and the heads of the sultan's guards as far as the main square for fear of being stoned by the mobs."[129]

This [sort of occurrence] illustrates how much the Coptic patriarch was personally interested in everything related to Ethiopia. One old narrative mentions that he used to write to the negus twice a year [with the approval of the sultan]. But this custom was discontinued in the reign of al-Hakim bi Amr Allah. Whenever the sultan of Egypt received a letter from the negus, he would ask the patriarch to assure the negus of his respect and to ask him to treat the Muslims well in his empire.[130]

It was a disaster if the patriarch were ever caught contacting Ethiopia directly without permission from the Egyptian authorities.

---

125. [One of the entrances to the Citadel. (Tr.)]

126. [Another gate that leads to the inside of the citadel. (Tr.)]

127. [R`ūs al-Nuwāb (sing. R`as al-Nawbah) were four emirs whose job was to control and discipline the mamlūks in the service of the sultan. They were headed by an emir in charge of one thousand mamlūks (*emir alf*). (Tr.)]

128. [The *mahmandar* was the official in the Mamlūk sultan's palace who was in charge of receiving ambassadors, chieftans and messengers, and seeing that they were taken care of as guests of the sultan. (Tr.)]

129. Ibn Iyās, *op. cit.*, 3:7.

130. Abu Salih, *op. cit.*, pp. 105–6.

"On Monday, the 20th of Jumada al-'Ula, a council was held with the sultan that included the four judges[131] and others, among whom was Sheikh Badr al-Din al-'Ayni, the brother-in-law of the Coptic patriarch, toward whom the sultan became angry, ordering him beaten and imprisoned in the *maqsharah*.[132] He also confiscated large sums of money [that belonged to the patriarchate]. The sultan ordered the patriarch to write a pledge that he would never write to the king of Ethiopia, neither personally nor through his agent, nor would he appoint a priest or someone else higher in rank in Ethiopia without the sultan's permission and without the sultan reading his correspondance. If the patriarch were to do otherwise, his covenant would be abrogated and he would be beheaded. The Maliki judge issued the decision and the other judges endorsed it. The pledge was read to the sultan and the council. The sultan ordered five copies of the pledge to be made. One copy was kept by the sultan and each of the four judges kept a copy."[133]

[It is worth noting that] the patriarch was not subjected to this sort of harsh treatment except rarely.

Sultan Jaqmaq was right to complain about the Ethiopians because during his rule he received a letter [from them] reprimanding him, even warning him, because of his position on the Copts. A letter arrived in 847 A.H. [1443 A.D.] with a delegation that carried gifts to him. One of the two chief delegates was a Muslim merchant called Abdel Rahman. After the ordinary expressions of respect and honor, the letter included among other things the following statement:

"In the reigns of al-Zahir Barquq and his son al-Nasser Faraj there was justice, especially for our brothers the Christians. We have been informed that these just practices have been changed by some people who have swerved from the road of justice and have walked in the road of injustice. Nowadays, if one of our Christian brothers dies, he is not buried until his relatives go through great difficulties. They are charged more than the customary [fees that were levied] during the times of former kings. God, may He be exalted, has not tortured anyone by

---

131. [Representing the four Islamic schools of law, the Shafi'i, Hanbali, Hanafi and Maliki. (Tr.)]

132. [House of detention. (Tr.)]

133. al-Sakhawi, *op. cit.*, p. 210.

depriving him of a means of livelihood. We have also heard of Christians being interrupted during their prayers in their churches and during their feast days. Those who interrupt them take away from them what they are not entitled to take. The Christians are in great distress because of this. Our father the patriarch and our Christian brothers who are now under your authority in your honorable kingdom are few in number, disadvantaged and poor in all regions. You, whom may God preserve, also know of the Muslims under our rule in our vast country over whom and over whose leaders we have full control. We have always been good to them. Their leaders in our country have crowns made of gold and they ride excellent horses. We do not impose *jizyah* or any other taxes on them. If you doubt what we say, ask the merchants and the travelers to our country to tell you the truth. It is also known to you that the river Nile originates in our country and we are able to prevent the annual rise of its water, that is used in irrigating your lands, from reaching you. Nothing prevents us from doing this except our fear of God and the trouble that this action might cause his servants. Our intention in writing you is only to achieve peace between us, as it was between our predecessors."[134]

Then the negus asked the sultan to issue orders for rebuilding the monasteries and churches that had been destroyed and for instructing everyone not to call Christians "dogs."[135]

Here again the negus was sending threats to Egypt, and the frightened sultan tried to deny the accusations of the negus. In response, he sent a delegation to the negus carrying gifts to him. The negus detained the delegation in order to show the delegates how Ethiopians take revenge on Muslims, exhibiting a corpse.

Taking revenge on innocent people [in Ethiopia] fired the anger of the sultan. An Ethiopian emperor named Seyfe Ar`id was able during his reign [1342–1370 A.D.] to force Egyptian authorities to release Patriarch Mark[136] from prison without resorting to the weapon of threats. Commercial relations between Egypt and Ethiopia were flourishing at the time, whether on land or by sea. Since it was impossible for Seyfe Ar`id to offer direct assistance to the patriarch, he arrested all merchants coming form Cairo and then sent his horsemen to terrify the

---

134. *Ibid.*, pp. 67–72.

135. *Ibid.*, p. 71.

136. [Mark IV (1349–1363) was the eighty-fourth Coptic patriarch. (Tr.)]

caravans and obstruct their progress. The traveler Bruce described this situation saying, "Because the reasons for these events were not secret and the patriarch was imprisoned to wrest money from him, the Ethiopians accused the sultan of injustice, forcing him to release the patriarch on condition that he re-establish peace between Seyfe Ar'id and Egypt. This was achieved in no time."[137]

As a result of the Egyptian empire's expansion into the Sudan and its consolidation during the reigns of Muhammad 'Ali, Said Pasha and Khedive Isma'il, several frictions led to war between Egypt and Ethiopia. The reasons behind these wars were purely political, which excludes them from our discussion. We should refer here to the noble deed of the Coptic patriarch [Cyril IV] during the reign of Said of preventing another war from breaking out between Ethiopia and Egypt.

These are the broad outlines of the relationship between the Coptic Christians and the Ethiopians. Co-existing with the Copts were the Melchites whose influence declined faster than that of the Copts. Of course, the Melchites were able to get Europe's attention during the reign of the Mamlūks. If we read Egyptian church history carefully, we notice that the Mamlūk sultans, followed by the Ottomans, treated the Melchites favorably. The reason for this was economic. Then came the crusades, widening the rift between Islam and Christianity but strengthening the political and economic relations between the East and the West and increasing trade in the Mediterranean. The privileges that the republics of Venice and Genoa obtained from Egypt indicate the interest of the Mamlūk sultans, and Turkish pashas after them, in creating a source of income of importance to their country and themselves. Moreover, Catholic Spain became unified, including the remnants of the Arab empire in the West, thus spreading its influence and increasing its wealth. Meanwhile France was playing the role of the defender of Catholicism in the East.

Although the head of the Catholic church was unable to form a new army of crusaders after the defeat of Louis IX in Mansurah[138] and Tunis, his influence continued to be strong and his word continued to be heard in Europe. Was not his order heeded when he threatened to excommunicate any Catholic who sold arms to Muslim countries? Did not he dictate conditions to the dissenting Byzantines

---

137. Bruce, *Voyage aux sources du Nil et en Abyssinie*, 3:115–16.

138. [A city in Lower Egypt, Daqahliya province. (Tr.)]

in the council of Florence in 1429[139] when they asked for military assistance from the kings of the West against the Turks? We have also discovered that the pope, in his capacity as the protector of Catholics worldwide, was interested in the destiny of the Egyptian Melchites, and his interference brought tangible results, especially after events of the reign of al-Nasser Muhammad ibn Qalawūn. Before these events, when the vizier of Morocco visited Cairo and the churches of the Egyptian capital were shut down, the Melchites took opportunity to gain the attention of western nations. They also explained to the Egyptian rulers that their decision to close the churches was unwise. al-Muffadal ibn Abi al-Fada`il said that "al-Ashkari [the sovereign of Constantinople] requested the hiring of Ahl al-Dhimmah in Egypt, as usual, allowing their churches to be opened. Churches were ordered opened and the Ahl al-Dhimmah were allowed to sit straight on horsebacks, although before that time they had had to sit on one side."[140]

To the above al-Maqrizi adds that in 703 A.H. [1303–1304 A.D.] the king of Barcelona sent a delegation [to Egypt] carrying valuable gifts to all high officials, requesting the reopening of the churches. The authorities agreed to open the Coptic church in Harat Zuwaylah and the church of the Venicians.[141]

The pope interfered personally after the painful events in 721 A.H. [1328 A.D.], and a papal delegation was sent to Egypt carrying a message from the pope asking the government to protect Christians. On behalf of the Catholic world, the pope announced that Europeans might treat Muslims hired in their countries in the same way that Christians in Egypt and Syria were being treated.

We must be satisfied by these three examples that explain how the Copts, who were in complete isolation, lost hope in Ethiopia's ability to help them and how they turned towards Europe after they saw the results of her interference in behalf of Melchites. We may ask ourselves once more whether the Copts were driven by material and moral despair when they sought participation in the council of Florence and explored joining the Catholic church.

Islamic Justice and the Copts.

We have little information about the justice of the Arabs towards the Copts because history has not recorded much about it. Although Arabs tended to

---

139. [The Council of Florence (1438–1445) was an ecclesiastical assembly noteworthy for its attempt to unite the Greek and Latin churches. See *The New International Dictionary of the Christian Church*, J.D. Douglas, general editor, Grand Rapids, Michigan: Zondervan, 1974, pp. 380–81. (Tr.)]

140. *Patrologia Orientalis XX*, fasc. I, p. 197.

141. *al-Khitat*, 2:499.

interfere in the legal affairs of Copts, as we mentioned when we discussed the colonial policy of the West, they gave the patriarch relatively wide authority. The savants of the French campaign [1798–1801] wrote that,

> "the patriarch makes decisions in all litigations among his subjects. But his decision is not final because, if they agree, the litigants can seek a decision from the [Muslim] judge, who usually supports the patriarch's decision. The patriarch also acts as a judge in offenses that require penalties. If a Copt were accused of stealing from a Muslim, the latter should complain about him to the patriarch, and visa versa. If a Muslim were the thief, the Copt should complain about him to the [Muslim] judge or ruler of the city."[142]

How did the patriarch make his decisions? Were there laws? Sisostris Sidaros Pasha, who studied the patriarchal system in detail, offers the following information:

> "Concerning orthodox Copts, the patriarch in Cairo and the bishops in the provinces were charged with making decisions in litigations that occurred among their subjects, and their decisions followed no specific rules. But if we were to examine certain documents, we would be inclined to believe that there were texts on which religious authorities depended to make their decisions. These authorities sometimes consulted the notables before issuing their decisions. There were no texts that concerned putting the decisions into effect. The patriarch and the bishops carried out their decisions without resorting to civil authorities. The result was that the decisions were carried out by agreement among the litigants."[143]

It seems that this situation continued without change. However, when Patriarch Demetrius II died in 1873 A.D.,

> "the notables discussed the situation and decided to prepare a plan for church reform before the election of a new patriarch in order that he approve it according to the church laws collected by Ibn al-`Assal in the

---

142. *Description de l'Égypte*, 2nd edition, 1st part, p. 17.

143. Sidaros, *Des Patriarcats*, p. 346.

thirteenth century. These laws stipulated that the patriarch should consult the knowledgeable and pious of the priests and laymen, especially those who had something to do with the sovereign, before making a final decision on important matters. Hence, there arose the formation of a council approved by the khedive in decree no. 17 dated February 5, 1874."[144]

This development indicates that the notables acknowledged implicitly that conditions were not good and that the Coptic community needed to follow the example of the reform movement led by the royal family. The purpose was also to limit the prerogatives of the patriarch in the interest of lay persons. It is not surprising that Patriarch Cyril V[145] tried to have this decree suspended. The [khedive's] law established—along with the national courts—community councils for every Christian denomination whose function was to make decisions concerning personal status [family] litigations.

Were Copts equal to Muslims in the eyes of the law? At the beginning of the Arab occupation justice was most probably flawless. The complaints of Copts were carefully and accurately investigated. We read an account of soldiers in the Arab army who claimed that they had the right to collect money from Christian villages. The wali, Qurah ibn Sharīk, requested that the governor of the province conduct an investigation at the place of the incident and send him a report to settle the problem in the light of accurate information.[146] Because such cases were heard in mosques, Christians and Jews were not allowed inside. al-Kindī mentions that judge Khayr ibn Na'īm used to look into Muslim cases inside the mosque. Then he would sit at the outside door of the mosque to look into the cases of the Ahl al-Dhimmah.[147] After some time—in 177–184 A.H. [793–800

---

144. *Ibid.*, p. 347. [This is a reference to the establishment of the first Coptic community council that consisted of twelve members and twelve adjuncts elected by general suffrage, with the patriarch as chair person. This council was also called *Majlis Millī*. See A. A. Bestawros, "Community Council, Coptic," *The Coptic Encyclopedia*, 2:580–82. (Tr.)]

145. Cyril V (Kerollos) lived from 1874 to 1927.

146. Lammens, H., "Un Gouverneur omayade d'Égypte," in *Majallat al-Majm'a al-Ilmī al-Misrī*, Alexandria, 1908.

147. al-Kindī, *op. cit.*, p. 351.

A.D.]—justice Muhammad ibn Qasrūn permitted Christians to enter [the mosque], but the procedure was considered an exception.[148]

On the other hand, no Christian could be a witness if one of the parties in the case were a Muslim. Justice Khayr ibn Na`īm permitted a Christian to be witness for a Christian and a Jew for a Jew.[149] This system was followed until the nineteenth century. Clot Bey mentions in his memoirs[150] that a student once assaulted him. A committee was formed, headed by the minister of war, to punish the assailant. The court listened to what the student and his colleagues had to say, and refused to listen to what Clot Bey wanted to say because he was a Christian and [therefore] was not allowed to make a statement against a Muslim.

The Decline of the Coptic Language.

The history of the Coptic language mirrors the history of the Copts themselves. The Coptic people retained their language during the era of Greek and Roman rule, paying scant attention to the language of the occupier. But they became interested in learning the Arabic language very soon after the Arab occupation of Egypt. It is true that they had their pragmatic reasons for learning Arabic. The proof is that, when the Arab rulers entrusted the natives [Copts] with the administration of the country, who had also served the Byzantine government, although the Copts did not care for learning the language of the Qurān, they were active in removing the Greek words from their language. Thus Greek names and the names of the capitals of the provinces disappeared [with the exception of the places founded by Greeks] and were replaced by older Coptic names. The Bible had usually been read in Greek with Coptic commentary. After the defeat of the Greeks, it was read only in Coptic. Writing came to be done in Coptic after it had continued [almost exclusively] in Greek until the sixth century A.D.[151] After that time, the Coptic language flourished.

But such progress was superficial. In fact the schism at Chalcedon eliminated the reasons for the renaissance of the Coptic language. We note that the language and its literature flourished between the two [ecumenical] councils of Nicea (325 A.D.) and Chalcedon (451 A.D.). The "genius" of the Copts declined and they produced little original literature. The Greek language

---

148. *Ibid.*, p. 390.

149. *Ibid.*, p. 351.

150. Clot Bey, *Memoires*, edited by Jacques Tagher, Cairo: The Royal Palace Library, 1950, p. 75 (in French).

151. Quatrèmere, *Recherches*, p. 15.

continued to be the official language, studied [only] by ambitious Copts. It also continued to be the language of religion, education and commerce. An [educated] Egyptian could neglect learning the Coptic language, but not Greek.

It is true that the large mass of the peasantry spoke Coptic. Hence, Christianity had to use it to spread its teachings among them. But when the Coptic language lost its position as a language of culture, the Copts resorted to Greek and borrowed a large number of terms which their language has kept to the present day. Over and above this, the Coptic language was never the language of government and administration. The employees who replaced the Greeks after the Arab invasion wrote in Greek, although they were Copts. When the wali `Abd Allah ibn `Abd al-Malik issued a decree in 87 A.H. [706 A.D.] making Arabic the official language, the Copts did not protest. They even hastened to learn the new language of the conquerors. Undoubtedly this change caused anxiety among [government] employees who used the Greek language. But we also learn from recently discovered papyri that the Arab ruler was unable to put his decree into effect right after its issuance. We discover that documents were written entirely in Greek until 164 A.H. [780 A.D.]. We also find documents written in both Greek and Arabic.

For this reason it would be difficult for us to learn the details of the development of the Coptic language from studying official documents. We should study personal [non-literary] documents to learn of the life and gradual decline of Coptic.

Why the Coptic Language Gradually Went Out of Use.[152]

Egypt spoke Coptic in the seventh century. By the twelfth century all Egypt spoke Arabic. The Arabs were able to make their subjects leave their old language behind and replace it with another, an achievement that the Greeks and Romans were unable to do before them and the Turks were unable to do after them.[153] There were two basic reasons that accelerated the disappearance of the Coptic language from public use. First, Coptic employees promptly started to learn the Arabic language to keep their jobs. Second, there was an increase in the number of people converting to Islam who abandoned the language of their forefathers immediately after conversion.

There were other reasons that led to the disappearance of Coptic from public use. The Arabs were not satisfied with invading Egypt; they wanted to

---

152. [For an excellent article on this subject, see L.S.B. MacCoull, "The Strange Death of Coptic Culture," *Coptic Church Review*, 10:2 (Summer 1989). (Tr.)]

153. *Dictionnaire d'Archéologie et de Liturgie*, article "Coptes."

occupy and colonize it. The colonizers mixed with Egyptian families encouraging them to speak Arabic. Moreover, conversion to Islam mandates the study of the Qurān, hence learning the Arabic language. The number of Coptic men of religion who kept the Coptic traditions and language alive began to decline rapidly. Monasteries that had flourished soon after the Arab invasion were eventually abandoned by the monks when authorities started to impose taxes on their occupants. After a short period of time the Coptic priests learned Arabic so that their flocks would understand them. As the monks gradually declined intellectually, they abandoned the study of Coptic when they realized that it was practically useless.[154]

The Stages in the Decline of the Coptic Language.
The decline of the Coptic language occurred gradually.

"The Arabic language suppressed the Coptic like a plant deprived of water and sun under the shadow of a huge tree. Coptic survived until the tenth century A.D. It even flourished in the monasteries. But from the eleventh century on, it was not taken care of, thus fading quickly. By the twelfth century it was on the verge of extinction."[155]

Events that support our claim are the following. In a dispute between Melchites and Copts in 132 A.H. [750 A.D.] concerning the ownership of certain churches, Patriarch Michael I[156] wrote a petition in Coptic to the authorities. But he attached to it an Arabic translation, on the advice of some bishops. Further, Deacon Yuhanna, who wrote the biography of Patriarch Michael I, related that while Musa the bishop of Awsīm[157] was on his way to an audience with Caliph Marwān, who had taken refuge in Egypt in 132 A.H. [750 A.D.], soldiers knocked him down on the ground and beat him on his neck and ribs with a copper rod saying, "Give us gifts and we shall release you." The historian added that "the

---

134. [See Emile Maher Ishaq, "Coptic language, Spoken," *The Coptic Encyclopedia*, 2.604–7. (Tr.)]

155. *Dictionnaire d'Archéologie et de Liturgie*, art. "Coptes."

156. [Michael (Kail) I (743–767 A.D.) was the forty-sixth Coptic patriarch. (Tr.)]

157. [Awsīm is a town in the Giza province that has a long Christian tradition. (Tr.)]

bishop did not answer them with one word because he did not understand their language. I had to translate for him every word that they said."[158]

In summary, the interest of the monks in learning Arabic was no less than that of others. Within one century of the Arab invasion, some monks were seeking the help of translators to read Coptic texts. When a Muslim wanted to convert to Christianity, he studied its principles with a priest who would explain to him in Arabic the Coptic text of the holy book.[159] The clergy in the lower ranks were the first to rush to learn Arabic and neglect Coptic. The higher ranks of the clergy put off learning Arabic for a long time. There was even a patriarch who was illiterate in both Arabic and Coptic, Michael V,[160] who lived in the middle of the twelfth century. In general, the clergy used the Arabic language from the beginning of the tenth century so that their followers could understand them. We know of the famous sentence with which Sawirus ibn al-Muqaffa started his *History of the Patriarchs*: "I sought the help of those of the Christian brothers whom I knew could give it, and I asked them to assist me to translate from Greek and Coptic into Arabic, which is known to the people in Egypt because most of them do not know Coptic or Greek." Sa'īd ibn al-Bitriq preceded him in this matter. Later the Copts wrote their history and religious texts in Arabic. Their most famous authors, such as Boutros ibn al-Rahib,[161] Makīn[162] and Abi al-Fada'il, did not know Coptic. It did not take long before the Coptic patriarchs gave particular attention to the Arabic language. Michael the Syrian wrote of Gabriel II [1131–1146] that he was excellent in his ability with the Arabic language and calligraphy. When he realized that the Egyptian people spoke and wrote Arabic because of the long period of Arab sovereignty, he translated the Old and the New Testaments into Arabic, as well as the Coptic rites, so that faithful Egyptian Christians could understand these books."[163]

---

158. Renaudot, *op. cit.*, p. 214.

159. Quatrèmere, *op. cit.*, pp. 34–35.

160. [Michael V was the seventy-first Coptic patriarch, 1145–1146 A.D. (Tr.)]

161. [See Aziz S. Atiya, "Abū Shākir ibn al-Rāhib," *The Coptic Encyclopedia*, 1:33–34. He was a historian and high official in the army, and the son of al-Rahib Anba Boutros who was a government secretary at the beginning of the thirteenth century A.D. (Tr.)]

162. [A Coptic historian (1205–1273); see Aziz S. Atiya, "Makīn, Ibn al-'Amīd al-," *The Coptic Encyclopedia*, 5:1513. (Tr.)]

163. Michel le Syrien, *op. cit.*, 3:235.

The activities of Coptic linguists such as Abu al-Barakat ibn Kabar[164] and the brothers al-Assal[165] can be explained not by their desire to facilitate learning the Arabic language by the people, but by their attempt to aid others in understanding the language of the Coptic mass and the rites of the Coptic creed. Although prayers were always said in Coptic, the religious lessons were explained in Arabic.

al-Maqdisi wrote that the Christians of Egypt spoke Coptic until 325 A.H. [985 A.D.],[166] and the French orientalist Quatrèmere says that "the upper class families distinguished themselves from the common people by their knowledge of the Coptic language. This language was wide-spread in Egypt, like Latin in Europe."[167]

In fact we cannot know exactly when the language went out of public use. We have referred to the twelfth century A.D., that is, after the fall of the Fatimid dynasty. But we believe that it flourished for a longer period of time in Upper Egypt. Abu Saleh al-Armani[168] notes a custom practiced in the city of Esna.[169] "The Christians of that city used to attend the wedding parties of the Muslims. They toured the squares and the streets in front of the bride groom cheering and shouting Upper Egyptian Coptic expressions."[170]

In the seventeenth and eighteenth centuries it was rare to find someone who spoke Coptic, a fact that led some travelers to believe that they had met the last person speaking this language. Vansleb[171] has said of Mu`allim Anistas that "he was the only man in Upper Egypt who knew the language of his nation, i.e.,

---

164. [He was a scholar born toward the end of the thirteenth century. See Aziz S. Atiya, "Ibn Kabar," *The Coptic Encyclopedia*, 4:1267–68, and Louis Cheikho, *Wuzara' al-Nusraniyah*, Beirut, 1987. (Tr.)]

165. [Known in Arabic as Awlad al-`Assal, they were three brothers who were historians, linguists and officials during the Ayyubid dynasty (1169–1250 A.D.). See Aziz S. Atiya, "Awlad al-`Assal," *The Coptic Encyclopedia*, 1:309–11. (Tr.)]

166. al-Maqdisi, *op. cit.*, p. 203.

167. Quatrèmere, *op. cit.*, p. 39.

168. [Abu Saleh the Armenian. (Tr.)]

169. [A city in Upper Egypt. (Tr.)]

170. Abu Saleh, *Churches and Monasteries of Egypt*, edited by B. T. A. Evetts, 1895, folio 9. [Aziz S. Atiya notes that the real author of this work is a Copt named Abu al-Makarim; see "Abu Salih the Armenian," *The Coptic Encyclopedia* 1:33. (Tr.)]

171. Vansleb, *Nouvelle relation*, p. 363.

Coptic." He adds that he could not make good use of his knowledge because he was a deaf old man of eighty years of age. In spite of this, "he enjoyed meeting the man after whose death the Coptic language would completely die." However, Du Mayée, the consul after Vansleb, wrote that people in some regions of Upper Egypt were still speaking Coptic, while the traveler Forskal claimed that he had met a Copt called Ibrahim Enash who was quite knowledgeable in the Coptic language.[172] However, even if there were those who knew the old language until the eighteenth century in some far away Upper Egyptian villages, there was no one who understood the contents of the books [written in Coptic] nor their authors.[173] It was recounted that in the second half of the nineteenth century the Coptic cabinet minister Boutros Pasha Ghali met with Pope Leo XIII.[174] The pope asked Mr. Ghali some questions in Coptic and Mr. Ghali had to acknowledge his ignorance of the language. When he returned to Egypt, he decided to learn the language of his grandfathers.

The Literary Value of Coptic Writings.

The Copts went through a long transitional period during which they neither spoke nor wrote well in Arabic or Coptic. We do not have the skills to evaluate the Coptic writings produced during the Islamic rule. However, the able translator Amélineau compared two documents, one written during the reign of `Abd al-Aziz ibn Marwān,[175] the other in the thirteenth century A.D. during al-Kamel's[176] reign. Amélineau said that the language of the first document reflected the atmosphere of an affluent era, exhibiting no signs of a decline. The other one indicated that the Coptic language had declined and become rough. It also

---

172. Niebuhr, *op. cit.*, p. 106.

173. *Dictionnaire d'Archéologie Chretienne et de Liturgie*, article "Coptes." [This was a very dark period of history for all Egyptians—Muslims, Copts and Jews. By the end of the eighteenth century the Mamlūks' absolute despotism, ignorance, cruelty, chaotic administration and wars had caused the destruction of the Egyptian economy, spread ignorance and superstition, and weakened the country so that it would fall an easy prey in 1798 to the French army under Napoleon. (Tr.)]

174. [Leo XIII (Gioacchino Pecci) was a Catholic pope (1816–1903). (Tr.)]

175. [`Abd al-Aziz ibn Marwān was the seventh Umayyād wali of Egypt. A half brother of Caliph `Abd al-Malik ibn Marwān, he ruled Egypt twenty-two years (683–705 A.D.). (Tr.)]

176. [The Ayyubid king al-Malik al-Kamel (615–635 A.H./1218–1238 A.D.). (Tr.)]

contained Arabic words that the writer had copied inaccurately, making it difficult to understand.[177]

Concerning the adoption of the Arabic language, we can say the same thing, but in reverse. The *History of the Patriarchs* by Sawirus ibn al-Muqaffa' was written in rather weak Arabic style with many mistakes and weak sentence structure. Eventually the Arabic [used by Copts] improved and became stronger than it had been before, in spite of grammatical mistakes that publishers of Christian manuscripts believed should be kept in, whether they were mistakes of the author when they were first composed or those of a scribe when they were transcribed.

Coptic Schools and the Study of the Coptic Language.[178]

History tells us little about the Coptic school system. What we know for certain is that these schools existed at various periods. But until the nineteenth century we did not know the kind of education offered in the schools. Dor Bey tells us about Coptic schools during the reign of Isma'īl. "The Coptic *katateeb*[179] were often forced to `hide' off the main thoroughfares by meeting inside houses. Nowadays, although the time of overt persecution is over, we find Coptic schools always hidden away in the narrow roads of the middle class districts between the main routes. The Coptic language does not play an important role in the schools. The teacher is satisfied with teaching Coptic writing to a number of children, some prayers, and religious hymns, because he himself does not know more than this. Thus the school teacher spends valuable time without really developing the minds of these young children. The basis of the whole educational process is the reading and writing of Arabic."[180]

177. Amélineau, "Deux documents coptes écrit sous la domination Arabe," in *Majallat al-Majm'a al-Ilmī al-Misrī*, Alexandria, 1885.

178. [For additional information see Sulaymān Nāsīm, "Education, Coptic," *The Coptic Encyclopedia* 3:931–33, and his *al-Aqbāt wa al-Ta'līm fī Misr al-Hadithah*, Cairo: Usqufiyat al-Dirasat al-Qibtiyah, 1980 (in Arabic). (Tr.)]

179. [*Kuttab* (sing.; pl. *katateeb*) refers to a Quranic school, but the Copts had the same educational organization. They first held classes in churches for teaching the Bible, prayer, arithmetic, and the Arabic and Coptic languages to Coptic children. Later these one-classroom schools were held outside the churches. (Tr.)]

180. Dor, Victor Edouard, *L'Instruction publique en Égypte*, Paris: A. Lacroix, 1872, p. 182.

The Arabs and the Coptic Language.

It was natural that Arabs establish the Arabic tongue early as the official language. We cannot say that they wanted to abolish Coptic, with the exception of al-Ḥakim bi Amr Allah who, during his persecution of Christians, ordered that Coptic not be used.[181] To be sure, the rulers wanted to know what people might be saying, particularly in patriarchal circles. Thus they were interested in translating Coptic prayers and [religious] lessons in order to be sure that they did not contain criticisms of Islam. They took the [further] opportunity of interfering by encouraging Copts to learn their own language and discouraging them from learning Arabic, especially when they saw their enthusiasm for learning it to keep their jobs. In a related vein, al-Maqrizi tells us that some Muslim students studied medicine and mathematics in Coptic schools. But this happened in the thirteenth and fourteenth centuries at a time when the use of Arabic was well established. Copts even studied the Qurān as a means of adopting the language of their rulers.[182]

---

181. [Butcher referred to this incident without mentioning her source. (Tr.)]

182. [For a detailed report on the development of the Arabic language and Islamic education, and on Egyptian culture in general and Coptic education in particular, see Ibrahīm Salama, *L'Enseignment islamique en Égypte, son evolution, son influence sur les programmes modernes*, Cairo: Imprimerie Nationale, 1939. (Tr.)]

Chapter 13

CONCLUSIONS

We have reviewed the historical events of thirteen centuries. But coming to conclusions at the end of this review is really premature in the light of the information we have.

We first noted that the Copts knew nothing about the Arabs when the latter invaded Egypt. They received them as liberators after the Arabs assured them of religious freedom and a decrease in the taxes they had to pay. When the Arabs had to collect more taxes because of their growing need for money, Copts did not hesitate to express disappointment. The Arabs could have maintained the loyalty of the Copts—or at least would have not disappointed them—if they had not added the names of the monks (who were only a few thousand) to the lists of taxpayers, forcing them to hide in monasteries to avoid paying taxes. In return for a few dinars to increase their income, the Arabs lost the support of those who then constituted the elite among the Copts and who could influence the behavior of their people. `Amr ibn al-`As was able to stop the attempted invasion of Egypt by the Byzantine commander Emmanuel, without protecting the rear of his army, because he had exempted the Coptic clergy from paying taxes. But the Umayyāds witnessed the Copts' support of the Abbasids because the former had imposed taxes on the monks.

Were the Arabs tolerant of the Copts? Surely the Arabs were not interested in the current religious disputes between Egyptian Christians. When they found that Copts constituted the [Christian] majority in Egypt, they readily supported them against the Melchites and granted them all that they needed, often at the expense of their enemies. However, they never refused the Melchites' offers whenever they found them beneficial.

At any rate, the Arabs eventually deviated from their principles and tended to become materialistic. Their wide-ranging invasions came to obstruct the application of laws that themselves could not be developed in tandem with Muslim expansion. As a matter of fact, Islam continued for one and one-half centuries without breaking the *shari`a* law of tax collection. But eventually the Arabs had to defend their empire which was threatened [by forces] from the outside and by revolution and conspiracies from within; and they further had to meet the financial needs of the extravagant court of the caliph, first in Damascus where the Umayyāds emulated the Byzantines, and later in Baghdad where the Abbasids emulated the Persians. It is no surprise that the rulers did not follow the orders of the Prophet, because if they had been satisfied with taxes as spelled out by the Qurān the treasury would have gone bankrupt. And if they had done away with the assistance of Christian employees, the administration would have become chaotic. In the beginning the Arabs were not ready to perform administrative chores because they were more interested in the arts of war than office work. Moreover, the Copts in Egypt had benefitted early on from the personal policy of `Amr ibn al-`As.

It may be said that the Egyptians were converting to Islam. Why then did the Arabs seek the assistance of the [remaining] Christians, even when Christians came to represent only a small minority of the population? We should remember that those who ruled Egypt after the Arab invasion were not Egyptians[1] but Arabs who were sent by the caliphs to rule Egypt in their name. The Ṭulūnids, the Ikhshīdīds, the Fatimids and the Ayyubids came from Asia and North Africa. The Mamlūk sultans were Circassian slaves or of other origin. The Turkish rulers never cared for the people [in Egypt or in any other country under their rule].

Muhammad `Ali the Great was the first to follow a nationalistic policy. The rulers before him had generally treated all Egyptians the same. Sometimes they threw a large portion of the burden on the shoulders of the Copts. But the Copts kept the secrets of land survey, and the arts of tax collection and bookkeeping. They reached the point at which they formed a syndicate of accountants. Although Muslims looked down on them, they could not do without them, and the rulers had to seek their help.

Moreover, the Arabs believed they were racially superior, and they were very enthusiastic about their new religion. They also believed that if they died for their sacred cause [of spreading Islam] they would have a high place in the hereafter. But if they survived the battle, they were entitled to divide the land of the enemy and his possessions among themselves. Invasions [of other countries] by the Arabs were similar to raids conducted by a tribe, whose members would enjoy the spoils of war and then resume their raids.

The Arab soldier went to war with this idea in mind. In point of fact the Arab leadership refused to divide the conquered lands among the invaders according to *shari`a*, Islamic law. However, they ruled countries as if they were not going to stay. For instance, they did not object to education in Egypt, but they did not establish one school. They did not try to reorganize the administration of the country, leaving it as it was under the Byzantines with some superficial modifications. Because the caliphs considered Egypt a supply center for their

---

1. [Nasser was the first leader of Egyptian origin to rule Egypt since the Persian invasion of Egypt in 525 B.C. (Tr.)]

empire,[2] the state agreed to meet the costs of repairing roads, but did not go beyond that. It did not supervise repair operations. Their main interest was that Egypt pay its taxes. Grohman states that "the caliphs and the walis paid such little attention to the administration that a register of the names of the tax payers, Muslims and Christians, was found written entirely in Greek with the sign of the cross on its first page."[3]

It is no wonder that income declined and Egypt became poorer. We may quote here some figures for Prince `Umar Tuson.[4] The [initial] total income from *kharaj* and *jizyah*, according to Arab historians, was twenty million dinars. `Amr ibn al-`As reduced it to twelve million. Abd Allah ibn Sa`ad succeeded in increasing it to fourteen million. But the income decreased to nine, then to five million dinars during the civil war of M`uawiyah's caliphate. The poverty of Egypt grew during the Abbasid reign to the extent that income [from taxes] decreased during Harūn al-Rashid's reign to four million dinars and leveled at that figure. Ibn Tulūn raised it to five million. During Khamarawayh's reign it was four million and during Muhammad al-Ikhshīdī's reign it was two million. During Kafūr's reign it grew to three and one-half million dinars, during al-Mu`iz li-Dīn Allah's to four million, then during al-Aziz's back to three million, during al-Hakim's three million four hundred thousand dinars, during al-Mustansir's two million (including the income from Syria), during al-Must`ali's five million (due to the rule of Badr al-Jamali and al-Afdal Shahinshah), during al-Hafiz li-Din Allah's one million two hundred thousand, during Salah al-Din's five million and a half and during Baybars's two million. When the French invaded Egypt the [government's] income was one and one-half million dinars.

These figures do not reflect exactly the degree of affluence in the country because the decrease in government income resulted from the decrease in taxes, as probably happened during Ibn Tulūn's, Muhammad al-Ikhshīdī's and al-Aziz's reign. But there is strong proof of the poverty of the country in terms of the reduction of the cultivable area: it was six million feddans during the reign of `Umar ibn al-Khattab, and in seventy-five years it shrank to three million feddans during the reign of Hisham ibn Abd al-Malik.

---

2. [The Arabs in this respect are like the Romans who called Egypt the granary of their empire. (Tr.)]

3. Grohman, *Aperçu*, p. 78.

4. [The figures quoted by the author in this section were selected from `Umar Tuson, *Kitāb Maliyat Misr min `ahd al-Fra`inah ila al-`An*, Alexandria: Matb`at Salah al-Dīn, 1931. (Tr.)]

Because the rulers were badly in need of money they regularly resorted to illegitimate means to obtain it. Ibn Jubayr,[5] who lived at the time of the crusades, did not hide his anger either for what he considered ill-treatment of pilgrims or for forbidding those who did not pay taxes from visiting the holy land. He wrote, "The house of God[6] is now in the hands of people who make a living unlawfully from it and use it as an instrument to gain money without justification." Then he added, "There is no [true] Islam except in the Maghreb [Morocco] because there they follow a clear line; there is no justice, no rights, no religion in the East."[7]

In fact religious considerations lose their effect after the religious zeal of a people cools down. Have we not read that Ibn Jubayr reprimanded the Muslims of the East for their manner of dealing with Christians during the crusades? Have we not heard of the pope threatening more than once to excommunicate Christian traders of Europe because they supplied Muslims with arms during times of crisis? Henry Lammens is not far from the truth when he reports the supremacy of politics based on interests as distinguished from policies based on sentiments, saying, "Egypt in the view of the Umayyāds had only an economic value. She produces grain, makes papyrus paper and pays taxes. These material considerations alone made the rulers of the time interested in her."[8]

These facts should be known if we want to measure the degree of Arab tolerance towards Copts. It is my view that we should look into this matter in the following way. If the Arabs were not in need of the Copts' help,[9] and if the public interest was not sufficiently important to make Arabs care for them, would the Arabs be tolerant towards them? It is clear that a Christian was not of interest to the ruler as an individual in society. Nevertheless the rulers broke Islamic law, they did not follow the advice of the *fuqah*, and they kept Christians in their jobs because they were in need of them. They remembered *shari`a* rules and the *fuqahās'* opinions when they wanted to ostracize Copts for financial or political reasons, either by their own will or under the pressure of public opinion.

al-Maqarizi reports the following incident from the events of 592 A.H. [1195 A.D.].

---

5. [The Muslim traveler Muhammad ibn Ahmad ibn Jubayr, 1145–1217 A.D. (Tr.)]

6. [He means the holy Muslim shrines in Mecca and Medina. (Tr.)]

7. Ibn Jubayr, *op. cit.*, pp. 77–78.

8. Henry Lammens in his work *Un gouverneur omayade d'Égypte* [previously cited].

9. [To manage Egypt's affairs. (Tr.)]

"There was a financial crisis related to the expenses of the sultan's palace, and the expenses of his dependents, and even what his children would eat. . . . To solve the problem, [his associates] had to consider unlawful income. Thus the production of wines made of maize and other alcoholic beverages were legalized and the sale of these products became public. They went on sale in stores to raise a needed 12,000 dinars. No one could object to this. This ill-gotten income was spent on food for the sultan and his other needs."[10]

What was the position of the people who remained deeply religious? In fact their situation did not affect the course of events except once during the reign of Sultan Muhammad ibn Qala`ūn[11] when he was forced to persecute Christians.

What was the position of the walis who ruled in the name of the caliphs? The interest of the people came second, and all means were legal with a view to embezzling money and becoming rich. But when these rulers ruled in their own names, they immediately considered the benefits of the country. Such a ruler did his utmost to develop the wealth of the country and protect the interests of the people, abstaining from making any decision that might disturb the peace. When the good intentions of rulers were augmented by a true spirit of tolerance, as was the case with Muhammad `Ali and his successors, religious affairs diminished and were replaced by national considerations.

It remains to describe the position of the Copts during this period of history. We can compare the Copts with other people who believed that, by partially or completely relinquishing their independence to the invaders, they would secure their safety and property. But gradually they were pressured to the extent that they lost the power of resistance. The Copts revolted only when their Muslim compatriots revolted and they always surrendered when their Muslim compatriots stopped fighting [an enemy]. We cannot consider the Bashmurian revolt an exception because the Bashmurians were of Greek origin, as indicated above.

The Arabs were characterized by patience. The *shari`a* helped Copts to convert to Islam and to assimilate into the Muslim community by exempting them from taxes (*jizyah*). The Arabs [in effect] helped those who remained faithful to Christianity to make a living by hiring them to supervise the state income.

---

10. al-Maqrizi, *al-Suluk*, 1:134.

11. [al-Nasir Muhammad ibn Qala`ün first reigned in 693–694 A.H. (1294–1295 A.D.); his second reign lasted from 698 to 708 A.H. (1299–1309 A.D.); he then resumed power from 709 to 741 A.H. (1309–1340 A.D.). (Tr.)]

In spite of repeated persecutions, Copts were able to re-accumulate their wealth. They rarely refused openly to pay additional taxes. It is astonishing that when Emir Ṣarghatmīsh[12] discovered that the Copts still owned 25,000 feddans, in spite of persecutions and the burden of new taxes, he immediately confiscated their land without justification. In such light, some orientalists have claimed that the history of the Egyptian church under Islamic rule was a history of conflicts over financial matters and that love of money was a prominent sin of the Coptic church.

* * *

Now that we have related events in a candid way, aiming at revealing the truth, we may ask how will relations between Muslims and Copts develop in the future. Should we be optimistic or pessimistic? Should the Copts [as a minority] seek the protection of legal safeguards to live among the majority?

The best answer to these questions can be found in the minutes of the meetings of the committee charged with writing the draft of the constitution of independent Egypt. In 1922 some voices were raised calling for a method of representation that was followed in forming the legislative assembly of 1933.[13] One of the members of the committee, Dr. Abd al-Hamīd Badawi Pasha,[14] told the other members, "If the minorities remember the past, and the injustices and financial obligations imposed upon them, they should remember that both the majority and the minority lived under a despotic government where the majority as well as the minority suffered injustices equally. We do not want to revive past history in our new system. Religious differences are growing weaker among us. Their effect will diminish until they completely disappear before long. We must not let the ghost of these differences become conspicuous among us—felt by everyone. I am afraid that this problem will cause us trouble in an age in which aspects of religious discrimination are decreasing and the ties that bind people together in their social life are now mutual interests rather than religion and sect.

---

12. [Sayf al-Din Ṣarghatmish al-Nasiri who was in the service of al-Nasir Muhammad ibn Qalaūn. This action of the emir was mentioned in al-Maqrizī, *al-Khitat*, 1:69–70. In addition to confiscating 25,000 feddans owned by the Copts and distributing them among the Mamlūk emirs, he ordered the demolishing of many Coptic churches. (Tr.)]

13. [This legislative assembly of 1913 recruited its membership from various groups of Egyptian society: notables, lawyers, merchants, religious leaders, Muslims, Christians, etc. (Tr.)]

14. [Abd al-Hamid Badawi (1887–1966) was cabinet minister and was later appointed member of the International Court of Justice in 1946, serving until he died in 1966. (Tr.)]

I hope that I shall see the day when all our affairs, even marriage and divorce, and other personal matters, are integrated into one [civic] system in which all of us live in one well-organized civic life. We need a purely national policy which disregards religions and sects, aiming always at achieving the interest of our country."

In fact we are now going through a transitional period that will come to an end. During this period we have discovered two currents that oppose one another: some thinkers—looking to the past—do not acknowledge the progress that has taken place in Egyptian society; others believe that modernism will eventually prevail over conservatism. Modern Egypt chose the right path when she adopted the 1922 constitution. Let us help her continue her critical experiment. The results, we shall learn, will be more expressive than our premature guessing.

APPENDIX I

SOURCES CONSULTED BY THE AUTHOR

Abdīn Palace Archives (Turkish, European and Arabic). Cairo.

Abu Salih, al-Armanī.
> *The Churches and Monasteries of Egypt and Some Neighboring Countries, attributed to Abu Salih the Armenian.* Translated by B.T.A. Evetts with added notes by Alfred Butler. Oxford: Clarendon Press, 1895. [This book was wrongly attributed to Abu Salih. The real author is Abu al-Makarim Jirjis ibn Ma'ūd who lived in the thirteenth century. See "Abū al-Makārim" *The Coptic Encyclopedia*, 1:23. (Tr.)]

Abu Yusuf Ya'qūb.
> *Kitāb al-Kharāj.* Cairo: Bulaq Press, 1884.

Academie des Inscriptions et Belles-Lettres. Paris. *Recueil des Historiens des Croisades. Historiens Orientaux.* Paris: Imprimerie Nationale, 1872–1906. 5 vols.

Ali Mubarak.
> *al-Khitat al-Tawfiqiyah.* Cairo: al-Matb'ah al-Amiriyah, 1886–89. 20 vols.

Amélineau, Émile Clement.
> "Deux documents Coptes." In *Majallat al-Majm'a al-Ilmī al-Misrī,* 1885.

Amélineau, Émile Clement.
> *Géographie de l'Égypte à l'Epoque copte.* Paris: Imprimerie Nationale, 1893.

Amélineau, Émile Clement.
> "Une Documente copte du Dix-huitième Siècle." *Journal Asiatique,* Feb.–March, 1887.

Awad, Ahmad Hafiz.
> *Fath Misr al-Hadīthah aw Napoleon Bonaparte fi Misr.* Cairo: Matb'at Misr, 1925.

al-Baladhurī, Ahmad ibn Yahya.
> *Kitāb Futūh al-Buldān.* Edited by M.J. De Goeje. Leiden: E.J. Brill, 1965.

Balawī, 'Abd Allah ibn Muhammad.
> *Sirat Ahmad ibn Tūlūn.* Edited by Muhammad Kurd 'Ali. Cairo: Maktabat al-Thaqafah al-Diniyah. Reprint of 1939 Damascus edition.

Belloc, J.T.
> *Le Pays des Pharaons.* Paris: Bourlaton, 1890.

Bemelen.

L'Égypte et l'Europe par un ancien Juge mixte. Leiden: E.J. Brill, 1882.

Blochet, Edgar.

"Mouffazzal ibn Abil-Fazaïl. Histoire des Sultans Mamlouks." *Patrologia Orientalis,* Tome 12, Fasc. 3. Paris: Firmin-Didot, 1919.

Blunt, Wilfred Scawen.

Secret History of the English Occupation of Egypt. London: T. Fisher Unwin, 1907. Arabic edition by Ahmad Hafez Awad, Cairo, 1907.

Bowring, John.

Report on Egypt and Candia, Addressed to R.H. Viscount Palmerston. London: W. Clowes, 1840.

Bruce, James.

Voyage aux Sources du Nil en Nubie et en Abyssinie, pendant les Années 1768–1772. Paris: Traduction Française, 1790.

Butcher, Edith Louisa.

The Story of the Church of Egypt: Being an Outline of the History of the Egyptians under their Successive Masters from the Roman Conquest until Now. London: Smith, Elder, 1897. 2 vols.

Butler, Alfred Joshua.

The Arab Conquest of Egypt and the Last Thirty Years of the Roman Dominion. Oxford: Clarendon Press, 1902.

Cabrol, Fernand (editor).

Dictionnaire d'Archéologie et de Liturgie. Paris: Letouzey et Ané, 1907–1953. 15 vols.

Chabot, J.B. (Trans.).

Chronique de Michel le Syrien Patriarch Jacobite d'Antioche (1166–1199). Paris: L'Academie des Inscriptions et Belles-Lettres, 1899–1905. Vol. 1, 1899; vol. 2, 1901; vol. 3, 1905. (Vol. 4 1910, Texte syriaque.)

Champollion-Figeac, J.J.

Égypte ancienne. Paris: Collection l'Univers pittoresque, 1876.

Charles-Roux, Francois.

Le Project français de Conquête de l'Égypte sous le Règne de Louis XVI. Cairo: Imprimerie de l'Institut français d'Archéologie orientale, 1929.

Charmes, Gabriel.

Cinq mois au Caire et dans la Basse Égypte. Paris: G. Charpentier, 1880.

Cheikho, Louis.
   Eutychii Patriarchae Alexandrini Annales. Corpus Scriptorum Christianorum Orientalium. Scriptores Arabici. Series 3, 6 and 7. Beirut: E Typographico Catholico, 1905–1909.
Clot, Antoine Barthélemy.
   Aperçu général sur l'Égypte. Paris: Fortin, Masson, 1840. 2 vols.
Clot, Antoine Barthélemy.
   Memoires inédits. Cairo: Publications de la Bibliothèque Privée de S.M. Farouk 1er, 1950.
Cromer, Evelyn Baring.
   Modern Egypt. New York: Macmillan, 1908. 2 vols.
Denon, Dominique Vivant.
   Travels in Upper and Lower Egypt during the Campaign of General Bonaparte. Translated from the French by E.A. Kendall. London: B. Crosby, 1802
Dauin, Georges.
   L'Égypte indépendante. Cairo: Société Royale de Géographie, 1924.
Description de l'Égypte. Commission des Sciences et Arts d'Égypte. Paris: Imprimerie Imperiale, 1809–28. 18 vols. in 19.
Devonshire, H.
   L'Égypte musulmane et les Fondateurs de ses Monuments. Paris: Maisonneuve, 1926.
Didier, Charles.
   Les Nuits du Caire. Paris: Hachette, 1860.
Dor, Victor Edouard.
   L'Instruction publique en Égypte. Paris: A. Lacroix, 1872.
Douin, Georges and Mme. E.C. Fawtier-Jones.
   L'Angleterre et l'Égypte (1801–1803). Cairo: Société Royale de Géographie, 1929.
Douin, Georges.
   L'Égypte de 1802 à 1804. Correspondance de Consul de France en Égypte. Cairo: Société Royale de Géographie, 1925.
Duff-Gordon, Lucie.
   Lettres d'Égypte. Traduction française par Mrs. Ross. Paris: J. Hetzel, 1869.
Durbin, John P.
   Observations in the East, Chiefly in Egypt, Palestine, Syria and Asia Minor. New York: Harper, 1860.
Duchesne, Louis M.O.
   L'Église au VIe siècle. Paris: De Boccard, 1925.

Encyclopaedia of Islam. First edition. Leiden, 1913–1936.

Fowler, Montague.
Christian Egypt, Past, Present and Future. London: Church Newspaper Co., 1901.

Géramb, Marie Joseph.
Pelerinage à Jerusalem et au Mont Sinai en 1831, 1832 et 1833. Paris: A. Leclere, 1839. 3 vols.

Ghurbal, Shafīq.
al-General Y`aqūb wa al-Faris Lascaris wa Mashrū`a Istiqlāl Misr in 1801. Cairo: 1932. In Arabic.

Goeje, J. de.
Memoires sur la Conquête de la Syrie. Leiden: E.J. Brill, 1900.

Grousset, René.
Histoire des Croisades et du Royaume Franc de Jerusalem. Paris: Plon, 1934–36. 3 vols.

Grohman, Adolf.
Aperçu de Papyrologie arabe. Publié dans les Études de Papyrologie. Cairo: Société Royale Égyptienne de Papyrologie, 1932.

Grohman, Adolf.
Arabic Papyri in the Egyptian Library. Cairo: Egyptian Library Press, 1934. 3 vols.

Hamont, P.N.
L'Égypte sous la Domination de Mehemet Ali. Paris: Collection d'Univers Pittoresque, 1847.

Harcourt, Francois-Henri.
L'Égypte et les Égyptien. Paris: 1893.

Haykal, Muhammad Husayn.
al-Farūq `Umar. Cairo: Maktabat al-Nahhah, 1944.

Heyd, W.
Histoire du Commerce de Levant au Moyen-age. Publié par F. Raynaud. Leipzig: Harrassowitz, 1923.

Holy Qurān, The. Sahīh al-Bukharī.

Homsy, Gaston.
Le General Jacob et l'expedition de Bonaparte en Égypte (1798–1801). Marseille: Les Éditions indépendantes, 1921.

Huzayyin, S.A.
Bilad al-Arab wa al-Sharq al-Adna. Cairo: al-Jam`iyah al-Jughrafiya, 1942.

Ibn ʿAbd al-Hakam.
> *Futuh misr wa al-Maghrib.* Edited by Charles C. Torrey. New Haven, Conn.: Yale University Press, 1922.

Ibn al-Athīr, Izz al-Dīn.
> *al-Kamil fī al-Tarikh.* Cairo: Dar al-Kutub, 1929. 12 vols.

Ibn al-Qalānisī, Abu Yʿala Hamzah ibn Asad.
> *Dhayl Tarikh Dimishq.* Leyden: E.J. Brill, 1908.

Ibn al-Sirafī, ʿAli ibn Munjib.
> *Qnūn Diwān al-Rasaʾil.* Cairo: Matbʿat al-Waʿiz, 1905.

Ibn Fadl Allah al-Umarī, Ahmad ibn Yahya.
> *Masalik al-Absar fi Mamelik al-Amsār.* Traduit et annoté avec une Introduction par Maurice Gaudefroy-Demombynes. Vol. I, *L'Afrique moins l'Égypte.* Paris: P. Genthner, 1927.

Ibn Iyas, Muhammad ibn Ahmad.
> *Tarikh Misr (Badāʾi al-Zuhūr fīwaqāʾi al-Duhur).* Cairo: al-Matbʿah al-Amiriyah, 1894. 3 vols.

Ibn Jobeir.
> *Travels.* Edited by Williams Wright. 2nd ed. edited by J. de Goeje. Leyden: E.J. Brill, 1907.

Ibn Kathīr, Ismaʿil ibn ʿUmar.
> *al-Bidayah wa al–Nihayah.* Cairo: Matbʿat al-Saʿādah, 1932–39. 14 vols.

Ibn Khaldūn, ʿAbd al-Rahmān.
> *al-Muqadimmah.* Cairo: al-Matbʿah al-Amiriyah, 1902.

Ibn al-Qalanisi.
> *Abu Ya'la Tarikh.* Leiden: E.J. Brill, 1908.

Ibn al-Rāhib.

Ibn Taghrībirdi, Abu al-Mahasin Yusuf.
> *al-Nujam al-Zahitah fi Mulūk Misr wa al-Qahirah.* Cairo: Dar al-Kutub, 1929. 12 vols.

Isambert, Émile.
> *Itinéraire descriptif, historique et archéologique de l'Orient.* Paris: Hachette, 1881–2.

al-Jabartī, ʿAbd al-Rahmān.
> *Tarikh al-Jabartī (ʿAjāʾib al-Athār fi al-Trājim wa al-ʿAkhbār).* Cairo: al-Matbʿah al-Amiriyah, 1904. 4 vols.

Jauna, Dominique.
> *Histoire générale des Royaumes de Chypre, de Jerusalem, d'Armenie et d'Égypte.* Leide: Murray, 1785. 2 vols.

Jesuits' Letters from Missions.
    Lettres edifiantes et curieuses, écrites des missions etrangeres. Paris: Société Bibliophile, 1837. 14 vols. *Missions du levant: Syrie, Égypte, Ethiopie.* vol. 5.

Jirjis ibn al-'Amīd, called al-Makīn.
    L'Histoire mahmetane. Traduit d'arabe en français par Pierre Vattier. Paris: R. Soubert, 1657.

Journal of Deputation Sent to the East by the Committee of the Malta Protestant College in 1849. London: Nisbet, 1854. 2 vols.

Kammerer, Albert.
    La Mer rouge, l'Abyssinie et l'Arabie depuis l'Antiquité. Cairo: Société Royale de Géographie, 1929–1935. 2 vols.

al-Kindī, Abu 'Umar Muhammad ibn Yusuf.
    Kitāb al-wulāt wa Kitāb al-Qudāt. Edited by Rufun Kast. Baghdad: Maktabat al-Muthanna, 1908.

Kitab al-'Unvān.
    Universelle ecrité par Agapius (Mahboub) de Menbidj. Editée et Traduite en Français par Alexandre Vasilief. Paris: Firmin-Didot. 1948.

Lane, Edward William.
    An Account of the Manners and Customs of the Modern Egyptians. London, New York: Ward, Lock and Co., 1890.

Lane-Poole, Stanley.
    The Story of Cairo. London: J.M. Dent, 1902.

Las Cases, Emmanuel.
    Mémorial de Sainte-Hélène. Paris: Gallimard, 1950.

Leeder, S.H.
    Modern Sons of the Pharoahs. London, New York: Hodder and Stoughton, 1918.

Lefebvre, Gustave.
    Recueil des Inscriptions Greque-chrétiennes d'Égypte. Cairo: Service des Antiquités d'Égypte, 1907. Printed by Imprimerie de l'Institut francais d'Archéologie orientale.

Maillet, Benoit de.
    Description de l'Égypte. Paris: L. Genneau et J. Rollin, 1735.

Malosse, Louis
    Impressions d'Égypte. Paris: A. Colin, 1896.

al-Maqrizī, Ahmad ibn 'Ali.
    Kitab al-Mawa'iz wa al-I'tibār bi-Dhikr al-Khitat wa al-'Āthar. Cairo: al-Matb'ah al-Amiriyah, 1855. 2 vols.

al-Maqrizī, Ahmad ibn `Ali.
> *Kitab al-Sulūk li-Ma'rifat Duwal al-Mulūk.* Cairo: Dar al-Kutub, 1896. vol. 1.

Marcel, Jean Joseph.
> *L'Égypte arabe.* Paris: Collection L'Univers Pittoresque, 1872.

Marcel, Jean Joseph.
> *Égypte depuis la Conquête des Arabes jusqn`à la Domination française.* "Sous la Domination française" par M. Amedée Ryme. "Sous la Domination de Mehemet Aly" par Mm. P. et H. Paris: Firmin-Didot frères, 1848.

Maspero, Jean.
> *Histoire des Patriarches de'Alexandrie, depuis la Mort de l'Empereur Anastase jusqu'à la Reconciliation des Églises jacobites (518–616).* Ouvrage revu et publié après la Mort de l'Auteur par Le Rev. Ad. Fortescue et Gaston Wiet. Paris: E. Champion, 1923.

Maspero, Jean.
> *L'Organisation militaire de l'Égypte byzantine.* Paris: Champion, 1912.

al-Mas`udi.
> *Murūj al-Dhahab wa M`ādin al-Jawhar.* Cairo: al-Matb`ah al-Amiriyah, 1927. 4 vols.

Merruau, Paul.
> *L'Égypte contemporaine de Mahamet Ali à Said Pacha.* Paris: Didier, 1858. 1st edition.

Michaud, Joseph and M. Poujoulat.
> *Correspondance d'Orient 1830–31.* Paris: Ducollet, 1833–35. 7 vols.

Michaud, Joseph Fr.
> *Histoire des Croisades.* Bruxelles: N.J. Gregoir and V. Wouters, 1841. 6 vols.

Minutes of the Committee on the Project of the Egyptian Constitution, The. Cairo: al-Matb`ah al-Amiriyah, 1922.

Muhammad, Abduh.
> *Risalat al-Tawhīd.* Cairo: al-Matb`ah al-Amiriyah, 1897.

Nassiri, Khosrau.
> *Sefer Nameh. Relation du voyage de Nassri Khosrau en Syrie, en Palestine, en Égypte, en Arabie et en Perse pendant les années 437–444 A.H. (1035–1042 A.D.).* Traduit et annoté par Charles Scheffer. Paris: Leroux, 1881.

Nicola ibn Yussuf al-Turk.
> *Mudhakirat Nicola al-Turk.* Cairo: Institut français d'Archéologie Orientale. 1950. 2 vols.

Niebuhr, Carsten.
    Voyage en Arabie et en d'autres Pays de l'Orient. Suisse: Traduction française, 1780. 2 vols.

Norden, Frederik Ludwig.
    Voyage d'Égypte et de Nubie. Copenhagen: L'Imprimerie de la Maison Royale des Orphelins. 1755.

Paton, Andrew Archibald.
    A History of the Egyptian Revolution from the Period of the Mamelukes to the death of Mohammed Ali. London: Trubner, 1870. 2 vols.

Porcher, E. (ed.).
    "Life of Isaac the Patriarch of Alexandria." *Patrologia Orientalis*, vol. 11, part 3. Paris: Firmin-Didot, 1922.

Qallini Fahmi.
    Mudhakirāt Qallinī Fahmī. Minia, Egypt: Matb`at Sadiq, 1951. 2 vols. (in Arabic).

al-Qalqashandī, Ahmad ibn `Ali.
    *Kitāb Subh al-`Asha.* Cairo: al-Matb`ah al-Amiriyah, 1913. 14 vols.

Quatremère, Étienne Marc.
    Memoires géographique et historique sur l'Égypte et sur quelques contrées Voisines. Paris: Schoell, 1811. 2 vols.

Quatremère, Étienne Marc.
    Researches critiques et historiques sur la Language et la littérature de l'Égypte. Paris: Imprimerie Imperiale, 1808.

Reinaud, Joseph Toussaint.
    Notice sur la Vie de Saladin, Sultan d'Égypte et de Syrie. Paris: Dondey-Dupré, 1824.

Renaudot, Abbé Eusebius.
    Historia Patriarcharum Alexandrinorum Jacobitarum. Paris: F. Faurnier, 1713.

Richardot, Charles.
    Nouveaux Memoires sur l'Armée française en Egypte et en Syrie. Paris: J. Correard, 1848.

Rifaud, J.J.
    Tableau de l'Égypte et de la Nubie et des Lieux circonvoisins. Paris: Treuttel et Wurtz, 1830.

Rigault, Georges.
    Le Général Abdallah Menou et la Derniere phase de l'Expedition d'Égypte (1799–1801). Paris: Plon, 1911.

Rouillard, Germaine.
    L'Administration civile de l'Égypte byzantine. Paris: Geuthner, 1929.

Sachot, C.

    Rapport adressé à S.E.M. Victor Duruy, Ministre de l'Instruction publique, sur l'état des sciences, des lettres et de l'instruction publique en Égypte. Paris, 1869 (dactylographie).

St. John, James-Augustus

    Egypt and Mohammad Ali, or, Travels in the Valley of the Nile. London: Longman, 1834. 2 vols.

al-Sakhawi, Muhammad ibn `Abd al-Rahman.

    al-Tibr al-Masbūk fi Dhayl al-Muluk. Cairo: al-Matb`ah al-Amiriyah, 1897.

Salama, Ibrahim.

    D'Enseignment islamique en Égypte. Cairo: Imprimerie Nationale, 1938.

Savary, Claude Etienne.

    Lettres sur l'Égypte. Paris: Onfroi, 1785–6. 3 vols.

Sawirus ibn al-Muqaff a.

    Historia Patriarcharum Alexandrinorum. Edited by Fred. Seybold. Beirut, vol. 1, 1904–10. (*Corpus Scriptorum Christianorum Orientalium. Sciptores Arabici,* ser. 8, tome 9.) Beirut: 1904–10 [Comprises the Arabic text of the biographies of the first 52 Coptic patriarchs, 61–849 A.D. (Tr.)].

Sharūbīm, Mikha'īl

    al-Kafī fī Tarikh Misr al Qadīm wa al-Hadith. Cairo: al-Matb`ah al-Amiriyah, 1898–1900. 4 vols.

Sidaros, Sesostris.

    Des Patriarchats. Les Patriarchats dans l'Empire ottoman et specialement en Égypte. Paris: Rousseau, 1907.

Silvestre de Sacy, Antoine Isaac.

    Exposé de la Religion des Druzes. Paris: Imprimerie Royale, 1838.

Silvestre de Sacy, Antoine Isaac.

    Troisième et dernier Memoire sur la Nature et les Revolutions du Droit de Proprieté territorial en Égypte. Paris: Academie des inscriptions et belles-lettres, 1824.

Sonnini de Manoncourt, Charles Nicolas.

    Voyage dans la haute et basse Égypte, fait par Ordre de l'ancien Gouvernement. Paris: F. Buisson, 1799.

al-Tabarī, Abu J`afar ibn Jrīr.

    Tarikh al-Rusul wa al-Mulūk. Leiden: E.J. Brill, 1964. 16 vols.

Tewfik, Habib.

    Souvenir de Premier Congrés copte. Cairo: N.P., 1912 (in Arabic).

Thevenot, Jean de.
    Relation d'un Voyage fait au Levant. Paris: Jolly, 1665.
Thibaudeau, A.C.
    Histoire de la Compaign d'Égypte sous le Regne de Napoléon le Grand.
    Paris: Huzard, 1839. 2 vols.
Vansleb (Wansleben), Johann Michael.
    Novelle relation d'un Voyage fait en Égypte en 1672–3. Paris: E.
    Michallet, 1677.
Wiet, Gaston.
    L'Égypte Arabe: dans Histoire de la Nation égyptienne. Gabriel
    Hanotaux, ed., vol. 4. Paris: Libraire Plon, 1931–40. 7 vols.
Wiet, Gaston.
    L'Égypte musulmane: dans Precis de l'Histoire d'Égypte. Cairo:
    L'Institut français d'Archéologie Orientale, 1932–35. vol. 2.
Zettersteen, K.V.
    Beiträge zur Geschichte der Mamlukensultane. Leiden: E.J. Brill, 1919.
Zotenburg, Hermann (ed. and trans.).
    Chronique de Jean, Evêque de Nikiou. Paris: Bibliothèque nationale,
    1883. Translated from Ethiopic.

APPENDIX II

SOURCES CONSULTED BY THE TRANSLATOR

`Abd al-Baqī, Muhammad Fouad.
> al-M`ujam al-Mufahras li-Alfāz al-Qurān al-Karīm. Cairo: Matāb`i al-Sh`ab, 1977.

Aziz S. Atiya, Editor-in-chief.
> The Coptic Encyclopedia. New York: Macmillan, 1991.

Bacharach, Jere L.
> A Middle East Studies Handbook. Seattle, Washington: University of Washington Press, 1984.

Encyclopaedia of Islam. 1st ed. Leiden: E.J. Brill, 1913–36.   9 vols.

Glassé, Cyril.
> The Concise Encyclopedia of Islam. San Francisco: Harper and Row, 1989.

Hughes, Thomas Patrick.
> A Dictionary of Islam. London: W.H. Allen, 1885.

Hyamson, Alliert M.
> A Dictionary of Universal Biography. New York: Dutton, 1951.

Kahallah, `Umar Rida.
> M`ujam al-Mu`allifīn. Damascus: al-Maktabah al-`Arabiyah, 1957–61. 15 vols.

King, Joan Wucher.
> Historical Dictionary of Egypt. Metuchen, N.J.: Scarecrow Press, 1984. (African Historical Dictionaries, No. 36.)

Mukhtar, Muhammad.
> Kitab al-Tawiqat al-Ilhamiya fi Muqarnat al-Tawarikh al-Hijriya bil-Sinīn al-Ifrankiya wa al-Qibtiya. Cairo: al-Matb`ah al-Amiriyah, 1893.

The Qurān.
> Arabic text with a new translation by Muhammad Zafrulla Khan. London: Curzon Press, 1971. Reprinted 1985.

Webster's Geographical Dictionary. Springfield, Mass.: Merriam   Co.,1969.

Webster's New International Dictionary. Springfield, Mass.: Merriam Co., 1954. 2nd ed.

GLOSSARY

Abbasids.

The descendants of Abbas Ibn Abdul Muttalib, an uncle of the Prophet Muhammed. The great grandson of Abbas overthrew the Umayyad Caliphate in 750 A.D. and founded the Abbasid Caliphate. His brother succeeded him and founded Baghdad, which became the Caliphal seat of his descendants until it was taken and destroyed by the Mongol Hulagu in 1258. This dynasty saw the highest development of the Caliphate during what is recognized as the Golden Age of Islam.

Ahl al-dhimmah.

Dhimmis, Christians and Jews (and may be Zorostrians and Sabians) who enjoy protection of and religious tolerance on payment of "Jizyah" to their Muslim rulers.

Akh. (pl. ikhwan)

Brother.

`Alim (pl. `ulema)

Arabic. An expert, one who knows - used, especially in the plural, to indicate those trained in the Sacred Law, and holding a diploma from a teaching institution, such as al-Azhar University in Cairo.

'āmil.

The Arabic for agent used in Egypt in the eighteenth century for an official in charge of a government source of revenue.

Ardeb.

Egyptian unit of capacity which is equal to 5.44 imperial or 5.619 U.S. bushels.

Baht al-Māl.

Treasury.

Bedouin.

Refers generally to Arabic-speaking camel nomads in the Middle East and especially in the Arabian peninsula.

Bey.

A Turkish official rank; inferior to pasha. Title given to high officials. It was given to the Mameluke chiefs who ruled as Suzerain princes in Egypt and Syria.

Caliph.

For Sunni Muslims, successor of Muhammad as leader of the Islamic "ummah, nation".

Capitan (Qabutan) pasha.

A high-ranking officer of the Turkish corps of Janissaries.

Copt.

The words Copt and Egyptian are identical in meaning. In Arabic it is Qibt which means the people of Egypt. Now this word menas a Christian Egyptian.

Dar al-Harb.

Literary, abode of war; non-Islamic territories (societies).

Dar al-islam.

Literary, abode of peace, Islamic territories (societies).

Darb.

Alley, lane. See Harah.

Dayariyah.

A tax on monasteries.

Dawadar.

The sultan's personal secretary.

Dayr.

Monastery or convent, used for Christian institution.

dhimmi.

"Protected" or people of the covenant; not-Muslim citizen (Christian or Jew) who is subject to poll tax (Jizyah).

Dhimmi.

Refers to those religions given special status in Islam particularly to Christians and Jews "the People of the Book".

Dinar.

A gold coin weighing 59.5 grains troy.

Dirham.

A silver coin weighing 47.5 grains troy.

Divan (Arabic Diwan).

A word with a long history and various meanings which generally was used in nineteenth-century Turkey to signify a secretariat or department or a council.

Druze.

A heterdox sect which developed out of Fatimīd Ismā`ilism. Druzes are centered in Lebanon and Syria.

Effendi.

Turkish title given to educated persons who were generally government employees.

Effendī

Turkish title derived from the Greek, meaning master.

Eid al-Adha
> The Muslim Festival of Sacrifice occurring at the time of Hajj.

Emir. (pl. umara')
> Prince; Mameluke of high rank; distinguished notable.

Emīr al-Hajj.
> The President of the Pilgrimage an Egyptian official whose function was to lead the annual pilgrimage to Mecca.

Eid al-Fitr.
> The festival of feast-breaking at the conclusion of Ramadan the month of fasting.

Emir El-Hajj.
> President of the annual pilgrimage from Cairo to Mecca.

Fatwa.
> Formal legal opinion or decision of muftī on a matter of Islamic law.

Faqīh.
> Islamic legal expert, Islamic juris prudent.

Feddan.
> Measure of land; 4,201 square meters or just over one acre (1.038).

Fellah. (pl. fellahin)
> Egyptian peasant.

Fiqh.
> Islamic juris prudence.

Firman.
> A decree of the Turkish Sultan.

Hadd. (pl. hudūd)
> Quranically, prescribed penalty or punishment for a crime.

Hadith. (pl. Ahadīth)
> "Literary: speech, report, account" specifically traditions relating to the deeds and ulterances of the Prophet as recounted by his companions.

Hadith.
> Narrative report of the Prophet Muhammad's sayings and actions.

Hajj.
> Pilgrimage to Mecca. One of the five pillars of Islam and the once-in-a lifetime obligation of the faithful given adequate health and finances.

Hajj.
> Annual pilgrimage to Mecca required of all Muslims who can afford it at least once in their lifetime.

Harah.
> A lane, a quarter or a district.

Hijira.

The migration of those faithful to Muhammad's preaching, from mecca to medina (then called Yathrib), from Mecca to medina (then called Yathrib), in 622. At Medina a full fruition of the political and social aspects of Muhammad's revelation took place.

Hijra.

Emigration of Muhammad from Mecca to medina in 622 A.D. where he established rule of Muslim state.

Ijmā'.

Consensus, or agreement of the community or interpreters of the Qurān a source of Islamic law.

Ijtihād.

Independent analysis or interpretations of the Quran and rules of Muslims law (Shari'a).

Iltizām.

Responsibility to exact taxes, usually on land holdings, imposed by the government.

Imam.

A religious teacher. Most often, the term refers to a leader of services in the mosque. In Shiism the term also refers to the leader of the Shiite community.

Jacobites.

The word is generally a synonym for Monophysite. The Coptic patriarch represented all Monophysites in Egypt, including the Jacobites. Jacobites are members of the Jacobite Syrian Church founded by Jacob Baradaeus, a Syrian monk who died in 578. This church is Monophysite like the Egyptian Coptic church.

Janissaries.

Known in Arabic sources as Inkishariyah. Corruption of the Turkish Yeni Cheri, the new troops. These formed the ottoman infantry who wire recruited. Christian boys for training conversion and eventual use in the military.

Jihad.

"Holy War." refers to the obligation of the faithful to extend the Umma and protect it from its enemies. Jihad has been variously interpreted as actual warfare or spiritual struggle.

Jihad.

Strine, effort, struggle, war to follow Islam, may include defense of the faith, armed struggle, holy war.

Jizyah.

Poll-tax on dhimmis (Christians and Jews) which entitled them to protection to practice their faith.

Kafir.

Unbeliever or infidel one who rejects the message of Islam.

Katib.

The scribe or recordkeeper in a Muslim administration. In Egypt katib means clerk.

Kharaj.

Land-tax.

Khutba.

Sermon delivered in a mosque at the Friday congregational prayer.

Kekhia.

An official in both Mameluke and Turkish times whose position was that of a second-in-command, a deputy or a lieutenant, to a more senior official.

Khutbah.

Muslim sermon in a mosque.

Mahdī.

Divinely guided leader who is to come in the future to establish a Godly sanctioned society on earth.

Midān.

Square.

Mihrab.

Niche in the wall of a mosque indicating the direction of Mecca which Muslims should face when performing their prayers.

Millets.

The religious groups given official status in the Ottoman Empire. In matters of civil conflict among members of the same millet, the conflict would be resolved by the traditional authorities and processes of the respective millet. Thus a Christian was governed by Christian laws in his dealing with Christians regardless of his physical location in the Ottoman Empire.

Miri.

From amiri, of the ruler; land over which the government has certain rights. Tax, mainly a land tax.

Minbar.

Pulpit from which sermons are delivered in a mosque.

Mudir.

Governor of province (mudiriya).

Muftī.

Specialist on Islamic law (Shar`a) qualified to issue "fatwas" or legal opinions.

Muhtasib.

Originally an inspector of markets who supervised and placed business transactions and practices. His responsibilities also include monitoring public morality.

Multezim.

A tax farmer. See iltizam.

Multazim.

Holer of illizām.

Ottoman Empire.

Founded by the Turkish leader Osman, the Ottoman state gave rise to the last great Isslamic caliphate. centered in Anatolia, the empire lasted from its founding in the late thirteenth century to the first decade of the twentieth century.

Pasha.

Title given to certain high civil and military officials in the Ottoman Empire and its provinces. All such titles were canceled in Egypt in 1952 and were replaced by one title al-Sayyid (Mister).

Porte.

Commonly used in the eighteenth and nineteenth centuries to designate the Turkish government. The residence of the Sultan in Istanbul, was call al-Bāb al-'Alī. "Sublime Porte", in French. La Porte Sublime.

Qadī.

Judge who administers Shari`a laws. Now the word refers to civil and religious judges.

Qal`ah.

Fortress, Citadel.

Ramadna.

The Muslim month of fasting. One of the lunar months of the Muslim calendar. Fasting during the daylight hours of Ramadan is one of the five "pillars" of ritual obligation of Islam.

Ruznamah.

Used in Egypt in the eighteenth and nineteenth centuries for the government office which kept the registers dealing with the land tax.

Shahada.

The declaration of faith in islam: "There is no God but Allah and Muhammad is his Prophet".

Sham el-Nassim.

Arabic for "Smelling of the breeze." A feast to celebrate the coming of the spring. It falls on the Monday after Easter.

Shari'ah.

Religious law of Islam.

Shaikh. (pl. mashayikh, shūūkh)

Elder; bedouin chief; religious dignitary; holy man. Shaikh al-balad village headman, native son.

Shi'ism.

The branch of Islam deriving from the belief that the true successor to the Prophet was the fourth Caliph 'Ali and that the Imamate (or Caliphate) belongs rightly to his successors. Differing on various points of doctrine from the Orthodox Sunni majority. Shiism, concentrated largely in Iraq and Iran, is divided into several different sects.

Sultan.

A ruler, king or sovereign specially in a Muslim state.

Sura.

Chapter in the Quran āyah: a verse.

Sunna, sunnah.

(The main or orthodox branch of Islam.) Literally "A path or way, a manner of life." The tradition which record either the sayings or doings of the Prophet Muhammad, adj. Sunni, Sunnite. All Egyptian Muslims are Sunnis.

Tanqimat.

Arabic and Turkish. Reforms, arrangements: commonly used to indicate collectively the nineteenth-century modernizing and Europeanizing reforms in the administration of the Ottoman Empire. From an Arabic root meaning to put in order.

Tanzimat.

Generally a series of attempted reforms in the Ottoman Empire from 1839–76.

Umayyads.

One of the most powerful and important of the Arabic families at the time of Muhammad. The Umayyad caliphate was founded at Damascus by Muawiya who was able to win the Caliphate in 661 after the death of 'Ali, the last of the four Rightly Guided Caliphs.

Ushr.

Tithe.

Umma.

The worldwide community of Islam which ideally commands a Muslim's loyalty above all considerations of race, kinship, or nationality.

Ushuriya land.

Paying `ushr and held in full ownership.

Vali.

Turkish (Arabic: wali) meaning ruler or provincial governor, directly responsible to the sultan.

Vizier.

Turkish (Arabic: wazir). An office of Persian origin whose holder, in Abbaisd times, conducted the affairs of state. In the Ottoman Empire the grand vizier was, in the nineteenth century, roughly equivalent to prime minister, except that, like most ottoman officials, he was often entrusted with military command. At present wazir menas a cabinet minister.

Waqf. (pl. awqāf)

Endowment of property for charitable purposes and institutions.

Waqf.

Endowed property not subject to normal transactions, its income begin assigned by the founder; the act of endowing waqf. Religious endowments usually made in perpetuity, which support a specific institution devoted to good works, such as a madrasah, a home for orphans or a religious building.

Zakat.

One of the five pillars of the Islamic faith, obligating the faithful to support the unfortunate and the needy.

Arbeiten zum spätantiken und koptischen Ägypten

Herausgegeben von
Prof. Dr. Martin Krause

1. *Cäcilia Wietheger,* Das Jeremias-Kloster zu Saqqara unter besonderer Berücksichtigung der Inschriften. Oros Verlag, Altenberge 1992, XVI+532 S., DM 94,80. ISBN 3-89375-044-4
2. *Katarzyna Urbaniak-Walczak,* Die "conceptio per aurem". Untersuchungen zum Marienbild in Ägypten unter besonderer Berücksichtigung der Malereien in El-Bagawat. Oros Verlag, Altenberge 1992, XV+263 S., DM 69,80. ISBN 3-89375-047-9
3. Die Verkaufsurkunden von Klosterteilen des Apa-Apollon-Klosters von Bawit (BM Or 6201-6204 u. 6206), herausgegeben, übersetzt und untersucht von *Martin Krause*
4. *Bernd Witte,* Die Schrift des Origenes "Über das Passa". Textausgabe und Kommentar. Oros Verlag, Altenberge 1993, 247 S., DM 65,80. ISBN 3-89375-089-4
5. *Siegfried Richter,* Exegetisch-literarkritische Untersuchungen von Herakleidespsalmen des koptisch-manichäischen Psalmenbuches. Oros Verlag, Altenberge 1994, XII+351 S., DM 80,-. ISBN 3-89375-091-6
6. *Bernd Witte,* Das Ophitendiagramm nach Origenes' Contra Celsum VI 22-38. Oros Verlag, Altenberge 1993, 163 S., DM 45,80. ISBN 3-89375-090-8
7. *Alexandr Khosroyev,* Die Bibliothek von Nag Hammadi. Einige Probleme des Christentums in Ägypten während der ersten Jahrhunderte. Oros Verlag, Altenberge 1995, X+195 S., DM 60,-. ISBN 3-89375-107-6
8. *Gregor Wurst,* Das Bêmafest der ägyptischen Manichäer. Oros Verlag, Altenberge 1995, VIII+258 S., DM 70,-. ISBN 3-89375-111-4
9. *Lucia Langener,* Isis lactans - Maria lactans. Untersuchungen zur koptischen Ikonographie. Oros Verlag, Altenberge 1996, XIII+223+199 S., DM 90,-. ISBN 3-89375-131-9

10. *Jacques Tagher,* Christians in Muslim Egypt. An Historical Study of the Relations between Copts and Muslims from 640 to 1922. Oros Verlag, Altenberge 1998, XX+294 S., DM 80,-. ISBN 3-8975-157-2